Dispatches from the World's Best Job

Robin Esrock

Dear Mokah,
The world without
the bugs *
Robin Esrock

ISBN-13: 978-1490485362

Author website: www.robinesrock.com
Word Travels: www.wordtravels.tv

For further information regarding this book or the TV series, please
contact: robin@robinesrock.com

Word Travels has been broadcast on *Travel Channel International,
National Geographic, Nat Geo Adventure, OutsideTV, CityTV, OLN,
Halogen TV, F/X Canada, TVB China, Delta Airlines, HULU* and
others, and is also used as an educational resource to inspire school
kids around the world.

For my Mom, Cheryl

FOREWORD

Word Travels would be broadcast in over 100 countries and 21 languages.
But we didn't know that then.

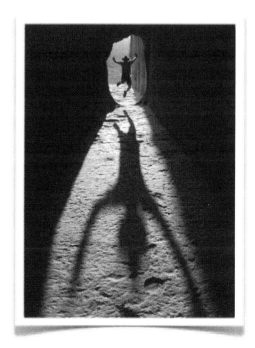

To be honest, I'm still scratching my head. How did my career turn from boring desk job to hustling backpacker to travel writer to hosting 3 seasons of an international TV show? It just doesn't happen every day, which I can testify to, years later, having failed repeatedly to make it happen again. There are so many moving parts at work, so many relationships and stars that have to align, it's enough to make you believe in fate, destiny, and the cosmic puppetry of someone with a jolly good sense of humour.

The stories and images that follow were filmed from 2007 to 2010, a journey to 36 countries on six continents. The series *Word Travels*, often misspelled as World Travels, follows the lives of two real-life working travel writers, Julia Dimon and myself. Each episode would usually have me chasing adventurous, physically oriented stories, while Julia investigated people-focused cultural stories. Two different beats was my idea, as was the original concept for a series, which pitched Julia and myself zipping around the world, literally living other people's dreams. This initial idea was called Dreamcatchers, which emerged from the gauntlet of modern TV development as Word Travels - a show about us just being us. Although I had travelled extensively before the show, everything was new: filming with a crew, being on camera, working with producers and directors, and throwing myself headfirst into one wild adventure after another, week after week, month after month.

The process of how one thing led to another can be read in the Appendix. Suffice it to say nobody had any idea what we were getting ourselves into, and how a life of almost non-stop action takes its toll. Case in point: during our first season, we filmed nine consecutive weeks, seven days a week, in eight countries on six continents. It's enough to make a person go insane, and some of us nearly did.

In 2005, I cashed in a $20,000 insurance settlement to solo backpack the world for a year. Once a week, I would diligently sit and record everything that had happened - in words, photographs, interviews and reviews. I called my website moderngonzo.com. Over 52 consecutive weeks, I produced an astounding amount of content, and a habit of recording everything I witnessed around me. I mined this skill while filming Word Travels, and this book represents what I managed to unearth in the process. Although many of the stories I researched for the show were only published years later (you can see a few in the Appendix), I wrote my "reports" once a week while the experience was fresh. Many of these words were used as narration for the actual show. I refrained from delving too heavily into personal relationships and production woes, focusing on the adventure itself, and the big, beautiful world unfolding before me. Julia and I researched and suggested our own stories, which is how we came to explore some pretty unusual destinations.

Each chapter in this book recounts the week's adventure, with a photo gallery and an additional Behind the Scenes blog, created for our show website. Of course, some of the wackiest stories didn't make my own cut, like getting roofied by flight attendants in Hong Kong (never accept a flaming drink from a pretty air hostess) or hallucinating in the wild jungles of Venezuela. Travel can be intense, especially with a punishing schedule and a job to do. This Truth Behind the Byline should more accurately be called The Truth Behind Filming a Travel Show, for the reality is that travel writers do not typically have a TV crew, move at this pace, with this schedule, and with our blessed amount of editorial freedom. Press trips usually find me travelling with half a dozen to dozens of other writers, creating a dynamic that unfortunately could not be explored in our show. The truth is that travel writing is a lifestyle, not a living, and certainly not a holiday. It's never been harder to keep up the lifestyle, either. Editorial budgets nowadays have been slashed, outlets shut down, and the explosion of blogs and social media has all but buried a once-glamorous, highly sought-after profession. Very few travel writers emerging today will be able to rack up the newspaper credits I did, purely because many of those newspaper travel sections no longer exist.

My favourite episodes were Ukraine, Sri Lanka, Lithuania and Ethiopia - countries where the road was bumpy, emotional, and often a little dangerous. It was surreal to return to Bolivia, Thailand and New Zealand to effectively repeat my adventures from a few years before. Although nothing was quite the same: A ten-minute stroll to the local market turns into an all-day shoot, waiting for a camera to reload, waiting for sound, waiting for the plane to pass over, the light to improve, the crowds to relax. All this adds to the hyper-reality and intensity of the journey.

Years later, our first season has a mythical aspect in the world of television production. Nobody in their right minds should have attempted what we did: 9 countries in 8 weeks on 6 continents, producing one episode a week? Some shows spend a year to make 13 episodes; others will only travel for a week or two. We had no days off. Just one wild experience after another, followed by a few hours' sleep and a tired drive to the airport, where it would begin all over again with a different language, culture and currency. Season two had us on the road for five consecutive weeks, which still took its toll. By the final season, we were seasoned pros, or so we thought. Expectations never help any traveller.

Since our journey, there's been tremendous upheaval in some of the countries we visited, while in others, things are exactly how they've always been. Facts change, places close down, people move on. All errors, inconsistencies and typos and are mine. No stunt doubles were used, so please be careful out there.

There have been many new adventures since *Word Travels* wrapped, both abroad and at home (I got married and became a Dad). Yet the show continues to air, and people continue to ask me: What's it like having the world's best job? Hopefully, this will give you some idea.

Robin Esrock
Vancouver, BC

Season One

COLOMBIA
BUSTING A REPUTATION

You're no doubt wondering why, when offered the opportunity to visit anywhere in the world, country number one on the list was Colombia. You're thinking. Kidnappings, Drug Cartels, Civil War, Murder, Unrest, Corruption, AK-47's, Moustaches, Scarface, Fedoras, and Food or Sex, because you've now been thinking for seven seconds and one of those is bound to come up. You might have read the *World's Most Dangerous Places* by Robert Young Pelton, which gives Colombia a maximum five out of five stars, symbolizing Hell on Earth (right up there with Chechnya and Liberia). Yep, Colombia sounds like fun for those who like death with their chocolate. So why am I here? Because two years ago, every backpacker I met in South America who had visited Colombia said it was their favourite country. Every Colombian I have ever met has been friendly, warm, and nothing like the media stereotype. So to reconcile these two images, a country so misunderstood it could be a washed-up former teen idol, I had to see it for myself. Pack your bags; we're off to Bogota.

Now let's start off by saying that Colombia is not Bolivia, or Guatemala, or Nicaragua - Latin American countries that have been known to put the banana in the republic. I knew this on the plane from L.A., which was jammed with the prosperous, the well dressed, the big-breasted. Oh, I was still on US soil when the wet rumour that Colombia has some of the world's best-looking women became hard solid fact. The girl behind me in line could have been Penelope Cruz's better-looking sister, and I was delighted to sit below two women loading their luggage, heaving their two considerable portable floatation devices a mere inch from my nose as they did so. Red eye flights are never fun, especially when everything you've read would make you believe your destination is a war zone, and the matter was further compounded by the fact that for the first time in years I arrived safely, but my luggage didn't. After somehow managing to drop my laptop from the security check-in conveyer belt, LAX also needed more than two hours to transfer our bags to the next plane, and thus, cold Bogota would meet Gonzo, and Gonzo would be dirty and cold and tired. Cold? Yes, cold. Twenty-six hundred metres above sea level, Bogota's weather in August is squid damp and dull gray, more so when your head is in the clouds and your clothes, somewhere else entirely. But adrenaline, the thrill of being back in South America (my favourite continent), and finding a hotel in the cobblestone colonial streets of Candelaria made the weather insignificant. That, and the dozens of uniformed man-boys holding one, two, three machine guns, on every corner of the street. The presidential palace was less than a block away, and in a country often at war with itself, leaders take their personal security seriously. Fortunately, this only made me feel more safe, since these man-boys seemed friendly enough, and there's absolutely nothing to be gained from harassing another dumb gringo with a stupid gringo hat.

Barely time to drop off the bags (oh, right, forgot, no bags) and I'm off on a bike to the Cyclovia - a weekly event in which long veins throughout the city of 7 million are unclogged of vehicles so that citizens can bring out their bikes. Instituted by a popular mayor several years ago, Cyclovia has been a huge hit in Bogota, allowing the rich (few) and the poor (many) to co-exist in a form of transportation utopia. Together with a friendly Cyclovia guardian named Julian, I rode the streets of Bogota and quickly realized that it's really not that dangerous to explore any city so long as there are heavily armed police/army personnel on every corner. The real dangers were the brakes (non-existent), gung-ho bikers with little patience for red-eyed writers, and potholes crushing my emeralds against the hard seat. I see a bike mechanic with an eye patch made from sunglasses. Kids in front, kids behind, expensive bikes, homemade bikes, cheap bikes, stolen bikes. Thin people, fat people, happy people, sad people, friendly people, nasty people, beautiful people, ugly people. Two wheels is a great way to promote democracy, and as a traveller, there's no better way to discover a city. Especially when you ride directly into a massive carnival procession, vibrating with passion as Bogota celebrates its 469th birthday.

But first, Colombia. Named after Chris Columbus, the explorer, not the guy who directed Home Alone. Like the rest of Latin America, it's been ravaged by the Spanish, disease, slave-owners, pirates, Reggaeton. Prosperous few, impoverished many. FARC me? FARC you! Civil war, death squads, and let's throw in cocaine, just for the hell of it, and what's this, cartels and corruption and assassinations, and now you're the mayor and now you're dead, and here comes the USA with its war on drugs, only it seems a lot more people are dying these days, or starving, and there goes another mayor, and a politician who thought he could take on the cartels, and where is the Romeo of Medellin and the Juliet of Cali? But hey, they got Escobar and Ochoa, only who's this new guy who likes to dismember anyone who looks at him funny, and the FARC, viva la revolution, take this land, but the army took that land and it sucks to be anyone who actually lives on the land, or the CEO of a petroleum company, because if you think picking your kids up from school is a bitch, try bargaining with kidnappers every other week - and here's paradise on the Caribbean, but international tourists are so scared they're teleporting themselves to Costa Rica, and 10,000 pesos is only 5 bucks, and a beer here costs six times more than a beer there, but what's this, this oldest democracy in Latin America, things settling down, the cities becoming safer, cleaner, international investment returning, and even the FARC (Che! Che! Che!) are becoming more attached to their villas than the jungle, and tourism is picking up, and what to do when you have the most beautiful women in the world, Afro-Spanish-Indian cultural soup and the genius of Gabriel Garcia Marquez, who invented magic realism here because it could be invented in no other place on earth?

It's magic to be walking these streets, considered among the most dangerous in the world, and feel safe, welcomed. A guy tells me in broken English that his friend, a pretty young girl, likes me and would like to have her cell phone photo with me. A scam? No, the only crime was that I quickly moved on to talk to two beautiful girls on stilts, and hello, a topless girl dances and shakes, painted in green atop something that looks like a papier mâché vegetable. People are smiling and saying, "welcome to Colombia," and I see NO other tourists around, which means I'm either doing something very wrong, or, most likely, very right. I take a picture of the fairy waifs, the industrial goths, the marching band playing Yellow Submarine, and all around there is a beat and a smile, and really, this is not what I expected of Colombia at all. Systems break down when there's no community, but judging by the amount of groups in the parade, this community is flourishing.

For Julia's solo story, she decided to investigate emeralds, which are sold here like opal is sold in India, jade in New Zealand, or whatever precious stone is sold in the back rooms of overpriced kitsch jewelry stores, marketed to tourists desperate for a deal on yes-sir-100%-real-sir gems they didn't know they needed before the tour bus dropped them off outside. I've seen it before, the Thailand hustle, hello-friend-want-to-buy-a-rug in Turkey, and so on. With the crew engaged nearby, I wandered into a local bar, where some university students were having lunch. In mangled Spanish and better English, we discussed how Colombia's image needs a desperate makeover. I might have heard machine gun fire from the bed of my hotel, but I felt more bad mojo in Rio or Johannesburg than Bogota, and trust me, the mojo in *those* fantastic cities is well worth checking out. If we fear the world, we fear ourselves.

Fifteen hundred words in here, folks, and I've hardly gotten to the good stuff. Like. Luggage arrives safely. And. The Bulletproof Tailor of Bogota, Senor Miguel Caballero, the Armani for moving targets, manufacturer of fine bullet-proof fashion wear. Here is the company headquarters, a squat, white low-rise building decorated with stylish discretion and armed with strict security. When your clients include the wealthy elite and world leaders, it's best not to advertise too much, especially in a city with the highest kidnapping rate in the world. The same way it's best not to advertise you're nervous of getting shot, which is why Caballero makes the only tailored bullet-proof suits, sweaters, leather jackets and hoodies in the world. Considering over 100 people work at the factory, it has shot to the top of the pile, exploded on the world scene, a real bang for the buck. The walls are covered in press - CNN, Wired, BBC - but I can't meet the man because Miguel's in Mexico, so instead I'm shown around by a guy named Andres and ballistics director Ignacio, and these guys are just great, answering my questions (yes, it can stop a 9mm bullet, yes, it can deflect a knife, no, it's not too heavy, yes, but only Mr. Caballero can make the shot that lets clients test the vests, no, it won't stop AK-47 rounds, yes, that is a bullet-proof tie, yes, the fabric is unique to the company, no, we can't shoot you, sorry, no, sorry, no, sorry, yes, we'll let you shoot a vest but only if you stop asking us to shoot you, por favor!). I try on various vests and outfits, and I feel powerful knowing that for a brief moment I could survive a shootout, providing I don't get hit in the neck, head, or groin. The aim, Andres tells me, is to save lives, not prevent injury, but even so he tells me that the impact of the bullet is no harder than a finger flick. He should know. All employees at the company have to put on a vest and get shot by Senõr Caballero, because they should believe in the product like he does. Considering everyone seemed happy and healthy, he's made a lot of believers. There's even a club for people whose lives have been saved by a Caballero vest, which makes a mockery out of St Andrews Golf Club membership requirements. Miguel Caballero only sells 20% of his product In Colombia, but, as Andres points out, a bullet proof vest made for life in Colombia is made for life wherever you want to take it. The company has boutiques in Bogota and Miami, and another one opening up in Paris. They lead me into the testing room, where a vest is strapped onto a square of soft clay. Here they scientifically test the velocity, the speed, the depth of the impact. After a demonstration, I'm handed an Uzi machine gun, loaded with a single bullet, and take aim a few feet from the vest. Wearing an armour-plated vest, holding a gun, for that moment, every misguided male hormone was going mad with mistaken machismo, and I fired, and oops, almost missed the vest but did manage to knick the bastard. We measure the impact, and fack the finger flick, there's a one-inch dent in the clay. Save lives. Not prevent injury. Now they nervously want to take the gun away, but I know I can land the shot in the middle of the vest, so I huff and puff and all eyes are on me, a small crowd gathered at the window in the hallway. Pressure's on. I have to make this shot, a true test to the nature of my testes. Fire! A blitz of violence, and Ignacio congratulates me. I think he's being sarcastic, since I could well have missed the vest altogether and sent a bullet flying through the wall, but instead, I've hit the vest panel dead center, a perfect shot. I strut like a proud killer, and then it hits me why young boys make the perfect soldiers, why there is so much gunfire and death - in the hands of a boy, a weapon becomes a toy, and death becomes a game. In the hands of a man it is no different.

Touchdown in the T-Zone! It's the night before another public holiday and the streets of Bogota are ablaze! A crowd has gathered outside the old church in Simon Bolivar Square, as we drive towards the T-Zone, an area of top-notch bars and clubs. It could be Miami, it could be Madrid, neon lights and silver service. New friends Ricky and Maria take me into a club called Giavanna, where I am frisked three times and enter to find what every man dreams of, but seldom discovers - a bar full of beautiful women (none of whom, I should add, are hookers). You can only buy liquor by the bottle, and everyone's slugging back *aguardiente*, Colombian moonshine, or, literally, hot water. I meet some guys in the lineup, and before long I'm partying in their extended crew, literally surrounded by girls so beautiful they're in my dreams days later. House music, Latin music, a little rumba, a little salsa, 80's remixed, lasers, smoke machines, a cannon fires confetti in the air, and girls, who all seem to be named Maria, take my hand and make me dance, and guys take my hand and give me drinks, and this isn't a scam or a setup, just the big night out. Except I have to catch a plane to the Caribbean in the morning, so I have to leave Maria-something here and say goodbye to Maria-something there, and any one of them would be reason to flush my passport. "Normally" I tell Maria-something-else, "I'd ask for your number, and we could go out, and I'd get to you know you and meet your family, but I'm a travel writer shooting a TV show, and tomorrow I fly to Cartagena, and that's it for Bogota." She can't hear this over the loud music, just smiles warmly, her eyes sparkling, and I take my leave, but my heart lingers and fades behind, until the music stops and everyone goes home, and it lies on the floor, like a discarded business card.

It's a relaxed one-hour flight to Cartagena, where Bogota's cold nights trade in for sticky sweat, its low-rise buildings become high-rise holiday apartments, and the green jungle hills of Colombia dissolve into the pee-warm Caribbean sea. It's the Cancun of Colombia, yet also a UNESCO Heritage Site that protects a historical walled city dating back over 500 years. From the plane window, I see the slums first, then Old Cartagena, and then the new Cartagena, and immediately I can see the different worlds that inhabit this beautiful town. Tourists pay European prices for hotels, meals and activities. Locals earn - and can only afford to pay - a fraction of that. Tourism drives the economy, and there's no problem with FARC (Che Che Che) and death squads, because everyone here appears to be making a killing. Sipping a ten dollar Piña Colada atop the old fortress walls, a warm ocean breeze so thick you could paint the notes of the Thievery Corporation tune in the air, it's undoubtedly stunning, if a little hard on the wallet. The cuisine is all fresh fish and coconut rice, the tropical juices squeezed and palm trees tall. I've seen this before, in northern Brazil, only there, it didn't cost $100 to buy a ticket on a boat to visit the islands, or $15 for fish and rice, or $6 a beer, or $7 an hour for Internet. But then you step one block beyond the tourism zone, or even next door to the hotel where old and young whores gather, and here are the locals, paying $1 a beer, $2.50 for half a roasted chicken, and 75 cents an hour for internet. Different worlds, same city. It's rainy season, so the sky is foggy and the humidity is overpowering. I jump into the Caribbean, and it's like swimming inside the bottle of water you left in the sun for half a day. On the patio of a bar, I'm looking at old Spanish forts, relics from when Cartagena was a pirate town, a major trading center of the old world. Colourful bustling party buses drive in the night, and the plazas in the old town are full of excellent outdoor seafood restaurants, weathered buskers playing traditional songs, dancers with hard stomachs as flat as a brick, hippies selling trinkets, pretty girls in short summer dresses. Basically paradise, providing you can afford it, and keep to the right parts of town. New developments in Cartagena pierce the sky with sky rise holiday apartments, but major hotel chains have yet to carve up the charm for their shareholders. I'd suggest you get in before they do.

I'm all over volcanoes. Hiking among their lava flows in Guatemala, climbing their slopes in Chile. So I had to make my way to the Volcan de Lodo, a mud volcano about an hour outside of Cartagena. The idea: You climb a ladder to the top, and inside the small crater find a pool of thick volcanic mud. Take a dip, rinse off in the lagoon. The bus arrives at the volcano, and the "volcano" looks more like a termite hill, an ant trap. I'm nursing a hangover from the previous night, during which the crew, inspired by Julia's appetite for destruction, partied with vigor. A few bottles of rum later, we ended up in a club called the Diva Bar, which is basically a clue, because that's one vowel short of what it actually was, namely a Dive Bar. My head was erupting when the bus arrived at the volcano, which on first impression resembled a seismic tourist fantasy. We took off our clothes and climbed into the thick goopy mud. Bye bye, hangover. We were floating in thick milk chocolate. Refreshingly cool, considering the furnace of the early morning sun, the mud invades every pore with pleasure. It's what we imagine it must be like to sleep on a cloud, only you'll fall through a cloud and freeze and die, where here the mud moulds around your body and cushions your head. It covers our skin like liquid latex, accentuating muscles and tone. Not only are we totally relaxed and cooled off, we feel like supermodels. Operated by an association from the nearby village, smiley men exfoliate me by rubbing my skin, and then, only then, do I notice the incredible view that surrounds us. Like the creature from Uranus, the mud covers me head to toe. It's all 100% natural, although the shape of the cone is maintained by villagers with sandbags. Legend calls this the "Volcano of Youth," where a man can enter at age 50 and leave as a 30 year old. Tourists have only been coming here for the last three decades, and the volcano does bubble up a small eruption of mud up to 3 times a year. We arrived early, and soon enough, the crater filled up with tourists. It was time for the lagoon rinse, whereby ladies from the village douse us in water, still and murky like the water in a latrine (which, unnervingly, are located nearby). More so, my Lady of the Lagoon had no problem ripping off my shorts to give them a thorough washing, and I almost lost consciousness holding my breath as she dipped me in and out with all the grace of a torturer. Julia was clutching her bikini for dear life. Thoroughly submerged in mud, rubbed, washed, shaken and dehydrated, the sun punching us with strong rays, I meet two English guys who have ridden through South America for six months and are two days from finishing their journey. "We haven't had a single problem," says Dave, "although we were nervous to ride through the jungle parts of the country." I repeat: Two bikers, long remote roads in South America, no problems. Here's Marina, with her two kids from Canada. Marina's Colombian, met her Canadian husband and moved to Toronto, and brings her kids back every year. "There's been a definite improvement in safety these last few years," she tells me, and I've heard this a few times during the week. "We invite our friends every year, but their parents are worried about the danger," says her daughter Melissa, and we both wonder why. Reputations can be nasty things, to people and places. "This is better than the Dead Sea," remarks Julia, and I can't argue. The mud volcano is the perfect type of unusual Gonzo adventure I'd expect to find in a place like Colombia, and possibly, the long-last cure to the vicious traveller's hangover.

I'm slowly getting used to the heat, the stickiness, the loud horns of the traffic, the second-hand smoke from the people in the room next door who blast their TV all day. Time to visit paradise: in this case, the Rosario Islands, an hour or so by speedboat from Cartagena. Today, I am inspired by lying up front, arms stretched over the bow, warm wind blowing hard through my fingertips, past my hair. All I can see is the Caribbean, turning brown, then green, then blue, then turquoise. Would Superman fly low to see the colours of the sea change? In the morning the sea is calm, and the speedboat hauls ass, pausing at the imposing walls of the old Spanish fort, connected by an ancient underground tunnel. On either side, six boys row up from nowhere screaming something in Spanish. Nico, our guide, blessed with an even wider smile than Danny Glover, explains they want us to throw coins in the sea so they can dive and retrieve them. This provides some cheap entertainment, but Julia feels we're taking advantage of them. She argues it's like begging; I argue it's a couple of kids having fun and making some coin in the process. To show solidarity, I dare her to throw in some pesos for me to collect, and sure enough, I'm diving into the sea to fetch it (admittedly, it was a lot easier to catch a floating note than a sinking coin). The engine kicks it up again, with the sun and wind to dry me off, and soon we arrive at the dream island of my reality - blue waters, palm trees, fine white beach. I once wrote about the cocaine-like sand of Sihanoukville, Cambodia, and here, that description would perhaps be more apt, since this particular island was once owned by the notorious Ochoa, a peer of the equally notorious Pablo Escobar. Today, it's all but deserted, allowing tourists to spend some time before boating off to another Rosario island, where tables and chairs sit beneath shade-tarps right in the shallow sea, and you can eat lunch half-submerged in crystal water, tiny fish swimming between your legs. Across the channel, on the island of Baru, I find the perfect backpacker paradise, only it costs a lot more than a backpacker could afford. Hammocks, lounge chairs, kayaks, chill music, fresh fish on the grill. I've seen something similar in Brazil, in Costa Rica, in Thailand, in Cambodia, only there they charge considerably less, and I still cannot make sense of the cost here. But whining about prices in paradise is like complaining about your grocery bill at your Academy Award speech. "Esrock, stop crying your velvet tears!" I understand now why those who have visited Colombia are so quick to sing its praises. The cities are as safe as any in South America, and unless you're desperately unlucky, don't count on getting into trouble. If you do, you'll be amazed at how quickly locals will be on hand to help you out. "Take New York City. People around the world know there are some bad places in the city, but they also know there are amazing places, too. Here, they just know the bad," sighs Maria-Jose, rolling her beautiful brown eyes. Back from visiting Monserrate, the mountain that overlooks Bogota, my taxi hits an armed roadblock. The soldiers frisked me, but upon finding out my gringohood were all smiles and innocent questions. It's when the soldiers are not on your side that you have to worry. Here in Colombia, a nation that prides itself on passion, on hospitality, on looking ahead and regretting the past, you can safely dismiss the bad news, and believe my hype.

Bogota's anniversary carnival

Old town Cartagena, a UNESCO World Heritage Site

Getting my Uzi on to test the bullet proof vests at Miguel Caballero.
Unfortunately, they wouldn't shoot me

Tourists in the legendary Mud Volcano, floating like shortbread in chocolate

BOLIVIA
RETURN TO THE ISLAND OF THE SUN

Not much has changed on the Island of the Sun. The same little girl is playing on the same sacred rock by the Sun Temple. The same man is rowing tourists to the south, weathered lines on his face barely betraying his immense physical effort. The most beautiful sunset in the world is still found by hiking the Calvario, the hill that overlooks the sleepy lakeside village Copacabana. And in La Paz, the air remains choked with diesel fumes and speckled noise. Former Eastern bloc countries have rapidly industrialized in Europe. India and China have become economic powerhouses, and the world has probably become even more flat in terms of communication and trade, but Bolivia remains as Bolivia was - the poorest country in South America, seemingly barred from progress just like it has been barred from the sea.

Maybe I'm just hallucinating, my oxygen-starved brain crying for drama that isn't there. Two years ago, I had weeks to acclimatize to the altitude, and when visiting the world's highest capital city (3600m) and highest navigable lake (3800m), your body definitely needs time to prepare for miserly air. This week, my preparation consisted of time in a plane, a short layover in Lima, and watching a man pass out from lack of oxygen on arrival in La Paz's very chaotic airport. Picking my backpack off the conveyer belt resulted in staccato breath, my heartbeat racing. Thirsting for O_2 at altitude literally makes you high. It was after midnight when we pulled into the city, and La Paz was freezing. Sprawled inside a dry, moon-like valley, half-built houses pockmarked the surrounding mountain, creating an atmosphere of undeniable urban decay. It is a city of only 1.5 million people, although it looks like it could easily accommodate three times that amount. Bright, revolutionary graffiti decorates cracked cement walls; modern billboards are few and far between. Driving from the airport, I see stray dogs chewing garbage. The highway feels as if 10 thousand pianos once dropped from the sky, and we're still driving over the keys. I cannot see a single crane, a single sign of urban improvement. Bolivia seems resistant to change. This is not necessarily a bad thing.

Before Thomas Friedman wrote the seminal *The World is Flat*, he wrote a book called *The Lexus and the Olive Tree*. It discusses how modernization battles with cultural habits, how assembly lines of products rub up against centuries of tradition. We can clearly see the world becoming culturally pasteurized, as multinationals and their invasive brands boil away the richness of local variety. Friedman did not judge whether globalization is for the better or worse, although his later books veer pro-globo. It has become the reality of modern life. To see where we're heading, just look to the mighty USA. Across an entire continent, every US city has the same stores, the same strip malls, the same same, hardly different. Travel across the developed world, ditto.

So I appreciate that La Paz conforms to some unwritten theory of urban chaos, where round ladies wearing round bowler hats sell just about anything you can imagine on the streets. Who can afford a cup of Starbucks when it costs more than a week's wages? Who gives a shit about Gap when you're more concerned about goats? I remember well the parts of La Paz that resemble parts of Miami, and certainly there are a few tall buildings (albeit desperately in need of a fresh coat of paint). These are small pockets of space serving the tiny upper-class elite, while in Sagarnaga, the backpacker ghetto, it's all Tour Operator and Internet and Hostel, and enough Hebrew to make you think you've popped up in the Middle East. Israelis, like Americans, Irish, Argentineans and English, come here because it is cheap. For travellers with US dollars, Bolivia is one of the cheapest countries in the world, easily comparable to India or Laos. Ear-splitting noise, rampant corruption, fake currency, scams, absurd regulations, tap water laced with fecal matter, minimal tourist infrastructure - just a few reasons most tourists skip the country for Peru, which has managed to recognize a foreign gift horse when it sees one. Yet visit Bolivia and you'll find some of the most breathtaking scenery you can imagine, untouched, well beneath the interests of corporate invasion.

We're back on the Island of the Sun, staring out over the water at a vista inspired by the gods. The quality of light at 3800m is immaculate, reflecting off the famously blue waters of Lake Titicaca. In the distance, the Royal Mountain range is painted white with snow, floating well over 6000m like a threatening cloud. It is a tundra on the south side of the island, the vegetation barely reaching knee high. The ruins of a temple that once housed priestesses still remain, a labyrinth of sunken rock. An old man walks past, his two donkeys loaded with wood, a few sheep padding timidly at his heels. Corporations would have to spend a lot of money to duplicate the authenticity of this old world, this theme park of the way things were, are, and probably always will be. "I'm surprised there isn't a hotel right here," says sound guy Zach, holding a makeshift broomstick boom pole with a furry microphonic creature at the tip. It's been hard to take him seriously since his boom pole "escaped" during the journey from Vancouver to Colombia. It currently resides in Acapulco, in a sordid relationship with a sexy pair of headphones. "Thank God there isn't a hotel right here," I reply, and we head off along the old Incan path, passing pigs, villagers and donkeys, to the rustic village below.

A fool might bike the world's most dangerous road once, so what does that make me, riding inches away from a 600m cliff for the second time? Actually, the death road from La Paz to Coroico is safer than it has ever been, thanks to a new highway that has stolen 99% of the traffic. Buses and trucks would frequently flip off the edge of the winding dirt track, resulting in an average of 150 deaths a year. Today, the 43km of jungle road, and the 22km of asphalt preceding it, sees more traffic from tourists on bicycles. When I was here last, seven tourists had died on their bikes. Today it was eleven, the most recent being an Israeli guy who flew off the cliff just a few yards away from the first fatality - an Israeli girl who complained about her brakes from the start and later slid off the edge. A monument in Hebrew reminds fun-loving tourists of the risks of this adventure. Her death was ruled a suicide by Bolivian police notoriously more accustomed to cash payouts than justice. She was 23 years old. The idea to commercially bike the death road came to a Kiwi with strange facial hair, named Alistair, and once again he was enthusiastically guiding me to the bottom. His company - Gravity Assisted Mountain Biking - was the first, and is the biggest, most expensive operator, with the best reputation. This counts for something when a brake is all that stands between you and a parachute-less freefall off a cliff. Injuries are still common, but Gravity has safely guided over 30 thousand people down the road without any fatalities. There were now over 30 companies assisting tourists to bike the death road, and as I discovered two years ago, there is zero regulation. Fly-by-night operators offer cheap prices to budget travellers, on sketchy bikes with little maintenance, and little or no instruction. That being said, Alistair can be overzealous with his warnings, reducing one girl in my group to tears with tales of imminent death. As he remarks, "If people didn't die, why would anyone want to bike the world's most dangerous road?" Because it snakes through stunning scenery, and, thanks to the new highway, is blessedly free of those rinky-dink trucks and buses waiting to terminate their journeys (and everyone on board) at every blind corner. The death road has become a fun bike ride through the mountains and lower-lying jungle, descending over 3.5km in altitude until you reach the bottom. Somewhere else exists the new "world's most dangerous road," and I'm happy to stay far away from it. Besides the obvious improvement of no traffic, Gravity now ends their trips at a wildlife refuge, home to rescued monkeys, cats and birds. What a thrill to play with a baby ocelot, a beast kitten with fur so soft it has been hunted to near extinction. A baby howler monkey - the loudest animal in the kingdom - sits on my shoulder, whispering sweet nothings into my ear. A spider monkey wraps its vice-like tail around my neck and hangs out, curiously peeking into the camera lens. I'm so distracted I fail to notice the mosquitoes and sandflies feasting on my legs. Later, I count 32 bites, a new Modern Gonzo record. Driving back along the same road to La Paz, the jeep up front gets a puncture, and the driver pulls out a bicycle pump (only in Bolivia). For a half hour we stand under a coat of stars, the Milky Way resembling a bright streak of pigeon shit across the car window of the universe. Finally we set off, drinking beer in the bus, listening to sing-along songs from my iPod, a group of exhausted international travellers aware that this is a once-in-a-lifetime kind of experience. As for me, with better bikes (a dual suspension $2,500 Kona), better weather, and better road conditions, Bolivia's death road was well worth hitting the repeat button.

Back in La Paz, and the chance to see a local derby soccer game in the national stadium. Football is religion here, and when the city's two top clubs meet each other it's bound to be interesting. The blue Bolivars, lions supported by the lower class, versus The Strongest, tigers in striped yellow and black, with a wealthier fan base. I accompanied the hostel's barkeep, Luiz, an avid Bolivar supporter, so screw the bourgeois tigers, and viva la Bolivar! Outside the stadium bi-partisan vendors sell all manner of swag, and $3 later I'm sporting a soft Bolivar Viking helmet, blue ribbons and a scarf. Thousands of people descend on the stadium from every direction, attacked by bowler-hat ladies selling thin sheets of foam for 5c to cushion the rows of cold cement. Bottles, plastic and glass are confiscated at the entrance, so the fans transfer their liquids to plastic bags to drink later. Luiz tells me this is the only game where fans are separated, and opposite our blue corner the yellow-and-black crowd is cheering loudly. It's warm in the sun and cold in the shade, the dry winter air blocking my nose as I breathe hard from the cross-city walk to the stadium. It cost $2 a ticket, and the stadium seems too big for the crowd, even as thousands of people continue to flock in. When the teams walk onto the pitch, a crescendo of drumming commences, fireworks explode in the sky, and a flock of birds is released, flying in circles for several minutes before realizing the way out is up. Kickoff is followed by a definite and enjoyable Latin flare in play. I cheer for the Blue, knowing full well that just about every sporting event I've ever witnessed is won by the opposing team. I am a sports jinx; nothing more to it. So when The Strongest score first, I am ready for the inevitable. The Blue crowd keep their spirits high, screaming "puta this" and "puta that." Then the tigers score again, and once again, in football as in life, the working class is crushed. At the final whistle, the Blue corner of fans exits first into a heavy barricade of armed soldiers. We walk along the human barricade dejected, but kids are smiling and wearing goofy hats, and judging by the amount of mothers, wives and girlfriends in the crowd, it has been a grand day out for the whole family, whatever the result. Teams win, teams lose, but as a means of interacting with the masses of La Paz, I achieved my goal.

With only a week in the country, there was not enough time to revisit the stunning Salar de Uyuni, so instead the crew hightailed it to Lake Titicaca. I was a little hung over from trying to over-impress two cute American girls at the hostel bar, and leaving before sunset would be the first of many groggy mornings to come. Yet when the sun broke the horizon on the Bolivian Altiplano, and my iPod shuffled Your Rocky Spine by the Great Lake Swimmers, it was more than the altitude that made the hair on my neck slow dance. There is something about the light in the Altoplano, the warmth of the winter sun, as if someone had focused the lens on the camera of my life. We arrived at San Pedro, where the bus drove onto a wooden barge for a short crossing to San Pablo. These two towns, separated by a channel of water and deriving most of their income from shepherding traffic, are the perfect setting for a novel of magic realism, a romance about the son of San Pedro falling in love with the daughter of San Pablo. I've been reading too much.

We arrive in Copacabana mid morning. Argentinean hippies are selling trinkets along the main strip; street vendors offer cheap traditional Bolivian ponchos, woolen hats and alpaca scarves. Two years later, the same restaurants blare the same music - Manu Chao, Bob Marley, the Beatles in panpipe. Garbage and the smell of sewerage litters the shore. Although I've heard Brazilians argue to the contrary, our guide tells me Bolivia's Copacabana is the original inspiration for Brazil's beach strip (and subsequently for Barry Manilow) and competes with Peru's Puno as the town from which to explore the beauty of Lake Titicaca. In Puno, I remember the water thick with green scum, polluted beyond repair. Despite the ever-present trash on the streets and shore, the water on the Bolivian side is blue and clear, and Copacabana faces the sunset, every night, disappearing under the horizon.

Sunsets symbolize many things to many people, certainly as evidenced by how many people have answered "the sunset" to my question about what inspires them. Like travel in general, the quality of a sunset depends on who you are, who you are with, and how you feel at that given moment. Top five sunsets to date that come to mind:

- The Calvario, Lake Titicaca, Bolivia
- Africa House, Stone Town, Zanzibar
- Sunset Dune, Jericoacoara, Brazil
- Anjuna, Goa, India
- Sihanoukville, Cambodia

It's a tough hike up the steps of the Calvario, a steep hill that overlooks Copacabana and the lake. Almost a religious passage, as it is for many Bolivians who offer tributes at the dozens of Christian/indigenous memorials found on the top. Sean was lugging his heavy A-cam; Zach and I taking turns with the awkward-to-carry tripod. A steep hike at altitude, without acclimatization, is nothing to scoff at. After waiting two hours for a chicken sandwich (there is never, ever any rush in Copacabana) we were hustling to reach the top in order to catch golden hour, when the sun glides towards the horizon, casting shadows over the cement crosses. Bowler women were burning oil in tribute, along with plastic cars, candles and candy. Oxygen was hard to come by. We made the peak, bought a beer, took a seat on the rocks looking out over the lake. I have never forgotten the energy I felt here the first time, when I climbed the hill listening to Dead Can Dance on my iPod. This time, reggaeton was blaring from a cheap vendor's radio, but light was fading and they soon packed up, leaving a handful of backpackers to watch the best sunset on the planet. Thin clouds burst into peach and pinks, a crescent moon appeared in the sky. The lights of Copacabana flicker on; it gets dark quick. Sean has got his postcard shot, Zach keeps muttering something about "Who knew, in Bolivia?" We carefully make our way down the hill and pop into La Cúpula for a superb four-course meal, beer and wine included, costing $8 each. Can't fault those Bolivian prices.

It's like a religious car wash. Every day, buses, trucks and cars line up outside Copacabana's conspicuous white church to be blessed by priests. Adorned with all manner of colourful and tacky plastic kitsch, it has turned into a cottage industry for locals, as even a backpackers' tour bus was in the lineup. Firecrackers, in the form of mini-dynamite sticks known as Tom Thumbs (made in China), explode every few seconds. Ah, Tom Thumbs. Long ago were the days I used to put them in milk bottles, or hurl them in shopping malls, or test a nine-year-old's nerve by holding onto them as they exploded at my fingertips. The very smell of their gunpowder triggered all sorts of youthful memories, and naturally I acquired a packet to satisfy my inner child's mischief. Meanwhile, owners are blessing their vehicles by pouring wine and beer all over them, and I wonder if there's a connection between christening a boat and this somewhat bizarre Copacabana tradition. A local lends me a light and I set off a strip of Thumbs, but my nerve has faded, because I'm backing away before the fuse is properly lit. Still, a small explosion hits my face as I retreat. God, I used to be fearless. After the spectacle, I set off for a local market, take a few photos, argue with some guy that I'm really not out here to disrespect his culture. I meet a backpacker from Spain who, in another world, I would probably end up backpacking with, because he's of similar age, attitude and direction. I flirt with some English girls I met the night before, shop for a poncho, play some pool on Bolivia's wonkiest pool table. There are only two bars in town, and according to Charlene, a South African girl working at one of them, both are owned by an Argentinean family. She also works at a lakeside restaurant owned by a German. The pizza place on the corner, another Argentine; the bar around the corner, yet another. Busloads of backpackers arrive every day, but by 10 p.m. the street is practically deserted. Just the smoky Sol y Luna is doing a fair trade. "Most of the backpackers chill out in the hotels," explains Charlene, who's been hanging out here for three months. "You never know if it will be busy or slow." I walk back alone to the hotel under a galaxy of stars, the déjà vu so thick it leaves me gagging for air. No, that's the altitude again. Back on Transturin's catamaran, a return to the Island of the Sun, playing with a big-eyed vicuña, dancing with a bowler lady on the boat. What are the chances - twice in a lifetime?

Will things change in this country? Will those houses ever get built, the glass, repaired, the vehicles fitted with exhaust filters? Will women finally take off their bowler hats? Will neon signs light up downtown La Paz? Probably not, and selfishly, this reassures me. My memories of Bolivia will remain as real as the country itself, no matter how much things change everywhere else.

The World's Most Dangerous Road: La Paz to Coroico

Cars being blessed outside the church in Copacabana

A Quechua priest making a blessing on the Island of the Sun, with
Lake Titicaca shimmering in the distance

VENEZUELA
AT PLAY IN THE FIELDS OF THE WARAO

According to the overweight missionary with braces, Jesus was coming to save me tonight, deep in the heart of the Orinoco Delta. Not an emissary, mind you, but Jesus himself, and he would save me, and save the primitive Warao people, because even though we're quite happy (me, the travel writer, them, the indigenous people of one of the world's remotest jungles), she knew, she just knew, that Jesus was coming tonight, not in spirit, but in person! I thought about the practicalities of this second coming, and made a fair attempt at some intelligent discourse, but when faith blinds people, it robs them of more than just vision.

"Do you know much about the Warao way of life?" I inquire. "Their respect for nature, the gods that make sense in their lives, as opposed to the god that makes sense in yours?"

"Oh, they practice witchcraft, but in their heart, they love Jesus," she replies, my words bouncing off her head like an over-inflated soccer ball. The Warao, it seems, will find Jesus whether they want to or not. But what is the difference between these blissed-out misguided missionaries, followers of a two-thousand-year-old Middle Eastern guy/Son of God named Jesus, and me, a gringo with a camera taking pictures in an exotic world that doesn't want nor need me? We're both using these people, this place. I came to learn and write, and they came to convert. Stuck in the middle of our argument - fragile, timid, lacking ideological filters and completely vulnerable to religious, cultural, physical or technological attack - are the People of the Canoe - the Warao of northern Venezuela.

****

I'm going to row the boat back, to my frenetic arrival in Caracas, where graft is thick, and with a few dollars one can skip the immigration lineup altogether. It was immediately clear that although the official currency is the Boliviano, this was not Bolivia. The airport was big and new, and when you have the fifth-largest oil reserves in the world, money counts for something, just as long as you don't use the banks. They'll give you a 2000:1 exchange rate, whereas just about anyone you talk to will gladly give you around 3200:1. The black market thrives, 70% on the dollar, despite the best efforts of president Hugo Chavez, of whom I'll return to later. There was no time to join in the fun of Caracas on a Friday night. Into a van, and we're off to the north, a six-hour bus ride to a beach town called Playa Colorado. From here, it's a further five hours (hopefully) to the world's second-largest delta, the Orinoco. Caracas showed all the signs of being a big South American capital: traffic, pollution, insane drivers, desperately poor and violent barrios, sexy mestizo girls, pounding reggaeton, neon-lit love hotels. After spending time in La Paz, I was desperate to get out of the urban jungle and into a real one. The six-lane highway slowly turned to four lanes, and finally into two. It was 11 p.m.; I'd been in transit for 16 hours, but the journey into the jungle was only beginning.

Fat chickens roast on a large rotisserie at the roadside buffet, and like the late-night air, the meat is hot and sticky. It reminds me of northern Brazil - the coconut trees, the humidity, the women wearing their sexuality the way a yuppie wears a tie on Wall Street. After a minor altercation with an SUV (a few dollars change hands; we drive off), we're back on the road. I'm DJing up front with my iPod, trying to keep Harold the driver awake, even though he hasn't been in transit for 18 hours like I have. At last, Playa Colorado, and welcoming young girls with skin the colour of brown sugar show us to a room with a few beds. Mosquitoes are in abundance, a warm-up of things to come. I climb into my sleep sheet, reposition the fan to blow away predators, and collapse in total transit exhaustion. I awake to the sound of kids playing in the garden, and a camera in my face. We've overslept, too late to drive to the Delta, but no worries; Chris has got plenty planned to keep us busy. And so, enter to the left of the stage Chris Patterson, the Scot of the Jungle, a real-life cigarette commercial man, host of this lush new world. After sailing in the Caribbean for ten years, Chris found himself the dream chaser for decadent Russian billionaires, organizing multi-million-dollar adventures around the world for oligarchs: from balloons over the Serengeti to castles in Ireland; from ice palaces in Iceland to heli-skiing in Whistler. How do the rich have fun? Chris knows the answer, but after a few years riding the perfect wave, he had earned enough to build his Jakera Lodge - backpacker heaven, school of life, one block away from Paradise, and just down the road from Dream Street. Wiping away sleep from my eyes, I wander over from the overflow house to Jakera Lodge to find a cage housing a dozen Scandinavian girls in bikinis, swinging in hammocks.

"We have mosquito nets around all the enclosures," explains Chris, "and we call this room the Bird Cage."

"You realize nobody will believe a word of this when I write it," I tell him in a low voice.

"Want to play with a baby river python?" he moves on.

"Sure, why not?"

The Jakera Lodge is a hostel of sorts (think hammocks instead of bunks), a Spanish school, a Salsa school, a Scuba school, a Climbing school, a Whatever school. The clientele is mostly European, although all nationalities breeze through at some point, and people stay for anywhere from a few days to six months. It's about immersion in a different culture and language. A few minutes away sits Playa Colorado, a beach of red-hued sand, coconut trees and turquoise water. "We had a big night last night," explains Chris's partner Brendan. "The guys are a little hung over." This explains the tanned limbs poking out of hammocks wherever I look. Tanya from England has been here for two months, and leaves today.

"Everyone thought it would be dangerous to come to Venezuela," she tells me. "But it's been totally safe. The locals are friendly, and encourage us with our Spanish. The people have been dynamic; there's always fresh travellers arriving; it's really a way of living."

I ask her how on earth she found this place.

"Google," she tells me. "I typed in 'Spanish' and 'scuba'."

I speak to some other students - Dutch and Swedish girls. They typed in 'Spanish lessons in South America' and 'volunteer travel'. I ask my travel partner Julia how on earth she found this place.

"I typed in 'jungle adventure' in Google," she answers.

I make a note to write a story about travelling through the power of Google.

After fiddling with the baby python and taking on the climbing wall before breakfast, Chris drops the D-bomb. In all my adventures, I have yet to swim with dolphins. There've been a few opportunities, but the weather turned sour (Honduras), the dolphins were migrating (Zanzibar) or were giving birth (Colombia). It's one of the few things left I have to do before I die, along with: heli-boarding, having a cheap pint with the Queen, tasting the perfect guacamole, sitting next to Bono on a long-haul flight, seeing Jennifer and Angela dump Brad for each other, flying in a luxurious private jet, finding a pen I can't lose, a beach without sand flies and a government without pork fat, speaking to an animal, slaying an Orc, mastering Time Crisis, winning a ballroom dancing competition, being weightless, starring in a Bollywood movie, mastering twelve languages (including Elfin), dating a supermodel, dumping a supermodel, playing tennis at Wimbledon, winning a bracelet at the World Series of Poker, seeing the world in peace for just one day, and cooking a gourmet vegetarian meal for world leaders in Timbuktu. But I digress.

The following day, Brendan organizes an old wooden speedboat from an old wooden pirate and we depart the beach, crowded with Sunday afternoon locals. There is nary a gringo in sight. The water has the sparkle of a paparazzi flash on the tooth of a movie star.
"Today's your day," says Chris enthusiastically, his thick brown curls an affront to balding 39-year-olds everywhere (the secret is aloe vera). And then we see the curved fin of a pilot whale breaking the surf just a few metres away from the boat. "Mucho queso estente vista tacos boutros boutros ghali," says the boat pilot, a weathered pirate of the Caribbean.
"He says it is a good omen for today, and the trip," translates Chris.
Sure enough, within minutes we encounter a pod of dolphins. Two of them leap in the air as if to welcome us. Chris grabs the knee board. I'm ready for the ride of a lifetime. But first, two bits of personal information for context:
1. I have had a shark phobia ever since I saw Jaws on a beach holiday when I was six years old.
2. I have ear problems that prevent me from diving, and have prevented me from swimming in the past. Thus when it comes to water I am a water baby.

I'm thinking about this when Chris tells me that a tiger shark bit half the ass off a tourist just last week. And another attacked a fisherman the week before that. Right here at Playa Colorado. Hungry tiger sharks, cruising around looking for tasty tourist butt. But, screams Robert Plant, "now's the time, the time is now," so I ignore the cello in my head and jump in. The water is as warm as the kiddies' section in a public pool. "Go Gonzo!"

The boat pulls off, and I'm being towed behind like a piece of bait on the end of a fishing hook. I read somewhere that dolphins protect humans from sharks. I know that sharks....whoa! A dolphin pops up a few metres to my right. Then another. Then they vanish together. The boat swings left in an arc. I'm looking this way and that way, and then three more dolphins break, and two of them leap in the air in perfect unison. We swing around again, but they seem to have disappeared, until a minute later, just as I begin to wonder if pilot whales are dangerous, two dolphins pop up on either side of me. For a fraction of a second I stare into an eye looking right back at me, a playful eye, an eye with soul. I know I am safe, I know I am alive, and I just connected with something, something real, something transcendent, and every muscle tenses up and hair stands up and screams and tears well up and organs chime and it's toccata and fugue on the strings of my soul, and in a flash it's over. They're pulling me towards the boat.

"You just swam with dolphins, as people are meant to swim with dolphins," says Chris. "In their space, at their welcome. Something else, hey?"

I blubber something in response to the camera that recorded it all, and after a few minutes realize I'm wading on my knee board like a big fat turtle in shark-infested waters. Moments after I pull myself aboard the boat, as unbalanced as the old, weathered pirate guiding the outboard engine, Chris decides he would be a good sport and take me canyoneering off a 28m waterfall in the nearby jungle.

We had driven about 15 minutes into the lush thicket, through a few villages, enthusiastically greeting the locals with shouts and waves. There's really nothing to worry about, so long as the ropes and harness do their job, and the people tying the ropes and harness do their job. I figured this out in Costa Rica, when I went off a 50m waterfall, dangling on a thread like a fly wrapped in dental floss. Reassuring me, I counted on the fact that there's nothing to be gained from dying at this early stage of production. Still, I was nearly pulled off the edge by accident before the safety rope was in place, the heavy rope tugging me forward resulting in a mad scramble and scream of panic, but hey, these things happen, so here goes nothing. The scene made the opening montage for the show. I look like a flailing albino chicken. Being wet season, the water level was high, and I certainly enjoyed myself bouncing off a solid wall of rock as fresh water crashes against my skin. Certainly better than, say, hanging around waiting to abseil, as thousands of sand flies attacked my shins with the hunger of starved wolves. Some local boys were swimming at the bottom, laughing hysterically at my gringo antics. I joined them for a swim beneath the waterfall. The only language we would communicate with is laughter, but it works a hell of a lot better than violence.

"It's really about day-to-day living out here," explains Brendan, a fellow Scot who joined Chris at Jakera about five years ago. "The locals trade or catch fish or do odd jobs and somehow make do. Girls get pregnant, families grow, another room is added to the shack, and that's the way it's always been. Simple." I don't ask about crime and social misery, because reggae music has a habit of making everything seem just wonderful, especially when you see a lot of people smiling under coconut trees.

I turn down the poker game at the lodge that night to prepare for the reason we're here - a weeklong jungle adventure deep into the heart of the Orinoco Delta. We'd be leaving at 5 a.m., packing light into dry bags. Accommodation would consist of hammocks, meals of camping basics or whatever we could catch. The second-largest river drainage system after the Amazon, the Orinoco has an average temperature of 27C degrees, and is 25,000 square kilometres of pristine, undeveloped eco-system, protected, owned and inhabited by the indigenous Warao people. But first, we'd have to get there, and in hot-blooded Latin America, this can become an adventure unto itself. All is well racing along the highway, until suddenly the cars in front stop moving, which is never a healthy sign for a highway. Chris pulls the Land Cruiser across into the oncoming lanes and makes his way at a steady pace into oncoming traffic, passing hundreds of stationery cars on the right. But then this lane becomes choked, too. There is a demonstration up ahead; a village has blocked the road to protest lack of civil services. Apparently, this is quite normal. Since the car isn't going anywhere, now's the perfect time to drive into the world of the continent's most controversial political leader, the outspoken never-a-dull-moment Venezuelan president, Hugo Chavez.

You may have heard of him. He's the guy who waved a Noam Chomsky book in front of the UN and compared George W. Bush to the Devil himself. He's best buds with the ghost of Fidel Castro, a huge critic of the US hegemony, the rare meeting of a left-wing radical with pockets so full of oil he can put his money where his mouth is. All around the country, large billboards of Chavez shadow the streets, graffiti and T-shirts comparing Chavez to Che Guevara, the ultimate symbol of the radical revolutionary. With his country's oil wealth, Chavez is not dependent on US business to float his empire, and is not afraid to say so. With Morales from Bolivia and Lula in Brazil, he's the spark behind the left-wing nationalistic fire that swept Latin America, much to the horror of US business interests, which would prefer everyone just stay at home, watch *Friends*, and buy a new blender. Instead, Hugo channels massive oil profits back into the country, which explains why a litre of gas in Venezuela costs a staggering 5c, or 2.5c if you use black-market prices. Chris fills up the 50-litre Land Cruiser, and it costs $3. Back home, gas prices are doubling. Nice one, Hugo.

Except, wait, what's this? Hugo shuts down the largest and most popular independently run TV station in the country for criticizing his policies. And now he wants to be El Presidente for life. These are not the signs of healthy democratic regime, which might explain why intellectuals and students are peacefully protesting in the thousands, and world media (with a wee bit of help from US business interests) are slowly but surely painting Chavez into a fruit and nut bar past its sell-by date. So what's the word on the street in the country itself?
"I hate Chavez," one guy tells me. "He's tricked us all and has become power-mad. He's going to ruin this country."
"Chavez has done amazing things for this country," says another. "He has given the poor a voice, improved the lives of the masses, and is putting the wealth back into the country and not into his foreign-owned bank account."

A nation divided. Everyone has an opinion, but everyone agrees that if a vote were held tomorrow, Chavez would win by a landslide. A populist, a voice for the silent masses - no wonder the small, wealthy elite are threatened and the Church is convulsing over Chavez's goal to permanently split the Church and State in this Roman Catholic country. He's pissing off the people who are benefitting from the status quo, in which millions live without running water or electricity, and dozens of people get murdered in the slums that border Caracas every weekend. Chris is on the fence, but has definitely seen improvement from Chavez's policies on the local villages around him. So very few of the right people step onto the historical political stage at the right time. Mandela, Gandhi, Churchill. Most arrive with good intentions, and leave bloated and disgraced with fat bank accounts. Chavez, a military man who spent time in jail after a previously failed coup, who had his own TV show, who is cozying up to the enemies of the USA because the enemy of my enemy is my friend - well, we're going to have to wait and see what becomes of him. In the meantime, there seemed little he could do to get us into the jungle, and the local governor wasn't worth a fart in a frat house since his wife busted him in bed with his male bodyguard. Ah, Latin America.

We could try to get there via the old route, but with the heavy rains of late, it might be a little dicey. So we fly along a cracked path until we hit a bridge, washed out in muddy brown water. Chris shifts the Cruiser into 4x4 and decides to take a chance. Have you ever heard the sound of a sinking car? Or seen water rise above the windows? He's revving it, and we're screaming, and God-Help-Us if somehow we don't find the smallest chunk of road for the tire to grip, and the car lurches forward to reach the other side. Shouts of victory! High fives all round! No other cars dare attempt this sort of madness. The roads will be clear for miles! Feeling well proud of ourselves, we gun down the old road, only to find the flood had done more than wash out the bridge. Villagers were crossing the river chest high in water, saving what possessions they could as the flood wreaked havoc on their homes. We stop on the side of the highway. A family sits with a TV, a couch, a chair or two. Their homes are destroyed. Now we continue into the jungle, less proud of ourselves. Past military checkpoints, giant gas plants burning the fires of the apocalypse from tall metal chimneys, stopping to watch a family rescue an armadillo. The road is flat and unrelenting; the journey has already delivered enough action for one day. When: the car begins to throb, the engine groans, the iPod goes dead, the battery fails, and the Land Cruiser comes to a hopeless halt. The alternator has been flooded by the bridge crossing, and we are stuck in the middle of nowhere, the mid-day sun batting us hard over the head. We hail a pickup, and within minutes they've tied a piece of rope to our Cruiser and are pulling us along, about two metres separating the two cars. Well and good, sure, except these guys decide to hit about 120 km/hr, overtaking big trucks on a narrow highway, and then, oh, yes, and then it starts to hail.

Fear is not jumping off a waterfall. Fear is not swimming in shark-infested waters. Fear is being pulled along at 120 km/hr on a dangerous road in a blinding tropical storm, without windscreen wipers, when a single brake will result in a massive rear-ender and almost certain damage to all occupants within. There was good reason to tighten my sphincter, because Jungle Chris, the kind of guy tough guys want to be, had white knuckles on the wheel and crazed animal fear in his eyes. We drove like this for an hour. All I could think about was that dying on a Venezuelan highway seemed somehow beneath me. Of course, the clouds parted just as quickly as they stormed, a brilliant sun burst forth, we finally had some vision out the front window, and the guys in front decided to take us right to the bridge, where we would meet our boat. J.P. would stay behind to sort the car out, we would load up the kayaks and the motorboat, and finally, this time I mean it, head into the Orinoco Delta.

****

Three days later. Red Army Karl must have spiked the drinks, because if I hadn't seen the photos, I wouldn't have believed we dove into piranha-infested waters at sunset to swim with the pink dolphins. Yet there it is on tape - us in the water, and a few metres away a rare pink dolphin leaping into the air. Memories of that night at the lodge are blurry. I played with a toucan, a macaw. I see a Palestinian flag, news clippings above the bar mentioning the Hezbollah. The lodge is owned by two Palestinian guys, and in my head, drunk from sun, from exposure, my liver fighting the toxins from spider bites on my mosquito bites on my sand flea bites, I concoct conspiracies and mad fevers of paranoia. A puma roars from a nearby enclosure. Wild parrots fly overhead. I remember strong jungle rum, playing classic rock on the stereo, passing out in the damp cabin, our one night of relative luxury. There is a hole in the net above the door handle. Someone punched through the door to get in; the bloodsucking mosquitoes are everywhere! I slap my neck and the corpses of a dozen sand fleas are on my hand. Outside, a giant black tapir runs down the wooden boardwalk. I look up in time to see the cow-sized creature in a sprint, chasing the girls into their rooms, the sinister cloppity-clop, cloppity-clop of its hooves on the wood. It is the largest mammal native to South

America. I feverishly dream of beasts and heat, sweat and danger. We are the only guests this night in the lodge. This is a good thing.

After just a few days, I had jungle joo joo fever, and I had it bad. Sleeping in my hammock took some getting used to, and even Chris's homemade repellent of baby oil, vitamin B12 and a dash of Deet was no match for the hordes, the armies, the full frontal invasion of jungle bugs. My back was bent out of shape, the mosquitoes perched on the small, surrounding hammock nets, waiting for a tiny part of skin to brush against the netting, and then, for what we're about to receive may the Lord bless us with this blood! I counted 136 bites on Julia's lower leg. Just one leg. The humidity sticks to you like Velcro, and swimming is not too advisable since these waters are home to man-eating piranhas, hungry for human fingers and toes. Add in the giant snoring of our Director of Photography, Sean, and lack of sleep, and, well, you've got the making of one unforgettable, incredible, now-this-is-the-real-shit Gonzo adventure.

We had 150km of river to get through, with a twin-engine open-roof speed boat, a couple of kayaks, a few days of food, and, invaluably, Jesus and Pina, two quiet but good-natured Waraos who knew these labyrinth tributaries the way a bus driver knows his city routes. Also, Chris has been guiding jungle expeditions here for ten years and has enormous experience with the Waraos, the elements, the challenges of life inside the planet's green lung. The wild beauty surrounding me is staggering. The water is a mirror to the lush tropical trees that tower above it, the sky as big as Dali's imagination. Wild macaws and parrots fly in love pairs above, while in the trees, cappuccino and howler monkeys swing on the vines. Fresh water stingrays gently float like orbs in a wet universe, the sound of the jungle at night becomes a hum of life, and yet 99 percent of it is beyond view, behind the curtain of darkness. And intertwined are the People of the Canoe, the Warao, a tribe who live by the river in open-walled wooden shacks, worshipping their tree of life, the *morichi* palm, which provides food in the form of giant worms, fruits and elixirs. Physically resembling the Asiatic features I encountered in Mongolia, the Warao talk in hushed elfin tones, communicating in what Chris believes is "jungle telepathy." Children learn to kayak before they can walk, families are nomadic, moving between different parts of the jungle. It's a beautiful dream, mixed up in the misguided concept of the noble savage, beyond the grasp of modern life. It's a beautiful dream that has been woken up. First came the engines: 500 boat engines given to the Warao in some sort of political maneuver for votes, resulting in a swift change in how they move, how they interact. Then came the villages, small concrete houses and generators, the government gathering the Warao into communities that never before existed (and the social conditions that come with poor rural communities, too). Some of these houses are used for chickens and feed, since the Warao way of life exists beyond four walls. Then came the satellite dishes and TV sets, the DVD players to napalm an unsuspecting people with messages of the west, without giving them the social tools to understand that advertising is all bullshit and television is television, not the real world. Then came the movement towards the towns and cities, the breakdown of family units. Then the tourists, taking pictures from their speedboats. Then came the missionaries to tell them that thousands of years of tradition are all wrong and they should all believe in a bearded white god who died on a cross. Like the indigenous tribes of the Amazon, like the indigenous tribes anywhere, these gentle people don't stand a chance. We head into the brackish water, the Black Water, where the salt of the sea meets the fresh water. The channels are becoming narrower, the trees, thicker and darker. The boat gently pulls along, barely sending a ripple in the water, as smooth as a polished granite. A small channel breaks to the right, and there is a half-naked boy fishing. It's the kind of photo you see in National Geographic, a vision of humanity that is both inspiringly and frighteningly different. I wonder what hope there is for the Warao. Wherein lies their future? Am I as complicit as the German tourists visiting on a day trip from the tourist island of Margarita?

I ask Chris what he thinks about tourists visiting the region, now that lodges are being built to accommodate them. "I want to bring less tourists here for more time. And if you kayak here, you earn the right to be here. The Warao are a completely passive people. With encroaching boats of tourists, they'll just fizzle and fade to nothing." What hope for a people that have no swear words in their native tongue?

We awake on the final morning in a small wooden camp on the water. Just two hours on the boat remain, to a small town and a waiting Land Cruiser. The rain held off, sparing us the torture of the heavy downpour at high speed we experienced a few days back. Waiting for the car, I walk in the village, houses painted in bright colours, past a missionary church. These "urban" Warao kids are wearing crosses, but one guy tells me it's just for fashion. A long drive back to a town called Barcelona, a short flight to Caracas, choking traffic to a nearby airport hotel, early morning flight to Houston. The jungle has disappeared, the bugs, the river, the piranhas, the Warao. I see overweight people for the first time in a week. "The Department of Homeland Security has declared the current terrorist threat level as: ORANGE. Please be aware of your surroundings and fellow passengers."

I fall back into my airplane seat, close my eyes, imagining the red beach of Playa Colorado, dolphins and waterfalls, the channels of water in the Orinoco, piranhas and tapirs, the gentle stares of the Warao. Not for the first time, I say a silent prayer in gratitude.

Eat me Mr Piranha? No, eat you.

BEHIND THE SCENES IN VENEZUELA

In this episode, you can see that GETTING to the adventure is as much an adventure as the adventure itself. The political road block, the washed-out bridge, the car breaking down, being towed in a storm by a thread of rope at 120 km/hr was probably the most dangerous moment for all of us in the first 13 weeks of filming. But the delta was worth it, of course; what a beautiful slice of life on our planet. Couple of things to mention. First, I was almost pulled over the waterfall by accident because the rope wasn't connected to a tree before it was flung off the edge. Pretty funny. Second, those were seriously shark-infested waters, and whenever I put my toes into the sea I hear the damn cello, even at the best of times. Mary, our director, interviewed me after swimming with the dolphins, while I was in the water, on the board, looking like a big, tasty turtle. All I could think of was, great, here's a wonderful take for *When Sharks Attack*.

The mosquitoes in the jungle chew on body parts the way Vikings once chewed on roasted pig. They feast. Blood everywhere. Then you have the gnats and the piranhas and the thorns and the wasps and the scorpions and all those wonderful things that make the jungle so graciously hostile. I was happy to let Julia eat the moriche worm in her segment; she eats, I jump. I think I came off better in that deal.

That scene when Julia gets stung by the wasp? Sean, our bold camera guy, got stung in the eyeball. Yes, the eyeball. Zach, our sound guy, had a thorn go right through his hand. Ouch. I mean it when I say Chris Patterson is a real-life cigarette commercial man. He's my bloody hero. He also runs an amazing backpackers' lodge, which is crawling with beautiful tanned Scandinavians. The bastard. Great place to learn Spanish, chill out, meet some people. Everyone sleeps in hammocks.We had a weird night of jungle fever, where leopards roared in the night and a giant tapir chased Mary down the wooden boardwalk. Might have been the jungle, might have been the rum and cokes, but I had a fever, and I say that like a Harlem preacher.   A fee-ver!   When I woke up I was covered in bites because someone had punched a hole in my mosquito net.   Nobody fessed up, but the size of the hole was very close to the size of Sean's fist.   He got the fee-ver too. It's a travel truth that the harder things are, the fonder you'll look back on them.   Venezuela was not always fun at the time, but every one of us would put it in our top five favourite destinations.

The People of the Canoe

Mural painting Hugo Chavez as a liberator of Latin America

Birds sitting on the front desk of the "Hezbollah lodge"

Sean follows us with the camera, floating up the Orinoco Delta

JORDAN
WONDERS OF THE WORLD

"I looked over Jordan and what did I see
Coming forth to carry me home..."

My week in Jordan was a pearl necklace of experiences. Instead of a beginning, middle and end, I'll string you along with some choice vignettes, scenes of life, atmosphere and adventure. If you print this out and shake the paper about, you might even hear the muezzin's call to prayer. Bring it to your nose, smell the smoky aromas of fresh-fried falafel. Lick it, and taste the bitter minerals of the Dead Sea. Just make sure you don't get a paper cut on your tongue, because that would hurt.

The Setting

Jordan, as in: The country that lies on the banks of the River, ruled by a popular king, with an inspiring and beautiful queen. Ally of the US, peace treaty with Israel, lacking in oil but faithfully greasing the wheels of the region's political machine. Population around 7 million, including over a million Iraqi refugees; no shortage of Palestinian refugees, either. "I want to be successful," a young guy tells me at a swank club called Nye that has heaving bosoms and pounding house music. "You don't want to be in this country and not be."   Most women appear to wear traditional *hijabs;* many don't. Chaotic traffic. Amman's malls are like any other - one is called - oh, the irony - Mecca. McDonald's. Starbucks. Popeyes Chicken & Biscuits. Two-thousand-year-old ruins in the skyline, Roman and Byzantine relics line the streets the way other cities parade waste. Package tours and backpackers, but it ain't all cheap; the US dollar is 0.70 dinar, but a dinar buys you here what a dollar buys you in the States. Press trip hospitality means five star all the way, and I could get used to sitting by a refrigerated pool if not to sipping the $10 beer, and I could get into politics, and I could get into truth, but that's the time for wisdom, and now's the time for youth.

Petra

I say Jordan, you say Petra, inducted into the sketchy marketing campaign that became the New Wonders of the World. *Indiana Jones and the Lost Crusade* really made the Treasury famous, but people have been coming here for years, or at least since it was introduced to foreign tourists through the efforts of a European explorer. The Treasury - misnamed because treasure hunters once thought the King's tomb housed all manner of riches - was carved into rock over 2000 years ago, yet looks like the facade of a 20th-century bank. A few minutes' walk from our hotel, I greet bored-looking touts with an enthusiastic "Welcome to Jordan!" as a sort of pre-emptive strike. From the amount of people who greeted me all week, they should print "Welcome to Jordan" T-shirts like the Thai print "Same Same." I walk down the canyon, along a well-carved gravel road, avoiding speeding horse carts loaded with sunburned tourists, and whistle the theme song. Da Da Da Da, Da Da Daaaaa. Each bend belongs in the chase scene of a historical adventure, almost distracting me from the fact that the rocks turn ruby with the early morning sun, lending the chasm an effect not unlike a CGI scene in a video game. I walked a half hour until a slit in the rocks stopped me in my tracks, revealing the glowing jewel of the Treasury. The memory card in my camera shuddered, knowing full well the abuse to come. Click. Click. Click. The people known as the Nabateans did all sorts of clever things two millenniums ago, mastering a water system to tame the harsh desert, building a trading post bustling with Asian, African and Middle-Eastern merchants. History rolled on, the Nabataeans didn't, but today their legacy is Jordan's biggest tourist attraction, and rightly so. I joined the throngs of French and Italian tourists to explore the temples and caves baking in the nuclear heat. Click. Click. Click. An hour to relax at the pool, then rush to catch the sunset in the Urn Tomb, a less-restored marvel with a massive chamber perfect for, say, the German tourists who broke out into spontaneous Gregorian hymn. I strike up a conversation with some friendly Jordanian students, even bump into Hollywood's Delroy Lindo. Sun streams into the chamber like spotlights on a concert stage, and I find a little spot on some nearby rocks to write some thoughts, like: "There's an energy in the Wonders, an element that triggers an emotion, an experience, an archetypal memory that resides in our human consciousness, just as sure as aroma resides in an ancient spice." Whatever that means. Then I look up and a murder (fraud? felony?) of crows is circling overhead. The sun sets, a donkey screeches, the tourists are gone, and Petra's colours deepen. Ghosts awaken and belly dance.

Petra Part II

Truthfully, I'd make a crap Marlboro Man. Born and raised in a city, I smell sales, not trails. Tools turn to fools in my hands, and I firmly believe the only way to start a campfire is with a can of fuel and a big pack of Lays (watch those potato chips burn!). So why have I taken so fondly to galloping on horses, without any lessons or technique other than holding on tight and trying not crush my gonads? It started in Mongolia, where I raced across the lush plains. Now I'm galloping an Arabian Seabiscuit across the desert, sweat drops forming on the hairs of its neck. I ride a horse the way I ride a story. Hang on; hope it takes me where I want to go. In this case, towards Little Petra, although Sean (tall, bald, camera) saw a time lapse, and Brown Stallion was exhausted, so I took to the hills, scrambled up a rocky boulder, and found a stairway to heaven. (God, this is all sounding so dramatic, the result of an unlikely Jane Austin movie being screened on the plane as I write this.) Stairs had been carved into rock, leading up to a couple of one-man caves, tailor made for people like me (or, according to local historians, Jesus) to meditate and ponder life. The landscape greatly resembled the Chilean Atacama, and the experience greatly resembled the time I got lost in earth's driest desert and climbed a hill to get my bearings. That day I was rescued by a lost Japanese backpacker named Ken. Today, I needed no rescuing. I see an old Bedouin man praying towards Mecca. Camels, donkeys, a loyal scraggly sheep dog. Some guys race a beat-up old car over dunes. Rose-red rocks live up to their reputation. Travel buzz.

Amman

The Coptic Church opposite King Abdullah's Mosque is welcoming in their new millennium. I'm inside, sitting on my knees, respectfully covering my shorts with a black cloak, feeling the spirit. A solitary man prostrates himself towards Mecca. A mosque official turns on the air conditioning. Ramadan is a few days away, and there is much to prepare. We deposit the robes, take off to see the Roman Coliseum downtown, a theatre over two millenniums old and still in use. I climb the stairs to the top. Take a break in the shade from the punishing mid-day heat. Strike up a conversation with a Jordanian guy who's been living in the US for a decade. His girlfriend in Florida tries repeatedly to call him on his cell phone, but he keeps hanging up on her. Our conversation is punctuated by ringtone. "My father lives here, but I wouldn't. (Ring Ring.) You need to know the right people. (Ring Ring.) The king is popular, but that's because nobody would ever risk criticizing him. (Ring Ring.) That's not freedom." Now I'm sitting by the pool at the InterContinental, a rare day to relax and breathe as Julia chases a story about modern Amman in a shopping mall. Filipino maids in tight pants dote on the young overweight children of Jordan's elite. A beer costs $10. I order water. Every major hotel has a metal detector, and all bags are screened at the entrance with airport scanning machines. In 2005, Islamic fundamentalists attacked several major hotels in the capital, killing over 55 people. Nobody wants a repeat. All week I am scanned, X-rayed, patted down. I keep telling people: "I fight only Salad Wars. I support only the Balsamic Revolution!"

Women

It's all about eyes. Jordanian women possess eyes that drown men like hot candle wax drowns mosquitoes. I'm reading a book about evolution (Jared Diamond's *Third Chimpanzee*), and it could say: "As religious Muslim women wore veils to cover their entire face save for their eyes, their pupils evolved to sparkle with rich colour as a means of attracting a mate". It doesn't. But it could. At a mall, I kill time in a food court staring at people. Seeing young women dressed in tight jeans provokes unconscious leers from men (including me). We can't deny the thrill of seeing what the other women must look like under their black cloaks. Some girls respond to the leer; others just as quickly disappear. With *hijabs*, they don't have to. Maybe that's the point.

Wadi Rum

I'm lying under the stars, deep in the stark, barren Wadi Rum desert. Riding a camel in the hot sun all day triggered a flu attack. Nose blocked, throat swollen, head pounding, chest burning with cough. I can't sleep, so I relax on a dusty bench near the fire (safe from scorpions and camel spiders), and scan the skies for shooting stars. I count 23. I'm in a Bedouin camp, protected from the wind by a cliff eroded to the point that the rock hills look like melted chocolate. It's a bouldering paradise. My energy is as low as a laptop battery at the end of a long flight, but earlier I had managed to scale a rock face to feel the warm wind blow in my *abaya*, a traditional Arab cloak. I felt like Batman, my cape dancing in the wind. I remove my red Jordanian *keffiyeh*, hold it in the wind, let it go. It does its best impression of the plastic bag in *American Beauty*. The scene would be cheesy if it didn't feel so damn alive. Ali buries lamb, chicken and vegetables in the ground, and three hours later they are perfectly roasted. He serves up plates of mezze; his tea tastes like sweet sage, briefly soothing my lungs. "I've been to many places in many countries," I tell our guide Ibrahim, "but few places are as magical as this." After a decade of being a tour guide, he tells me he is bored of all Jordan, save Wadi Rum. In the morning, it feels as if a truck has driven over me, reversed, and parked right on my body. The camera is rolling. A TV show about my life shows no mercy. During my brief period of outdoor sleep, I dreamed of spiders and refugees. Nerves were crawling. Feeling barely alive, there is one more item on the menu: the Dead Sea.

Food

My plate is always stuffed. The hotels serve up a buffet of dreams. They even have their own Tabasco. The hummus is creamy, the *tabouleh* is crunchy, *baba ghanouj*, fresh pita, falafel, and olives as juicy as fruit. I make a right mess of the mezze. Sheesh, another kebab. Why not? Grilled chicken, beef, lamb on the same plate. Chili paste, pasta, salads, onion soup. "For a little guy, you eat a lot," says Sean, one of the bigger guys I know. That's because the worm in my gut needs to be fed. All week I'm never far from a toilet. Montezuma's Revenge. The Belly. Gypo guts. Call it what you will, I punished the buffet and lost 6 pounds. The Modern Gonzo Diet.

Dead Sea

The lowest point on earth, 430m below sea level. A sea with zero life in its waters. A sea where you float effortlessly. A sea that is receding at a rate of one metre a year. A sea that will one day disappear. A sea that divides two countries of two faiths. A sea that heals skin conditions, arthritis, this-and-that-itis. A sea with hotel resorts, of which the new Mövenpick is surely the top of the pile. Final day to relax, heal, reflect, float, burn. The mineral-rich mud has got to be good for you; they sell it for a fortune back home. Breaking from the afternoon sun, I write an article in the lobby, easy listening music over the speakers, drinking in the wealth of the resort's tasteful extravagance. Press trips have a habit of making me feel like Cinderella, giving me a brief glimpse into how the others live - hotel suites, porters, yes sir, Mr. Esrock - and then midnight strikes and I'm backpacking again, hustling away, dusting roaches off the bedspread. But I'm floating way out now, the sun setting between my feet, the dead salty water supporting me like a soft, watery pillow. An unusually clear day, I can see the lights of Jerusalem begin to twinkle less than 35km away, ushering in the Jewish New Year. And on the right, I see Jericho awake, the first evening of Ramadan. I hear the gentle lapping of waves, and as I drift away between the world's biggest conflict, all I see, feel and hope for, is peace.

A slit in the canyon reveals Petra's Treasury

BEHIND THE SCENES IN JORDAN

So we arrive in Jordan, and on the plane are a bunch of US mercenaries flying to Baghdad. Seriously. Big stocky guys with shifty eyes and army haircuts, I overhear the name Blackwater, and less than a week later there's a scandal involving the dubious US private army Blackwater and the killing of innocent Iraqis. This is the kind of Gonzo that follows me that is not fit for a travel show. The flight was a red-eye killer, but we arrived on the one night that Amman's club scene would be firing, so after dropping off the bags it was off to the party to film Julia's story.

As you can see in the show, what we found was not what most people think about when they hear about the Middle East in the news.

The name of this episode is Press Trip Cinderellas, and because there's so much to show and do, we don't go into press trips in too much detail. Basically, travel writers are amongst the worst-paid writers anywhere. Simply put, we cannot afford to travel on our own dime. So tourism boards and companies offer free trips in the hope that we'll write something positive, which of course we usually do, because most travel writing is positive. There're various opinions as to whether or not this constitutes an act of literary bribery, but given what travel writers earn, it's a reality of the job. I pride myself in remaining independent, writing as we see it, and every profession has a behind-the-scenes etiquette and unspoken rules that, if revealed, might be misunderstood by those outside it. Travel writing is no different. Meanwhile, we relished the chance to stay in nice hotels and eat in nice restaurants before heading back to reality - hostels and cheap street noodles. If I lived in luxury all the time, would I be able to appreciate it?

Our Bedouin campsite in the Wadi Rum

Floating in the peace of the Dead Sea

Exploring Amman's Great Mosque

ETHIOPIA
BREAKING OUT OF THE HUMAN ZOO

The Nigerians on board the flight from Dubai to Addis Ababa were losing their minds. Pushing, shoving and screaming at each other by the check-in counter, one woman ran her overloaded trolley directly into my legs; another woman shoved my back while waiting in line at security. There was nowhere for me to go; Dubai Airport was slammed from all sides, and both women were unapologetic. Adding to the chaos, our names weren't on the e-ticket list. Someone forgot to tell someone something, and nobody knew anything about nothing. We rushed to board the plane with just seconds to spare. A fight broke out a few rows down, and women started screaming at each other, their babies hollering along in solidarity. Of course, given the frenetic rush to get on board, our plane stubbornly sat on the tarmac for an hour. When we finally took off, Ethiopian Airlines served up chicken curry, and the pretty flight attendants, battered by verbal abuse, somehow managed to smile. At this point, I realized that I was returning to Africa, and, well, I better get used to it.

With no disrespect to Nigerians in general, I was relieved that 98% of the plane continued onwards to Lagos, depositing us in Addis Ababa just two days after the country celebrated its millennium. Ethiopia does more than follow its own Christian calendar (the Julian, as opposed to our Gregorian), they also tell the time differently, with 12 hours of day, and 12 hours of night. We arrived at eight p.m., but it was really two p.m. Thus, I arrived in the country a full seven years younger, and way ahead of my time. Our luggage, on the other hand, took an hour to make its way to the conveyer time, or, if you prefer, just a few minutes in Africa Time. Oh Africa!   Birthplace of Humanity, Land of Beauty, the Place that Progress Forgot (or at least, Overlooked). I had missed the Millennium Party due to scheduling, but Addis was still aglow with festive coloured lights, its roads wide and dusty, snaking through tin shacks and creaky wooden scaffolding holding up leaky cement construction. The Greeks called this the Land of Burnt Faces, a politically incorrect term that has nevertheless given the country its name. It is one of only two countries on the entire continent that has proudly never been colonized, but it is also a highway lined on either side with war and famine - the tragic car wrecks of history. There is no time to explore the capital just yet; an early morning flight is ready to take us north, to the little-known, incredible rock churches that still survive the ancient kingdom of Lalibela.

Cars break down, boats break down, I've been on a train that broke down, and, once, a gondola I was in got stuck, too. So it came as no surprise when the twin-prop Fokker 50 takes off after a quick stop in Bahir Dar, circled over Lake Tana - the source of the world's longest river, the Blue Nile - and bumpily lands again. According the pilot, the plane had broken down. The two-dozen passengers, made up of adventurous international tourists, Rastafarians, and a few locals, walk back into the airport to be served up coffee, bread soaked in spicy *berbere* sauce and rain drops of misinformation from the airline. It was the weather. No, the weather instrument. No, we're not sure - more coffee? Five hours later, a replacement plane arrives, but unfortunately, it breaks down, too. So the passengers from the replacement plane are transferred to our plane, which apparently now works, and we will have to wait for a replacement replacement plane. I don't mind so much, because one of these Fokkers is bound to crash, and my bet is on the one that "suddenly" fixed itself. The airport toilets don't flush and there is no water, but I sit through my first Ethiopian coffee ceremony (which can take an hour) and unplug the cafe fridge to do some work on my laptop. Three hours later, an unmarked Fokker lands to the cheers of the by-now-somewhat-irate passengers. The airport staff, with whom we'd been mindlessly bantering all day, turn professional and empty our bags as a security precaution, barring us from going outside, and requested the tape from our cameras. It is all rather odd, but a few hours later the plane takes off from Bahir Dar, and, where was I, oh yes, the ancient kingdom of Lalibela.

It must have come as a surprise to uptight European missionaries arriving on the Dark Continent, eager and ready to convert heathen savages, to discover that someone had beaten them to it. Ethiopia was the second country to adopt Christianity as a state religion as early as the 4th century. An ancient kingdom known as the Aksumites was one of the largest, most civilized and prosperous nations of its era, benefiting from its position as a vital trading post between Africa, Asia and the Middle East. While Europeans were living in caves and sleeping in hogshit, northern Ethiopia had sophisticated art, architecture, music and commerce. The Aksumites faded with the rise of trading posts along the Red Sea, but a new kingdom arose in the 11th century, led by one King Lalibela. He decided to build a New Jerusalem in Africa, just in case the rising Islamic empire swept the real Jerusalem into the paper shredder of history. And thus began the construction of the churches of Lalibela, hand-carved into red volcanic rock, a mind-boggling human accomplishment. Jordan's Petra is similarly carved into a rock face, but the eleven churches of Lalibela stand on their own, like the finished masterpiece of a sculptor. Built alongside its own renamed River Jordan, Lalibela is rich with symbols, icons and religious images from the 11th century. They have survived and are still in use to this day.

Lalibela attracts tourists - Italians, Spanish, Japanese - with the trickle barely supporting the town that surrounds the churches. The Ethiopian word for foreigner is "*ferengi*", and be it an accident from decades of foreign aid, or just irresponsible tourists who should know better, *ferengis* in Lalibela (and elsewhere, as we'll soon discover) appear good for only one thing, and that is: handouts. Seconds after departing our van, my ass still vibrating from a staircase masquerading as a stone road, I'm surrounded by children asking for birr (Ethiopian currency). Prodded and poked, I stare into dozens of upturned hands. An old toothless woman walks up from behind and gives me a sloppy wet kiss on my arm. Years later, I still feel the phantom moisture of her saliva.

A guard walks up, raises a stick, and the children scatter. We enter the main gate, buy $20 tickets and pricey $30 video camera permits, and are assigned a compulsory guide, as well as someone to watch our shoes when we enter the churches. UNESCO, in an attempt to preserve the main church of Bet Medhane Alem, has installed ugly scaffolding around it, designed, no doubt, to ruin all photographs. Still, the fact that this huge building was carved top-down from solid rock is staggering. We take off our shoes and enter inside. It is dark and cold and still has some of the original carpeting on the ground (we were warned to wear long pants because of fleas). Light streams in from small windows, the ceiling blackened with centuries of candle smoke. Voices echo, dark corners hide stacked carpet and wood, angels and demons. Forget the polished gloss of Europe's superstar churches. Here, you can feel every one of Lalibela's 800-plus years, breathe in the past (along with the thick dust). A robed priest is happy to pose for pictures for a few birr, protecting the sacred inner chamber, housing a replica of Ethiopia's holiest object, the legendary Ark of the Covenant.

Recall *Raiders of the Lost Ark*: Indiana Jones gets wind of a Nazi plot to find the ancient Ark of the Covenant, built by the Israelites to house the tablets of the Ten Commandments, given to Moses by God. The Nazis want it because, according to Biblical history, the Israelites were invincible in battle so long as they possessed the Ark at their side. Legend believes it unleashed a powerful light that decimated their enemies. Moses himself had to wear a veil after he gazed at the Ark, as it burnt his face. The Nazis believed the Ark to be nothing less than a powerful weapon, and they were right, the suckers, as Indiana cleverly looked away and the Ark unleashed its supernatural power, killing all the bad guys and melting the creepy Nazi guy with the glasses (which gave me nightmares for months). A classic movie, mixing myth and history.

I first became inspired to visit Ethiopia after reading *The Sign and the Seal* by Graham Hancock. An English journalist formerly with *The Economist*, Hancock spent over a decade sleuthing the real whereabouts of the Ark, becoming a real literary Indiana Jones in the process. The resulting book is a fantastic mix of history, research, speculation and adventure. What became of the Ark remains one of history's greatest unsolved mysteries. Its disappearance has been linked to the Knights of Templar, King Solomon's relationship with Queen Sheba (which resulted in the birth of the first great Ethiopian ruler, Menelek), and all manner of conspiracy theories. Is it an accident that Ethiopia's holiest object is the Ark of the Covenant, its language shares many Hebraic commonalities and the country even held tribes of "lost" Jews? Hancock spent much of his time figuring out how this all came to be. His logic and conclusions are controversial but sound, and having briefly met the guy many years ago, I can testify that he's definitely no cracked conspiracy hazelnut. In Ethiopia, the real Ark (or an ancient replica) is believed to exist in the town of Aksum, north from Lalibela, where priests zealously guard it. Not even the President of Ethiopia is permitted to see it. An Israeli traveller tells me her investigations lead her to believe the Ark was destroyed, or maybe it's sitting in a big warehouse somewhere in Washington, D.C. We'll probably never know. But here in Lalibela, where the Ark supposedly passed through, you can still feel the magic of the mystery.

I explore the rock churches, walking inside carved rock tunnels, peering inside doorways to find weathered priests reading leathered bibles. If only I could blink and take photos with my eyes. Fortunately, my photographs will do. Bet Golgotha, another dark and dusty rock church, houses the tomb of King Lalibela and is forbidden to women. The priests don their robes and display ancient crosses while the surrounding 11th-century religious paintings still hold their bright colours. By lunchtime, I am escorted out of the three main churches and head over to the House of Saint George, by far the most visually impressive of the lot. Shaped like a Greek cross, it is carved into a gash of surrounding rock, and it is blessedly scaffold free. The bones of mummified 14th-century pilgrims protrude out of "hermit holes", where holy men once meditated. Channels have been carved for rainwater to flow, and a priest points out King Lalibela's olive tree wooden treasure chest from eight centuries ago. The sun breaks between the clouds, the god-rays lighting up the church, along with my goosebumps.

As we exit out an open tunnel to the street, I see the open hands again, pleading and begging. Julia and I walk down the main street, and the harassment comes thick. We're warned that children speaking good English will tell heartbreaking stories and ask for money to buy school books, only, it's a scam; the books are actually exchanged for money, or are never bought at all. Kids want *ferengi* email addresses, to email about their lives in Ethiopia. Sounds great, only we're warned it's another scam, since their real intention is to guilt you into sending money. The kids surround us like a swarm, fighting among themselves for priority. It's hard to keep things in perspective. I want to connect with locals, I always do, but I also want to connect with real people, and I want the communication to be authentic. I don't need to buy friends.
A boy named Jordan gets to the front and tells me, it's OK, he doesn't want money.

"Look, Jordan, I want people to visit this amazing place, but you guys make it very difficult and uncomfortable, and then nobody will come, and that hurts everyone."

"We are not all like that," he explains, somewhat annoyed. So we begin to chat. He tells me that his parents are farmers, and he looks after some crops, and is never hungry, and is going to school. I begin to feel awful about my earlier sweeping generalizations - here I am, another white, rich, western asshole ready to dismiss the natives as beggars and thieves. Everyone's not out here to use me, to get a buck. Then Jordan tells me, after a half-hour chat, that he needs some schoolbooks. The ball drops, and it's the same old scam.

Damn. I sweep, I generalize.

Africa can be like a beautiful, possibly dubious girl you meet at a party. There's an incredible connection, you laugh, you cry, you open your heart, you embrace. Then she puts out her hand, and tells you to pay up for the privilege. I told Jordan to stay in his fictional school, and decided then and there to find a real charity and try and make a real difference.

My cynicism retreats that night thanks to a guy named Kassa, whom I meet at a hole-in-the-wall bar selling 40c beers. That's a new record - the cheapest beer I've found in any country. Local reggae music spiced with Bollywood is blearing from the TV as I attempt some Ethiopian dance moves, which consists of twitching my shoulders while keeping my legs still. I've got a nice buzz from the *tejj* - local fermented honey wine. There are no girls in the bar, since no decent Ethiopian girl would ever go to a bar unless they are willing to sleep with you for money, which I am told is perfectly acceptable in this part of the world. Kassa and I talk about life in Ethiopia, in Canada. We sympathize, we laugh, and naturally there's no financial arrangement at the end of the conversation. But if I thought I'd made peace with being a walking dollar sign, I was yet to experience the true *ferengi frenzy*. For that, I'd have to fly back to Addis, and drive five days into the southern Omo Valley.

I wake up to the sound of a women screaming in sexual climax. Unfortunately, she's not in my room, but rather, in the room next to mine, although with the cardboard walls she may as well be lying in my bed. A cockroach runs across the floor. It's six a.m. The plane from Lalibela made it back to Addis late last night, a few hours late. Not bad, considering the first flight. I had hoped to check my email, but the email is down at the hotel, and everywhere else. Ethiopia is still using dial-up, and it takes a few hours to check my inbox from an internet cafe down the road. There is only one service provider, the government. There is only one cell phone provider: the government. There is one TV station: the government. After decades of brutal communist rule, in which thousands were murdered and starvation was used as a political weapon, the current left-wing liberator is conforming to the typical pattern of African rule - when power comes, so does corruption. Recent elections were declared a farce by UN observers. Most people voted for the opposition. The opposition lost. Sounds like the Bush-era USA, so who is to judge?   Anyway, on ETV the president is talking and talking and talking, and hours later, he's still talking. The Derg, the horrific previous government, pretty much killed anyone who didn't like Red, including Haile Selassie, Africa's most recent emperor. Born under the name of Ras Tafari, he crowned himself Emperor Haile Selassie, spawning a religion in Jamaica and forever making Ethiopia a popular destination for those with dreadlocks. After being unceremoniously strangled, His Highness's remains were subsequently found to be buried under the incoming crackpot dictator's toilet. I think about this while the woman behind the cardboard veil continues to scream in ecstasy. It's a different kind of early morning rooster, a cock will doodle doo.

It takes three days by Land Cruiser to the Lower Omo Valley, one of the most culturally diverse regions on the planet. 53 nations live in Southern Ethiopia, most with unique customs and traditions, as different from western life as whales are to Shih Tzus. We take a while to navigate out of Addis, stuck behind trucks and buses puking thick black smoke directly into the back of our throats. There are cows in the middle of the road, herds of goats, overloaded donkeys. Children run in front of the car, and before long we see the first of many road kills, a donkey, split in half in the middle of the road. Our driver Ayalew honks repeatedly, at animals and people. The road is an obstacle course requiring absolute concentration. Bob Marley on the iPod, we leave the city behind, the lanes become narrower, but the countryside is lush with various shades of green from the rainy season. After a few hours the asphalt disappears into a strip of never-ending craters. Tin shacks become mud huts with thatch ceilings. Small villages are crowded with people and livestock. Kids play ping pong and foosball under the shade of trees. Shacks sell everything, and the only structure that looks like it is from this century belongs to the ominous-sounding Ethiopian Insurance Corporation. Hand-painted street signs show drivers to watch out for donkey carts, to celebrate "Happy Millennium". They also show a dead baby, and the only word I can recognize is AIDS. Ethiopian writing is all dashes and squiggles, with English words appearing occasionally and usually misspelled. After 250km, we drive through the town of Shashamane (gifted by Haile Selasssie to the Rastafarians), welcomed by a hand-painted billboard of Bob Marley. Rasta colours are prominent, as are tall dark foreign men, their dreadlocks towering over locals.

Each kilometre along the bone-shaking acacia-tree-lined dirt highway seems to wipe another century off humanity's recent progress. No glass, no cement, no electricity, or phones, or wide-screen TV's. No tennis courts and swimming pools, no basements, no driveways, nor cars to drive on them. No windows or patios, or dishwashers and washing machines. Forget about laptops, battery-powered toothbrushes, mattresses, linen or bathtubs. Throw out the microwave, blenders, futons, cabinets and sofas. Here we are exactly how we were, before words like Globalization, or Renaissance, or Industrial Revolution, or Cyberspace. Living in huts, working fields during the day, sleeping around a fire in the dark, using wooden headrests as pillows, on a bed of thin, dried animal skin. We were driving forward, back in time.

A mosque appears, with a single minaret. Huts now have a crescent towering over the thatch. After the Eastern Orthodox Church, Islam is the country's second-largest religion, but unlike the civil war in neighbouring Sudan, Christians and Muslims live in relative peace. The purpose of our road trip is to visit some tribes along Ethiopia's Rift Valley, and the Muslim Alaba are the first. The Land Cruiser pulls up, and immediately aggressive, impoverished villagers surround us. Children are wearing western-style clothes that resemble rags, torn and filthy. Hands are out. "Birr!" "Birr!" I feel sick to my stomach, and yet I continue to walk through the metaphoric turnstile of the Human Zoo.

However moral and well intentioned, the fact that you are expected to pay money to locals for photographs has hideously backfired in

Ethiopia. I see nothing wrong with remunerating someone who appears in my photographs. It's only fair to reward them for the right to capture their image, and later sell some photos. The problem is that it has become a business in Ethiopia, encouraging desperate people to appear in tourist photos as a means of making easy money. When I take pictures of locals in foreign countries, I aim to capture an image that speaks (a thousand words?) about life and the people who live it. It is never the intention to manipulate anyone, or take photos of them without their consent. I look for the authentic, the real, the moment. So consider the impact of a mob demanding I take their photo and pay up seconds after I do. Gone are the moments of locals in their natural element, replaced by locals doing whatever it is that will get foreigners to pull out their cameras and their wallet. It's undeniable exploitation, by both parties, and the result left me taking great photographs with an accompanying memory I'd rather forget. One of many examples: We stop to join a group of locals on a donkey cart on the side of a highway. I ask first for permission, followed by how much it will cost for the fare. I am told 20 birr. I get on the cart and the poor donkey heaves on; a few photos are taken. People are laughing and smiling and I feel generous, so I pull out a 50 birr note (about $5). What ensued was amateur wrestling hour, the group physically turning on each other, demanding more money, grabbing me from all directions, literally ripping the money out of my hands. I was threatened, shoved, and had to run for the safety of the car. All because I wanted a photo, for which I was prepared to overpay the agreed-upon price by more than double. How could it not taint an experience?   As one guy told me in the town of Jinka:
"The money makes everybody go crazy!"
"All they know of *ferengis* is NGO's and tourists," Da Witt tells me over coffee in Addis. He's a local nutritionist who works for an NGO. Like our guides and drivers, he laughs off the harmless Ferengi Frenzy, as it is called, even though it has left a negative impact on our experience. He tells me there is an Ethiopia where it is customary to refuse gifts and handouts. There is an Ethiopia where people care and support one another, are warm and open and friendly to strangers, eager to learn from each other. Unfortunately, if you're a tourist in town for two weeks and plan on visiting locations suggested by a tour agency, chances are you won't see it.

I needed to find a way break through, and while music may be the international language, football trails a close second. We stop in a town and I buy a soccer ball. For the Konso people, known for their agricultural terraces, I was determined to break the cage of the human zoo. Right away, things were different. Tourists pay a fee up front and are assigned a local guide. Chu Chu is young but well spoken, and assures me the tourist fee is split with the tribe (apparently this is not always this case with other similar operations). Although children flood us with their familiar hands out, Chu Chu keeps them in line. He explains the significance of tribal walls, how unmarried men live together and serve the community, how bundled tree branches are used to determine the age of the village. At last I am learning something. I pull out the soccer ball and learn a whole lot more. Whether I am merely distracting the kids or tapping into their desire to genuinely interact with a strange *ferengi*, we choose sides, play some soccer and have some fun. I might be deluding myself or seeing the truth, but for a half hour I'm not a human handout, just a traveller in a strange land, trying to connect. Chu Chu shows me a traditional game called *grayka*, involving a piece of wood and a lot of jumping. Everyone has a riot. It is only once we began to make our way to the car that the frenzy takes hold again, the calls for money, or "Highland" - empty bottles of packaged water. I tip Chu Chu well, he responds with genuine sincerity and I leave feeling a little better about the way things could be. It's a Catch-22 in any country. Tourists want to interact with indigenous locals, but the process of interaction changes the way locals live.

Another long day in the car, on bulldozed roads that would beat a suburban SUV into teary submission. We pass curious baboons brave enough to jump on the hood and bare their teeth. Vultures and large hawks sit on acacia trees, postcard Africa perfect. I meet man-sized marabou storks, their guilty beaks red from the blood of gutted catfish. Bright blue and yellow birds play chicken with the car's front grill, and everywhere are cows, donkeys, goats and children loaded up with backbreaking hay, screaming "Highland!" with hands out as we pass. Many are naked. A couple even wave their little peckers at us. A few break dance, hoping we'll stop and take a picture. Instead we break for the night in Arba Minch, a university town that overlooks two fine-looking lakes connected by a hill called the Bridge to Heaven. This is Africa - beauty wearing its heart on its countryside. We're in malaria country, so there are mosquito nets over the bed of my modest hotel room. There are also four condom packets on the bedside table. The hotel makes no pretensions, much like the nine sisters I meet when trying unsuccessfully to get online at a small internet cafe. The oldest is unnervingly direct about what I might get for a few dollars. Holding her hand is her youngest sister. She is two years old.

One more day, and like a pimple on your prom date, the dirt road somehow gets worse. It takes nearly three hours to drive just 27km, and this time, we're attacked by a swarm of tsetse flies. There are easily over a thousand flies clinging to the side of the Land Cruiser, their syringe-like needles ready to puncture our skin and suck our blood. These little bastards are deadly to cattle and humans, although we are reassured that right now they were harmless since "nobody is dying in the area." Perhaps they're just waiting for *ferengis*? Our destination is the Mursi Tribe, nomads famous for their women with lip plates, aggressive stick fighting and all-round "am I on planet Earth?" cultural extremes. We are warned that this tribe is particularly aggressive when it comes to photographs, demanding 2 birr for an adult, 1 birr for a child, and 3 birr for a woman and baby. Yes, you can put a price on people after all. We are also advised not to visit in the afternoon when the tribe becomes intoxicated on fermented milk and potentially violent. Running late after a fascinating visit to a cultural museum in Jinka (in which I learned much about female circumcision and the cultural traditions of the varying tribes), we finally reach the camp around 3 p.m. Since we would be camping overnight in the bush nearby, we decide to leave the cameras and experience what might happen if the photo frenzy is removed. The cruiser pulls up to a small village made up of a dozen or so huts built of twigs. Men are hanging about under a tree, some with AK-47's. Soon enough, we are besieged by a full-scale Mursi offensive.

Still in the Land Cruiser, we are attacked by children with white face paint, and men with patterned scars, and bare-breasted women clutching babies, and women with bottom lips hanging below their chins, and women with clay plates, and men with sticks, and everyone is screaming, "Take picture! Take picture! Take picture!" We hold up empty hands and show them no cameras. I was naturally hesitant to open the door, to embrace this alien world.

Our guide Mulu, mild mannered with the kind of face that just begs for implicit calm, begins a form of negotiation. We are invited into the chief's hut, welcome shelter from the oppressive sun. It is no bigger than a three-person tent, with a blackened fire pit in the middle. A tied-up live chicken sits to the side, along with some basic wooden cooking utensils. The chief, Shalima, introduces us to his three topless wives. Two of them hold babies, one with a horrific burn on his hand. One wife holds an AK-47. Shalima chawks and spits in the middle of our crowded circle. Outside, the tribe gathers, playing with Julia's hair through the thatch. The smell is intense, sweet, pungent and metallic, like dried blood diluted with semen. Mulu negotiates a price for us to come and film the village the following day. I attempt to ask the chief questions, but the communication is stilted and sharp. Mulu rolls his eyes, says the chief is talking gibberish, drunkalese. Jerry cans of strong fermented moonshine lay about. My legs cramp. Our director Mary holds one of the babies, and the baby begins to scream. His mother takes him with the universal look of care in her eyes. Seeing the interaction somehow puts me at ease. I may be a polka dot banana painted on the Mursi's abstract canvas, but we are all human beings. We get up to leave, and the tribe heaves forward in unison. A tall drunk man grabs my arm. The chief now wants 50 birr for letting us in his hut. Mulu continues to negotiate as I pull away and make for the car. Children are hitting the window with their fists. No sooner have we managed to close the door than our driver Ayalew floors the accelerator. I look back and see the drunk man screaming at the chief, who promptly turns around and punches him hard in the face. We speed into the bush.

The Mursi are embroiled in a conflict with the Africa Parks Board, which is turning their natural habitat into a national park. Armed scouts patrol the region looking for poachers, and the Mursi are being increasingly confined and restricted on their own land. Fights with neighbouring tribes occur periodically, and with the flood of AK's arriving from the Sudan, so do fatalities. The tribe survive by drinking milk and animal blood, grinding corn into a powder, and herding a few animals. Lately, they have been turning to tourists, who arrive daily in 4x4's, take photos for 15 minutes, and leave hastily in a cloud of dust. The band we visited apparently consisted of one extended family, related to a guard at the Parks Board who bulldozed a road and set up the village purely as a means to cash in. The next Mursi village is another 20km away, which on these roads can add an hour or two to the drive. But this is no act. This is the real deal – full blown tribal Africa.

The growl of baboons wakes me the following morning, which is marginally preferable to the sound of neighbours in sexual climax. Long-tailed colobus monkeys play in the trees above. We're camping in the bush alongside the Omo River, and I'm nervous about the day to come. I didn't come this far, three days of tough travel, not to get photographs of what I can hardly believe I'm seeing. And yet how could I ethically photograph this tribe, which parades as an exotic exhibit in a human zoo? We drive back to the village, but this time, it is 9 a.m. It is strangely quiet and passive when we arrive. Villagers are waking up, painting themselves in streaks of white. Some recognize us from the day before, but nobody attacks with quite the same gusto. Mulu and the chief arrange for several dozen women to sit together and show Julia how they make their clay lip plates. I stay back, take photos, start peeling back my thick roll of one-birr notes. It feels awkward, and it is awkward. The strangeness of the scenario leaves me numb. I take a picture of a woman and her baby, and she demands only new one-birr notes (some of the money in Ethiopia is so used it could crumble in your hands). "Take picture!" I am prodded and pushed, and when I start talking to one person, six more join in, hoping to get in on the photo. A young girl holds an AK-47. To take the picture, she wants 2 birr. I agree. Even with the nuclear sun, the photo is incredible. I take the shot, pull out two notes. "Three! " she says. "But you said two." "Three!" "Two." "Three!" I am arguing with a child who has a loaded AK-47 about the fact that she just added 15c more to the price of her photograph. Do you see how ridiculous this is? No wonder some tourists don't even get out of their cars. Eventually, it becomes so intense I have to retire to our Toyota bubble just to escape the constant harassment. Children tap on the window. "Photo photo photo photo photo" they yell, persistent like tsetse flies. Meanwhile, Julia's period of female bonding comes to an abrupt halt when another Land Cruiser arrives with some Italians, and Japanese, and Polish, and English. The tribe vibrates into a feeding frenzy, money changing hands everywhere, ripped away, all desperation, no gratitude. In order to shake things up, I try stick fighting with a Polish guy, to distract the commerce with something as amusing as two white guys whacking each other in the (hopefully) traditional manner. It works, for a few minutes. A tribesman even comes over and shows me how to hold the stick. Then he wants money. The tourists I speak to are dumbfounded, although fully aware that we are all the reason this has happened. If tourists stuck around longer, there wouldn't be the feverish desperation of the tribe to get their money. If the tribe didn't attack tourists with their feverish desperation, tourists would stick around longer. And so it goes...

A UN Land Cruiser pulls up with a small film crew revolving around a remarkable Mursi man named Oli. Having spent 11 months in Australia, Oli is filming a documentary about his tribe, and in turn is being filmed by an international UN TV crew. It's just like Word Travels, art recording art. I'm thrilled to meet someone local to communicate with about all that I have experienced. He tells me that due to the Parks Board, the Mursi are forced to live like beggars, like animals. But this village, he relays, is an anomaly, not the norm. It is dependent on tourists, who take their pictures and leave as soon as they can (by this time, half a dozen cars have come and gone, and we are the only ones left).
"I want tourists to see we are human, not a zoo," says Milisha, Oli's friendly brother.
"But how can they, in this environment? There needs to be a program, a structure, that allows two cultures to communicate and benefit from each other, without this mayhem," I respond.
We agree, pondering the fate of indigenous people around the world. Communication, respect, understanding - I suddenly have enormous respect for anthropologists. The tribe has calmed down now, the scorching afternoon has come and men are in the shade of the tree, drinking from plastic jerry cans. We retreat into the van and drive off for the last time, the image of the lip-plate forever burned into my memory. It is the eve of Yom Kippur, and I am preparing to fast as I have done since I was 13 years old. We all belong to tribes, and we all follow our own peculiar traditions.

There is much to think about on the drive back to Addis Ababa, along the exact same road we took to get to the Mursi. As much as I try and ignore it, every time I hear "1 birr!" or "Highland!" I'm saddened. In countries like India, Albania, Tanzania or Bolivia, I've never encountered a local population so eager to take advantage of me. After another regrettable encounter with some kids on the side of the road - I gave them double what they asked for a photo and they mobbed me, fighting and pushing to the extent that they tore the ten-birr note in my hand - I am disillusioned and, for the first time in all my travels, falling into a trap of negative judgment and western generalization. And then I meet Joseph Kabir.

I call it the People Chain. It's like Facebook, offline, with edge. The idea is to get random contacts in random places and see where it leads you. Might be a palace, might be a dark alley, but knowing anyone here who knows anyone there can sometimes lead everywhere. In this case, an old friend I bumped into in Vancouver passed on the details of Joseph in Addis Ababa. I knew nothing about him, who he is, and what he does, only that we had a mutual friend. Since the rest of Addis Ababa's population of five million were complete strangers, that was a start. I called Joseph from the hotel bar and we arranged to meet the following evening over coffee. I'm still grappling with the Ferengi Frenzy, this sense of wanting to give back but not perpetuate, when Joseph rolls in, sent from above to answer my prayers. Born in Ethiopia, Joseph immigrated to Canada at a young age, settled in Montreal, and later Vancouver. He became the Canadian cross-country champion, competing in the World Championships against Ethiopian greats like Haile Gebrselassie, and then made a fortune in the dot-com boom as an entrepreneur. Able to retire in his mid-30's, he decided to pack his family up and return to Ethiopia to give something back. Investing in various start-ups, he's founded a charity called UniqueProjects.org to support orphans, and most recently has become passionately involved in sponsoring a group of young kids from impoverished backgrounds who show promise of becoming professional runners. Many consider Ethiopia to be the Home of the NGO. So it's inspiring to find Joseph independently making a difference, one kid, one dream at a time.
"Is it challenging to live here?" I ask him, as a local minibus taxi narrowly avoids smashing into us from the left, another from the right, one in front, and, for all I know, one above us, too.
"I'm a long distance runner and entrepreneur," he replies. "I'm made for challenges, but sometimes I think it's hopeless." He talks about the crippling bureaucracy, the constant corruption, the pollution, the problem of "thinking poor" in a country with so much potential. But Addis, he explains, is the kind of city that grows on you, the

kind of city you come to miss. We're climbing up Entoto Mountain, 8000ft above sea level, one of the few forested areas that remain in the area, offering a stunning view of the city below. Joseph has arranged for me to go for a run with some of his sponsored runners, along with Askale Tafa Magarsa, one of the country's top female athletes, who won the Paris, Milan and Dubai marathons. I wanted to find out more about his programs, plus it would be a great opportunity for the kids to meet their hero Askale, and leave my *ferengi* ass in the dust.

"If you can beat these guys up the hill, I'll give you a million dollars," Joseph offers with a glint of seriousness. I begin to entertain the idea of being a millionaire. My backpack will have golden zippers. Then the group takes off, running their "normal" pace, which translates into Robin's full throttle, push-every-muscle-to-the-breaking-point-dash-to-save-my-life sprint. Less than a hundred metres later, I'm hacking my small intestines out and the kids are laughing. Workeneh was a shoeshine boy, Tibebe was homeless, and Kidest a domestic servant. Now they have a trainer, shoes, a place to stay, a basic allowance, and a shot at running on an international level.

Joseph explains. "Look, even if they don't get to the Olympics, running encourages them to succeed, to discipline themselves, to focus on good, healthy behavior. I understand what it can do for an individual. These guys were training with no shoes, no homes and one meal a day. This will give them confidence no matter what they decide to do."

Joseph's idea has caught the attention of friends and fellow athletes back in Canada, who are assigned a runner and can literally watch their charity run for gold. It's an alternative to making a donation to an aid organization, where vast sums of money seem to get swallowed into a bottomless hole. And while every NGO needs donations, here was a small, unassuming man making a big difference in the lives of kids who showed him their dedication to succeeding. I dropped to my knees after the first kilometre, but the kids ran back and carried me up the hill on their shoulders to the car. If I had won the million dollars, I'd have a much better idea as to how to give it away.

I gave Joseph a hundred bucks to do with as he saw fit. It paid off my conscience for every kid who showed me the palm of his or her hand, and I genuinely felt like here was a guy who could take the donation and put it to good use. Later, he told me he used my money to buy a new pair of running shoes for Kidest, and as a direct result her time improved significantly enough for her to win a major race and qualify for the Olympic National Team.

We travel to learn. We travel to challenge ourselves, our expectations, our thoughts of the world. If I want a holiday, I'll book an all-inclusive hotel on a beach. If I want museums, I'll go to a major city. It's never easy travelling in developing countries, and harder still in a country where foreigners are largely associated with financial aid. Yet Ethiopia's landscape is inspiring, its culture and history fascinating. As more travellers discover it, perhaps the frenzy will subside, or perhaps it will get worse. Either way, the country just might be the very reason I started travelling in the first place.

House of St George, Lalibela

BEHIND THE SCENES IN ETHIOPIA

I was born in Africa, and so it's always special going back. It generally takes a while to get used to how things work, if they work, and then you get in the rhythm and really start learning so much about yourself and the world around you.

This episode starts with a frantic flight and only shows the tip of the logistical iceberg revealed when we discovered that the flights we booked three months ago didn't exist in the airline system. We were catching a connection through Dubai, and other passengers were pushing and shoving their way forward, mostly Nigerians bringing back huge bundles of merchandise to sell back home. It was pretty intense, but the plane always takes off, and somehow we always seem to be on it.

Something that truly separates this show from other travel shows is that we film and discover mostly on the fly - sometimes we have no idea what our stories will be or if they'll work for both travel and TV editors. There is little time, and no research team travelling ahead of us. It adds a lot of pressure. The People Chain was pure luck - meeting a guy like Joseph and being able to learn about his wonderful work to help impoverished athletes was so unexpected and amazing for all of us. I got his number from an old friend in Vancouver who I just happened to bump into on Commercial Drive - a chance encounter, and the next thing you know you're shooting a TV show about it: that's Word Travels. Joseph offered me a million bucks if I could beat his runners, and whether he was serious or not, I was serious about getting some fat extra zeroes in my skinny bank account. I lasted about 3 minutes before I wanted to collapse from exhaustion. We were running hard, and we were running at altitude. But I kept moving because I knew it would be a great part of the show. The scene at the end, when the guys pick me up and carry me up the hill, was spontaneous (and much appreciated; I wouldn't have made it back to the car without them). What a great jump shot, too. My T-shirt (pg 73) has a symbol on it; it's the number one in Aramaic. As if.

Like the rest of Ethiopia, Lalibela was vivid. Those churches are so dark and old, and far removed from the restored gloss factor of many other historical wonders. It sees a fair bit of tourism, and they make you pay for it, with the surrounding village basically feeding itself off the tourists who pass through. The issue of giving to beggars was something that again materialized on the fly, and we knew we'd have to be careful on how to portray it. We were warned about various tourist scams, and I was frequently disappointed that encounters with locals would inevitably lead to them. But the churches, and the stunning countryside, not to mention late nights drinking in tiny shacks with pounding Ethiopian rock music, were unforgettable.

In a high-speed world that's increasingly wireless, I really struggled with the dial-up connections, when we could find one working. It was expensive and slow, and a real sign of just how much I've come to rely on being online, both as a living and as a socially networked person. We all struggled a bit, but if we wanted things to be like they are at home, then why bother leaving in the first place?

Oh, and I love Ethiopian food. One of my best cuisines, there's nothing like some spicy "tibs" stew dumped in a large plate of soggy injera...

Meeting the Mursi in the Southern Omo Valley

Jumping with Joseph Kabir and his inspiring runners in Addis Ababa

The Mursi kid with the gun

Priest reading a bible in Lalibela. An Ethiopian viewer in Canada emailed me to say it was his uncle.

The Ferengi Frenzy

DUBAI
BEHIND THE BOOMTOWN EPISODE

We filmed in Dubai a couple of years before its inevitable economic meltdown. It was in the midst of the biggest boom the region, if not the planet, had ever seen. The scale and ambition of the various developments boggled the mind, and in terms of comfort, food and service, everything was so top-notch, tourists were making their way over in droves. It was completely unsustainable, and just a few years later many of the grandiose developments were sitting empty, including many of those villas we explored on the Palm. We had flown in after Ethiopia, and the contrast between the two countries gave us cultural whiplash. You may notice on the show that each episode stands alone, i.e. there is no mention of where we were before, and where we are headed to next. So you can't really grasp how happy we were to see a modern, beautiful hotel after our time in Ethiopia - it's like going from instant noodles to a steak house. The excellent Qamardeen hotel we stayed in is owned by the South African hotel chain Southern Sun, the same hotels I used to holiday with my family in when I was a kid, so there was a weird sense of nostalgia, too. The hotel even gave me some biltong (South African beef jerky). How hot is Dubai? The temperature cracked 40C degrees when I went sandboarding. You don't have to be mentally prepared for the challenge; you have to be mentally insane. I was practically dry heaving after the first run, and we did a couple, because as you can see in the episode, the board didn't exactly deliver the thrill-a-minute adventure I had hoped for. I had fine desert dust piled up in every orifice you can think of (and ones you can't), a bad cold kicking in, and the heat pounding me - ah, the things we do for TV! And, of course, the sequence looks amazing, Sean (camera), Mary (director) and Peter (editor) once again making me look like a bloody superhero. I'd do it again in a heartbeat. After crashing in the blissfully air-conditioned hotel for a few hours, it was off to the snowboarding, which was the first time I'd strapped in for a few years, so I wasn't about to attempt any daring tricks. Sean is one of the top ski cameramen on the planet, so he thought nothing of skiing backwards down the hill holding his expensive camera, and all the time I'm just seeing him falling backwards and destroying our A-cam. Not likely. Living in Vancouver comes with a few advantages, and one of them is that it takes about 30 minutes door-to-door for me to snowboard the local mountains, which are pretty big, and have loads of runs. Ski Dubai was great for the story, but kind of like playing tennis with a four year old...fun, for the first few minutes

My story wrapped up, the show switched to Julia, who was hurting on her story hunt. Although she was going through hell, you really get a glimpse into the pressure we were under to find things to do that work well for both a newspaper article and a TV show. Sometimes you have to take what you can get, and no irony that it turned out to be a shopping mall - there's one everywhere you look in Dubai. You also see part three of Robin getting woken up with a camera in his face (see Venezuela and Colombia). We must have left hair and makeup in Africa. Exploring the Palm development was interesting, actually seeing the reality of a concept that I truly did think was a joke when I first heard about it. And we could see The World in the distance, too - dozens of islands shaped like the continents, so that they resemble a map of the world from above. The ambition is contagious, although those islands would soon enough remain empty in the real estate bust a few years later. After the meltdown, the project was abandoned. I contacted the local Gulf News, the only daily newspaper I've ever seen printed on thick glossy paper, and pitched them some stories. That later turned into a regular column. Whether Dubai will continue its evolution and turn into a major world financial and tourist center, or remain a boomtown gone bust, we'll have to wait and see. I ended up publishing dozens of stories for the Gulf News, until they too felt the pinch and fired their travel staff. Tough times for us all.

Sandboarding: it looks more fun than it is

Snowboarding indoors: it looks more fun than it is

LITHUANIA
TRAVELLING WITH GHOSTS

Ike joined me at the hip Double Coffee shop on Pilies Street. Abie was running late. It took me a few moments to acknowledge his lanky frame, my attention being focused on the buxom black-clad brunette waitress with the short bangs carrying a tray full of large beers. Ike cleared his throat, whiplashing my attention, and I turned to face a thirty-two-year-old guy - my age - with a stern face, thin channels of life already carving themselves around his eyes. He's somehow managed to instantly get a pint of Utenos beer, so we raise our bushy eyebrows and take a sip in silence. Seconds later, Abie comes in, smiles at the waitress, deposits his hat on the hook James Bond style, dances across the room and takes his seat next to Ike.

"So what are you doing in Lithuania, anyway," he asks me, heavily accented.

I begin to explain. My grandparents on my dad's side were both Lithuanian (although my Dad's mom was born in South Africa, her parents were Lithuanian), and my grandfather on my mom's side, also Lithuanian. Through fate, luck and mercy, I've been given a ticket to travel the world, so why not see where they come from, and by extension, where I come from, too?

"It's not going to be all fun and gaming," remarks Abie, drops of rain still falling from his curly hair onto his stylish leather jacket. They really know how to dress in this part of the world.

"Most people don't even know where Lithuania is," says Ike, one eyebrow curiously arched.

"Then, as a travel writer, it's my job to tell them," I say, signaling the waitress for another beer.

I thought it was a small Baltic country (population 3.3 million) in northeastern Europe, but scientists have determined that the geographical center of Europe lies just 26km south of Vilnius, the nation's capital. Twice the size of Belgium ("and we all know the size of Belgium," ribs Abie), it borders Latvia, Poland, Belarus, Russia and 99km of the Baltic Sea. Picture flat green farmlands, fresh lakes and pine forests, towns with medieval cobblestone squares, aristocratic palaces and fairy tale castles. Similar to other countries in Eastern and Central Europe - Poland, Czech Republic, Hungary - only a little cheaper, less recognized, and with fewer tourists. History dates Lithuanians back to the 11th century, mired in an ongoing series of regional wars with larger neighbours Russia and Poland. The country was also the last remaining pagan outpost in Europe, although today it is mostly Roman Catholic. Jewish history begins in the 15th century, and due to brilliant scholars and large Jewish schools, Vilnius became known as the "Jerusalem of Lithuania." Lithuanian is one of the world's oldest-surviving languages, regarded by linguists as the oldest link to the original Indo-European tongue that gave birth to most of the languages of Europe and beyond. It is also closely related to Sanskrit ("that might help me find myself, should I get lost in India," mutters Ike). Lithuanians, a proud and industrious lot, have given the world actors Sean Penn, Sir John Gielgud and Charles Bronson, singers Anthony Kiedis of the Chili Peppers, not to mention Bob "Zimmerman" Dylan, fictional serial killers like Hannibal Lecter, and writers like Nadine Gordimer and Antony Sher. "And, although it remains to be seen, maybe you," says Abie.

Autumn has lined the streets with red, yellow and green leaves, which incidentally match the colours of the national flag. The October sky has been watching a tragic love story on cable TV, and frequently cries raindrops (when it blows its nose, a chilly wind rushes up the streets of Old Town). I'm looking at the Litvaks Abie and Ike (*hukking* about the *kakameyme schlep* to get here in free-flowing salty Yiddish), and realize that, for once, I'm a physical fit in a foreign country - pale, blue-eyed, average height, biggish nose. I'm told Lithuanian girls love foreign men, but that doesn't help me, since I don't look foreign at all. We're on to our third deceivingly strong unpasteurized beer, so I order a round of a local herb-based liquor as a sort of yardstick. The waitress brings them over swiftly. I'm trying to flirt, but Abie seems to be doing a better job."There are three Abrahams in my family, so they call me Abie Bachelor, since I'm already in my 30s and not yet married," he says. "I have been thinking about this Polish girl I met, but hey, if I was in a hurry, I would take a bus."

" I suppose that makes sense. Hey, l'chaim!"

We touch glasses, make eye contact, snap our heads back, drain the elixir. I've always thought that anything that tastes this disgusting has got to be good for you.

"So, you both come from Vilnius?"

"No, I was born in a little village called Kupiskis, or, Kupishok, or Shuk, or Shik, or however you want to say it," Abie says, chasing the shooter with a sip of beer.

"I am from nearby, a bigger town, Panaveyz. Today it's the fifth-biggest city in the country; used to be bigger. But I suppose a lot of things used to be something here," adds Ike, glancing over at Abie, who looks down into his glass. It is quiet for a moment, but the uneasy silence breaks and Abie continues to talk.

"Look, Gonzo, this is not all party time. This country has seen a lot of pain... We...have seen a lot of pain. What is it you are looking for?" His face take a serious turn.

I answer him: "People around the world are travelling to see where they come from, digging for roots, trying to understand a little about where they sit on the family tree. Hell, it's become an industry, with software, websites, tourist agencies specialized in helping westerners trace their European heritage. It's a good article to write for my travel editors, and better yet, I get to figure this stuff out, too."

Ike purses his lips, says something in Yiddish, Abie shakes his head, a brief discussion, then a grimace, a smile.

"OK, you like, you want, it can be arranged," he says, "but first, let's give our regards to Broadways".

The three of us are sitting at a wooden table at Brodvejus (pronounced Broadways), which one moment was just another bar, and the next a better-than-average high school talent show. There is singing and dancing, all tongue in cheek, the dancers flirting and flapping on the dance floor. A short, squat guy with a goatee, looking very much like a repressed computer programmer, steps forward with a microphone and commences to sing *Yesterday* by the Beatles. The bar sings along with him; the scene is so Europe, so Unlike-North-America. "Oh I believe, in Yester-Day," we bellow, arms on each other's shoulders, and I decide then and there that I like this country. I walk back to the guesthouse on Bernadino Street, tripping and slipping on the wet, uneven road, giving those even drunker than myself a wide berth. My new Lithuanian friends had agreed to pick me up in the morning, and together we'd drive out into the countryside to see where it all began.

"She's a chariot, no?" says Ike, standing beside a rusted Mitsubishi minivan, the fan belt squealing like teenage pigs at a rock concert. Lithuania has the highest rate of accident fatalities in the European Union, but they're excited for me to take the wheel, to really feel the journey. It's an old stick shift, or, more accurately, stuck shift, but after driving an East German Trabant in Berlin earlier this year, I feel confident I can drive anything. I narrowly avoid scraping a truck that almost blocks the narrow street, and we head off out of the city. Although local drivers constantly pull in front of me, tailgate and overtake into oncoming traffic, I am well armed with a dented piece-of-shit diesel minivan that couldn't possibly sustain any more damage than it already has. The speed limit in the countryside is 70 km/hr, which would be useful if my speedometer actually functioned.

"If you're in a hurry..." starts Abie.

"Yes, yes, yes, I know," I cut him off, just as someone cuts me off. It doesn't take long to leave the streets of Vilnius; the city only has a population of half a million. Having experienced the minefields of Ethiopian highways in recent weeks, it's a pleasure to drive on new four-lane highways, if not to see out the cracked window with wipers that somehow managed to collect the rain as opposed to clear it. As we make our way to Kupiskis, I see fertile green fields and fat healthy cows. Old wooden barns and signs with place names I couldn't begin to pronounce. Ike and Abie are in the back seat looking pensive, dark rings beneath their eyes.

"You guys look as hungover as I am," I say, trying to lighten things up.

"We're just thinking about the recent past, you know, the things that happened in this country."

The things that happened in this country are difficult to discuss, difficult to understand. In 1939, two of mankind's greatest villains - men deranged by power and hate - carved up Europe in accordance with their megalomania. By the time they were finished, and after they went to war with each other, Adolf Hitler and Josef Stalin were responsible for one hundred million innocent deaths and the systematic genocide of people and cultures across three continents. In 1939, Lithuania as an independent country ceased to be, as Stalin, in agreement with Hitler, bullied a de facto Red Army coup.

Soviet forces occupied the country, soon replaced by the Nazis, who took control over all aspects of the country and went to work to systematically murder Roma, partisans, intellectuals, and over 200,000 Jews - a staggering 94% of the country's Jewish population. Although there were terrible pogroms throughout their past, Jews had thrived as a community in Lithuania, living in bustling shtetls, building world-renowned Talmudic schools and synagogues that produced some of the age's most influential religious scholars. In the space of three years - 1941 to 1944 - all that was wiped out, no mercy shown to men, women, the elderly or children. Disturbingly, it was not the Germans responsible for the actual killing of these innocents. Responsibility lay with brainwashed and hate-filled Lithuanians, seizing the opportunity to murder off a population they had long envied for their wealth and business acumen. Anti-Semitism has always been around, and will always be around, but it is the speed and brutality of the Lithuanians that renders many of today's few remaining survivors unable to talk about their childhoods, or dare to consider returning to the country of their birth. There were those who saved Jews at the risk of execution, and not everyone was a Nazi collaborator. Yet entire towns, where Jews and Gentiles co-existed peacefully for centuries, watched thousands of Jewish citizens being marched into the forest, stripped, shot in the head, and pushed into hand-dug mass graves. Towns like Kupiskis.

"Say, any of you guys might know how I come to be South African? I mean, why my great-grandparents ended up in South Africa? It seems a little random."
Ike clears his throat, speaks softly with a certain amount of authority.
"From what I can gather, and I'm not sure 110% on this, there was a shipping company that took luxury goods from South Africa to London. They figured the best way to pay for the cost of sending an empty ship back to South Africa was to fill it up with people. So they sent a representative to Northern Lithuania and gave 15 free-passage tickets to young Jewish men. I don't know why Lithuania, I don't know why Jewish men, maybe someone at the shipping company was Jewish with Lithuanian connections."
"Sounds like," interrupts Abie, "I mean, it's very good business. Shlomo goes to his son, asks him what two plus two is. His son

replies 'that depends; are you buying or selling?' Ha ha ha," and Abie has cracked himself up.

"Anyway," continues Ike, unamused, "these fifteen men go over to South Africa, to the mines, and things are just about to boom there, the Gold Reef, and these guys make good money, so they bring their families out. Well, within a decade, thousands of Jews are leaving Lithuania and heading for South Africa. Less hardship, better weather, lots of opportunity. Men first, to save up, then they bring over who they can. That's what your great-grandfather did; that's why you're South African."

I think about this for a while. Two generations later, I've packed up and left South Africa for Canada. Similar opportunities maybe, but far less violent crime, corruption. Worse weather, but I'll take Vancouver's snow-capped mountains and beaches in exchange for Johannesburg's inland urban sprawl. Definitely better lifestyle. Hey, I'm just like my great-grandfather! Only I didn't have to work and save up for 10 years (10 long, lonely years) before I could afford to bring over my wife and kids. It's been a lot easier for me in every respect, but at least I can understand why he travelled to the other side of the world. I wonder if my great-grandchildren will emigrate somewhere else, too, and one day return to South Africa, to Johannesburg, to see where I grew up.

"Hey, this is bigger than I thought it would be," I yell back to Abie. "By the way you described it, I thought it would be a horseless one-horse town."

"Today there are about 8000 people in Kupiskis, more or less," he says, shaking his head, a little surprised, too.

The two steeples of the main church are the highest points, dominating the skyline. I circle a roundabout and pull into town. In 1897, a census declared there were 2661 Jews in Kupiskis, 71% of the total population, but many were already emigrating overseas in search of better lives. By 1938, there were only 1200, 42% of the overall population. Today, there is not a single Jew in the area. Abie becomes quiet, begins to reminisce:

"My father Meyer was a grain merchant. Here in Kupiskis, there was a thriving Jewish community. Everyone looked out for each other; nobody went hungry. If you couldn't pay? Too poor? That's OK. He told me about Shabbat, Friday night, the shamus announcing 'To the synagogue!', the excitement on the street as people prepared for the Sabbath. The smell of food would float out of houses, fish from Yudel the Fishman, homemade challah, potato latkes. He spoke of boys and men constantly studying Torah and debating and arguing into the night, of celebrations on Jewish holidays, when people would sing and dance and pray, and of hunched old men and women who could still remember everyone's names and birthdates (like Blind Zalman, who worked for the credit union and never lost a letter). Everyone was very religious, the boys going to yeshivas around the country to learn, their mothers begging train passengers to take parcels to their children in this place and that. We got along with the Christian townspeople, traded with them flax, grain, coal, crafts and goods from Germany, sewed their coats, we helped them out, too, if they were in trouble. There were problems, like anywhere, conflict between two sects, the Hasidism and the Mitnagdim, problems with the bank, but there was always financial support from overseas Kupishokers, and no pogroms in the town itself. Jews had lived here since the 16th century. It was a pious town, a peaceful town, and then the war, and then... well, there is nothing Jewish here anymore, just a few memorials recently built by those overseas, the killing sites. Come, you need to see."

He directs me a few hundred metres past the town centre, tells me to park on the road adjacent to a supermarket. Opposite is the Freethinkers Cemetery. Grim, ashen iron gates surround the park, and inside I see a white Soviet statue standing over Russian tombstones. We walk to the back, and there are five long rectangular strips of grass, each enclosed by foot-high cement walls. In late 1941, local white-banded Nazi collaborators marched over 1000 Jewish men, women and children to this site and brutally murdered them. Babies were hit against trees to save bullets. The shots could be heard by everyone in town; the mass graves themselves are in clear view of houses and the church steeples. Ike and Abie put a hand each on my shoulder, steadying me.
"I don't... I don't understand. Tell me, what goes through a person's mind when they kill children, shoot an old lady through the head...?" My companions remain silent. Tears have welled up, along with anger burning inside my chest. I visualize the victims, hear the ghost echoes of gunshots, look towards the town, the supermarket, walk around each grave in the soft rain. The October Sky is watching the same show, and crying too. Finally, Ike speaks up. "Come, Robin, there is more."

We drive over to the civic center, where they introduce me to a local journalist named Eugenja. She has gray hair and kind eyes. The rain has stopped (a commercial break, perhaps?), so we walk down a street alongside century-old yellow painted houses. An old Soviet-era Lada is parked by an oak tree; maple leaves are coloured seasonal red. The scene is entirely picturesque, the definition of autumn charm. In the early 90's, after Lithuania became the first Soviet republic to bravely declare its independence from the Iron Curtain, Eugenja wrote a series of influential articles examining the complicity of the country, of Kupiskis, in the aftermath of the Nazi genocide. It was simply not something that could be swept under the rug. People were living with enormous guilt, and for a future to be bright, they had to make sense of a dark past. She tells me about Luva, a German in Kupiskis who was taken in by local townspeople claiming to have escaped the Russians. He turned out to be a Nazi spy, organizing local militias and henchmen, and instigating the massacres of the town's Jews. Local townspeople did all the killing under his supervision. I asked Eugenja what became of this Luva. "He died of old age in Cologne, Germany," she tells me.

And what became of the henchmen, the killers? What happened to them?" She explains that many were captured, arrested or executed by the Russians. Collaborators and their families were scorned by the community, ostracized and known as "Jew Killers."

"Their children were forced to leave; they could not have normal lives here," she says. People, she tells me, looked back fondly on the Jews, the way they cared for each other, cut people breaks when times were tough. But with no survivors, there was nobody to rebuild a community, nobody to demand revenge or justice. And so Kupiskis continued under a new occupier, the Soviets, who later bulldozed the Jewish cemetery, and with it centuries of local Jewish presence.

There is one cobblestoned street left, Sinagogo Street, whose name recalls this history. It leads to the surviving synagogue, which has been converted into the town's library. The old Jewish cemetery is now a park with a giant water tower, but a memorial has been built, and a dozen jagged 19th-century Jewish tombstones lie under an ominous tree, Hebrew letters faded with time. The descendants of Kupiskis have not forgotten, and in 2004, a group of 50 people from the UK, Israel, Denmark, Australia, the US and South Africa returned to unveil a memorial plaque on the walls of the old synagogue, as well as at the killing sites. In 1997, it was discovered that a group of midwives had assembled a handwritten list of 808 Jewish residents who were murdered during the war. Why this list was compiled is not clear, but it is unique within the entire country, the only list that names some of the town's victims, and their ages. This led to a project to create a Kupiskis memorial, a Wall of Memory, identifying and honoring the vanished Jewish community. It rests protected inside the library, on the walls of the old synagogue, and it is late afternoon by the time I get there. I find it impossible to make sense of a figure like six million. Six bazillion! Six Trazillion! But standing in front of 808 names, I imagine a rock concert, or a sporting event, or morning assembly at a high school. I can see the people, their faces, their tragedy. What strikes me instantly is the ages: 14, 8, 7, 1, 20, 18, 32 - my age. And then I run my fingers up the list, and find Ezrochovicius, Ezrochoviute, Ezrochas, Ezrochiene, variations of my name, all relatives, all murdered. A group of kids come out of the library, their voices echo in the gloom. I walk over to Abie and Ike, faces in their hands, and together we sit on a table in silence. Emotion strangles the life out of me. The memorial quotes Isaiah, in Hebrew and English: *I will give them an everlasting name that shall not be cut off.*

Over 3000 people were murdered in Kupiskis, from the town and the surrounding areas, with the biggest massacre occuring at mass graves dug in the Jewish cemetery, once again located in the heart of the town. Nobody here can claim they did not know what was going on. In June 1940, when Russians took over the town, Jewish life was immediately attacked. Many Jews looked to escape to nearby towns, or into Russia itself. When the Germans moved in, local townspeople were agitated and encouraged to join the anti-Semitic purge. Those that tried to protect or harbour Jews were eventually ratted out and executed, including Catholic priests. Rabbis were tortured, Torahs were burnt, houses and businesses confiscated. Wealthy Jews bribed their way to survival for as long as they could, until they, too, were led into the forest. All across Europe, a cloud of evil reigned hell on earth. Genocide is a distinctly human trait - this cruel desire to murder an entire people.

From Tasmania to Rwanda, Cambodia to Darfur, we are the only species on this planet that undertakes such heinous acts, perhaps because we are the only creatures smart, or dumb, enough to justify our actions. Chimps, our closest relatives, have been known to attack and murder rival clans, including infants. Females are usually absorbed into the new clan, and the violence is based around territory. Greed, ambition and military conquest have similarly resulted in the mass murder of people - North and South American Indians - but there is no rational reason to explain man's inherent and unstoppable bloodlust. 2 plus 2 = 808; it doesn't add up; it doesn't make sense.

We drive into town to the ramshackle yellow wooden house of Veronica, a 91-year-old woman who can still recall these terrible times. Ike and Abie are having a smoke outside. Popping in and out of lucidity, Veronica sings me a Yiddish lullaby in her dark, cold room, recalling her love for the Jewish children she once babysat. Suddenly, she leans forward, whispers:
"The Jews were better than the Lithuanians! They cared for each other; they helped each other." Then her milky blue eyes glaze over and she sings another song, somehow burnt into her memory. Being poor, the Church granted Veronica and her husband some land, which overlooked the nearby Freethinkers Cemetery. Veronica watched the Jews marched to the pits, stripped to their underwear. Veronica watched the Jews being slaughtered.
"I cried," she tells me. "I cried and cried. But what could I do? I still see their faces."
I shiver. The musty smell of age in the house is thick. After a moment, she smiles, and then:
"I tried to save one family's children. To hide them. But the family wouldn't let me."
"But weren't you afraid that if you got caught, you would be killed?" I ask.
"No," she says. "No." She drifts off. I pop outside, see Abie playing with an old dog. Ike is looking out over the cemetery. There is no joy to breathe in the air.
"I have seen good times, and I have seen terrible times," Veronica says when I re-enter the house, rubbing my hands to get some life back into them. "Good people, and terrible people."
"Are there more good than bad?" I ask.
"About the same," she says.

She sings another song, this time in Lithuanian; her granddaughter and great-grandson are visiting, and the toddler adds some energy to the cold room.

Veronica died just a few months after I met with her. Who is left to remember?

The only hotel in town is being repaired, so we retire forty kilometres away to Rokishok for the night. It is Friday night, and while I'm not religious, I feel compelled to make Kiddish, a blessing over the food. All three of us have had an emotional day, and nobody is in the mood to visit the nightclub that has opened a few doors down. "How about Panaveyz? Did the same happen there?" I inquire of Ike.

"The same. Everywhere, the same," he says softly. "Same stories, all over Europe. Only difference between Panaveyz and Kupashok? 10,000 people, not 3000. More people, so first, a ghetto. A few weeks later, into the forest, and then, gone."

In the morning, we visit another site of mass graves, just outside of Rokishok, at a clearing cut into a beautiful pine forest not far from the highway. 3000 Jews were shot dead in this site alone, their bodies later exhumed by the Russians, counted, and reburied in the graves. A small granite plaque stands at the foot of the enclosure, carved with a Star of David and the words: Holocaust Mass Graves. It has been vandalized, the top chipped and broken off, and someone has fired bullets into it. The enclosure fence has been damaged. What kind of person defaces a mass grave? I expect the same kind of person who digs one. These people are still here. They are still everywhere. I don't agree with its politics, and I often question its leadership, but when Abie pulls out an Israeli flag, my heart swells with pride. So long as that flag exists, there will not be another Jewish genocide, because, after thousands of years of being victims, Jews will no longer let it happen. If only we could stop it from happening to others. I understand why the Darfur protests back home in Vancouver were first instigated and brought to public awareness by members of the Jewish Community.

Ike, Abie and I stand alongside a mass grave in a forest. It is raining again, but birds are flying overhead; red mushrooms grow from the earth. Here, surrounded by tragic death, I am more grateful for life than I have ever been. I think about my family, no doubt currently wondering where the hell I am in the world, and wish I was with them so I could embrace them. I whisper a thank you to my great-grandparents, who bravely decided to leave this green European forest for the wild African veldt, and say a prayer of thanks for whoever or whatever helped them along the way. I think about what might have been. Would I have been the mere dream of a person buried beneath my feet?

I suppose branches get cut down, but it takes more to kill a tree. Hmm, that's pretty good. I turn around to tell Abie and Ike, only to find my grandfathers, walking arm in arm into the forest, aging fast, talking Yiddish, slowly evaporating amongst the autumn leaves of my imagination.

In Memory of my Grandfathers:

Abraham "Abie" Esrock
15/10/1909 – 13/11/1996
Samuel Isaac "Ike" Kalmek
10/12/1910 – 04/10/1980

BEHIND THE SCENES IN LITHUANIA

Lithuania was always going to be a personal story. When the opportunity arose to go travelling again, it was one of the first places I thought of. We didn't know much about the country, but I had a hunch it would be beautiful, and for me, a vital piece in my jigsaw puzzle of life, since it's where three quarters of my grandparents come from. A couple of years ago, I travelled to Poland to find my grandmother's village, and it was one of the most rewarding stories I've ever written. I was hoping Lithuania would be similar, and while we only spent a week in the country, I wasn't disappointed. Our schedule at this point was beyond insane. Ethiopia to Dubai, Dubai to Lithuania - three countries in three weeks on three continents in three climates. After the heat of Dubai, we relished the cool autumn in Vilnius, and the city was exploding in colour. Vilnius charmed us immediately, a catwalk model of European style parading on cobblestone. After a couple of days exploring the city, my wonderful guide Regina came by in the "Rustbucket" and it was off to find Kupiskis. There was a brick in my gut during the drive. I knew I would find nothing left about my family, because I knew the history. My great-grandparents managed to leave for South Africa in the early 1900's, but other family members didn't, and all were murdered during World War II. I volunteer for Jewish seniors back home, and the war stories I'd heard from them about Lithuania were beyond shocking. Some of them could not believe I would want to visit at all - the wounds still run deep. Walking around those mass graves, the horrors of the Holocaust left me choked. It is one thing to learn about 6 million dead, another to see the names of your family engraved on a wall of victims. At this point,my being here shooting a TV show became irrelevant. I just wanted to record as much as I could, so I could share my experiences with family and readers. This is truly the gift of my profession. I get to share my world, words and images, with those who don't have the opportunity to follow in my footsteps. We shot loads of footage and other amazing interviews. The clip has been shown at several Jewish film festivals, and is even on display at a museum in New York.

By the way, that's me, the blond kid playing with my grandfather in that old Super 8 shot. I thought it would make the personal connection that this was really my life, not something we were doing for a TV show. The music in my sequence is a song called Shine from a fantastic Victoria-based artist named Vince Vaccaro. On a lighter note, I scaled the roof of a shed alongside an old grain mill to get a cool writing shot. Thing is, by standing on the shoulders of Sean and Zach, getting down became somewhat problematic. Fortunately, there was a forklift on hand to rescue me. The things we do for this show! Like: driving a crackly old van on a highway with a broken speedometer in a strange country where you don't even know the speed limit. Not to worry; I'm a professional.

We stayed in a B&B in the old town, and my room was in an attic of sorts. I remember writing my story, looking out at the wet sky, reflecting on how lucky I was to be doing what I do, and to have been born in the time I was. My article was about genealogical tourism, and my conclusion was true: Genealogical travel has all the rewards of travel anywhere: encountering beautiful landscapes, interesting new cultures, people, food and history. However, when you journey into the land of your heritage, it makes those rewards all the more relevant.

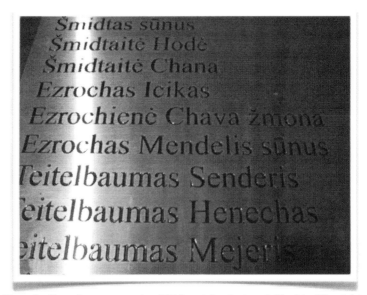

Esrocks listed amongst the 808 Jewish victims killed in Kupiskis

Walking into my past, the town where my grandfather was born

Vandalized memorial at mass graves in the forest outside Rokishok

LATVIA
MY LIFE IS A CIRCUS

Location: Airport, Paris
Destination: Riga, Latvia (via Prague)
Mental State: Emotionally spent
Physical State: Brain throb, congested chest, sore eyes, back pain

I'm thinking about air travel on the four-hour bus ride from Vilnius (Lithuania) to Riga (Latvia). Remarkable. Truly incredible stuff. A century ago, it would take four hours to get from one village to the next. On this bus, in Europe, I'll get off in a different country with a different language, currency and religious philosophy. On a plane, four hours can deposit me on a different continent. It's the planes that have turned cities like Riga - rich with history and culture - into European nightclubs. Budget airlines offer rack seats for the price of a DVD. Countries like Latvia were initially keen to welcome an influx of tourists from the UK and Ireland, flush with their pounds and euros. They came from Glasgow, they came from Liverpool, they came from Dublin and Oslo and Cardiff. Only instead of middle-aged potters with twee pipes and "Gosh, Richard, isn't this just too quaint?" sensibilities, the fledgling Latvian government got a little more, em, Britain than they bargained for. When Latvia's reputation for beautiful ladies, cheap beer and dynamic nightlife met the cheap tickets of the budget airline boom, the result brought it plane loads of excessive horny hooligans - stag parties and boys' weekends made up of Britain's finest, if by finest you mean the kind of guys who end up pissing on each other in an alley while sexually molesting an iron gate. Inebriated men with no respect for anything, much less each other, can quickly turn a charming medieval old town into a center of vice, where prostitutes, drug dealers, casinos and everything in between (card-betting drug dealing hookers?) gather to do business. I've seen it in Prague, once the jewel of Europe, now a playground for loud, sunburned idiots. Vilnius, Krakow, Budapest, Zagreb, Eastern and Central Europe opened their doors to the West, and the West dumped its trash in their living room. Thus, as the bus crossed the border and the gentle melody of The Weepies song

92

Riga Girls harmonized my iPod, my impressions of Riga were of a beautiful city plagued with the kind of foreign influence I do my best to avoid.

Just a few steps into Old Town, carrying my backpack towards an excellent hostel named the Argonaut, I had barely adjusted to the cobblestone before seeing a peroxide blonde dancing on a pole in a bar with open windows. It's a cold, windy October night, a practice performance for the long, cold winter to come. When it starts to rain, we quickly head up the stairs to the Argonaut, and I'm relieved that the off-season has left the summer-slammed hostel free of roving groups of obnoxiously tanked manboys.

"Actually," says the lovely Ance at the Argonaut, "we no longer accept stag parties. They're not worth it: breaking things, vomiting on things; we just don't need it." They stopped booking stags about 18 months ago, but owner Dean mentions that hen nights (or stagettes, if you will) are welcome.   When one of the city's best hostels bans what must once have been its core clientele, you know things have gotten out of hand. In the hallway I notice a hole in the wall that perfectly matches the size of my fist. I've stayed in party hostels before: Picture screaming voices, loud music, breaking mirrors, beer bottles, heavy footsteps echoing in the passageways. Forget about sleep. Any sort of attempt to control the mayhem results in further inconsiderate rebellion. You can either join it, which can be fun so long as you don't mind acting like a complete arse, or leave the hostel and find somewhere quieter - and usually full of lovely people who have escaped, just like you. Bags unloaded, a quick walk towards a nearby square in search of food was further proof in the perogy. I count a half-dozen strip clubs, a half-dozen drug dealers, two casinos, several ladies offering a massage and an assortment of tough-looking heavies with whom I'd very much like to not encounter in one of Old Town Riga's many dark alleys. As with dating, first impressions count when meeting a new country. Riga, tonight, looks like a beautiful girl who's been hanging around too long with the wrong crowd.

By morning, all the less-desirables had scampered off to their mouse holes, and the city is bustling. 800,000 people live in Latvia's capital, and just about all of them dress like rock stars. You'd have to troll Melrose Avenue in L.A. to find long leather boots and new-wave nouveau haircuts worn so naturally. Riga has style, and beautiful *Riga Girls*, as The Weepies song goes, make me wish I was someone else. It's as if God poured a bucket of blonde paint over their heads, etched in sharp angles for cheekbones, and used only the tallest, narrowest and curviest canvas for this portrait of hip European razzle-dazzle. If the locals look good, the buildings do too. Riga is the capital of Art Nouveau, the 18th-century art and architecture movement that aspired to break rules. Although much was damaged during World War II, today the city has the largest collection of Art Nouveau buildings anywhere. When I first heard this, I confess I was less excited than amused. After so much travel, it seems like every destination has the largest this and the largest that, and buildings don't hold my attention for too long. I appreciate creative art in construction, mourning the lack of it in just about every new development sprouting like Viking facial hair in downtown Vancouver. So my expectations were not exactly stellar when I heard that legendary Russian filmmaker Eisenstein's dad built one of the most ambitious Art Nouveau buildings ever. Until I saw it.

What possesses a man to adorn a building in fantastical sculpture, to place neuro-engineered science-fiction motifs in archways, and lace cement with outsized techno widgets? What made him sculpt the large heads of a king and queen, staring into opposite corners, sitting above the building as if it were merely a chess piece? And who, in their right mind, would pony up the cash for this grand creative vision? I've been awed by the modern audacity of Dubai's skyscrapers, but never before by the sheer ballsy building artsiness on display in Riga. On Albert Street, admiring the attention to detail caused my neck to ache - sphinxes or naked beauties or faces screaming in agony. With the right lighting, Albert Street would be a perfect set for *Lord of the Rings*, *Star Wars*, *Metropolis* and *Batman* - all at the same time, without changing any of the facades. As it stands, many of these buildings are mere apartment blocks, with "For Rent" sales displayed outside. Some are crumbling with time, some have been magnificently restored (including the Irish, French and Russian embassies). Building watching provides a good morning out, one only slightly eclipsed by that other passion of mine - beautiful women watching. Back in the square, in the shadow of the Freedom Monument, it's hard to believe this is the same place I explored last night - it looks perfectly cosmopolitan, as well-attired as any major European city.

I'm still coming to grips with the fact that the Latvian lat is worth double its amount in dollars, and the country is nowhere nearly as cheap as I'd expected it to be. The Double Coffee - a chain of high-end coffee shops ubiquitous in Lithuania - are here in Riga, but even with the same menu, the items are 50% more expensive. Long-term travellers who become accustomed to paying $1 for a beer feel a sense of moral outrage when it's suddenly $2. Meanwhile, for Brits and Scandinavians, it still costs a fraction of what they'd pay at home. I hoped to investigate the Stag Plague that evening, so to kill time and steal a few laughs I head off to the Riga Circus. As one of the world's oldest running circuses this being its 119th year in operation - the circus is housed in a somewhat decrepit old building downtown. Like an ancient pub stained with the smell of smoke and beer, the circus has a compelling odour of popcorn, candy floss and elephant shit. It's not very PC to talk about the circus these days, what with animals (through their self-appointed voices, the activists) demanding more rights than starving babies. Surely any animal performing for our entertainment has had to have been beaten and tortured in order to learn how to do so, as opposed to, say, a dog being asked to sit and roll over. Personally, I believe there are bad people and there are good people, and there are bad circuses and there are good circuses, the latter treating what few animals they still employ with the utmost love and respect in a mutually beneficial relationship. The only way I could find out if Riga Circus fit into that second category was to go and see it, and get a rare tour backstage to see its inner workings. Immediate impression number one: Everyone working here is absolutely and stunningly gorgeous (in a city of gorgeous people, that says a lot). Moreover, everyone has a super power, of which I am insanely jealous. Here's a girl who can tie herself into a pretzel, right in front of me, no problem. Here's a guy who juggles with a dozen balls, and then has the patience and humour to watch me struggle with three. Looking at the circus folk - the performers, the administrators - I see 14 books, 17 screenplays, 22 love songs and an opera.

Goddess Number 7 brings out an iguana, which looks as healthy and happy as any iguana, I guess, although I'll admit I'm not the one to be able to tell otherwise (but then neither are most self-righteous animal fundamentalists). The highlight was meeting Aleksandrs Slaugotnis, a legendary Russian clown who has been wearing face paint for 37 years. He was trained by Oleg Popov, which in Clown World is the equivalent of saying you were trained by Michelangelo. Clowns are funny and clowns are scary, and watching Aleksandrs apply his smile and red makeup to his nose ("I don't need a clown's nose; my face is funny enough," he tells us) was a special, privileged glimpse into this mysterious shadow world. A man in full Arabian prince regalia walks past, together with a breathtaking blonde woman in a pink carnival outfit, her bosom bursting - who said circuses are only for kids? A couple of black guys are hanging out, muscles ripping through their street wear (these, I later find out, are the African acrobats, only one of them tells me he's from Denmark). The building is flaking with paint and damp and all manner of colourful stories, 119 years of freaks, the human extraordinairies, people who do things with their minds and bodies that we can only classify loosely as entertainment. I finally get my opportunity to ask a real clown: "Are you happy?"

"It is what I was made to do," says Aleksandrs, but his eyes nevertheless speak of a lifetime far more complicated. Like the rest of the performers, Aleksandrs is Russian. Last year I visited the Moscow State Circus, and was blown away by the acrobatics, if not by the Ron Jeremy lookalike cracking his whip during the lion finale. I wonder if these acrobats dream of being scouted for Cirque du Soleil, which had the ingenious idea of removing the "distasteful" animals and then charging $80 a ticket. I also recall warm, misty childhood memories of my grandfather taking me to see the Boswell Wilkie circus in Johannesburg, and it makes me think that the Cirque du Soleil spectacle, however incredible, has removed, financially and in spirit, those innocent days of popcorn and carnies. The ringmaster announces the performance, and a pretty sizeable crowd has gathered, mostly kids with their parents. Together we'll laugh and yell and ooh and aah and eat peanut crepes and stare at mammoth hairy camels, the two-hour show awash in laughs and thrills. Aleksandrs in particular is a hit, as deft with slapstick as he is on a tightrope. High-pitched blonde kids are screaming in approval. It's as Aleksandrs says:"People will always need clowns, and people will always need the circus."

It's time to hit Riga's famous nightlife, and get to the bottom of this stag business. Ance at the Argonaut gave us a list of clubs, and off we go. First stop, an Irish bar (surely the choice for Irish stags), but all I see are drunk locals being hastily escorted out the door.

Latvian police are patrolling Old Town, ready to fine anyone caught drinking on the streets. The next bar is quite empty, but I'm told things only get going at midnight. A drunk guy sees our camera and freaks out. I try chill him out, and he threatens in strained English to "shoot my head" with his gun. Oh well, that didn't work out. The next bar, the Cuba Room, is heaving with reggae and dub, an artsy young crowd, peanut shells on the floor encouraging a dance shuffle. I speak to a pretty local girl who's in marketing. She hates foreigners, but we shoot back some vodka anyway. We meet some Norwegians, and they're just as festive as anyone else. A sign on the door says: No Stag Parties. En route to the next club, I'm accosted by a half-dozen girls well into their evening, and arm in arm we cross the cobblestone singing *Do Wah Diddy Diddy*. This subsequently causes significant licensing issues for the show, so we later overdub the song backwards, which somehow still seems to work. I ask them about the stags, and they too, hate the foreign men who invade their city. "The English, the Iri… no, the Scottish are the worst!" they tell me. Inside a new venue, eclectic dance music is blaring and people are rocking out and having a great time, and still I don't see the gangs of stags. Instead, just a cool city with cool clubs. At dinner earlier, a group of English twits were making right asses of themselves, but now that I want to see them in action for my on-air story, they have vanished (probably into the many strip bars). It's cold, wet and slippery when I finally meet some English guys outside the Double Coffee during a pee break. Only they're nice English guys. "I've been coming here for years," says Buddy, "and they're really trying to get rid of the stags by closing down the strip bars. The government knows they messed up when they opened up the country to those cheap flights."

The opportunity to crash a stag was running out because I had to catch a plane to Paris at 4:30 a.m. Oh yes, I decided to go to Paris. Almost forgot about that. At the last bar, I meet a group of Scottish guys (and one Canadian), drunk and happy and in good spirits. We end up dancing on tables, play-wrestling, generally acting ridiculous. "Guys, I'm trying to do a story here on Riga the stag capital, on cheap European flights turning charming cities into dens of sin, and you lot match the description, but you don't seem very horrible at all." They tell me they've been travelling as a group of friends to a different European city every year for 12 years. Their favourite so far is Tallinn in neighboring Estonia. What happens when visiting a foreign country becomes as common as visiting a local pub? Either way, my stag hunt concludes unsuccessfully, but I later hear stories of roving English guys molesting blow-up dolls that very night. And before the weekend is out, I'd have more than my fair share of the English. I guess it all depends on people, and how they behave, where they draw their moral centre. It's not like every stag party is made up of a bunch of schmucks, but too much booze mixed in the wrong kind of person can spoil any good party, in any good city.

This brings me back to the wonders of air travel, and the fact that before dawn hit the streets of Riga I was on my way to Paris to watch the semi-finals of the Rugby World Cup. My old friends and long-time Gonzo associates Brad and Tamar had secured tickets to the game, which would take place at the end of their two-week vacation. Now there's no direct flight from Riga to Paris, nor is Riga, the meat in the three-state Baltic sandwich, just a hop, skip and jump away. But $350 (a steal, considering the match tickets were going for well over $450 each) later and I have a flight to Charles de Gaul, routed through Prague, where I pick up a bottle of 70 proof absinthe and helplessly fall asleep on the cold, hard floor of the airport during the stopover. There is not a patch of carpet anywhere, because if there was I would have found that patch, and it would have been the equivalent of finding a soft leather sofa. Under the shadows of the Duty Free, I bruised my hips trying to catch some sleep, knowing full well that a weekend in Paris is not about relaxing, and also, I had gone directly from the nightclubs in Riga to the airport. No sleep, an address scribbled in my notebook, the promise of a ticket to a major sporting event, and perhaps some (carpeted) floor at a crusty hotel. What more do I need for the Modern Gonzo?

I should briefly furnish some details about Brad. Friends from high school, we travelled to Europe together when we were 18 (which he painfully reminds me is 15 years ago), and then again for a couple months to Kibbutz in Israel in the 90's. We've met up for a Gonzo weekend in Copenhagen, attacked the good life in South Africa, London, New York, Vancouver and most recently Tokyo, where he works for a major bank and lives with his wife Tamar. Brad is the only person I know who has lived in London, New York and

Tokyo, and he should throw Paris in there just for laughs. If travelling is about the people you meet, than travelling to meet the people you know means good times.

The Arc de Triomphe was glowing in the late afternoon sun, the sky a crisp blue. For the first time, I realized just how unusual my destinations have been of late - Lithuania, Ethiopia, Colombia? Paris was packed with thousands of tourists, many of whom wore national rugby shirts. France and England have a rivalry that can only be put in the context of centuries of warfare, and here together they would contest the first semi-finals, the French favourites to win. I heard that 35,000 English were crossing the channel for the match, which might explain why they weren't in the clubs of Riga. Fortunately, rugby is not soccer, so the true hooligan did not make the journey. Spirits were high. We stopped at the Eiffel Tower, sparkling in lights, a giant screen broadcasting the game live. Brad and Tamar had tickets to the England-France match, so I resigned myself to a festival tent set up outside the Stade de France, surrounded by thousands of French, English, a smattering of South Africans and disappointed Kiwis and Australians, who had surprisingly been knocked out the tournament. The atmosphere was worth the journey alone: Viva les Blues! Many nations argue about many things, but just about everyone wants the English to lose (everyone, that is, except the English). Of course, being a sport jinx, they didn't. A devastating upset took the wind out of the Parisian sails. English supporters painted in white and red went berserk and the French, shoulders hunched, went to sleep to ponder what might have been. This night I learn that it is nigh on impossible to catch a cab at 2 a.m. from the Gare du Nord, and also that the French can be very accommodating when they want to. I crash out hard in the hotel, on the floor, by the door.

Go Bokke! It's the Springboks vs. Argentina, an unlikely matchup for a semi-final, but the Argentines are undefeated in the group match (including a surprise win against the French - it's been the most bizarre World Cup in rugby history). After I reignited my South African taste buds in Dubai (thanks to a handful of South African chain restaurants), my national pride was stoked seeing so many Green and Gold jerseys. I don't write about it much, but I grew up South African and will always consider myself South African, no matter how much my accent bastardizes into some sort of globalized pidgin. I grew up watching rugby, rooting for the

Bokke (The Springboks), and it doesn't come bigger than the World Cup. Sport, it has to be said, has long driven ordinary people to go to extraordinary lengths. I was among thousands of sleep-deprived sport-tourists, outraged by $9 bottles of Coke, $400 tickets, and loving every minute of it. The spirit of a major sporting event should be experienced by everyone at some time in their lives. It makes travel all the more sweet.

The game comes, the game goes, the Bokke winning comfortably, the crowd appreciative of both teams, blue and white and green and gold. Fully attired in Springbok gear, a jersey, a bright green wig (my gween rig?), the French are high-fiving us, too, because they can't wait for us to beat the English in the final. Champagne has been drunk, absinthe suffered, victory seized, old friends connected, old roots unearthed. Brad wakes me up on the floor early Monday. Tamar has taken off to New York to do some green card chores, he's off to Tokyo, and I have to catch my flight back to Latvia in order to meet up with the crew and fly to Bangkok in two days. My life is a circus. And a rather international one at that.

Splitting the Freedom Monument in downtown Riga

BEHIND THE SCENES IN LATVIA

Here was another case of a story that didn't quite pan out as I had hoped, but as you can see in the show, I don't seem to mind too much. I had heard that Riga is the stag party capital of Europe, so the plan was to hit the streets and crash a stag, getting inside the story, as is my custom, in order to experience and understand it, and, most likely, get blindingly drunk.

Admittedly, it was freezing and wet off-season, so there wouldn't be as many stags wandering the cobble as there would be in summer, but I was optimistic. EasyJet was offering flights from Bristol to Riga for 10 pounds - hence the line "less than the price of a DVD." So off I go, in my backpacker fashion (oh, there's nothing hotter than a blue rain jacket!), but wouldn't you know, I can't find the stags. I hear about them, I occasionally even hear their screams, but I can't seem to find them. In the end, I do meet up with groups of guys from Norway, Scotland and England who have come to Riga specifically to rip it up. Can't blame them in the least - the clubs and bars are excellent, the drinks are cheap and the women are gorgeous. Unfortunately, as I wrote in my report, opening the doors to the stag industry brings in some unwelcome guests, and I had several conversations with locals who were determined to clean the city up. Downstairs from our hostel we were greeted by a pole dancer in a strip club. They're pretty prominent in Old Town.

Julia was off to the prison, and then I did something outrageous that I hoped would make the show, but in the end it just didn't fit. After partying in the clubs until 4 a.m., I took a camera, hopped in a cab, went to the airport, flew to Prague, passed out on the stone hard airport floor, woke up, bought some absinthe, and flew to Paris to meet some old friends from Tokyo who had secured me to a ticket to the Rugby World Cup semi-finals between South Africa and Argentina. For 48 hours I explored a sunny autumn Paris in a sports-mad stupor, crashing out on a hotel room floor, wearing a green wig and brushing up on my "viva les bleus!", who we were hoping would beat England, but instead, the

French lost (what a downer) and it was left to South Africa to beat them in the finals, which we watched on TV in Thailand a week later. I flew back to Riga just in time to meet the crew, hit the airport again, and this time fly to southeast Asia. Thus is the life of a travel writer.

I would have loved to spend the night in the prison hotel, if you can love to do that sort of thing, but sometimes it's my job to hit a multitude of clubs and party hard to get a story. I know. Sometimes, I don't know how I do it either. As a footnote, you hear us in the show wondering if we can sell this story about architecture in Riga. A few months later, I sold it as a feature in the South China Morning Post. So yes, to answer our own question, buildings do make great stories.

Motifs on Riga's buildings look like sets for science fiction movies

Mikhail Eisenstein's incredible Art Nouveau masterpiece

Legendary clown Aleksandrs Slaugotnis backstage at Circus Riga

THAILAND
THE STORY OF MAX

With his towering height, Max was always going to attract attention. Born in 1962, many people claim he might be the tallest male in all of Thailand - even after so many years of hope and pain, all the ups and downs of a rolling jungle hill. His adventures begin in the jungles of the north, where he is born into a poor family of festival performers. Max's earliest memories paint a picture of loud parades, holidays and weddings, being covered in bright robes to greet friendly smiles. But, like many others in the region, once he came of age Max was sent to work. His mother and aunts cried, but his father was always a loner, and so young Max would have to learn many things about life all by himself. Family ties are close, but survival clings closer. To put food in his mouth, Max found work at a logging camp, where tough men would work long hours in scorching temperatures and torrential rain, clearing and cutting down thick jungle for wood. Here, Max developed the thick-skinned approach to life that would see him through many more hardships.

Conditions were terrible, but soon enough another opportunity came his way, this time in the form of the exploding tourism industry. Help was needed to accommodate and transport the ever-increasing number of tourists heading to the region. Having being ripped from his family and sent into the brutal, harsh world of forest labour, Max discovered that tourists don't break and splinter when they fall – they shout and scream and complain and threaten to sue. He was never a social creature, never one to roll over to those he didn't respect (with his enormous size, it would have been difficult for anyone make him budge at all). Simply put, he was stubborn, arrogant with youth and drunk on strength. One unfortunate day, a group of sunburned Englishmen pushes him too far, and he reacts violently, his intentions merely to scare, but his actions as clumsy as an octopus in a giggling fit. The tourists get a few bumps, complain and screech in outrage, the authorities get involved, and Big Max, Big Clumsy Aloof Max, is sent away for the minor offense. His frustration is almost as large as his eyes, wide with injustice – nobody should have to be treated the way he was – a play thing, a slave for the pleasure of foreigners.

Refusing to remain chained up for long, he used his wits and power to escape, heading deep into the forest. Here, he would rely on the lessons learned from his youth, how to forage for food and berries, find shelter. Under the stars, he made raids into the fields of a nearby village, drank from their irrigation systems. Survival was possible, but the villagers soon discovered this new unwelcome stranger, and called in the monks to help. They coaxed Max out the jungle and into the temple, offering him a spiritual life in keeping with their strict Buddhist practices. This quiet life of meditation and thought pacified him for a while. Although there was some peace here, at last, there was also not enough food to support this giant personality, enclosed after so many months in the forest. His weight dropped dramatically, his skin flapping on his giant frame like the canvas of a tent. Max began to feel trapped, restless, hungry. Villagers could see that the temple was too small to keep him tied down for too long, and demanded the monks release him instead. Max was put in a truck and sent away to the city.

And so a new adventure begins, as Max is taken into a strange new world, the biggest city with the brightest lights of all, Bangkok. He doesn't know who made what deal, but with no food and no place to stay, Max ends up on the streets, begging for scraps, living in parking lots and rummaging in garbage scraps. This concrete jungle is not like any jungle he has ever known. The constant noise vibrates in his skull, making him tired, irritable, unable to sleep. The lights burn his eyes like pin pricks, the choking pollution gripping his lungs, slashing his throat. His stomach rotting with whatever he can find to put into it, the days and nights pass in blurs of screams and punches, a blend of violent animal instincts and docile submission. He is dying, and then he is almost killed. Wandering the streets one night, dazed by lack of sleep, an 18-wheel truck clips him on the side of the highway, dragging him underneath its wheels for a few meters before coming to a halt. Miraculously, he survives, but his right front leg has snapped in half.

Throughout his turbulent life, strangers had come to Max's aid, appearing like angels in a dream, briefly holding back the demons of reality. It is these strangers who help Max recover, regain his strength, feeding him what little there is to go around, putting his leg in a makeshift wooden splint. After a few weeks, he is able to limp again, and all wonder: was it his size or spirit that helped him survive the accident?   And, in hushed tones: *would he have been better off dead?*   What is there for him to look forward to?   More begging?   More angels, more demons?   Luck finds him first, in the form of a tribal family who take pity on this homeless giant, bringing him back to the jungle where he can work for his food instead of slowly dying on the streets of Bangkok. A warm, kind woman named Lek finds him second, horrified by his physical condition and the sad story of his life. Lek Chailert had just started a refuge for the homeless, the hurt, the sick and the poor, and with the cooperation of the tribal family takes Max under her care.

Five years later Max has recovered his strength, his weight, his pride. He stands tall, dignified, like a political prisoner being released respectfully into the offices of power. His right leg will always be bent, making him walk slowly, thoughtfully, with purpose and self-esteem. Others at the camp regard him highly, revering his experience and the wisdom he has learned from it. Gentle with the babies, popular with the ladies, here he resides as an elder statesman, an example of how we can all conquer our adversity, temper our demons and believe in hope. Max is still weary of the few tourists who visit the Nature Park. His memory is as fresh as that of an elephant.

Max is just one of the dozens of elephants supported through donations at the Elephant Nature Park in Northern Thailand. This unique wildlife reserve protects, rehabilitates and houses elephants rescued from abusive conditions such as elephant camps, illegal logging, and street begging.

BEHIND THE SCENES IN THAILAND

We thought we'd switch it up a little this episode. Me punching bags and Julia cooking curries would have been a little too predictable. Change the beats and soon enough you get Julia surrounded by panting half-naked men and me clutching a large knife and an empty wine glass, chewing thermo-nuclear chilies. I love to travel, and I love to eat. Favourite destinations for food: Malaysia, India, Argentina (meat meat meat), but number one is Thailand. Cooking is an art form here; every taste should include sweet, sour, spicy and salty, and I just love the sweet and spicy in life. Khao San Road, Vegas for backpackers, has grown since I was last here a couple of years ago. I remember arriving late at night, completely overwhelmed by the colour and people and smells and loud music. Well, there's more neon today, but my old haunts are still here, crowded with backpackers from around the world. Ladyboys still serve evil Chang beer at the Central, Burmese women peddle wooden frogs, and charming men want to sell you suits. Booze buckets are as strong as ever, and the 50c street pad Thai still delicious. But you can only stick on Khao San for a few nights before it either drives you insane or grabs hold and never lets go. It's off to Chiang Mai.

Despite the famous beauty of the islands in the south, I've always preferred northern Thailand. Something about the jungle, the culture, the chill of it all. The cooking schools were fantastic, as you can see in the show, and I passed the green curry, pad Thai, cucumber relish and even hot and sour soup tests with flying colours. Yummy. The story has done pretty well for me; I managed to sell it while we were still filming. It was a delicious one after all.

After 7 hectic weeks on the road, we had a couple days off and the crew took the opportunity to give each other some space. Some went south; I went further north to the sleepy backpacker town of Pai. It was a much-needed decompression. Surrounded by gorgeous landscape, I hired a scooter and spent 4 days zipping around, discussing life with travellers and locals, catching up on some sleep, even teaching some kids at a local school. I was shocked when I heard that just a few weeks later one of the guys I met in Pai, a Canadian, was shot dead by a drunk local cop. A tragic, unfortunate incident, and my heart goes out to his family, his girlfriend (who was also shot), and the tight backpacking community in Pai. The inevitable fallout followed. Travel *must* be dangerous because look what happened! Well, it's not. Shit happens at home, and shit happens abroad. For every one tragedy the media attacks, there are hundreds of thousands of happy stories they don't. Don't let the bad stories scare you away from realizing your dreams of travel. And on the slight chance you find yourself in a situation, smile and walk away. It's just not worth it.

Finally, the elephants. The Nature Park was inspiring in every sense of the word, funded and operated through the efforts of volunteers and the remarkable woman who founded it. I could have gladly stayed there a week. The story about Max wrote itself, and it's all true. One more thing: Julia and I both picked up ear infections from our water fight in the dung-drenched river water.

A spontaneous water fight looked like fun on TV, but gave us both ear infections

From roasted silkworms to mouthwatering curries,
Thailand has the world's best cuisine

Eye to eye with with an elephant at the Elephant Nature Park

HONG KONG & MACAU

LIFE IS A RUSH

Just my luck that AJ Hackett, the lunatic who introduced bungee jumping to the world, decided it was time to really push the limits with the highest commercial bungee in the world. Right here, in China's gambling (shh, don't mention gambling) Special Administrative Region of Macau. I hate bloody bungee jumping. It's way too intense, too short and too bloody bad for my knees, which start shaking and don't seem to stop when I'm even just thinking about it. Of all the stupid crazy looks-like-fun things I do, I'm petrified of bungee jumping the most. I don't know why - it's as safe as playing with a yoyo - but the psychological impact of throwing oneself off a bridge is not the same as launching oneself out a plane, or sandboarding down an active volcano. Did I say bridge? What about a TV tower, piercing the sky at 233m, a full 50m higher than the previous World's Highest Bungee Jump from a Building, the kind of daredevil activity reserved exclusively for fruit-nut bars like Hackett. He held that record until breaking it with this one. So, here I am, of course, standing on the edge of Macau Tower, about to equal the Guinness Book record for the world's highest bungee jump from a building. Talk about taking it to the edge, and then jumping right off the son of a bitch.

Before taking the hour-long ferry to Macau, I spent a few days in China's other Special Administrative Region, Hong Kong. China has a "one country, two policies" mandate towards Hong Kong and Macau, which essentially means it allows Hong Kong to be a capitalist leviathan and Macau to be a gambling (shh, don't mention gambling) behemoth just a few miles from the heavily controlled Communist People's Republic. The Kong's stock exchange is the 7th largest in the world, generating over one trillion dollars, and Macau is the only place in China where it is legal to gamble (shh) and boy, the Chinese love to gamble. Macau has surpassed Vegas as the world's biggest gambling center, generating an incredible US$7.2 billion in gaming receipts, compared to US$6.6 billion in Vegas. It's a given that a fair percentage of that moola flows straight to Beijing, and if you've got two golden geese, who's stupid enough to let a little thing like political ideology get in the way? Yes, it's hypocritical and pokes a giant, beautifully corrupt hole in their entire system, but shut the hell up and keep feeding the bird. Ooh, Vegas is investing $2 billion in another casino; come on, birdie, *lay that sweet, shiny egg*!

Hong Kong in early November was refreshingly cool. I'd say the autumn leaves were falling, but I hardly saw any leaves. Just people, people, people, everywhere. Neon signs and sharp sky rises lit up like a Christmas trees, stalls selling their mothers for a digital camera in Tsim Sha Tsui, the smell of fried duck mixed in with the smog and grease. It's loud and bright, men selling suits and fake watches, and restaurants buried in giant buildings with dodgy wiring and grating air-conditioning. At Chungking Mansions, it's reported that over 120 nationalities regularly pass through - a squat building made up of hundreds of cheap flophouses and over 2000 rooms. The sizzle of hallucinogenic neon and steam rising from god-knows-what and technology slams into history, and it's no wonder *The Dark Knight* Batman movie was filmed in the city - Hong Kong is all science fiction, a melting pot of world culture driven by commerce, shopping and service. Hookers are aggressively grabbing my arm in Wan Chao, and I tuck into Fenways, where hundreds of freelance Filipino whores battle to land a client for a "short time," and thick US Navy boys with their crew cuts and dumb stares seem only too happy to oblige. In Lan Kwai Fong, expats and foreign workers gather in the steep streets, drinking themselves silly and shouting themselves hoarse over the barrage of beat breaking out of the outdoor patios. Everyone I speak to loves it here - the action, the pace, the cash. This city has the kind of edge that cuts and leaves a scar. Who wouldn't want to be a part of it, even if you have to live in expensive hamster-sized apartments? I don't want to think about the underbelly of this beast, the sex and drugs and filth, because open that door and you're bound to disappear. In the news, *Batman*'s producers cancel a stunt in the harbour because they could not, in good conscience, allow a stuntman to drop from a helicopter into the water. E-coli, fecal matter, harmful bacteria - it's that polluted. In Hong Kong, you don't bury secrets, you drown them.

The lure of the underground is the story here. I don't want to hop on a bus and see a temple, visit this museum, that building, here's a market, there's a garden. I want edge, and that's how I come to be sprinting on a single-gear bike into a costumed crowd of thousands, revelling in the pagan festival of Halloween. Two friends of mine are making a movie in Hong Kong, and through their contacts I connect with Brian and Calvin, the organizers of Hong Kong's first Alley Cat race. Alley Cat racing emerges from the North American bike messenger scene - those guys you see racing about cities with walkie-talkies and shoulder bags. They tend to look scruffy and completely alternative, making us wonder who the hell would do this for a living, and why? Surely there are safer ways to earn a living. As usual, it's all a lot more dynamic than it seems. See, those couriers have their own sub-culture, complete with websites and heroes and uniforms. There are those of New York, Toronto, Philadelphia, Vancouver, DC and Chicago who have carved out legends, survived tragedies, getting that damn package there on time. There is music, there are parties, there are groupies, there are casualties, and it's all done on a bike with no brakes and no gears. Fixed-gear bikes are favoured by couriers because they're simple to maintain, and when your job involves sprinting into buildings in urban centers, they detract thieves, since these are no ordinary bikes. With fixed gears, the only way to stop is to control the pedals, but they aren't like the back breaking bikes you had as a kid. It requires precision skill, control and balls. Jeff, a veteran DC courier who planned HK's first Alley Cat race, tells me: "It's a Zen-type thing; the key is to never stop. If you run into a problem, you turn right." It didn't take long for each messenger community to develop races, called Alley Cats, designed to test each courier's knowledge of the city, speed and endurance. Typically, each race consists of checkpoints. Riders get there using whatever route they choose, and on arrival must perform a task. Their manifesto signed as proof, they bike off to the next checkpoint, avoiding the traffic, crowds and cops as they do so. Thing is, Hong Kong has no messenger community. Long underground tunnels that connect the main island from Kowloon prohibit bikes, and couriers are quicker on subway and foot. So Calvin and Brian, two hip thirty-something dudes, have taken it upon themselves to introduce fixed-gear bikes to the city, having followed the sub-culture online for some time now. My buddy Greg is also a fixed-gear nut, but to ensure I survive he provides me with a feather-light single gear racing bike with brakes. We meet up with a half-dozen other enthusiasts and grab our checkpoint route and manifesto. I get lost on the way to the starting line, so I trail Greg all the way. Thousands of angels and devils are in the streets, hot Chinese girls in tight maid mini skirts, black leather and fake blood in abundance. Traffic is heavier than ever; alert cops are on every corner. October 31: the perfect night for an illegal street race.

I follow Greg into the sticky fried duck night. Buses, taxis, cars, mini-buses, and when he pulls into the tram tracks, I feel a gust of wind as Hong Kong's famously thin trams pass by within inches. If my wheel gets caught in the track, if I lose my nerve for a second, I'm tram meat. We sprint across, a sharp corner, straight into thousands of confused pedestrians. Left, another sharp right into oncoming traffic, I hear a cop scream at me but screw it, if I brake I'll probably flip, and besides, try and catch me, you bastard; I'm two blocks and an alley away before you've got your walkie out. There are no waiver forms here, bucko, no safety lines and rope checks, just me on a fast bike sprinting towards the headlights of a bus. You can bite hard on this thrill, chew it in your mouth, taste the risk. First checkpoint has two hotties outside a coffee shop, and to complete the task I have to tell them they're "sooo beautiful!" They are, I do, they sign my manifesto, and I'm off. Next stop, the White Stag. I find a big guy named Glenn, call him a ...., and do 10 pushups to the cheers of the bar patrons. He signs my manifesto; I'm off. Rub 9-ball's head, drink a beer, end up back at the Stag, and nobody cares who won or lost; it's more like who survived and didn't get arrested. We all get props. We all get drunk. The night gets stupid.

****

Damn it, Hackett. I don't know if I can hack it. The plan was to jump off the Macau Tower connected by wire; they call it a Decelerator here (or Skyjump); in New Zealand, they called it Base

Jumping by Wire. I tried it in Auckland, and it was a blast; the wire slows and steadies your descent so that you're fully aware on the way down, slowing gently so that you land on your feet below. After playing around on the Skywalk, in which I circle the Tower's rim by foot, I convince Julia that the Decelerator is no big deal, even if it is the world's highest. But then Hackett has to go and introduce this bungee, and now, TV cameras and all, I have to do it. How could I not and call my blog Modern Gonzo? It's about pushing yourself to do things you're not sure you're capable of - from hang-gliding over Rio to eating bugs in a Thai market. To make matters worse, we head out to Macau and find the Macau Tower closed due to bad weather. Returning to Hong Kong for a few days, now I have to think about the jump, revisit the Skydeck, where I saw exactly how high 233 metres is. Jetlag, booze and fear - I don't sleep for days in the tiny white cupboard-sized hotel room at the perfectly named Fook King Mansions. Fook me. It's a perfect day at the tower on our return. Julia does the Skyjump (she loves it), and I follow her just for kicks. I return up the world's 10th tallest free-standing structure to turn it into my Gonzo playground. Anyone will tell you that it's the waiting that kills you. Once you jump, it's over. So let's break the wall here; I'm being followed by a TV crew, and a TV crew needs angles and set-ups, and that means I'm going to be standing on the platform, outside in the wind, for a half hour, legs tied up. The fear is kicking my kidneys; a large crowd of Chinese tourists have gathered to witness the spectacle. And then Sean needs a practice, a dummy hop to the edge and a 3-2-1, before pulling back to set up another angle. Pure psychological torture. Knees are jelly, head is spinning. I know that I'll be safe; shit, this is a commercial jump, after all, but there's something else at play here, a force that has grabbed hold of every sensible cell in my body to squeeze the life out of it. I am choking, and then the wind plays up and I have to wait some more.

Macau looks beautiful, bigger than you'd imagine, the brand-new MGM and Grand Lisboa casinos glittering in the sun. Although it is the world's biggest gambling center, the tourism guys don't want to talk too much about gambling (shh, no cameras on the casino floor, please). With its rich history of sea trade and Portuguese heritage, it's made up of two islands covering only 27 square kms, located 64km from Hong Kong. Large parts of the city have been declared a

UNESCO Heritage Site, and it's odd to be in China and see bilingual signposts in Chinese and Portuguese. The Grand Lisboa looks like something out of a Godzilla movie, a weird, distinctly Asian sky rise with a Power Ranger design that spectacularly lights up at night. Behind me is the new Venetian, which is the largest hotel in Asia and currently the second-largest building in the world (although Dubai, Macau's Middle Eastern, less whorey cousin will no doubt challenge that shortly). Costing US$2.4 billion, The Venetian is the brainchild of Vegas mogul Sheldon Adelson and is designed to attract mainland Chinese with the biggest casino in the world. I got a tour, and the design is all Vegas - full frontal assault of kitsch and painted pomp. The smallest hotel room, at 700 square ft, is decadent enough; the next room up is 1800 square ft. High rollers are comped 6000-8000 square-ft rooms, which conjures up images of pure excess. Beyoncé is playing in the arena tomorrow night and the Venetian's 3000 rooms are all occupied. Later this month, the Venetian has an exhibition tennis match - Roger Federer vs. retired great Pete Sampras. Money is no object. Julia and I hop on a gondola, complete with a flaming gay Italian gondolier singing bad opera through his bad teeth. The frontage is all fake, fake, fake, but the Asian market is loving every plastic brick of it. Around us, the shopping mall is huge, getting huger, and the casino floor is simply enormous, mostly made up of baccarat tables, electronic roulette, blackjack and Caribbean poker tables. It's too pricey to play even the cheap tables, and while the casino accepts Hong Kong dollars, they pay out in Macau dollars, which are only accepted in Macau and not in Hong Kong. Someone is making ridiculous money out of all of this. Eventually, Zach and I find a 5c digital slot and I win $80 Macau, about US$10, and raking in my huge take I leave the Venetian shaking my head at the latest example of humanity's urge to entertain and gamble to excess. $2.4 billion could have educated a lot of children and fed a lot of hungry people.

Back on the platform, I'm thinking about what a great war story this bungee jump will make, about all the people who would actually love to do this but will never get the chance. I think about an editor who requested the article I'll have to write about this, I think about this jockstrap schmuck who used to intimidate me in high school. Charlie the jump master finally signals it's time to go. Arms out, fall forward and enjoy the ride. 3...2...1...

Insert the BIGGEST MOFO FREAKING SCREAM HERE. 20 seconds of a 200km/hr plummet, and then the recoil, and for a second I'm floating, and then insert the SECOND-BIGGEST MOFO FREAKING SCREAM HERE. I have a camcorder duct-taped to my hand, and all I can think of is relief: it's over, it's OH VER! Blood rushes from my feet to my head, turning me into a human beetroot, and I feel like a city that just got nuked, only the H-Bomb didn't detonate. It feels like winning the cup, the promotion, the girl and the race in the space of three seconds. It takes a minute for the bungee contraption to lower me to the ground below, and my throat is scarred from all the screaming. Holy Gonzo. Hong Kong and Macau. That, my friends, was a rush.

Old and new worlds at dusk in Victoria Harbour

Alley cat racing on Halloween, probably the most dangerous activity of the season

BEHIND THE SCENES IN HONG KONG

I've said it before and I'll keep saying it until people start believing me. I am not a gung-ho skateboarding thrill-seeking adrenaline junkie cranked-out lunatic. I just tend to find myself going to amazing places and doing amazing things, like Macau, and the world's highest bungee jump from a building. Oh, you would jump, too, if you had a TV crew there to capture it for posterity, or maybe to capture your last remaining moments alive. Maybe not.

Anyway, I didn't know there was a bungee jump at Macau Tower until we got there, and figuring it would make a great story, I spent the night before psyching myself up to believe that I could, in fact, take the leap without browning my shorts for high definition TV. The night before, I went out to Central, where I was offered a flaming Lamborghini by two flight attendants, only someone had actually offered it to them first, and slipped a little something in for good measure, which subsequently was passed on to me, and I therefore passed out, and were it not for a lovely girl who's name or face I cannot remember, I would not have gotten back to the hotel at all, and would have missed the opportunity to travel all the way to Macau Tower and find out that weather had canceled play that day. After all the hyping and psyching, that did indeed suck balls, or more accurately, Halls, since I was sucking a throat lozenge when we were informed of the bad news (which is why I have a lump in my cheek). Julia was thrilled, but I knew that all the fear and apprehension and anxiety would only be delayed for a few more days, and all I wanted to do was jump off the damn thing already. It's the waiting that kills you, and boy, I would have to wait. My friend Greg was working on a bad Hollywood movie called Push starring Dakota Fanning which was being shot in Hong Kong, and he picked up on this fixed-gear madness. The Alley Cat race was a stroke of luck, really, because it was a perfect story for me. If he had given me a fixed-gear bike (with no brakes), I surely would be a dark splash of maroon on a Hong Kong street today. It was Halloween night, and the streets were packed with people in costume. Halloween in Hong Kong? Believe it, the vamps (and tramps) were out for blood. We raced around, with the poor crew following in a taxi, weaving and darting through traffic. You only see two checkpoints in the show; some of the others were not considered family entertainment. Truth is, biking in heavy traffic at night with no helmet or sense of local custom is far more dangerous than bungee jumping with a professional company that has strictly enforced every safety regulation you can think of.

A segment that didn't make the final cut was of my meeting a travel editor for the first time. The *South China Morning Post* has published dozens of my stories, and just before he skipped over to the Books desk, Stephen McCarty was the travel editor. Over excellent curry at Chungking Mansions, and along the bustling streets, I asked him about the other side of travel writing, the business side, and why editors today are looking for riskier stories than ever. Steve was a great sport with some killer zingers; unfortunately, with a 24-minute show, so much of the good stuff just doesn't go through to the final edit. Still, it was great for me to finally put a friendly face to one of the names I constantly bomb with pitches. As for Macau, the new Grand Lisboa is a building straight out of Buck Rogers, especially when it lights up at night. I'm not sure how I felt seeing Vegas kitsch applied to a former Portuguese colony. Heritage used to mean more than gambling and glitz, but who am I to judge? It's definitely a place worth visiting, if only to see signs in Portuguese and Mandarin, a flame- grilled peri-peri bok choi of culture. Julia and I were awkwardly serenaded on a gondola in the fake canals of the Venetian, to the soft stares of tourists who figured we must be on honeymoon or something. Our singing troubadour was so camp we could have pitched a tent.

5.4.3.2.1. I was only going to do this bungee once, so thank God the camera duct taped to my hand (1002 uses) worked to get that shot of me scarring my throat with scream. Julia was not so lucky. Her camcorder malfunctioned on her Skyjump. Some days, the camera is just not your friend. As much as I wanted to just walk to the edge and jump without looking down, there were shots to be gotten, and then the wind picked up, and all in I was standing on the platform for close to a half hour, absolutely and entirely petrified. You can't fake fear. Know that I was never in doubt that the bungee would work, but I did doubt that my mind wouldn't cross some barrier of sanity. And the camera would be there, as always, waiting to capture that moment. The things we do for our jobs! In the end, it was terrifying and fun and life affirming, and sure, I would do it again, if you put a gun to my head. See you at the next platform then.

Sean Cable and Zach Williams go to the edge to get the shot, and the audio

The crew watching an early draft of the second episode of Word Travels,
sent to us on DVD. The only place we could find to watch it was in
a small alley selling porno

Displaying perfect form at Macau TV Tower. At 233m, it's the
world's highest commercial bungy jump

NEW ZEALAND

THE GREAT GONZO BLOWOUT II

*T*ired. *Exhausted. It's been a long journey. Many rivers crossed, many miles stamped with the fist of Gonzo. My eyes are burning crimson, stained with red wine, and it's clear to everyone: I need to liven it up. Something to put me back inside the travel bottle, shake it up, pull out the cork and let me fizz all over the green fields of New Zealand. What's this? Rotorua. Ro-to-rua. The name sounds like a machine designed to trim the weeds of boredom. Cut the hedges, take out the whacker, Modern Gonzo is coming to town, and the long grass is quaking in its roots. Rotorua. Maori Country. It means "second lake" and is a quiet town surrounded by volatile geothermal geysers, lush forests and crystal lakes. Located just a few hours from Auckland on the North Island, it's small with a big heart, fast building a reputation as an adventure capital to rival Queenstown in the south. Here, even the land is extreme, the ground bubbling with volcanic heat, the earth blowing off steam right in the heart of town. The air smells of sulphur, but you get used to it, the way you can get used to anything, and the sulphur, well, that just reminds you to use all your senses, and that the earth, Mother Nature, well, she can be a cold, hard bitch if she wants to. So if you're going to jump out a plane or raft over a waterfall, it's best you pay your respects. With New Zealand laws the way they are (good luck suing anyone), I'll be lucky to escape the next week unscathed. But then luck has followed me the last 11 months, attached itself like a charm to my backpack. Nothing to lose. Time to wake up and smell the adrenaline. Go for it, Esrock. Go for it.*

Zorbing

Kiwis are insane. Just look at the Zorb. Invented in Rotorua, a Zorb is a giant plastic ball with a hollow core. It's spin spin sugar, spin the black circle, and spin me round like a record round, round. Zorbing was my chance to finally hop inside the tumble dryer (every kid has thought about it – better check on yours now). Inside, the heat was sticky, and the light filtered in as if the PVC bubble were made of jellified pee. I opt for the Hydro Zorb - no harness, just a puddle of warm water in the middle. I manage to stand for about a second before the Zorb tosses me around on its zigzag course, like that one sock you always lose at the laundry. I wish I have a couple of young lady friends inside to distract me – three people can go at a time in the Hydro Zorb. But no wet T-shirt contest for me, just tossed lettuce, a whipped egg of Esrock. Soaked, rinsed and spun out, I lay in the sun to iron out my creases, catch my breath and ponder life as a garment. Which way is up? Which way down? Either way, I'd be keen to give it another spin.

Bodyflying

Bodyflying, or extreme freefall, involves a modified DC-3 prop, rubber padding and catch net to prevent budding Gonzo flyboys from taking off over the 12-metre-high platform. It's the only contraption of its kind in the southern hemisphere, designed to blow you away, literally. I felt like a big magnet repulsed by its pole, a plastic bag in the wind. The considerable rush from below has me floating in mid-air, although it's quite a feat to remain front and center for more than a few seconds. I drift out of the circle and fall over like a sack of meat, despite the best efforts of the guides on either side. My cheeks blow into a frozen smile, the loose-fitting overall inflated with air to create the impression, however short, that I really was a superhero coming to save the day with steroid-monkey muscles at the ready. After just a few minutes, I am exhausted. Wouldn't it be neat to master the art of the hover? Unfortunately, that would take more time, and a lot more money than I would ever have to spare.

Swoop

I climb into the canvas cocoon, a hang-gliding harness zipped and secured to a crane that is raised until the pod dangles 40 metres above the ground. With me is the Swoop's marketing manager, and I hope she gets some kind of danger pay. It doesn't sound like much, but believe me, it's high enough to get the nerves revolting. All I have to do is pull the ripcord and we'll freefall for a second before the wire catches and we hurl forward at 130km/hr, as fast as Superman rushing home because he forgot to turn off the stove. It's a G Force factor of 3, and I don't know what that means, really, except it is fast, it is furious, and I leave my vocal chords back at the ranch. "Don't be afraid if I scream like a girl," I yelled shortly before pulling the ripcord. And I did.

Jet Boating

A New Zealander named Hamilton invented jet boating in the 1950's. He wanted to zoom around his farm on shallow river water, fast and easy. Today, jet boating has evolved into a sport with aquatic rocket ships powered by engines with up to 1000 horsepower and with the acceleration of F-16 fighter planes. There is nothing on land or water that goes faster than a souped-up jet boat. I tagged along for a ride on Agrojet, the fastest commercial jet boat in New Zealand, able to hit 100km/hr in 4.5 seconds. The 1km purpose-built track did not seem large enough for a normal boat, and it isn't. For an Agrojet, spinning 360 degrees on the head of a needle, it's just fine. The acceleration pinned me back in my seat and sent my eyes to the back of my skull. No engine in the water means the jet boat can fly over water only inches deep, and the spins and doughnuts performed by the pilot literally robbed me of breath. It's already running on aviation fuel - fix wings to this sucker and it could fly to the moon.

4x4 Safari

I'm impressed by the Suzuki 4x4. I do everything I can to kill the bastard – tip it on its side, drown it in deep puddles, gun it up hills. As my friends will testify, putting me in control of any car is dangerous. Allowing me to run wild on a terrain course, and then hurl the jeep off an 80-degree vertical drop, well, that's just the Kiwi way. With the brakes on, the handbrake up, the Suzuki goes down hard, a c-c-c-runch as it hits the bottom. It must have sounded worse than it was because these cars do this all day, every day. As for the drivers, well, Off Road NZ provides fresh underwear back at HQ. Then it was time to Sprint Car, driving the full-sized roll-caged racing machine like I stole it, which I kind of did for a couple of laps when I didn't see the red light. Burning rubber must be hardwired into a man's gonads. That's why women drivers, despite popular male wisdom, are survivors. On my final lap I execute a screeching, smoke-burning doughnut, completely unplanned, of course. Next, I hop aboard a Monster 4x4 with front and rear steering for a wheel-bound rollercoaster, including a descent into a modified mine shaft. All I had to do was strap in and enjoy the ride; the Monster truck stuck to the ground with a loud roar. Suitably covered in mud, I'm looking forward to getting back to my 15-year-old Honda Civic to really put it through its paces.

Sledging

River rafting is fun and all, but why raft when you can sledge? Take a plastic kickboard, a pair of mermaid fins, hold on tight and throw yourself off the same rapids that rip those large industrial-grade rafts. No teamwork. Just you, in the soup, and you better start dealing with it. As you fly over the edge, you push in, turn your head to the side, brace for impact. Rocks are everywhere, undertows and whirlpools, so keep kicking and whatever happens, don't let go. At one point I find a neat little rapid, pointing my Sledge upstream and getting caught in the ride. It's got me screaming at the sheer bloody fun of it all. Then I try a barrel roll, get pushed downstream and kick my way out of it just in time to hurtle over the next waterfall. Incredibly, I emerge unscathed. Unscathed, and completely elated.

Luge

Another world first designed and built in Rotorua, the luge is a small three-wheeled plastic cart with a low centre of gravity and a simple steering and braking system. Push back the handles to brake; otherwise, ride these babies down three mountain courses as fast as your nerves can handle. A modified ski lift returns you and your luge to the start of the course. The 2km scenic route looks over the town and lake, but things start getting interesting with the intermediate and advanced tracks, with dips, twists and steep corners. One traveller showed me his impressive road burn, earned by ignoring the speed warnings and tipping himself down the concrete track. I push it as much as I can, but I am racing against myself, which is never as much fun as racing against someone else. By the last descent, I am pushing it for the thrill, but a near-wobble reminds me how long it takes skin to grow back. I coast to the bottom, watch a meathead and a stripper make out on the return chairlift in front of me, and head back down the gondola into town.

Shweebing

It could well be the answer to the nightmare of urban traffic, and once again, it's up to tiny Rotorua to bring it to the world. The Shweeb's inventor, inspired by the crawl of Tokyo's gridlock, has created the world's first human-powered monorail. Inside a plastic pod, I sit, pedal and power the orb forward along a steel circular track. Capable of reaching speeds in excess of 70 km/hr, faster than I could ever pedal it, the pod zips around the track, a cross between a bike and a rollercoaster. All the while I'm thinking how a Shweeb track linking key areas in any major downtown core would ease congestion, get people from A to B, and be a lot more fun than sitting in a car looking at the exhaust fumes rising in front of you. Environmentally sound, it's more of a concept than a thrill ride, but well worth doing to appreciate the idea, and the engineering ingenuity needed to make it a reality.

Maori Culture

Rotorua has a large Maori population with a rich heritage, eager to share and educate visitors about their unique traditions and history. They are one of the few indigenous populations ever to fight back, and win, against impeding colonial armies. New Zealand's Maori population give it a unique edge, a rich world of folklore and national pride.   There are several tours to the local villages that surround Rotorua, now evolved into super-slick tourist operations offering cultural shows, model villages, outstanding art and geothermal wonders. We rope in some help to learn two Maori dances, the Poi and the infamous Haka. The Poi, traditionally performed by women, involves the use of small pom-pom-like balls attached to each other by string. No surprise, they are inspired by an ancient weapon. The haka, reserved for men only, is the traditional war dance performed by Maori, made famous by New Zealand's rugby All Blacks, who terrify their opponents with the performance of the haka before the start of a match. The haka includes intense postures, clenched fists, big eyes and scary expressions, all designed to intimidate. Akama Te Kama Te Kia-or Ki-ora – performing the ritual literally makes you want to go out there and kill somebody. I slap my thighs and stick out my tongue (which symbolizes aggression, and that Maori warriors would looking forward to eating their opponents), veins popping. For a brief moment I'm transported to a world of tribal battle. Then we finish up, and once again I'm just a skinny white guy looking kind of ridiculous. At the Te Puia complex, the Prince of Wales is the name given to a particular geyser that sprouts regularly over 30m into the air. The ground here literally bubbles with heat and the resulting formations and colours are stunning, even with the stink of sulphur in the air. This geothermal wonderland has been attracting tourists for centuries, drawn to its healing hot springs.

BEHIND THE SCENES IN NEW ZEALAND

Nine countries in ten weeks across six continents, and you start to lose your mind a little. What I needed was a good boost of adrenaline, and New Zealand didn't disappoint. I was here a couple of years ago, and knew that Rotorua, located on the North Island, would provide plenty to keep us busy.

It's all about having fun, even when you pack in so many activities in just a few days. But I was always aware that given the cost of these activities, there would be slim chance I'd be able to do even half of them if I wasn't a travel writer. The job might not pay well, but no one can argue with the perks.

To congratulate the team for surviving our journey, I decided to treat everyone to a skydive. Even Julia. Fortunately for her, the weather played havoc the last couple of days, gusting strong winds and rain, and nature decided that jumping out of a plane would have to wait for next time. Of all the thrill sports I've done these last couple years, jumping out a plane at 4500m takes pole position.

I was a little hesitant to try the *haka*. South Africa and New Zealand are fierce rugby rivals, and I grew up fearing and respecting the infamous Maori war dance. And here I was, smacking my chest and shaking my hands with the best of them. No wonder New Zealand are such a good team. After doing the *haka*, you feel pumped up enough to kill someone (or at least make a good tackle). I got myself a double-page spread with my Rotorua adventures, in what I called the Great Gonzo Blowout. It ran in a couple of papers, and no doubt anyone who read thought: Wow, I'd love to do that - and - What a lucky bastard. Less lucky was a woman who was killed sledging the same river a couple of weeks later. There's always risk when it comes to these things, but folks in New Zealand are notoriously good at managing them.

Learning the art of the hover atop a DC-3 engine

Sledging. It's like white river rafting, only you have a kickboard and flippers

Swooping at Rotorua's Agrodome

YUKON

DOGSLEDS AND SOUR TOES

The winter! the brightness that blinds you,
The white land locked tight as a drum,
The cold fear that follows and finds you,
The silence that bludgeons you dumb.
The snows that are older than history,
The woods where the weird shadows slant;
The stillness, the moonlight, the mystery,
I've bade 'em good-by, but I can't.

- Robert Service, The Spell of the Yukon

The severed human toe splashes into my glass tumbler, spilling drops of sweet Yukon Jack whiskey on the bar counter. It sinks, the nail still attached, scraping the glass with post-amputee growth. Brown and withered, there's no doubting that this-here toe once belonged to some not-here person, and all these years of being kept in salt and soaked in honey whiskey have kept the skin intact. I'm in the Downtown Hotel in Dawson City, lost in the Great Canadian North, and the weather outside is a balmy -30C. That's minus thirty, in case you thought that was a dash. Captain Al, tonight's Toemaster, has a creepy grin, with coffee-stained teeth. As I look on in a blend of one-third disgust, one-third morbid fascination and one-third fear, he commences the ceremony, reading from a prepared text with great fanfare. Although there is nobody in the bar, this freezing night in the north, he draws the attention of the unimpressed bartender, along with the ghosts of the saloon's former gamblers and whores. Finally, he reaches a climax. "Drink it fast, or drink it slow, but either way, your lips... must touch... this gnarly looking toe."

Never one to shy away from a challenge, even when it involves what might be considered cannibalism, I raise the glass and tuck my head back. I've been to bars before in the hope of meeting a nice girl and getting her digits, but this is just outrageous.

There's a magazine out here in the Yukon called *North of Ordinary*. Fitting, for this is a harsh, breathtaking land of natural beauty and pioneering human spirit - what happens when an extreme climate meets an extreme population. Bordering Alaska in the northwest corner of Canada, the Yukon Territory is bigger than Germany, Belgium, Denmark and Holland combined, yet has a population of only 32,000. Most people live in the capital of Whitehorse, which can hit 30C plus in the summer, and has recorded temperatures as low as -52C in winter. Don't get sunburned. Snow-capped mountains and pristine lakes, a sparse sub-arctic dry climate where moose outnumber people two to one, and people who drink 50% more beer than those in any other province or territory in Canada. The Yukon would probably have remained an isolated northern region, populated by small indigenous bands who have survived on caribou for thousands of years, if not for a mineral rich in value but poor in practical use. In 1896, gold was discovered on the Klondike River, and when several dozen miners arrived in Seattle loaded with their takings, word spread as fast as the fading career of an American Idol finalist, as loud as a sonic boom in a bathroom, as clear as the skin of an android. Within a few months, some 40,000 people raced feverishly to the Klondike to stake their claim: the miners, the cowboys, the hucksters and gamblers, along with the riff-raff and rabble needed to serve them. Bonanza Creek, Eldorado - few fortunes were being made; more dreams were lost. Legends were created; it was here that Jack London wrote *White Fang*, and where Robert Service wrote epic poems like *The Shooting of Dan McGrew* and *The Cremation of Sam McGee*. Charlie Chaplin starred in *The Gold Rush*, Mae West in *Klondike Annie* - the wild west became the wild north, as saloon doors swung to the tune of can-can dancers. Dawson City became known as the Paris of the North, the largest town north of San Francisco, as lucky strikers would blow their earnings on all manner of wonders designed to separate a fool from his gold. Railways were built to shuttle the stampeders, and the Canadian government created a new territory to deal with the influx. Even though the gold strike was significant, it was not large enough to support the amount of those seeking it out, and when winter arrived, freezing rivers and blackening hands with frostbite, the rush ended, with the population draining like water from a tub. The government consolidated mining interests, and built highways that devastated aboriginal bands, which had no resistance to western illness or alcohol. The rush lasted just two years. Today, the mining of lead, silver, gold and copper still brings in the moolah, but the government is by far the largest employer - almost one in three people in Yukon's labour force work for the Man. The second-most important industry is tourism.

Whitehorse is not in the Arctic Circle, so there is no Arctic Night at this time of year. Instead, it gets light around 9 a.m., and dark around 3 p.m., and in between it's too damn cold to want to be outdoors too long anyway. Unless you want to go dog-sledding, in which case you have to speak to Frank Turner. I can see my friends, the animal activists, frothing already, sitting with their Great Dane in their small apartment, wondering how anyone could dare harness a half-dozen huskies and have them pull them through the snow on a sled. They don't see dogs treated with love and respect, not to mention the latest in homeopathic and naturopathic food and medicines. Here are those few huskies living life as they were born to, in the right environment, with the right exercise and purpose - not for a half-hour daily walk in the park. For contrary to what you might think, it's the doggone dogs in control, not the guy on the sled. If the dogs are not happy, if the rider and pack don't work as a team, then nobody is going anywhere. Including me, since Frank was taking me out to frozen Fish Lake for my chance to mush. Frank's Muktuk Kennels has around 120 dogs, all named, loved and cared for. He doesn't sell puppies or dogs; the old guys are retired and remain free to run around, sleeping indoors on blankets, becoming part of the 102-acre ranch. Joined by Japanese and German volunteers, tourists, large black ravens and Frank's wife Anne, who keeps it all together. Each dog has their own kennel, and is chained up in "streets" according to gender. It's quite the site, arriving from Whitehorse to a ranch and being greeted by a hundred dogs going berserk at your presence. Puppies are reared and exercised, and each dog is as friendly as a family pet (which, in a way, they are). They have names of composers or birds, previous guests and heroes. Bet your life there's going to be a Gonzo.

It's nearly 9 a.m. and still dark as we gather the huskies for the drive to the lake. Friendly Frank is a legend in the Yukon and beyond; he's the only guy to have raced the Yukon Quest 23 consecutive times - a grueling solo 10-day dog-sledding race whereby competitors have 4 hours' sleep per day, travel 1000 miles through brutal conditions (cold enough to literally freeze a dog's balls), and have to ensure that canine and keeper reach the finish line healthy. Frank has more stories than whiskers on his thick gray beard, and you just know that here is man who has stared into the very depths of his soul, and found a husky barking right back at him. They have saved his life, and he theirs. As I pick up a lab-husky cross named Livingston, Frank tells me about the sport, the art of keeping the dogs happy, and how to survive in the wilderness. He's kitted me out head to toe because all the warm stuff I brought along would ice over in these 20C climes. Meanwhile, he hasn't put his gloves on yet. He teaches me to slow howl at the dogs, and soon enough there's a chorus of howls echoing in the forest. I learn to say "Gee" for right and "Haa" for left and "Whoo Whoo" to stop. The sleds have brakes and foot pads, and it takes a while before I get the hang of it. Breaking is key: if the dogs run too fast they might get injured. I have six dogs harnessed to my sled, and, as the saying goes, unless you're the lead dog, the view is all the same for them. As the rider, I gawk at the low tundra mountains surrounding the frozen lake, tears freezing on my cheek, passing Frank on the left, yelling "Gobuy Gobuy" so the dogs don't get themselves tangled. It's exhilarating, and thrilling, and one of those things you read about and think: I wish I could do that. Which, of course, you can. We spend a couple of hours racing along the snow and ice, and I slowly get to know my dogs, their personalities, their strengths. Val is a firecracker, Falcon a steadying force. Incredibly, a healthy Quest pack can travel around 160km each day at a speed of around 15 - 20km/hr, depending on conditions. I imagine Frank's experiences, wrapped up freezing in the sled for a few hours, under the hot-ice stars and glowing northern lights, and wonder if I could ever do it. Then I remember I'm a city boy, and will probably succumb to hypothermia within hours, which will leave the dogs in a fix, so they'll have to eat me. But all is not lost; Frank is originally from Toronto.

Back at the lodge, the dogs fed and sleds packed away, Anne and her volunteers cook up a feast of BBQ'd bison and elk, with Arctic char and salads. We end up playing late-night poker in the cozy lodge, listening to classic rock, talking about life, relishing the coziness of winter. I'd go star gazing, but my eyeballs might freeze over, and so we finally retire to the cabin, feed the wood stove for the night and crash out. I'm struck by how, in cities, dogs bark in the night, driving everyone bonkers, and yet out here, surrounded by hundreds of huskies, there is only silence. Frank and Anne's Muktuk offer various packages for tourists, from one-day to week-long treks, and always with the utmost appreciation and respect for the dogs driving their business. "We get to do what we love; what more could we ask for?" says Frank. I understand completely.

We hop on Air North's small twin-prop Hawker Siddeley for the hour-long flight to Dawson City, 800km of snow, mountains and frozen river away. When I first heard about the Sour Toe Cocktail, available only in the Downtown Hotel in Dawson City, I assumed it was joke. I mean, seriously, a drink with a human toe in it? You've got to be kidding. Then I Googled it, and was shocked to discover it was true, and the perfect thing for me to do in a late-November pre-season Yukon winter. The opportunity to get this on film could not be missed, plus I have a little bit of a foot fetish anyway.

The former Paris of the North has a population of only 2000 today, a quiet old frontier town along the banks of a frozen lake. Tourists come here in the summer to learn about the Yukon's gold rush heritage and enjoy the pristine scenery and national parks found throughout the territory. In 1973, a character by the name of Captain Bill bought an old wooden cabin and found an old pickled toe, assumed to have once belonged to a frostbitten miner. Over drinks at the local pub, pondering the legendary (but fictional) ice worm mentioned in Gold Rush epic poems, he cottoned onto the idea of the Sour Toe Cocktail, originally drunk in a glass of champagne. Well, the Toe was a hit, and so the Sour Toe Club was founded, with various rules drawn up for becoming a member. You could have it in any drink save milk or pop (including Red Bull; yes, I asked), and the Toe has to touch the lips in order to qualify. Now there have been various toes over the years. Drunk cowboys have accidentally swallowed some, others have been lost or stolen, which is possible since the defining principle here is that not too many people are sober when joining the club. And we're talking about some 65,000 people - yes, there are at least that many lunatics in the world. Various toes have subsequently been donated, and the latest, a big toe, apparently belonged to someone who lost it in a lawnmower accident. The local health board took Captain Bill to court and lost, since what people choose to add to their drinks once it is poured is a matter of their own concern. It costs the price of a drink plus $5 to join the club, and afterwards you can drink it as many times as you like. You are also presented with a certificate and card for your wallet, which is bound to impress (or, more likely, scare) the hell out of anyone who sees it. The toe itself is safely locked away and stored in a glass container with salt. It smells of liquor. Captain Bill had hightailed it to Mexico, so Captain Al, a teetotaler, was filling in. The toe nail was pretty disgusting, but for some reason I found it a lot harder to think about the deep-fried crickets and silkworms from Thailand a few weeks back, and certainly a lot easier to stomach. Maybe it's because you don't want to believe that this brown fetid thing is, in fact, what it is, while a cricket will always look like a bug. Anyway, I tilt my head back, suck up the whiskey, and the toe hits my lips. Not to be outdone, I put it between my lips like a cigar just for effect. I had now joined the Sour Toe Club. You may vomit now.

The weather kicks in and the plane can't land in Dawson City (which should perhaps consider changing its name to Dawson Village), so we're stranded at the Downtown, playing pool in the smoky bar, eating chicken wings, doing anything but going outside. Once it dips into the -30C's, even the locals start to bitch. We put a couple of beers outside the hotel room window to chill, and an hour later they were frozen solid. Old wooden buildings are sinking into the ground, and if I listen hard I can hear the drunken screams of no-luck miners, the wails of whores and the creak of the saloon door in the wind. I read about the guy who struck it rich and had four dancers from Frisco play poker for the right to be his wife. I read about the cremation of Sam McGee, whose spirit welcomed the flames because his soul had frozen over. Perfectly understandable; the vast frozen Yukon winter can do that to a person.

Finally we could leave, a day late and the ATV ice-fishing trip cancelled. After a bumpy flight (which had Zach sweating, because the last thing I said to the camera was: "This could be the one that crashes") we pull back into Whitehorse, eat overpriced pasta (things are noticeably more expensive out here), and take in a movie, because the clouds had settled in again and the chances of seeing the northern lights are slim. They only come out in ideal conditions, and clouds ain't one of them. The streets are flat and wide and frozen over, and it's hard to breathe without inhaling ice crystals into your lungs. Clearly, I am made for warmer climes. But since the flight is only two hours from Vancouver, Yukon is one of those "who the hell knew - right here in your own bloody backyard" kind of places I'll be thinking of often. In summer, for the unspoiled wilderness, and in winter, for the chance to meet up with Frank, crack some beers, join the dogs and enjoy life at the very extremes.

Falcon greets us at Muktuk Kennels outside of Whitehorse

The buildings in Dawson City, sinking into history.

BEHIND THE SCENES IN THE YUKON

It was -50C. It only got light at about 10 a.m., and dark at 3 p.m., and in the meantime, Julia and I were both wondering why on earth we chose to do outdoor stories at this time of year.   I was thrilled, and far less chilled, since she was the one who had to sit around a hole waiting for a fish to bite.   As for the dogsledding, well, the experience was everything I was hoping for, and more.   Truly the stuff that tattoos your memory. Now, the Sour Toe, the real human toe in a drink: It looks like a toe; can't say it tastes like a toe, because I'm not familiar with the taste of severed, shriveled human toes (live ones, I confess I have an inkling about). This story is the definition of quirk, the kind of thing that people won't believe, because who can blame them, and yet when you're there, well, it's just one of those things people do in an old saloon in the middle of the Yukon. I had a pretty tough time selling the story because my editors were grossed out, and no doubt readers would be too. I'll take the toe over the *moriche* worm in Venezuela any day.   The weather turned sour and we were stranded for a few days in Dawson City.

Air North were great, though; they seem capable of landing their planes in just about anything, and we watched it arrive from the control tower, happy that we were one step closer to getting to anywhere that wasn't -30C. How cool would it have been if the Northern Lights had actually come out to play? I wish we had a production manager in the sky who could arrange these things. In the end, Sean left the camera out overnight (how it survived the cold, I'll never know), and you see a few glimpses of the sky lighting up in a green mist.   Best time to see the lights is around 1 a.m., and after waiting around for a couple of hours, on two separate occasions, we gave up.   That's OK; it's always nice to leave something for next time.

Dogsledding on a frozen lake

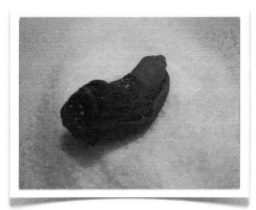

The infamous human toe, dropped into a glass of whisky as the key ingredient for the Sour Toe Cocktail

Jumping on thin ice

Season Two

VANCOUVER ISLAND
CLOSER TO HOME

Since the show is broadcast worldwide, we didn't want to stress too much about the fact that Vancouver is actually my home. It should also be said there is nothing fake at all when Julia comes and gets me for our trip to Vancouver Island. I was crashing in the downstairs nook of a legendary party house on Commercial Drive called the Foxy House. Living out of backpacks and boxes is a reality for travel writers, even ones with TV shows. Even as I write this, I've spent the last four nights crashing on an air mattress and a couch, although I'm very excited to finally rent my own place in a couple of days. It's a welcome change from the glorious chaos of the Foxy House (ruled by the Chihuahua you see named Margaret Thatcher, I kid you not), but on the same street, just a few houses away.

Vancouver and Vancouver Island are easily amongst the most beautiful places on earth, which is one of the reasons why I moved here. It also rains a lot, and while we were hoping for a blue-sky day to really make the colours pop for the camera, we got the clouds and the West Coast drizzle. On our schedule, when it comes to weather, we either get lucky or we don't, so I was bummed we couldn't show off the city, the ferry across the fjord, and even Tofino in all its sunny glory. I've been to Tofino many times, as have most people who live in Vancouver. It's wild, it's remote, it's got this great hippie-logger vibe. Usually I camp further up the beach, so it was a serious treat to stay at the luxurious Pacific Sands. "One day I'm going to come back here!" I swear, as I always do, although Tofino is a little more doable for me than, say, Ethiopia.

We talk about it a little in the upcoming Philippines episode, but I have a bum ear that has pretty much ruled water sports out for me since I was six years old. Hence I don't know how to surf even though I grew up in South Africa. I've tried a couple of times before and have never gotten up, so it's to Krissy and Tia's credit that I got up, even if it was for a brief second, on those puny waves. I once started writing a book that looked at the rise and fall of apartheid through the eyes of a South African surfing community. This experience kind of inspired me to get that project going again, along with a thousand others.

I didn't grow up in British Columbia, so I still get a thrill watching bald eagles soaring above me. For the crew who were born and raised in British Columbia, it's like seeing a seagull. A of couple years ago I did the West Coast Trail, a seven-day hike up the coast of Vancouver Island. The only animals you might see are bears, wolves and cougars. Now that was a hard hike!

As for the yacht, it all came together quickly through word of mouth. Nick and Cory are impassioned British Columbians, proud of their beautiful backyard. Pearl Jam had rented the Pacific Yellowfin boat a few weeks before us, so we truly were living like rock stars. The water was freezing, though, so doing those jumps damn right nearly gave me hypothermia. But there were always delicious cocktails on hand to distract from the cold. When you see Julia wake up – well, the night before, we'd gotten carried away with Captain Colin's homemade brew, and one of the many attractions of that magnificent yacht: a trunk of masks and costumes. Trust me, it was a very good thing, for everyone involved, that the cameras weren't filming.

The Surf Sisters teach me how to Surf. Years later California's Scuba Diver Girls would teach me how to scuba dive. Clearly water and women go well together

The $12,000 a night Pacific Yellowfin

Why they call it "glamping"

TAIWAN
BACK ON THE ROAD

I am that guy. The one you see on TV and think:
- *That must be the luckiest guy in the world.*
- *Can you imagine having his job?*
- *Boy, I hope there's a commercial break soon; I need to pee.*

Sunday night, the band is still playing when I kiss my friends goodbye, climb into my car, deposit it in the underground parking lot of my parent's apartment and get dropped off at the airport at midnight. My mom and dad are used to my comings and goings. I might as well work at the airport. The crew gathers for the two a.m. EVA Airlines flight to Taipei. There are six of us in total. Other than a slight shake-up of directors, these are the people I'll be spending just about every waking moment with over the coming months. Four of us are veterans of Season One, which took us to twelve off-the-wall countries, including Venezuela, Ethiopia and Lithuania. We know the score of a life in motion. My co-host is Julia Dimon, who writes a weekly travel column for *Metro* in Canada. We met in Turkey on my first trip around the world, and have become unlikely partners on this escapade. The fact that we are so different, as people and as writers, gives the show its appeal. Shooting us is Sean Cable, a tall, shiny cameraman of legendary status within the industry. Although Sean is known as one of the best sports shooters going, he's also an artist capable of capturing images that saucer the eyes. Paul Vance (pronounced as one word, Paulvance) is our sound guy, our ears. He was born and raised in Whistler, and is therefore laid back to the point of horizontal. Chris Mennell is our production packhorse. Nicknames abound, as they do on these kind of shows. Chris is called Chewie, although I confess I can't remember why. He looks like a young Tom Berenger, and lives on an orchard in the B.C. Interior. Directing a couple of episodes, including Taiwan, is Jordan. He's a former comedy writer, sharp with the wit. I round out the crew. Esrock. Ing. The Free World.

Monday disappears, somewhere between jet lag hell and the international date line. I know very little about Taiwan, other than I once stopped here en route to China and spent a painful night at a golf resort. We arrive in Taipei at five a.m., meet and greet, and breathe in the soup they call air over here. It's already cracking 30C, the humidity sheening everyone with a flattering glow. Too early for traffic, we arrive sooner than expected at the Grand Hotel, billed as one of the world's finest. It is. Built in 1952 as the fledgling nation's flagship hotel, it looks like a massive Chinese temple. Between the giant halls, seven restaurants and exquisite traditional design, the hotel is in itself a major tourist attraction. We come to stay here because the Taiwanese tourism board is supporting our production, and we are all grateful for it. It's important for the production (and for us as travel writers) that *Word Travels* maintains its editorial independence, and does not sink into becoming a tourist promotional video. We love travel, and that love is reflected in the show, and my writing. If something warrants negative observations, I will make them. Travel writers are notorious for becoming jaded bastards, but my unique journey to this unlikely career will hopefully keep me immune. Meanwhile, if tourism boards offer to support us, who am I to say no? Admittedly, this is not backpacking, but does that make the experience any less authentic? Some of you might argue yes, or no, but that is a debate for another time. When you live out of a backpack in perpetual motion, you appreciate being treated in style, and when you're filming a TV show, you appreciate all the help you can get.

There are only twenty-three countries that recognize that the Republic of China (also known as Taiwan) has a right to exist. For a democratic country with a free press and healthy economy, it bespeaks the awesome power and influence of its neighbour, the People's Republic of China. Confused? Here's a quick history lesson: Originally discovered by the Portuguese, the lush tropical island was known as Formosa, a fertile paradise located a few hundred kilometres off mainland China. The Japanese occupied it for decades, using it as an important base during World War II. When they lost the war, they lost the island. In 1949, mainland China was embroiled in a devastating civil war that pitted the communist forces of Chairman Mao against the incumbent, Chiang Kai-Shek. Kai-Shek lost and fled to Taiwan, where he proclaimed Taipei to be the new capital of the Republic of China. Mao established the PRC and was about to wipe out his sworn enemy across the Taiwan Strait when the United States got involved as a means to establish a presence in the region. Two million people fled the mainland for Taiwan, mainly intellectuals and supporters of the previous government. China had essentially been split in half (although China's population of one billion, compared to Taiwan's 23 million, articulates the split was nowhere close to even). Neither country would recognize the legitimacy of the other to exist, and for a while Taiwan became an important piece on the Cold War chessboard, backed by the US, China backed by the Russians. China's threatening to invade poised the world on the brink of war, and Taiwan's outspoken criticism of its ethnically homogeneous neighbour did little to help. But as China descended into agrarian communist chaos, Taiwan embraced a free market, rapidly industrializing and pouring in cash. It became the fourth leg of the powerful economic Asian Tiger. Time passes like gas, and things change. The Asian Tigers were wounded in the 1990's, and China has embraced economic reform. Although China still has between 700 and 800 missiles aimed at Taiwan, a defrosting of tension is inevitable. Taiwan elected a new government, which has placed more emphasis on economic development and less on independence posturing. The first high-level talks in decades have opened up Taiwan to Chinese tourism. Still, just about every major country in the world refuses to acknowledge Taiwan's independence for fear of pissing off the Chinese, who have a billion potential customers for their products. When I ask some locals what they think the future holds for Taiwan, they look to Hong Kong. Might Taiwan become another Special Administrative Region of China, part of the whole, yet undoubtedly different? Manufacturing has shifted to the mainland, but Taiwan remains one of the world's leading suppliers of electronics. The country remains prosperous, democratic and optimistic, despite being under threat. It is a strange glimpse into what China may have become if the communist forces had been defeated. Or, perhaps, what China may become in the future. Class over.

For our *Word Travels* in Taiwan episode, I am here to meet Master Hsieh Ching-long, the creator of Fire Therapy. It's a hot story, allowing me to understand what a steak feels like when thrown on a grill. Using open flame, Master Hsieh (pronounced Shay) realigns the energy in your body, healing muscle ailments and sports injuries. Judging by the Polaroids of the Master posing with dozens of local celebrities, the hour-long treatment seems to work. First, he applies a technique called cupping, using heat suction to massage the airplane seat out my back. Then he has me lie down, pastes my back in a thick gooey mixture of herbs, covers me with a towel, douses me with alcohol and set me on fire. What does it feel like to be lit up like a BBQ? It feels warm, in a pleasant sort of way. I am more nervous about the other Polaroids on display in the small clinic depicting people's reactions to the treatment. Some of his clients look like well-done steak. The clinic is suffused with the smell of various Chinese herbs, and Master Hsieh oozes confidence – important qualities in a doctor that literally plays with fire. He looks like Jet Li, and developed his practice after years of doing martial arts and a medical school stint in Beijing. To prove his inner strength, he rips an apple with his bare hands, and then hands me a sledgehammer. Sandwiching his hand beneath two bricks, he asks me to smash the top brick over his hand. Who am I to argue? My first swing breaks the brick over his hand, but does not transfer the energy to break the bottom brick. Master Hsieh wants me to give 'er. So I take another swing to the replacement brick, which shatters over his hand, the sledgehammer ripping a piece of skin as it does so. Now there's blood, but Master Hsieh is determined to demonstrate his power, and his belief that I can actually pull off this stunt without killing him is flattering. Another swing, and thank God, the bottom brick crumbles. Scars and burns on his arms exhibit that the good fire doctor has had much practice honing his art. "Now, for the dangerous part," says Vic, the Master's brother, acting as an able translator. This would involve me, an open flame, and the potential for Esrock mignon. It's amazing what one will do when there is a camera around. Britney Spears forgets her panties; I set myself on fire.

From my home base at the Grand Hotel, with its outrageous buffet and sinister underground evacuation tunnel (not open the public, but travel writers have perks), I spend the week exploring Taipei. There are some eighteen universities in this city of 2.6 million, and more scooters and bikes than I've ever seen anywhere. Narrow streets are lined in neon, the smell of deep-fried fish and pork dishes smoke up the white, wet Asian sky. It will take some time to adjust to the humidity. Even the cameras keep fogging up every time we exit an air-conditioned bubble. I was on the Chinese mainland last month sailing up the Yangtze River, and although Taiwan and China share the same language and culture, there are differences. People here appear friendlier, less pushy. I hardly encounter the infamous Chinese "chwark" spit, and while traffic is wild, drivers afford each other more respect. Longshan Temple sparkles in the peaceful prayers of candlelight, the spiritual home of the country. Shops are colourful, plastered in cute, brightly-coloured cartoon characters that remind me of Japan. Characters like the comic poo people on the menu of Modern Toilet.

I read about this toilet-themed restaurant online, and I've become quite fascinated with proving that sometimes you *can* believe what you read on the Internet. So here we have a restaurant where customers sit on designer toilet seats, eat from toilet-shaped bowls, drink from urinal-shaped cups and buy poo paraphernalia. I ordered the Number Two, a delicious chicken curry. It arrived in a miniature porcelain toilet bowl, and the carrots floating in the brown stew reminded me of the last time I drank beyond my talent. I'm not taking the piss, but the potential for puns here is endless. Rock-bottom prices fit for a king on a throne, the food was anything but crap, which explains why there are now ten outlets across the country. I ask the owner what inspired such a scatological take on dining. "Just for fun," he says. Ask me why I chose to eat here and I'll give you the answer.

What I won't eat is snake, and I won't drink the bile of snake bladder, either. Snake Alley was once home to whores and superstitious inequity, but today it is the home of tourist stalls, out-of-place sex shops and somewhat distasteful (and therefore thoroughly fascinating) snake kitchens. Drinking the bile is supposedly good for virility; eating snake soup is good for skin conditions. Since I owned a pet snake once (albeit one that bit me), my gut sank watching them hung up, skinned and split for this bizarre serpentine cocktail. Large cobras atop a cage were taunted by a creepy old man, and he picked one up and threw it towards the camera. For a big man, Sean moves quick. Our tourism board guide Wen showed remarkable and admirable restraint. Normally, government officials do their best to sanitize the experience of a travel writer, and we often have to break rank to see this kind of thing. It's pretty horrific, but it's there for the locals, not for the tourists. Real travel often offends the sensibilities. That's what makes it so much fun.

There are some interesting rock formations at Yehliu Geopark, up the scenic north coast, eroded into spongy phallic shapes by wind, water and time. The coastline is beautiful, but there are no leisure boats to be seen, for reasons of national security. A large number of surfers are in the still ocean water, waiting for a freak wave from a typhoon nailing the Philippines to the south. It's a rare blue-sky day during monsoon season, when heavy rains unleash themselves onto all those poor scooter drivers. Like on the mainland, the sky here is mostly a haze, fogging the view from way up high. Taipei 101 is not a lecture class; it was the world's tallest building. An engineering marvel with 101 floors, it has only recently been pipped to the post by the Burj Khalifa, but remains a symbol of Taiwan's economic power. Women give birth to life; it appears men give birth to phallic symbols of longstanding greatness. Inspired by the flexibility of bamboo, the building is covered in symbols, from massive coins on the exterior for good fortune to stylized dragon gargoyles for protection. It has the world's fastest elevators (at 60km an hour, you reach the 85th-floor observation deck in just 37 seconds) and four massive damper balls to stabilize the building from strong winds and earthquakes. Architectural porn, if you're into that sort of thing.

This has been fun, but now I've got stories to write, pitch, and, hopefully, sell. Hosting a travel show is one of the best jobs in the world, but there's more work than you realize setting up those beauty shots, improvising decent dialogue, shlepping from one place to the next. It's 10-, 12-, 14-hour days, every day, and then comes the writing, the photo galleries, tying up interviews, and frayed nerves. Not that I'm complaining; I've got two hours to finish an article and then we're off to Korea, where a new adventure begins.

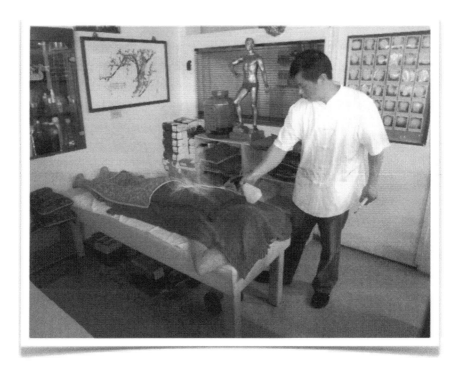

Master Hsieh, the Fire Doctor of Taipei, sets me alight in his consulting rooms

(l)Taipei's Grand Hotel, our living quarters for a week.
(r) Standing outside Taipei's 101 building

BEHIND THE SCENES IN TAIWAN

Television is a mighty beast, and a moving picture is worth a few thousand words, but there are a couple of limitations as to what it can do. For one, it was impossible to convey just how hot and humid it was during our visit in Taiwan. Stepping out of the stunning, air-conditioned Grand Hotel was like getting blasted by a jet burner. We were all dripping in sweat, especially when we drove up the coast. Taiwan was our first international episode of the season, so there we were, dealing with the heat, figuring things out and coping with the overall weirdness of being in China, yet out of China.

The Fire Doctor scenes were as wild as it looks on TV. Except I couldn't see my back being lit up like the Human Torch (probably a good thing). Master Hsieh definitely had an air of power about him. There were Polaroids on the wall of him posing with celebrities, so I figure if they'd put their trust in the guy, why shouldn't I?   Of course, there were also those pictures of people with their backs grilled, and since we were just starting out on our Asia leg, I was naturally concerned that I'd be toast for other episodes too, with strips of burnt skin down my back. So we asked him to take it easy with me, which was a wise thing to do considering I didn't have any back problems to begin with. The breaking the brick over his hand incident was hilarious. He hands me a heavy sledgehammer and tells me to whack his hand. I break the brick, but not hard enough to transfer the energy through his hand to the one underneath. In the show, you see the second attempt, in which the sledgehammer breaks the brick and tears a chunk of skin off the Master's hand. It's raw and bloody and I'm naturally horrified, hence my reaction on camera. But he insisted on me doing it again, and I did, and it worked, finally, although now he was going to light me up on fire and I had just caused the man considerable discomfort. I can attest, ultimately, that fire on the skin causes pain, too, but not as much as when you wake up two nights later with a back spasm. It might have been because of the clicking twists at the Fire Doctor, it might have been because I overdid it at the gym that day, but either way, it's the only time during the filming of all three seasons I'd ever seriously considered being rushed to hospital. The pain went away a few days later. As did we.

We show a little of what it's like to be on an actual press trip, but the Taiwanese Information Office were fantastic about it. It always takes a couple of days before hosts and writers figure each other out, but there's genuine respect and gratefulness on our part that they appreciate. Most travel writers, it has to be said, are a little older than Julia and I, and our enthusiasm for doing what we do goes a long way.

A meal served up in Modern Toilet. I believe it was Number 2 on the menu

The bizarre geological formations at the Yehliu Geopark, caused by erosion

SOUTH KOREA
MEAT FOR THE SOUL

The irony of looking for a steak restaurant in the frenzied height of a protest about beef did not escape me. The citizens of South Korea were out in force, vocalizing their discontent at their government's decision to allow US beef to be imported into the country, after being banned for fear of importing mad cow disease along with it. If cows were being infected in the fields of the United States, you can bet Americans would be dropping like the flies feasting on their corpses. But here we are, thousands of people on the streets, riot police, water cannons, blockades – you can also bet this is about an issue more complex than just bovines going bonkers. And I had a window seat, since the action was taking place below my hotel window at the Somerset Palace in downtown Seoul.

Reputations are funny things. You hear something about somebody, read something about some place, and instantly you form an opinion that creates a mountain on the landscape of your opinions. "I heard it's dangerous," or "She's a slut," and the only way you'll ever know for sure is if you go there yourself, or get to know her. All I knew about Korea was from what I had seen on *M*A*S*H* as a kid, heard from a family friend about doing business there, and the odd story from fellow travellers who'd taught English in the country. *M*A*S*H* taught me there was once a war in Korea, that suicide is stupid, that it's possible to hook up a martini machine in a tent, that nurses are naughty, and that life is a bittersweet comedy. Did you know the actor who played Radar only had tiny fingers on his left hand? Anyway, my family friend told me Korea was grey and industrially bleak. It's quite possible he was doing business in a grey and industrially bleak area. The various ex-English teachers who have come my way have mostly been folks looking to escape, save some cash and defer making any serious life-changing decisions. In other words, people I can relate to. Teaching English in a foreign country is a deposit that has sat in my travel bank for some time now. All you need is a degree, some enthusiasm, no criminal record (a recently instituted measure), and off you go to nurture the minds of another nation's youth. I really had no idea where the real beef was with South Korea, and although I only had a week to find it, I was determined to try.

The crew bade farewell to director Jordan in Taipei, and in Seoul we would meet Michael, our director for the next eight episodes. Having directed multiple seasons of the popular travel show *The Thirsty Traveler*, I was eager to glean something from his ample well-trampled travel show experiences. Certainly the shows are designed so that everyone who watches them automatically thinks: I wish I could be there! Michael reckons every travel show needs its "holy crap" moment, when the viewer sees something that inspires them to explete in their respective manner. What you don't see are the 16-hour days, the frenetic schedule, the enormous amount of work being put in by the guys back in the office, the barrage of emails and phone calls, equipment issues, editing, paperwork, permits, post-production hermits, editorial quagmires, shlepping, shlooping and shipping of tapes and discs, deal making, breaking, back aching, faking, reputation staking superhuman effort to produce a life of seemingly endless leisure. Not that anyone is complaining, mind you; it's just that Einstein's Theory of Relativity applies to travel shows, too.

As with dating, first impressions count on the road, and my first impression of Seoul was that it reminded me very much of Tokyo. Clean, busy, civil, modern, extreme: I love Tokyo. However, the Japanese brutally occupied Korea between 1910 and 1945, denying Koreans basic rights while squeezing its resources and technical know-how. I wonder if the similarities I see today between Japan and Korea are a result of that, and if so, who absorbed what from whom? Massive LCD screens project advertising onto the streets, while high-rise residential buildings line the highway, large numbers marking them like inmates in a prison. You've heard of Korean motor brands Hyundai, Daiwoo, Kia and Ssangyong – but never have you seen such a diversity of models. Given the history, good luck finding a Japanese car in Korea. Then there's Samsung and LG, multinational electronic firms that sharpen the country's cutting edge. And the other edge, the 38th parallel – the line that separates the prosperous south from the destitute north. The line that has cost millions of lives.

I just taught my first class of eleven year olds, and I've got a major case of teacher buzz. So here's a brief paragraph on Korea's modern history: After the Japanese were defeated in World War II, the Russian-backed communists established a government in the north; the US-backed government was in the South. The UN recognized the South, not the North, and the North, flush with Russian arms, invaded. At first the South were losing, then UN forces (comprising mostly US troops) were sent in, along with Hawkeye, Hunnicutt, Hot Lips and mobile army surgical hospitals (i.e. *M*A*S*H*). The UN forces pushed the communists all the way home and beyond, until China decided to support its communist neighbours with 1.2 million troops. By the time an armistice was declared along military lines in 1953, some 4 million people were dead, including 900,000 Chinese troops, two million civilians split equally between the North and South, and some 37,000 US soldiers. One third of the country's homes were destroyed, along with about half of Korea's industry. As a pawn on the Cold War chessboard, the peninsular of Korea developed quickly with the aid of its respective kings, the US in the South, the Russians in the North. Kim Il-Sung, the grandfather of North Korea's current lunatic, rolled the progress-o-meter back in his country. Today North Korea is a world apart separated by the 2km Demilitarized Zone (where video cameras are not permitted). In flourishing South Korea, people are not protesting for food. They're protesting because they can.

For my "teaching English in Korea" segment for the show, we arranged to meet a Canadian English teacher named Matthew at his school in Seoul, where his principal kindly agreed to let me teach a class on camera. I figured geography would be a good line to take, and, hooking my laptop up to a projector, I packed up the kids for a 'round-the-world adventure with my photographs. The Gowon Elementary School has over a thousand students, and is spotless and modern (classes have a state-of-the-art digital monitor as well as a chalkboard), with cute kids eager to learn and play. On my hastily assembled slideshow, I added the names of creatures and places. "This is Malaysia" is followed by a chorus of kids saying, "Malaysia!" with a lot of oohing and aahing, since the photo shows me holding a crocodile's tail in a den of man-eating saltwater crocs outside Malacca. I figured Machu Picchu was a little complicated for Peru, so I added "Lost City of the Inca" instead.

Says precocious eleven-year-old kid: "Machu Picchu!"

It's not every day you get to open the minds and hearts of children, and while it may not be bungee jumping, showing them bungee jumping was just as thrilling. I told them, sincerely, that travelling the world is just about the most wonderful thing anyone can ever do. That for the most part, travel is safe and friendly. That the next time their parents go on holiday, they should scream crocodile tears until their parents take them with them. Aside from the one kid slumped over in a daze (there's always one, isn't there?), I captivated their attention, answered their eager questions and was sad to hear the chanting over the speakers that signalled it was time for the next class. Suddenly I understood why teachers do what they do, at least before they become bitter and jaded and start handing out detentions to kids named Robin.

For a more dynamic on-screen interview, we took Matthew along to the Sea La La Spa and Waterpark, a somewhat plastic example of Koreans' love of bathhouses. Rotating between salt saunas, ice rooms, private caverns and traditional baking hot rooms, it's a good example of how something supposedly relaxing becomes far more challenging when shooting television. Between random sounds, rogue people on camera (we call them *bogeys*), setting up creative shots and whatnot, it's a case of hurry up and wait, and not nearly as relaxing as it would look on the show (as poor Matthew will testify). That being said, when Michael called for me to get a traditional massage from a beautiful Korean girl, who was I to argue? And the power Jacuzzis did go a long way towards untying the sailor knots in my back and neck. Is it wrong for me to say that on the same day that I inspired three dozen kids to become citizens of the world, I got the greatest thrill from Dr. Fish? These little fishies (Garra ruffa from Turkey in the one pool, larger Chinchin from China in the other) eat the dead skin on your feet and hands, sort of like harmless piranha. The sensation is one third pins and needles, one third tickle and one third "holy crap, I'm being nibbled on by hundreds of carnivorous fish!" It's just the sort of "holy crap" moment Michael looks for, although ironically none of the footage made the final show. Anyway, I've eaten my fair share of fish in my time, so it's only fair that I offer some callused skin as a form of giving back. Here, fishy fishy!

A rock narrowly misses Sean's head, slamming into the armoured police bus barricading the road to City Hall. He's encouraging me to get closer to the BBC/CNN cameras, which are mobbed up front around an important protestor spokesperson. The police "chicken buses," as the locals call them, are covered in eggs, spray paint, stickers and the overall discontent of the masses. I estimate there are over 50,000 people protesting tonight, after the government declared that it would in fact go ahead and lift the ban on US beef. A long line of people form a chain to bring sandbags up front, creating a makeshift bridge to walk over the buses into the thousands of armed riot police waiting on the other side. A water cannon rises threateningly, a couple of youngsters hightail it through the masses, but the sandbags keep coming. A few rocks get hurled, but besides an eerie female voice telling everyone to "Go Home," the cops seem content to wait it out. Fortunately, tear gas is banned in South Korea. Members of the press are wearing hard hats and protective gear. Everyone, that is, except members of *Word Travels*, who, shamefully, are just enjoying the thrill of being close to their first major urban riot. I'll admit that things like this can turn dangerous very quickly, but there was a buzz being a part of democracy in action. Plus, the protestors were mostly calm, if a little angry. If this were China, or the US, rubber bullets would be flying, and trust me, I would be enjoying the view from the Jacuzzi on the rooftop of the Somerset. Danger on the road is a judgment call, and we all rightly judged we were not in harm's way.

Meanwhile, word and gushing water on the street indicates there is more action just a block away, and here, in a narrow alley, a robotic water cannon is spraying a mass of determined protestors. A stream of water rushes over my sandals and there's a peppery smell in the air, possibly because the water is laced with an irritant. After drenching the faithful up front, the cannon stops and a large rope gets picked up and pulled in a tug-of-war to tip the buses over. I take hold of the hard rope to figure out what the chances are of it actually tipping, and since the buses are no doubt anchored on the other side, chances are slim. Ripping the grates and wooden boards off the chicken buses is an easier task, and inside I can make out the shadows of riot police no doubt shitting beef patties in fear of the thing actually overturning. A girl next to me tells me she is studying in North Carolina and flew home specifically to take part in the protests. "I can't believe this is happening in my country," she says, dismayed, as the chanting kicks into another gear and the water cannon renews its projectile into the crowds. She blames the government for not listening to the people, but since Korea is America's third-largest beef importer, I imagine it's less about people and more about money. It's getting late, so we decide to head back to the hotel, which sits behind the barricade. Riot police let us through a small crack (oh, the things you can get away with, being a tourist!) and we walk back to the hotel through the dark, eerily quiet streets. We see the anxious faces of young policemen, eyes as innocent as on calves to the slaughter. South Korea's mandatory conscription has all men serving in the army or the police force. It is highly likely that these kids have friends on the other side of the barricade, girlfriends, family. If they were not in the police force, they might be there, too. Instead, they sit on their shields, row after row, five cops deep. We walk without hindrance, even stopping to play around with some of the riot gear. We can hear the livid chants of the protestors on the other side of the buses. It is one of the most surreal and tense scenes I have ever seen throughout my journeys. And it is all about meat, and where it comes from, while just a few hundred kilometres away, North Koreans are dying in a famine. Like the rest of us, Koreans live in interesting times.

Another irony: travellers like to get lost in order to find themselves. Korea Tourism has been pushing spiritual getaways to temples around the country: "temple stays" for tourists wanting to experience the tranquility and order that comes from living inside a Buddhist monastery. We headed over to the Lotus Lantern International Meditation Centre, a few hours' drive from Seoul, to try on a little monkhood. First, I had to try on grey overalls, to be worn at all times. A young shaven-headed Russian monk gave us an introductory talk in spotty English, although it was impressive how he switched to Korean for the horde of local university students also spending the night. Alexander gave us a brief introduction to Korean Buddhism, a constant, peaceful smile on his lips. We would chant and meditate, bow to the Buddha three times upon entering the temple and exit facing the Buddha. Meals were vegetarian and eaten in silence, although the head monk's cell phone did interrupt him for a few minutes. We tried meditating atop soft pillows in a long hall, emptying our heads, counting to ten, focusing on our breath. I confess I'm one of those people who constantly buzzes. I've got fire ants in the pants and Speed Racer neurons triggering thoughts, with soundtracks of music in my mind. I quite like it that way. But I hate mosquitoes, present here in abundance. I ask if mosquitoes constitute a sentient life form, a sly-handed way of enquiring whether it's OK to squash the buggers in a Buddhist temple. "Monks do not kill mosquitoes," says Alexander, waving a couple away from his face. This could be the single biggest obstruction to my ever becoming one. I spend the meditation session swatting, staring out the window into the forest and using this rare moment of silence to reflect on all I have to be grateful for. A half hour later, I emerge from the hall relaxed and jovial, a believer in the benefits of taking a "time out" to stop and think about the things that matter, or even nothing at all.

Physical challenges have somehow become my forte, so performing 108 prostrations in a Buddhist temple at four a.m. should have been easy. Bend your knees, touch your head on the mat, raise your hands, stand up, repeat. By number sixty, however, I was dizzily sweating, my knees trying to topple the chicken buses of my tendons. As a form of meditation, prostration takes practice and is a sign of devotion. A golden statue of Buddha looks on approvingly, eyes half closed, dragons above his head. Behind me, some of the students are giggling in agony.

Things you're not supposed to do on TV:
1. High five.
2. Say the word "awesome."

When the bowing stops, Julia and I rock an awesome high five.

By five a.m., we are back in the meditation hall, facing outwards, fighting the attack of thoughts. This time, I think about countries and the adventures I had within them, the people I met, and anything that will prevent me from falling asleep. Pickled cabbage and radish and porridge for breakfast, a dash of calligraphy, and we return to the city for a meal of ginseng chicken soup, various time-lapses along the busy streets of Insadong and the canal of Cheonggyecheon, Gyeongbokgung Palace, with the 360-degree views atop N Seoul Tower showing us just how massive this city is. I catch a martial arts display and some interesting public art. We spend a night in a beautiful traditional guest inn called Rakkojae, a pocket of Korean history amidst the latest slick city fashions. I sleep on the floor off the manicured gardens, half-expecting to see the silhouettes of attacking ninjas through the light screen doors.

Finally, a visit to the World's Largest Congregation, a mega church that, according to the Guinness Book of Records, has some 780,000 members. Yoido Full Gospel Church looks like a stadium and holds 12,000 people at a time. Seats are so in demand that people arrive hours early, and little old ladies barge past me on their way to the pews. On Sunday, there are seven packed services, featuring a band, full orchestra, choir, giant TV screens, and thousands of little old ladies waving their hands in the air. There's a special section for foreigners, where it is their "godly pleasure" to serve us with headphones and translation services in eight languages. The elders, all men, sit on comfortable leather couches on stage, stoically facing their adoring audience. The dome above looks like a snail's shell, a molluscular ceiling of faith. The production value of the service is top notch. A short film about mentally ill children supported by the church has the ladies reaching for donation envelopes, stuffing them with 10,000 won notes. If they needed to get some more, I noticed there were ATM's and a bank in the lobby. Behind me, three women are raising the roof, one with the tears of the faithful. It's our lucky day, too, since Pastor David Yonggi Cho, the retired and globally renowned founder of Yoido, is giving a sermon in aid of the church's charity. He's a slight man, blown up to mega proportions by the mega screens, speaking with a seemingly divine ability to take no pauses. There are more Christians in South Korea than Buddhists, and Korean missionaries are common around the world. Fascinating stuff, but the segment didn't make the episode.

One week in any country can hardly make you an expert, but admittedly we pack in more than most people. Racing about in our bus, our driver Mr. Kim slamming on the brakes and pulling U-turns as is the custom in Seoul traffic, our wonderful local guide Sarah showing patience beyond anything we deserve. I've barely got time to catch my breath, let alone write three articles to pitch, and once again my little diary has run into thousands of words. Time to gather up the innards of my backpack and catch the early morning flight to the Philippines. As for South Korea, what else can I say? It's been a riot.

BEHIND THE SCENES IN SOUTH KOREA

We film a lot for a half-hour show, and so much ends up on the cutting room floor (or more accurately, the bin system in the edit suite). We had found a young Canadian ESL teacher named Matthew James, and it was his class that I got to pounce on with my makeshift geography lesson. Matthew and the school were terrific about my invasion, but unfortunately there was no space to throw in more info, or even Matthew and I chilling in the relaxation caverns at the spa. As for the kids, well, it truly was terrifying to go up and entertain a class of 11 year olds. There was no rehearsal or setup (there never is on our show); we arrived, I plugged into their very modern projector system and away we went. Having finally placated my mother by getting a TV show (being a travel bum was never going to cut it), she's now on my case that I should become a teacher.

As for the 108 prostrations, by number 63 my knees were creaking, I was sweating and an auspicious wet spot was on the mat where my head touched every time. I've found that it takes a couple of days to adjust to being outside of your comfort zone, be it in a monastery, an ashram, a kibbutz or a jungle. Once you do find that new routine, it can be very peaceful, and very chill. Naturally, we crammed as much as we could into the two days we had, and were back to Seoul before our souls could acclimatize.

Seoul was in the midst of a full-scale riot. The people were protesting the fact that the government were relaxing the ban on US beef imports. Koreans take their meat seriously. The ban came after cases of mad cow were reported in the US, and Korea is a major US beef importer. The already-unpopular government unleashed the fury of the people, and well over 100,000 protestors gathered downtown every night. The riot police were out in force, and our hotel was right in the thick of it. We'd go down every night and speak to the masses, pull a rope or two, get water cannoned. It didn't make sense to include much of it in the show because we're not a news show, and demonstrations fall outside the travel sections. Plus, the gear would have been destroyed. But it was interesting to see a mobilized population protest an apparent injustice. Considering how many people were involved, it's amazing nobody was seriously injured or killed in the clashes. South Koreans are passionate, but wonderfully civilized, too.

Reading the riot act at the beef protests

A monk calls everyone to service

Teaching the class

Saving mosquito souls

THE PHILIPPINES
LIFE IS A BUFFET

I wonder if it's something in the air. Some places, you arrive and you just *know* it's going to be good travel, the way you know the outcome of a first date in the first five minutes. I had barely left the airport, the scent of fresh jasmine filling my nostrils, and I was already thinking: *How come it took me so long to visit the Philippines?*

I love South and Central America, perhaps more than any other region on our planet. So much history, so much passion. North America has its big ideas and western lifestyle. Having experienced 300 years of Spanish colonial rule, followed by four decades of the United States, the Philippines falls somewhere in the middle – a meal of hamburgers served with *ceviche* and eaten with chopsticks.

Manila, the capital, has two seasons: hot and hotter. A yellow glare beats down on us, the light sharing the faint colour of manila envelopes (originally made from an indigenous plant fibre). I'm here in rainy season, when torrential downpours soak the stickers off the loud chrome Jeeps that shepherd the population around the city. These customized "Jeepneys" growl like engines trying to dispel pieces of chickens in their throats, shepherding Metro Manila's 12.8 million population for a couple of pesos a head. Yes, pesos, here in Asia, where soy sauce is mixed with vinegar and floating fresh chili, and where people's names combine Spanish, English and the local Tagalog. For a city established by the Spanish as early as 1571, there's a definite lack of historical buildings to prove it. The Philippines, named after the Spanish King Phillip II, is the world's third-largest Roman Catholic country. Pillaged, bombed, colonized, rebuilt and pillaged and bombed again. The Americans took it from the Spanish in the Spanish-American war (the same war that inextricably gave the Americans Guantanamo Bay in Cuba), the Japanese brutally took it from the Americans in World War II, the Americans took it back (bombing most of Manila into splinters) and gave it to the Filipinos for their independence in 1946. Since then, governed from the main island of Luzon, the country has repeatedly slipped off a tightrope of political instability. It's been battered by up to a dozen typhoons every year, loan-sharked by one-sided US naval base deals, prodded by Islamic insurgencies in the south and kept afloat by regular remittance cheques from the world's largest diaspora: some 11 million Filipinos live and work abroad. Yet, much like its Spanish-influenced cousins across the Pacific in the Americas, its people are friendly and genuinely welcoming, impassioned by the sun to dance the fiesta of life. Perhaps it is this dichotomy of tragedy and joy that draws me to the Latino culture, and the dichotomy of a Latin Asia that has drawn me here.

As usual, I only have a week, and spending a week in a country is like having only one bite of one dish at an endless five-star hotel buffet (more on that later). As much as Manila has to offer, the most delicious slices of life are always, in my experience, found off the plate of a big city. One bite, so I'd better choose wisely. It's my dream to snorkel with whale sharks, the ocean's largest fish, but not only are they tough to find, they've also been covered by another travel show on our network. From fellow travellers, I've long heard that the Philippines have some of the world's best tropical beaches, scuba diving, rock climbing and surfing. So I call over the waiter and order a plate of Palawan, a narrow archipelago of 1780 islands located to the southwest of the country. If I'm only going to be able to take one bite, I may as well chew on paradise.

Palawan has the highest number of islands, the least amount of people, and is proudly referred to as the "last ecological frontier" due to its wealth of protected areas. In 1967, the entire province was declared a fish and wildlife sanctuary, and while Ferdinand Marcos was looting the country's economy in the 1980's, he still passed a number of presidential decrees safeguarding Palawan's environment. With this commitment to national parks and reserves, there's a slick irony that huge deposits of natural gas have been found off Palawan, leading to the single-biggest investment in the history of the country's economy. It's always interesting to see how governments react when a previously worthless tract of land ("Hey, let's declare it a national conservation park!") suddenly attains mineral value ("Hey, let's mine the crap out of it!"). Hopefully, the remoteness and vastness of Palawan, coupled with a political desire to maintain it as such, will see it through.

It's a one-hour flight to Puerto Princesa, the capital of Palawan and the nation's fastest-growing city. On board, there are around fifty girls wearing bright orange shirts asking me if I'm pregnant. A pharmaceutical company called BioFemme is having a conference in the city. Last week, a massive typhoon blew through the southern Philippines, killing dozens of people, tragically capsizing a ferry that drowned another 700 more. Other than some towns in the north of the main island, I'm relieved to hear that Palawan is typhoon-free, since this is slam-bang up the yin-yang of typhoon season. Not that I'd be getting away from the rain, mind you; this is rainy season, and let me describe what a Felipino tropical downpour is like with bullet points:

- The rain falls with the force of angels using power hoses to put out a fire on earth.
- The rain falls as if the clouds have overfed their fat bellies and have burst at the seams.
- The rain falls like bullets from the sky.

Palawan boasts two UNESCO World Heritage Sites, and it was only a few hours' drive to visit the World's Longest Underground Navigable River. The road was a rutted, crunchy pretzel; our guide called it the "free Palawan massage." Air conditioning is cranked in the minivan as we worms our way around flooded potholes, so no surprise when the engine overheats. Fortunately, we had two minivans to hold crew and equipment, and proceeded towards the Subterranean River National Park in the backup van, arriving just in time to watch traditional wooden boats head out into the crystal sea, the wind tickling the coconut balls hovering over the white sandy beach. After two weeks exploring some of the world's biggest cities, this, my friends, is much more like it.

Navigable. I've always enjoyed the way the word sounds on my tongue, forcing it into four positions within my mouth. At 8.2km, we'd arrived at the longest navigable underground river in the world, drifting from the mouth of a cave beneath the limestone mountain above it into a narrow sanctuary for eight species of bat and striking rock formations. Tourists only get to paddle up the first kilometre with a guide, using a car battery power spotlight to see the sights within. While some of the stalactites and stalagmites have the usual cute-cave names common in caverns around the world (the Jesus, the Candle, the Naked Lady), refreshingly absent are bright coloured lights and wooden walkways. With the acrid smell of bat shit in the still-eerie darkness, I felt like I was being swallowed by a beast, prodded along beneath stalagmitical teeth, ingested further towards something powerful, something black. Cave exploring is fun, but not as much fun as seeing light at the end of the tunnel.

Back on the beach, there was no time to explore the wooden monkey trail, so we hopped aboard the boat to get back to the vans, witnessing an inspiring sunset, the warm sea breeze caressing my fingers as I stood up front at the bow. Paul took a photo from the other boat. It has leapfrogged to cruise among my top Gonzo photos of all time.

I was meditating to an eclectic iPod shuffle, stretched back in the van, so fortunately didn't see the dog get splattered up front. The guys who did were pretty shaken up, and not even an outstanding seafood meal and the perfect pina colada back in town helped much. Late check-in, a night in a hotel where my head is asleep before it hits the pillow, only to wake up confused because nothing about this room is familiar. It happens often enough now that I enjoy the brief confusion, the fear of absolute lostness, before my brain reactivates to remind the rest of me that I'm in Puerto Princesa, and have to wake up early so I can go to directly to jail.

"Originally known as the Iwahig Penal Colony, 23km outside town, it is a one-of-a-kind prison. Built like any normal community, Iwahig's system allows detainees – called colonists – to work and live without being bounded by walls. Tourists are welcome to visit and to purchase souvenir handicraft made by prisoners." So sayeth the Palawan Traveler's Guide produced by the provincial tourism office. It sounded like a perfect story to investigate, a great segment for the show. Unusual, weird, one of a kind, an open-walled prison holding murderers and thieves in one utopian community. As it turns out, tourists are welcome, possibly even travel writers, but travel writers with a TV crew? Forget about it. Whatever permits we had were not the permits they wanted, and whatever reason we gave was not reason enough. With a tight schedule, this was to be a key story in the show, and here we were, barred at the gates, as curious prisoners in tattered work shirts looked on from the surrounding rice paddies.

In truth, of course, all is not nearly as airbrushed as the pamphlet might suggest. There are more than 3000 prisoners here, ranging from minimum to maximum security status, a chain gang of assorted criminals. Some escape after being locked up in sinister-sounding "orientation areas" for up to 18 months before being allowed in the "work brigades" outside the fence. Families were once allowed to live with their convicted breadwinner, but according to a recently released prisoner, this is no longer the case. He did prefer serving his two-year sentence for robbery here because it beat the city jail, and there is a good relationship between the guards and the prisoners, who wear T-shirts colour-coded to indicate their security level. Brown for minimum, blue for medium, orange for maximum.

Meanwhile, we're desperately trying to shoot something, anything, for the show, and in the end decide we'll focus on the challenges of travelling with a TV crew versus travelling by yourself, especially when it comes to getting those edgier experiences. We left the cameras behind and went into the 30,000-hectare compound and directly to the gift shop, where a bizarre assortment of beads, crafts, heavy wooden batons and nunchakus were on sale. Maybe it's just me, but prisoners and weapons should perhaps be kept apart. But I did score the Weirdest Souvenir of All Time. An effeminate prisoner working in the souvenir shop (medium risk, according to his blue shirt) said he could score us authentic prison T-shirts in a hush-hush-say–no-more deal. In a quick exchange out back, we bought four Department of Corrections T-shirts for $5 a pop, but were warned to not wear them anywhere in the Philippines. Only later did I realize there's really nothing cool about walking around in the dress of a convict. For someone who has built a career on personal freedom, there's really nothing cool at all about being locked up. Ironically, the afternoon's production headaches were for naught: for some reason not a frame of it made the actual episode.

Julia, my co-host, has guts of such iron she can consume *balut*, the local delicacy I once saw labelled number one on a TV show about the Top 10 Most Disgusting Things You Can Eat. *Balut* is a fertilized duck egg, an egg you eat with a baby duck still in it, chewing the pliable half-formed bones, crunchy beak and all. Her fearless culinary adventures do not extend to the air, however, which is why she let out a high-pitched yelp when our 19-seater LET-410 gut-kicked us during heavy turbulence in a tropical storm. The heavy rain was somehow getting through the pilot's window, and as we bounced around the sky en route to El Nido, I suddenly recalled the "flying coffin" scandal, where a small plane carrying a bunch of Australian tourists crashed off Manila a few years back. I thought about what song I'd like to be listening to if the plane were to go down, and thought that it's not like anyone could ever accuse me of not living my life to its fullest. Still, it would be awfully inconvenient to check out just now, especially since we were on our way to arguably the most beautiful spot on the planet. The plane arrived safely on the dirt runway in El Nido, but the propellers of my nerves took a few hours to stop spinning.

Alex Garland wrote *The Beach*, an amazing book later adapted into an overblown Hollywood production starring Leonardo DiCaprio. For those of you who haven't read it, it concerns a young English backpacker in Thailand who hears about a "secret" beach, a backpacker utopia free from the hordes of Lonely Planet-clutching tourists. Dramatically, it turns into a *Lord of the Flies*-ish nightmare thriller, and the movie, filmed on the Thai island of Phi Phi, takes the now-American hero Leo into the heart of budget travel darkness. But here's the funny bit: The remote, breathtaking beach that inspired Alex Garland to write his novel was not in Thailand. It was in El Nido.

Start with the seaweed wrapper of warm, crystal seawater. Roll in sharp limestone cliffs, hundreds of tropical fish, turtles, private beaches, emerald lagoons, coconut trees, pina coladas, sea kayaks and world-class diving beneath the stilts of your cabin. Add wasabi and soy sauce, and you've got paradise sushi.

I've travelled far and I've travelled wide, so when I say that El Nido's Bacuit Bay is probably the most beautiful place I've ever seen, you've got to realize the scale here. There are 45 islands in El Nido, mostly deserted, most protecting The Beach of Dreams. Besides the town (also named El Nido), there are a couple of high-class luxury resorts in the Bay, and I got the chance to stay at the oldest and grandest, the El Nido Resort on Miniloc Island. Its environmental policy is impressive; they even give guests biodegradable plastic bags to collect any trash they may find during their stay. A delicious daily buffet with several dozen homemade condiments, stilt and beachfront cabins, snorkeling and diving gear and sea kayaks and yachting and happy hour at the beach bar and a spa. It didn't matter that it was rainy season; it mattered that somehow I had managed to find this place, and from the second I arrived all I could think about was, *How on earth am I going to get back here?*

Heavy rain had pretty much killed my rock climbing story, but I did manage to kayak the limestone channel of the Big Lagoon in a few hours of sunshine. Photos could never do it justice; words (considerably less than a thousand of them) are insufficient, too. We take a boat out to explore some private beaches and a big cave, where I felt compelled to jump into the sea and swim right into it. Apparently, in the twenty years the resort has been open, I'm the first guy to attempt such a thing, which somehow scares the hell out of me. Why am I not scuba diving? Because I've got a bum right ear. Hell, it's only been a couple of years since I had a big ear operation and have been able to put my head underwater, never mind taking a week-long PADI diving course. It occurred to me that if a tandem instructor can help you skydive without any training, maybe a tandem instructor can help me dive, just deep enough to get the experience, but not deep enough to do any serious harm (I hope). So I grab Rommel and Jeff, the two resort activity studs, and they kit me up, walk me over to the pier and drop me into a sea of tropical fish. Rommel carefully steers me around the coral and clown fish, controlling my breathing apparatus and depth.

For those of you who have dived before, you know the feeling. For those of you who haven't, well, the buzz is so huge that the risk of the bends, lungs bursting, ears exploding, shark attacks and anything else you can think of is not risk enough. Intimidating bully jack fish, luminous flighty parrotfish, fish that look like dogs, fish that look like frogs, fish that look like monsters, fish that look like beauty queens, fish that look like Republicans, fish that look like Democrats, fish that look like musical instruments, fish that look like tools, fish that look like the sun, fish that look the moon, fish that salsa, fish that play chess, fish that are tidy, fish that mess, fish that are nerds, fish that are jocks, fish that can make everyone laugh, fish that are too shy to come out, spiky fish, smooth fish, naughty fish, nice fish, scary, sporty, posh, ginger and baby fish, everywhere I look I see fish, fish, fish, fish… and me. Tropical fish in the warm, light-blue sea, the rain pounding its keys on the water above my head, a toccata and fugue of sea life. El Nido is nothing less than a tropical El Dorado.

I just took a lunch break at the Dusit Thani hotel buffet. You could feed a mid-sized school with the food on offer, and everyone would still get a different dish. I sampled a little bit of that, a little of this, and left feeling satisfied, but I kind of wished that I had the time (not to mention the appetite) to try it all. After just a few days in Manila, and a few more in Palawan, all I can do is look forward to a second helping of the Philippines.

Yes, this will do.

BEHIND THE SCENES IN THE PHILIPPINES

We film a lot for a half-hour show, and so much ends up on the cutting room floor. That's why you won't see the prison in the show. El Nido was absolutely spectacular, although once more it felt like we were sabotaged by off-season weather. To do a show like ours, on a budget like ours, off season means we can afford to get to where we need to go, and also get into the places we'd like to go (a place like the El Nido Resort gets booked up pretty fast in high season). In the show, there's a fraction-of-a-second shot of me swimming into a cave. We had parked the boat alongside it; the water was crystal blue, and it seemed like the thing to do: you know, swim into the cave. Later, a guide tells me, "In fifteen years, you're the first person I've ever seen do that. Legend has it a big anaconda lives in that cave." Proving, once and for all, ignorance is bliss, and it also makes people do things that, in retrospect, are obviously stupid.

Since my bum ear keeps me out from under the water, I had originally planned to go rock climbing amongst those fantastic limestone islands. Rain and rock climbing mix like pit bulls and kindergartens, so we had to scramble for a replacement story. Compared to other shows on adventure travels, I knew my first time scuba diving wouldn't be very impressive in terms of what you, the viewer, might see beneath the surface. But my reaction, and the pure thrill of doing something I've always wanted to do, would be as real as it gets. Being real has held me in good stead these past few years. After all, if I was actually a gung-ho thrill-seeking adrenaline junkie, what fun would that be? Half of the time I'm scared to death; the other half I just reassure myself that people don't get hurt too often filming television.

On the other hand, Julia can eat all the *balut* she wants. She seriously did chase me around the hotel with that fertilized egg in her hand. You have to be a serious nut to eat that. Swimming with anacondas is like playing with puppies in comparison.

For someone who spends a lot of time in planes, I make a concerted effort not to think about plane crashes. This is not easy when flying through a tropical rainstorm. Rain was pouring in through the windows, and we were bouncing around like lottery balls, the propellers making that growling sound you hear in war movies just before a big explosion. I've got to think that the more I fly, the more I increase the chances of going down in a fiery ball, but statistically, it's more dangerous to drive your car. Did you know more people are killed every year from bee stings than shark attacks?   Fear exists in nature, and irrational fear is human nature. So here you have someone who's been set on fire and bungee jumped off TV towers and hiked erupting volcanoes, but show me a plane in a storm or an exotic egg delicacy and I'm wrapped up in the corner blubbering for mercy.

Looking out over Bascuit Bay, El Nido

Paul snapped this tremendous shot of me having a
moment up front in the boat, the warm South China
Sea breeze flowing through my fingers

Kayaking on impossibly blue water in
the Big Lagoon, along Maniloc Island

Balut - fertilized duck
egg is a local delicacy

THE MALDIVES
HONEYMOON FOR ONE

Lets chase those island screensavers, enter the world of the paradise wall calendar, taste the soft milk of the tropical coconut. During university, I once tore the photo pages off an old calendar and plastered the images over my desk. Bored with my studies, I'd inspire myself with images of crystal white seas mirrored by deep blue skies, coconut trees flirting with silky white beaches. There might be a hammock, a yacht or a sunset, but whatever the variation, the symbol remained the same. This is freedom. This is warmth. This is success. Sitting at my desk, weighed down by the pressure of an school assignment, I couldn't feel the intense heat of the sun, the life-draining humidity, the mosquitoes or sand between my toes. Instead I could simply gaze up every few seconds and embrace paradise, the Garden of Eden, a longing to find myself at home on a tropical beach, even though I grew up in a city surrounded by mine dumps. The title of the calendar was *Islands of the Maldives*, and 14 years later I'm still working on an assignment. Only this time I get to leave the desk, rip apart the fabric of my cosmic dream wall and finally put myself in the picture.

The Republic of Maldives consists of 1200 coral islands: the smallest country in Asia and the flattest country on the planet. With only 200 of the islands actually inhabited, and with the highest land point being just 2.3m high, word on the Indian Ocean is that rising sea levels will result in Maldivians being the world's first environmental refugees. One People, Under Water. In the meantime, it's a strictly conservative Islamic country that bans tourists from bringing in any other form of non-Muslim religious worship, nor any dogs (deemed unclean), pornography or alcohol. All major credit cards are, however, accepted. Since hotels are known to mark up liquor by up to 2000%, I bought some rum at the duty free in Manila only to find it confiscated by Maldivian Customs at the airport. I could retrieve the bottle before my return flight, and had the small consolation of knowing that Maldivian custom officials will not be getting loaded in the same way female US airport security nowadays only wear expensive perfume. If you come to paradise, you play by its rules. Foreigners in the capital of

Male are only permitted to buy alcohol with a special permit, and are limited to sixty cans of beer a month. But catch a sea taxi or powerful speedboat to one of the luxury resorts and anything goes. Fortunately, that's exactly where I would be going, leaving Male minutes upon arrival, and beelining it from the airport to the Soneva Gili, one of the world's most luxurious villa resorts.

Oh yes, there are perks to this job: jetting around the world; one exotic adventure after another; endless gourmet meals; a wealth of experience (but, says a fellow travel writer I met in Costa Rica, "Experience never paid my rent."). No doubt this is a dream assignment: the chance to sample life within a $2000-a-night ocean villa, happily attended to by an army of resort staff in its immaculate surroundings. After the beaches of the Philippines and the service at the Grand Hotel in Taipei, you can bet I will not be easily seduced. This will *not* be a case of a teenage girl hanging around with a college grad on a motorbike (or, more accurately, a backpacking travel bum hanging around a five-star luxury resort). See, I pay attention to detail and notice the quirks about the other side of the coin, the surface that shines with wealth and privilege. I am here to be critical. Well, it's a few minutes after my late-night arrival, and you can call me Tiffany, and watch me giggle on the back of the older boy's Kawasaki. Oh my!

There are forty-four villas, built over turquoise water and crammed with every luxury, yet full of space. Total privacy, embraced by a seemingly rustic aesthetic that only comes from spending wad-loads of money. Hear the gentle lapping of the transparent sea against a beach as fine as stardust. Listen to the warm breeze blowing notes through flute holes in the palm leaves above your head. The over-water bar is glowing with candles as wooden jetties tentacle into the ocean, lit up like runways to land every romantic dream flying in the air.

Using the high speed Wi-Fi somehow available in every villa, I Skype up to give anyone who's online a tour. It's about one a.m., and my producer Deb in Vancouver can't see much, but that doesn't matter. I waltz around the 250-square-metre residence illuminated by the glow of my MacBook.
"And here's the bathroom. Look at the size of it!... and check out the glass bottom, and the walkway to the glass-walled shower...

and the ladders into your own private sea pool...you can snorkel inches from brushing your teeth!... and the Bose surround system with an iPod adaptor... nice touch... and look at the upstairs deck with a bed you can roll out and sleep under the stars with overstuffed pillows... how could you not?... and the air-conditioned master bedroom with the Arabian Palace mosquito net... love it... and the living room with the backgammon and chess tables and waiting bottle of chilled champagne and fresh tropical fruit and couches and pillows and abundant big soft towels... check out this private deck, where you can dive right into the sea, and there's stingrays, and tropical fish, and even cute reef shark pups, and..."

"Robin, is that you? I can't hear you. You're breaking up... something about a bathroom?"

I sleep outside beneath the shooting stars, the sound of the wind gusting through feverish dreams of red-haired aliens, blowing away any troublesome night bugs. It is off-season here at the Soneva Gili on Lankanfushi Island, but all I need is a thin sheet to keep me warm in the night. I fall asleep smiling, but in the most romantic place on earth, on the upper level of an open-roof, over-water honeymoon villa, I fall asleep alone.

They take away your shoes in this part of the world. Put them inside a canvas bag labelled "No news, no shoes." It takes time to adjust to living barefoot, to the idea that nothing you can step on is going to hurt you. You eat barefoot; you ride the villa bikes barefoot. You fall in love with your forgotten feet, those stubby wubby toes that haven't seen such action since childhood. The bike pedals are cushioned, of course, and the long jetties are lined with water jars to cool your feet off when the wood gets too hot. You have to admire the attention to detail in the design, the faultless execution – a resort as a work of art. Look at the wine cellar, holding over 500 bottles of handpicked wine, and home to a resident sommelier. My director Michael, a veteran of the travel series *The Thirsty Traveler*, calls it among the most exquisite he's ever seen. A large tree, washed up during the 2004 tsunami, has been incorporated as the centrepiece of the cellar, a graphic demonstration of the resort's impressive sustainable environmental policy. Outside the cellar, a large on-site organic herb and vegetable garden delivers fresh produce to the kitchen and buffet, which twice a week drowns you in five-star gourmet choice. There's a cheese room and a meat room holding imported hams and cold cuts . Even in a strict Islamic country, allowances are made for the resorts so crucial to bringing in foreign income. Soneva Gili is one of twenty-two luxury resorts owned by the husband-and-wife team of Sonu and Eva Shivdasani, surely the Brad and Angelina, the Zeus and Hera, the Sonny and Cher of the luxury hospitality industry. You get the distinct impression they spare no expense creating their vision, and to enjoy it you won't spare much of your own. $2000 a night, an extra $150 per person per day for meals, $150 per person airport transfer, $8 beers... the cheapest bottle of wine is $65 from the cellar. This is no place for a young travel writer who lives out a backpack, and yet here I am, toasting myself over a magical dinner (a film crew recording it all, of course).

I'm writing an article about ultimate honeymoon destinations, which serves as an interesting platform to demonstrate what I have earlier referred to as Esrock's Theory of Travel Writing Relativity; yes, I have somehow found the back door to an exclusive club that, given what I earn in my profession, I could never afford to even think about approaching, much less ring the door bell.
The door is open; here I am enthusiastically welcomed by the staff, who sincerely go out of their way to make me feel welcome, graciously providing the canvas to paint my honeymoon story. But I am not on honeymoon. I am not like Texans Trevor and Kathryn who are spending a week in the Maldives absolutely glowing with love and happiness. Or the couple from Prague, or the couple from New Jersey, or Spain or Japan. I am sharing my villa with a 50-year-old married director from Calgary, who is admittedly in the same boat. "If my wife were here..." says Michael, knowing full well she couldn't be. It's like being treated to the finest wine, the richest chocolate, the deepest kiss, and then having it taken away, the taste forever on the lips of your desire.
Better to have known love than never have loved at all? Better to have experienced a honeymoon paradise on your own than never to have experienced it at all? The chocolate is bittersweet, the wine extends a few hooks as it slips down my throat, and as for the kiss, well, there isn't one at all.

The honeymoon, derived from an ancient practice in which fathers-in-law furnished their new sons with a month (moon) of honey mead, is described as a period of unusual harmony immediately following the establishment of a new relationship. For five days, I soaked in the harmony of my new relationship with the Soneva Gili. Trevor and Kathryn rave about the spa, so I take along the film crew to see how honeymooners get pampered. I get a few blissful moments courtesy of a beautiful Swedish masseuse, watch baby (harmless) reef sharks swim beneath me through well-placed floor windows as Katarina pulls apart the hard cement putty of my shoulders. "OK, got that, thanks," says Michael, and I move onto a quickly assembled facial, a manicure and a body wrap, all to demonstrate the pamper, without the pampering itself. The Theory of Relativity says I am not on honeymoon, I am merely researching a honeymoon, which has its perks (feel those strong Scandinavian fingers!), but, unlike for the rest of the couples in the resort, there's no happy ending.

We head out to snorkel the surrounding reef, seeking schools of fish and hoping to see turtles (nope), sharks (nope) or stingrays (nope). No matter, it's still life in a fish tank, letting the chill sink in as tropical marine colours explode from the overhead sun. More successfully, Julia and I did manage to see a giant manta ray gliding along a reef, but unfortunately the cameras weren't with us as this massive creature dove into the deep. On a catamaran, we rolled and rocked our way along the blue, giving us views of the Crusoe Residences – seven villas accessible only by personal motorized boat. Apparently, some people prefer absolute privacy on their honeymoons. And then you get the Russian gazillionaires who rack up $200,000 bar tabs in the 1400 square foot Private Reserve, which consists of five separate buildings, all over water, a private island unto itself. Apparently, some guy once arrived with ten girls for a week-long stay. Now that's a honeymoon!

This close to the equator, the heat and humidity are overpowering, and although we're here in rainy season, we are denied even brief respites of showers. But since I am barefoot and in shorts pretty much every waking moment, I can always just dive into the sea, which I do repeatedly throughout the day. In the evening, we have the opportunity to join some of the staff in the staff quarters, and discover life beyond the white wall where some 250 people live to serve. It's a village unto itself, seldom seen by the clients, with its own shops, a bar and a school. There are folks from England and

Austria and India and Sri Lanka and Sweden and Scotland, and they're living on the other side of paradise, gaining an income while guests across the wall shed it. Over heavily discounted drinks, there's no doubt that the TV crew feel more at home here. We're all working in paradise, after all. What happens when you live in paradise? Paradise becomes meaningless. The Theory of Relativity kicks in. It always does.

They set the clock forward at the Soneva Gili, a chance for guests to enjoy extra daylight, another opportunity to literally leave the world behind. Four nights pass quickly, the days busy with getting the images that will leave our viewers salivating. We overstuff ourselves with fresh fruit juices, outstanding breakfasts, dream salads, themed buffets – a quality of food that will continue to nourish the mind long after it has fed the body. I give a couple more Skype tours, and my dad reckons I'll never be able to go back to normal living. I don't have much of a choice. We bid farewell to our dream villas, the long jetties, the ever-smiling waiters, the white numbered bikes, the chilled cellar, the healthy organic farm, the dive shop, the pontoons, the pup reef sharks, the playful hermit crabs, the lone coconut tree in the lagoon, the water hammock, the table tennis hut, the catamaran, the tennis court, the cocktails, the stingray that feeds below villa number 41, the water, the stars and the photos on the college dorm wall of my imagination. Yes, it is better to have tasted paradise, because that's what you hold onto when you find yourself in a dark, musky el-cheapo hotel, a grating ceiling fan blowing reality straight back into your face.

Male' is small, busy and overcrowded to the point of rotating residences. 100,000 people, half of all Maldivians, live on this small island. Narrow spaghetti streets are crammed with shops selling mobile phones and knock-off Ray-Bans. Without the sea to dive into, the heat burns a cavity in my chest, the black exhaust from scooters browning with the spit of the Bangladeshi labourers drilling outside my broken window. We are told to carry our passports at all times; a man accosts us minutes off the island shuttle and pleads with us to tell the world about the political corruption in the country. Our overpriced hotel reeks of mothballs, the leaky shower sits above the toilet, the pillows are hard and lumpy. At least my room doesn't have the smell of a decomposing corpse, although Paul, our sound guy, was not as lucky. Chris gets a fever, Sean loses his appetite. Fortune graces us with Canadians Leta and Gerard, who live in Male', where Gerard is a floatplane pilot. They treat us to a night of domestic normalcy (superb Thai takeout and some of their limited monthly liquor supply), holding back the weight of reality that might have crushed our spirits entirely. We've been put back in our place, taken back to our station. Yet I can always close my eyes and see myself biking slowly along the illuminated narrow wooden jetty towards my villa. The mercurial turquoise sea laps against the pylons; a cloud streaks across the sky beneath small lamps of stars.

Then I open my eyes, call up the schedule for next week's assignment in Sri Lanka, and realize the honeymoon is far from over. My relationship with the road, while no longer quite new, is determined to maintain its period of unusual harmony.

Abandon shoes all ye who enter here

BEHIND THE SCENES IN THE MALDIVES

More so than with most other episodes, you really do get to peek inside my head here, and hopefully you'll understand how a dream assignment and a dream job can kind of backfire if you let it. After all, what's the point of being in the world's most romantic destination, where everything is designed "for two", while being alone?   Well, not quite alone; I was sharing my exquisite villa at the Soneva Gili with Michael, my director, but let me assure you, two grown hetero men were not the intended occupants of such an ocean palace.

Here is a glimpse into the kind of destination you usually can only read about in celebrity magazines. The manager of the hotel, a wonderful fellow South African named Kurt Berman, made us feel right at home, and his terrific staff realized that, like them, we were also workers in paradise. In fact, we ended up sneaking away to the staff quarters – a sort of mini-village – to join them for drinks at the more affordable bar. The hotel back in Male', with its cranky ceiling fan and dusty yellow cracked windows, was more along our budget.

For a couple of days it was *Lifestyles of the Rich and Famous*, but the loneliness was definitely not fake. I had a girlfriend at the time, and I was genuinely reflecting on whether I'd trade this experience to be with her, and what the cost is, emotionally, of always being away. Well, most travel writers will tell you it's nigh on impossible to hold down a relationship unless you can incorporate your partner as a companion. My own relationship didn't last much longer after the episode was filmed, so it's painful for me to watch as I literally tried to salvage it on camera. Well, you wanted the truth behind the byline, and you got it.

In contrast to Julia's experience, I found Male' to be the most boring and repressive capital city I've ever been to. There isn't even a cinema! No nightlife at all; no fun. It's overcrowded, overpriced, and not worth more than a day on a visitor's agenda. Julia has a different opinion. We're two very different travel writers, and that's why whatever you read, you should always be aware that it's just one writer's experience, and that experience is subjective, personal, and could completely differ from your own.

We touch on the traveller/tourist difference, and it's important for me to stress that however you choose to travel, make sure it's the right way for you. Nothing irks me more than travel gurus who'll dismiss your experience because you failed to travel in their particular footsteps. If you want the comfort and ease of a package tour, go for it! If you want to rough it, camp on the side of highways and travel without any money, go for it! There is no right or wrong way, and the only person you should be trying to impress is yourself.

The Soneva Gili really is the ultimate honeymoon destination for people who can burn thousands of dollars per night on such an experience. Personally, I don't think I could enjoy myself knowing that I could use that money to travel for months in a developing country, but, as I mention above, we do whatever floats our own particular boats.

Hanging out at the Soneva Gili

SRI LANKA
A NICE CUP OF SERENDIPITY

Note: We filmed shortly before the defeat of the Tamil Tigers and the end of Sri Lanka's long-running civil war.

Serendipity. Defined as: the faculty or phenomenon of finding valuable or agreeable things not sought for. Such as: getting nailed by a car and turning it into a career as a jet-setting travel writer. Or: meeting a Dane in China and being advised to visit a magical little country called Sri Lanka. Further: Having the opportunity to act on such advice and visit this little-known country a few months later. And: bumping into one of the handful of foreigners at a 100,000 strong religious festival who just happen to know of an insane Gonzo ritual involving knives, holy men and self-mutilation.

Serendipi-tea?   Ceylon, renowned the world over for having the world's best tea, and the abovementioned Dane in China, who happens to be friends with someone whose family owns possibly the best (and certainly the most ethical) tea company in the world.

Serendipity: the warmest smile in a war zone, a bolt of lightning in a shoebox, a romantic kiss from a blood-sucking leech. Ancient Greeks called a lush island in the Indian Ocean Taprobane. The Portuguese had it; the Dutch took it from them until the British moved in and renamed it Ceylon. When ancient maritime Arab traders discovered this fertile teardrop to the south of India, they gave it a different name. They called it Serendib, and we still use their word, and their meaning, to this day.

Travel advisories are like overbearing mothers. They tell you where you can't go, what you can't do, which food to eat, which clothes to wear, and which kids you really should stay away from. The travel advisory for Sri Lanka screams, in red letters, "Avoid non-essential travel unless you have critical business or family reasons to do so." Yes, a civil war had torn the country apart for decades, and bombs had a habit of exploding in the capital of Colombo. Yes, Sri Lankan presidents had the life expectancy of an opened milk carton. But let's be honest: it's cool to sit with the bad kids at the back of the bus. It's cool to eat too many chocolates. It's cool to wear weird clothes, open the door marked authorized personnel only, and take calculated risks for the inevitable and thrilling rewards they bring.

Admittedly, it's not cool to get maimed or killed, but travel advisory notwithstanding, if you stay away from the well-known hot zones (which is easy enough to do), there's more of a chance you'll be attacked by an elephant than by a terrorist. Now Sri Lanka, an island of 20 million people, certainly has its hot zones, known to boil over. North, where Tamil rebels control an entire region. East, where they're prone to attack military bases. The capital, where they'll get the most column inches (and innocent bystander carnage) for an explosion. That's why I head south, to learn more about a religious pilgrimage, and into the central highlands, to learn more about the far more civilized life of tea. Along the way I meet some of the friendliest, most welcoming people on the planet. Sri Lanka is tropical, hot, and just a little wild, the way I like my adventures.

There was a time when soldiers looked like brave hard men with thousand-yard stares. Now, I see frightened young boys with twitchy fingers on the triggers of their machine guns. Security is tight in Colombo. Road blocks, bag searches, trepidation blasting through the air-con. As tourists, we are waved through – Very Important Persons – for although my stubble and rat-red eyes fit the profile of trouble, most foreigners are anything but. They're most likely tourists with a taste for adventure, or English tourists reliving the glory days when Ceylon fed the coffers of the Empire. Sri Lanka's colonial hangover is evident all around me, from billboards promoting its cricketing superstars to the dusky smell in my room at the grand Mount Lavinia Hotel – a former British governor general's palace. School kids wear uniforms and education is prized, and judging by the signs and adverts in English, many here feel that even though the ink has faded, the British influence tattooed across the country still looks good. Since Ceylon's independence in 1948 and subsequent re-naming to Sri Lanka in 1972, the country has been battered by politics, storms, political storms and disbelief that its bowlers are spinners and not throwers. (For non-cricket fans, you'll have to look that one up). With ancient kingdoms dating back before Christ, Sri Lanka is a holy land for Buddhists throughout Asia, with the ethnic majority of the population, the Sinhalese, still worshipping the words of Siddhartha. Tamil Hindus and Muslims make up the rest, and it's not my job to explain how it all fits together, only that for the most part it does – excluding the north, where it doesn't. Hot climates breed hot tempers, and like the Middle East, South Africa and Northern Ireland, Sri Lanka is still paying for the aftertaste of British colonialism. In the meantime, I watch big waves crash against the rocks outside the Hotel Lavinia, the massive fruit bats lurking in the sky, and look forward to the road trip south to the holy town of Kataragama.

Serendipity: Arriving somewhere just in time to catch an incredible festival. One day, I'll travel specifically for festivals, but as it stands, it's more a luck-of-the-draw kind of deal. The dealer hands me a pair of pocket aces when I arrive in Kataragama, a small town that nevertheless acts as an important pilgrimage site for Buddhists, Hindus, Muslims and the Vedda communities of the sub-continent. Although it's only 228km from Colombo, driving Sri Lanka's Rice Krispie roads is an all-day affair, blind corner after blind hill, and littered with cows. We wanted to visit the two-week-long Esala Perahera festival, where 100,000 Hindus gather at the full moon to devote themselves to the gods, make oaths, prove their faith and enjoy colourful evening parades. There's no thrill like walking into a mass of people in a country where you've been strongly advised to avoid large crowds.

I write this report a few days after a pretty wild music festival in the mountains outside Whistler in Canada (less than a week after events in Sri Lanka took place; yeah, I get around). 20,000 Canadians were camping for a couple of days; the place looked like a hurricane sat on a tornado and exploded into a plane crash of garbage. Surrounding the Hindu temple in Kataragama, I see thousands more people crammed up against each other, yet they were quiet, respectful, a gentle sea of human beings. Wave after wave of faces. The festivities begin at night under the bright LED - like light of the full moon. I count three foreigners. We acknowledge each other; a nod to say, "You're brave," and "Holy crap, isn't this just this most amazing scene ever?" Locals react to our crew with either curious smiles or complete ambivalence, as if we're ghosts. Even as I crush up against the men in the male line to get in, nobody thinks it strange that a solitary pink gringo is slammed against a wall of brown faces. Security is tight. A soldier gives me a full body search, alarmingly checking my scrotum for weapons of mass destruction. This may or may not be acceptable in a country where it's completely normal for men to hold hands (apparently Sinhalese men were renowned by the British for their softer feminine qualities). Inside, I surf the wave of the crowd, cross a bridge over a sacred river and emerge into the parade area, which is glowing with orange lights. A parade of fire dancers, performers and musicians, and elephants dressed like Mexican wrestlers, make their way around the crowd towards the holy Kataragama shrine, which legend dates to the second century BC. I squeeze into the masses amidst crescent smiles, curious eyes and mesmerized kids. Thousands of people sleep here during the festival; some are sleeping right now even as firecrackers and drums and horns blast into the warm, dusty night. The firecrackers are actually whips, snapped hard by a group of boys leading the procession. I've seen my share of fire dancers at raves and hippie parties, but nothing like the naturalness with flame I saw on display here. Then came the peacock costumes, more shrouded elephants, and the man with the hooks in his back.

Call it religious masochism; call it a true test of faith. One of the many aspects of this festival is a show of devotion in the form of physical challenges and self-inflicted mutilation. There is also some legendary fire walking, of the kind that burns to the bone. But as it turned out, we had missed a lot of the extraordinarily wacky stuff, and even in such an atmosphere I was pretty bummed to have been so close to the Gonzo, yet to have missed it by a day. That's when Serendipity struck, slicing her way across the night, jamming her edge into the proceedings. 100,000 people, and I find myself standing next to Dee, a native of Ohio, part owner of a local guesthouse. He came to Sri Lanka as a tsunami volunteer (more than 40,000 souls were lost in the devastation) and stayed after the country got its hooks in him. Dee asked me if I'd seen the Muslim ceremony, and in a massive Hindu festival in a largely Buddhist country, the appropriate response is: What Muslim ceremony?   So we head over to a Muslim shrine located within the temple compound and seat ourselves in the dust before several men in a semi-circle. They are skinny and bearded, and in front of them rests a large hookah and several ominous-looking weapons. Small fires burn; there's the smell of smudging sage.

The drumming starts, followed by the chanting.

"I saw this last night; it got a little gory," says Dee. A few feet away, the crew, with permission from the imam, set up cameras,. The beat gets more intense. Something crazy is going to happen, and then, it does.

Holy men and crazy men have always walked the same thin line. A skinny grey-bearded man with long stringy hair was about to jump right off it. Half naked, bones squeezed against his skin, he dances in circles barefoot, and then selects a wooden-handled knife. Picking up a heavy stone, he places the knife above his skull, and to my slack-jawed horror proceeds to bang it in. Whoa. After dancing around some more, he picks up another knife, and once more jams it into his cranium. A thin trickle of blood runs down his face, but he is alive, swept up in a trance that clearly requires no use of the brain. Another knife, this time used to slice his tongue. I see Paul, our sound guy, his eyes and mouth forming O-rings of shock. I, too, can't believe what I am seeing, and I can't believe we're actually capturing this on film. Bloodied, the holy man begins wildly slashing his chest, the drums and tambourines reaching fever pitch. Finally, the imam walks over to the entranced holy creature, who is now shaking on his knees, and attempts to pull out the two knife horns on his head. They are stuck firmly in place, giving no budge. So another man comes to help, and together, they pull the blades out the holy man's skull like Arthur pulling Excalibur out a rock. The imam sprinkles some ash onto the wounds, pressing his hand down. There is no blood. The holy man is dazed but takes his place in the semi-circle, and the next guy gets up. For the next hour, I watch men pierce themselves with thin spikes: through their necks; through their arms. I see a man jam a thin blade into his forehead, a do-it-yourself lobotomy. I see two men hooked back-to-back with spears through their arms. Nothing is sterilized, and all the while there is very little blood. The imam points in my direction.

"They know me and want me to join," says Dee, standing up. For a brief moment, I ponder the idea of joining him in the ritual, just as I ponder a life with hepatitis, and the fact that neither of us are anywhere near being in a state of trance. Still, Dee is making the effort to "fit in with the community," and the imam takes the spear and pierces the centre of his tongue. He pulls the spear out, dabs on some ash, and Dee sits down. He's putting on a brave face. It hurt, and will hurt for some days to come. I have done many silly things in the name of my adventures, my friends, but self-mutilation in a mystical Islamic ritual will have to wait.

For all the masses, the festival quietly dissipates, the throngs flowing into the adjacent night market. It's been a big day, so our guide, the venerable Mr. Ashraf, calls the bus, and we return to the hotel. Normally, it would be slammed with mostly Indian tourists, but tonight, as we eat a late dinner in the restaurant, it is quiet. The "troubles" are keeping people away. The week before, a bus was fired upon on the road outside Kataragama and three people were killed. Politics smashes into religion, the war barrel flips, and everyone gets hurt. Michael Franti sings, "We can bomb the world into pieces, but we can't bomb it into peace." I remember visiting Dubrovnik and being shocked that the Serbs had bombed this historic city, considering it had no strategic value. Is it in anybody's interest to target tourists, ambassadors of the world, the juice of foreign currency? I have my opinions, but whether the Tamil Tigers ever achieve their independent homeland of Eelam through the use of violence, and whether the Sri Lankan government ever stops them through the constant "disappearances" of troublemakers, is beyond my limited scope. But it is in neither party's interest to go after travellers, those brave enough to discard the warnings and visit a beautiful country with open hearts and minds. I'm not booking a ticket to the Sudan just yet, but nothing makes you appreciate peace like driving through a war zone.

The road outside Kataragama is normally lined with thick jungle. We pass a tense military checkpoint just outside of town, and suddenly, the jungle vanishes. In just a few days, the army has bulldozed trees for 50m on either side of the road to prevent another attack. It's an intimidating show of strength, the scorched earth littered with upturned trees and hastily assembled patrol bases. For a half hour, we drive in this Mad Max hellscape, the green placidity of the countryside vanquished by fear and violence. The road is narrow and serrated, and there's a collective sigh of relief when we reach a village and the danger has passed. "It's all good from here," says Mr. Ashraf, and it is.

As the van makes its way to towards the mountains of the central highlands, we pass milky waterfalls, muddy sapphire mines, manic monkeys, and elephants pressed against the fence of a national park, eyeing bananas held by those passing by. Kids in school uniforms wave and smile, and grinning old men bathe themselves in village streams. A flat tire, but our driver and our attendant (buses in Sri Lanka always have a driver and an attendant) make short work of it. Mr. Ashraf tells me about one Major Thomas Rogers, the infamous elephant killer. Charged with the task of ridding the island of its native elephant, the Major killed over 1500 glorious beasts in just four years, until one day, after having been warned that he had killed a sacred elephant near the shrine at Kataragama, he was struck dead by lightning. In a country where millions worship a god with the head of an elephant, justice was served. Legend has it that lightning also struck the grave of the Major, who is no doubt currently being trampled by 1500 elephants in hell.

We pass the town of Nuwara Eliya, where old colonial English houses line a dilapidated racetrack. Small villages are jammed with people on bikes, buses, foot. I get the chance to play some cricket with local kids, all of whom are familiar with South African cricketing heroes. I run up to bowl a fast delivery and get clobbered for a six. For those of you who don't know cricket, you'll have to look that up, too.

Nine hours later I'm doing a phone interview with CBC Radio in Canada, a national segment appropriately called *Far-Flung Canadians.*

"So, last night I was at a festival where I watched a bunch of holy men stab themselves in the head. After driving through what could technically be called a war zone, I zigzagged along a steep mountain pass until our van had a minor accident with a bus, causing a massive public commotion, which almost led to a riot. While we waited for things to be sorted out at the local police station, we got hit with a torrential downpour, and screamed along crazy narrow roads to get here just in time to make the interview. It's pretty much been the best day ever."

"Em, sorry, Robin. We're running a half hour late. Can we call you back?"

They did, at which stage I had consumed two stiff gin and tonics to relax my nerves, and peeled off a leech that had fastened itself to my little toe, sucking the nerve-shot blood right out of me. Common on the side of the road, leeches bite with an anticoagulant so the blood will run freely. I must have picked up Robin Leech while I was making a pee pit stop. Lifestyles of the Rich and Creepy.

Colonial tea farmers lived in bungalows, and we were guests in one such colonial bungalow called Tienstin, part of the fabulous Tea Trails bungalows built for tea estate managers in the 1800's. You say potato, I say potatoe, you say bungalow, I say glorious country mansion. Recalling an opulence of another time, the large one-storied bungalows come complete with butlers, four poster beds, massive bedrooms and baths, manicured gardens, a sensational chef, and immaculate round-the-clock service. We arrived late at night and I collapsed in the bed of my dreams (seriously, one day I will own a four-poster bed like this), eager to wake up and find out everything there is to know about tea. For we had arrived in the Ceylon Highlands, famous the world over for the quality of tea. And who doesn't enjoy a good cuppa?

Of all the places I've travelled in the world, of all the varied landscapes I've had the privilege to gaze upon, the emerald carpet of tea trees that covers the hills of Sri Lanka's central highlands is easily amongst the world's most striking. Tea plants are plucked (not picked) like Bonsai, manicured to a size and shape that ensures optimum growing and plucking conditions. Left alone, they would grow to 25 feet, and you'd need giants to pick the desired "two leaves and bud." Although Ceylon tea is known the world over, it is not native to the island. The British first cleared the jungles for coffee plantations, which yielded positive results until a crop blight put an end to coffee on the island. Faced with ruin, farmers experimented with other crops and were delighted when tea took to the highlands like syrup to a waffle. Some of these original mid-nineteenth-century plants are still being picked, lining the hills, shaded by a lone tree.

Like everything we know nothing about, the production of tea is an exact science incorporating wacky machines, time-brewed techniques, and a multiplex of grades and quality controls. My guide into this world is Andrew Taylor, an ancestor of the Ceylon's first-ever tea planter. Call him a tea sommelier, call him Mr. Tea, because once you meet him you'll never be able to drink a cup in quite the same way again.

We start in the fields, where waves of tea plants break against the hills, shaded by solitary trees needed for growth. Each sector is plucked once every seven days for a period of four years before it is allowed to recover. Short, skinny local women are the front-line tea pluckers, selecting the "two leaves and a bud" with lightning speed and depositing them in heavy wicker baskets strapped around their heads. The tea pluckers will pick around 16kg a day, receiving wages according to the weight of their tea. Watching them bent over in the plantations, dressed in colourful saris, chattering away as their hands pluck and refresh the plant, is to witness a scene that has changed little in 150 years. Andrew enthusiastically explains the hows and whys, the origin of teas like Orange Pekoe (pekoe is a Chinese word meaning "newborn shoot with hair still on," and orange refers to Dutch nobility), how 20 tonnes of leaves make 5 tonnes of tea, how soils, climate and altitude impact taste and quality. I pluck this wealth of information for an article brewing in my head. I also try my hand at plucking, and to the smiles of the ladies realize the basket is heavy and my pluck rate, non-existent. Still, next time you have a cup of tea, there's a remote possibility I was there at the beginning.

Back at the factory, Andrew takes me through the processes of withering, rolling, fermentation and drying as the leaves get classified and graded, and slowly but surely are ground down into the drink we know and love. He walks me through tea tasting, taken as seriously as any wine tasting I've been to, where I ruin the genteel nature of the event by spitting out the tea and missing the pontoon. Did you know that tea-seeped water is known as liquor? I learn how tea was discovered by the Chinese thousands of years ago when an emperor drank boiled water enriched by a wayward wind-blown tea leaf. I learn about its health benefits, from preventing hardening of the arteries to preventing various forms of cancer, and learn how to make the perfect cup (water just to a boil, one spoon of tea per person, and one for the pot). Back at Tea Trails, I enjoy the finest tea in the world in possibly the finest setting in which to drink it, and ponder another lesson learned.

From tea plantation to tea factory, the tea is packed in 50kg bags and sent to brokers who bargain over price and quantity. It is next sent to multinational marketers, who typically blend dozens of different teas of varying quality to get a tea bag that tastes OK for the lowest possible price. Then you get Dilmah, a family-owned, family-run Sri Lankan company that prides itself on producing pure, single-origin tea. Since its founding by Merrill J. Fernando, Dilmah's vision has always been to create a company that gives something back to the communities in which it operates. It supports an incredible 1500 community projects, from childcare and prisoner rehabilitation to programs for the aged, abused women and education – it's overwhelming and completely inspiring. I'm typically skeptical about this sort of thing: companies that suddenly market green to take advantage of the prevailing consumer climate. But Dilmah have been giving back since its inception, and maybe it's karma, but the fact that it now exports tea to over 80 countries means its success is being spread around through its MJF Charitable Foundation. I visited one such empowerment project, where women from an impoverished village had been taught how to make pottery and were being paid by Dilmah to make various items for their marketing. Everyone wins.

I have a moment to relax on the balcony of the bungalow before the long drive back to Colombo. A cup of tea has been brewed, and for the first time in my life I'm drinking it without sugar, as advised by Andrew (it negates all the health benefits). I wonder what songs Paul Simon played when he stayed in this same bungalow with his family, and kind of hear his guitar playing in my head. A cloud drapes over the hills, a soft wind blows, and distant cries of kids playing cricket sounds can be heard in the distance. In a country that people are afraid to visit because of a tragic civil war, it is a scene of peaceful serenity. Finding something valuable not originally sought after? Serendipity, indeed.

BEHIND THE SCENES IN THE SRI LANKA

So I'm scheduled to do a live radio interview with the CBC in Canada, and we have about a 150km drive to get from Kataragama to the central highlands, and eight hours in which to do it. No problem, right?

Like the rest of the Asian sub-continent, it helps to never be in a rush. Ever. I was once on the train back from the Taj Mahal with two Israeli backpackers who had budgeted a few hours to get back to Delhi and make their plane home. Bad decision. I was thinking about this as we wound our way on potholed roads, topping off around 30 km/hr, stopping off to get the shots we needed. We were actually doing OK until we came to a bridge where there was only space for one moving object, but the driver of the oncoming bus had decided there could be room for two. He crunched into our bus, which damn near caused a riot as an entire village came to see the fuss, and every single one of them had an opinion on how to resolve the situation, none of which involved moving the buses off the bridge. Our driver, who had right of way, needed to clear this up for insurance purposes. Otherwise, his family might end up on the street. Meanwhile, there's a crowd of young men steaming up the window staring at Julia. Then there's a torrential downpour, and a little bit of pushing and shoving, but we finally make our way to a police station. Missing a live national radio broadcast is not something you want to do too often, but we managed to scream around hairpin bends into the central highlands, almost making it on time. Eventually, I had to use a cell phone to call the CBC and apologize, only to find out a: they're running late, and b: the interview is a taping, and not live at all. It was only once I had a gin and tonic in my hand at the Tea Trails country house that I noticed I had also picked up a hungry swollen leech, which was draining the blood out of my foot. By the time I did the interview, I was spinning from the stiff drinks, the smell of tea, the pace of the day, and the undeniable fact that I loved this country.

Sri Lanka is a beautiful, friendly nation desperately in need of some good PR. A long civil war has damaged its reputation and tourist infrastructure, which is so sad because everybody is so welcoming. There were just a handful of tourists at the Kataragama Festival, a spectacular event, and we were fortunate to be invited to the wild ceremony where men pierced their skulls with knives. I'd do just about anything for this show, but picking up hepatitis isn't one of them. We literally couldn't believe what we were seeing, and hopefully you'll notice that we're as shocked as you are. I love this photo with our sound guy Paul's mount forming a perfect O. As in: Oh. My. Gawwwd.

It was hard to capture just how tranquil the central highlands were, the patterns of bonsai tea trees weaving across the landscape. I wish we could have stayed longer, but soon, we were off to Colombo – heavily patrolled; a constant threat in the air. Sometimes we have an internal battle about whether we're a travel show or a news show, the same way we battle about whether we should be filing stories in the travel section or the world news section of a newspaper. Sri Lanka constantly skirted that line, but I personally focused on travel, because here's a country that really needs to make its way out of news and into leisure. And we didn't even get the chance to visit the amazing beaches in the south. The moral of the story: don't let the headlines fool you.

A wonderful Hindu temple, located next to a Mosque in Colombo

The wild Muslim ritual we stumbled across at the Kataragama festival. Paul's expression on the right says it all

A dad holds up his kid at the Kataragama so he can see the action

Tea pluckers at work in the fields of the Central Highlands

Buddha statue outside a temple in Colombo

ROMANIA

HASH 'N' TRANSYLVANIA

I'm as guilty as the next Vlad. When it came to Romania, I thought mountains and vampires, petite gymnasts and bloodthirsty dictators. I expected women with razor-sharp cheekbones and rock-bottom prices. Well, at least I was right with the last two. Romania is the first stop on Season Two's European leg, and after a long flight to Amsterdam, we found ourselves with eight hours to kill. Due to the eruption of a volcano in Alaska, the cross-continental flight flew us as south as possible, extending the journey aboard the old KLM jet, making King Fu Panda on the old TV sets up front an unusual highlight amidst the tedium.

At Schiphol Airport, a bottle of water will set you back five bucks, so we catch a train into Amsterdam to kill the time, drink some coffee, and tap Morse code on the glass to the daylight whores in the Red Light District. Back to Schiphol, back on the plane, welcome to Bucharest at midnight, where I'm feverishly having visions of small children with long, skinny fingers. Julia wanted to do a story about the Roma – or Gypsies, if you're less PC – but was met with indifference from local Roma organizations, and stern advice from locals about the reality of wandering into a tent city. For the record, Roma are not from Romania. In fact, a local politician dug himself a pile of donkey shit by suggesting that Roma should be spelled "Rroma" to avoid confusion. Regardless, Romania takes its name from the Romans, who occupied the country for a brief century or so but left their mark in the form of the name and language, the only Latin-based tongue in the region. Romanians are also well known to be blessed with a passionate, fiery Latin spirit, too.

After our adventures in Lithuania and Latvia last year, we have a saying on the road: Welcome to Europe. Meaning:
- A land where men wear white pants and pink shirts.
- A land where supermodels work in bakeries and coffee shops.
- A land where you can drink in public.
- A land of cobblestone, outdoor cafes and flashy wealth among abject poverty.

Welcome to Europe. We use it as a catch phrase for anyone who makes a comment pointing out the obvious, like: That church is really old and impressive, or, Bucharest has over 100,000 stray dogs, and one is ripping its teeth through my thigh muscle right now!

Bucharest is big and cosmopolitan, like any capital city, although it does have a pretty turbulent recent history. The country was practically pillaged during decades of the corrupt communist crackpot Ceauşescu, until it shook him off in a public rage that resulted in him and his loony wife Elena being tried, sentenced and executed within a few days of fleeing for their lives from Bucharest's fed-up population. A thousand people lost their lives in the turmoil of the revolution, as the army at first tried to keep the people back before turning their rifles around and pointing it at their megalomaniac boss. I'm standing at a monument where the army opened fire on protestors, killing hundreds. Now I'm standing by the old Communist Party headquarters, where 100,000 people gathered to watch Ceauşescu flee by helicopter. This was in 1989, and I remember reading about the revolution when it happened, although it would be nearly twenty years before I would come to understand it.

Today, since the fall of communism, Romania's economy has recovered and it has joined the European Union, although it has yet to adopt the euro. Ceauşescu's House of the People, the second-largest public service building in the world after the Pentagon, sits at the top of a wide boulevard like a giant ivory elephant. It houses parliament, an art gallery, functions and banquets, and the remaining 1000 or so rooms sit dormant, an echo of greed and power run amok. To build it, Ceauşescu practically demolished the historical Old Town, displacing thousands and burning what little remained of Bucharest's past after it was bombed by the Allies in World War II. Like their Latin counterparts, the Italians, the Romanians initially sided with the Nazis in the war, before the highly regarded King Michael switched sides and they joined the Allies. They were rewarded by having the Communists move in, purging educated intellectuals and liberals, and introducing decades of a corrupt one-party fear-based rule. But this is water under the bridge, or, more accurately, the water that flows in the fountains of central Bucharest, which sit beneath a sweltering mid-30's summer sun and are encircled by crazy traffic.

A while ago, my friend Katherine told me about this "drinking group with a running problem" called the Hash House Harriers. Apparently people meet and have a human "fox hunt" involving lots of running, beer chugging, dirty name-calling and outrageous fun. Kat is a diving instructor, and I thought maybe she had the bends. Then I looked online and found that the Hash House Harriers exist in 178 countries, with over 8000 clubs organizing weekly Hash runs, which are open to all and sundry. Born out of, and largely followed by, the expat community, the first Hash took place in 1938 in Malaysia, and has since grown into the worldwide phenomenon it is today. There are even Hashers, and their female equivalents, the Harriets, running wild in Antarctica. A story that would let me see the city, run about, drink plenty of beer, sing dirty limericks and meet people who are doing the same is right up my alley, so I arranged to join the Bucharest Hash House Harriers for a late afternoon run, with the TV crew in tow. The spirit of Hashing is one part college dorm, one part teenage prank, one part marathon training and one part adults behaving badly. Needless to say, I ran, I drank, I was initiated with beer and flour, I sang, I drank some more, and hung out with an assortment of characters fielding Hash names like Tampon Jelly, Midnight Itch, Holefinger, Moby Dick, Gutentight and Canny Fanny. The Religious Advisor, Crash Test Dummy, was instrumental in setting it all up, gathering the group of Scots, Americans, English, Swiss, German, Australian, and even a Romanian for our viewing pleasure. An upcoming article will explain more in further detail; suffice it to say that I was given my own Hash name, which will be with me for life as a punishment for wayward research. With its own vocabulary and titles for members of the mis-management, I read about the Grandmaster and the Cash Hash, the Front Running Bastard (FRB) and the poor sucker who is DFL (Dead Fucking Last). I also incorrectly read about someone known as the Big Wanker, so when I asked who the Big Wanker was, well, naturally, that would be me. Soaked in beer and flour, they took me to a local pub, and on my first night in Bucharest, jetlagged to a fate worse than hell, I ended up drinking beer from my sweaty shoe and scrubbing solidified flour from my ears.

I can't wait to get home and join the Vancouver Hash House Harriers, because seriously, who knew grownups could have so much fun?

Happy to report that razor sharp cheekbones are the order of the day, and Romania's plethora of beautiful women also seems content to walk about in thin dresses with no bras. Pre-euro prices offer bargains wherever you look. We get dropped off at the train station for an overnight journey north to the regional Transylvanian capital of Cluj-Napoca. For some reason, I felt compelled to watch *Lost Boys 2* on my laptop, a decision I regretted the second I saw the washed-up flabby shell of Corey Feldman battling hip surfer dude vampires. The train was pleasant enough, always preferable to a bus, and we arrived at four a.m. just in time to be whisked off into the Transylvanian countryside. It's important here that we dispel some myths.

1. Dracula is a fictional character created by an Irish novelist who based the castle on a Scottish fortress and who never set foot in Romania.

2. Vlad the Impaler (not to be confused with Vlad the Impala, a buck in the African bush) was a Transylvanian hero and king who fought back the Turks as they attempted to conquer the region. That he enjoyed spiking his prisoners on a sharpened pole that entered their anus and missed all their vital organs while they died a painful miserable death over two days was apparently no more unusual than any other leader's methods at the time. From which we can deduce it's a good thing to live in the age we do.

3. Vampires do NOT exist, although there is a blood disorder that causes a tiny percent of the population to have receding gums, pale skin and a thirst for iron, easily found in the consumption of blood. Local folklore did once blame vampires for this and that, and they also appear in Hindu and Buddhist culture, too. Bram Stoker invented the bits about garlic, mirrors, inviting them into your home, bats, wolves, necks, and the children of the night.

4. Dracula's Castle is a tourist attraction designed to separate mainly-American tour bus passengers from their hard-earned dollars. Dracula never lived there because Dracula never existed, although Vlad the Impaler did stay there once. He stayed in a lot of places – no doubt wherever the view of Turks spazzing in agony on spikes was exceptional.

5. There are no transsexuals, from transsexual, Transyl-vani-ya…

What is not a myth is that the Kazakhstan portion of the hit comedy *Borat* was filmed in rural Romania, and this is where I was headed. To get away from all this vampire myth bullshit, I searched online and found Carpathian Tours, which promised authentic cultural encounters with people in the region, steeped in folk music and dance. Ethnic Hungarians form the largest minority group in Romania, and most of them are located in the region of Transylvania. Fertile with forests, farmland and mountains, Transylvania has been used as a pawn on a geo-political chessboard for millennia, being annexed here, gaining independence there, attacked and conquered everywhere. Today it is part of Romania, awash in small villages that continue to exist as they have for centuries. There are also thousands of horny students who descend on the colleges in the capital of Cluj-Napoca, the third-largest city in the country.

On her first visit, an Australian musician named Sally fell in love with the music of the region, and subsequently spent the next fifteen years doing whatever she could to return and learn from the masters. As she formed friendly relationships with local villagers and musicians, she found that many Australians were fascinated with the region and culture. Carefully trying to avoid any form of exploitation of either party, she started Carpathian Tours a few years back, taking small groups into the countryside, where they stay in village homestays, encountering real people and real culture. Her packages are basic (most villages don't have plumbing), sincere, fascinating and probably the best European excursion I've ever been on. The potential for cultural faux pas is rife in this part of the world. Push your plate of food away, or offer to help with the dishes, and you'll be indicating disdain, and insulting your hosts. Working largely with ethnic Hungarian musicians and their families, Sally has smoothed over the cultural differences, and has opened the door to another world few travellers get to experience in this day and age.

We pulled into the town of Ture, dumped our bags into a 250-year-old stone house and drank some strong coffee brewed by an old lady in traditional dress, hobbling on a crutch. It would be unthinkably rude to help, but we all offer anyway. Cowbells sound in the distance, so we head off to watch the cows come home, before a failed effort to try to milk a water buffalo. It is all very traditional for the times we live in The sun breaks behind the hills as another old lady, this one in her mid-80's, her fingers like fat pork sausages, strains fresh warm milk through a cloth for us to taste. Roosters crow, dogs bark, a horse-and-buggy crunches along the dirt road. Not much has changed in centuries, although houses do have electricity and satellite TV. Julia and I help two seasoned old men shovel hay, total city slickers that we are. Later, I see the same old guy busting moves in the village hall to the sounds of a local band jamming away on violins, double bass and accordion. I am struck by the sincere warmth of the villagers, the authenticity of the experience, the enthusiasm of our tour guide Sally, and the fact that the best travel always happens when you burst the tourist bubble and connect with real people in real life.

A few days later, I'm back in Cluj-Napoca, a name I just love repeating for the way it sounds in the mouth. Julia and the crew take off to shoot her story about a haunted forest, and I discover that some asshole has hacked my website and inserted some malicious code on every page. It's probably all automated, as these things are these days, but Google has flagged my site, and it takes me hours to re-upload everything, cursing away as I do so. If you haven't changed your passwords in a while, you might want to look into that.

My sleep pattern resembles that of a spider on acid, but it's Saturday night in a student town, so I rally my emotional troops, ask for some suggestions from the receptionist at the Retro Hostel, and head out into the night. People here only go out at midnight, and by eleven p.m. I've been walking around and still haven't found what I'm looking for. Naturally, the last spot on my list shows immediate promise. La Gazette has the smoky air of a student bar (although in Romania, where everyone and their infant seems to be smoking, that's not saying much): lacquered newspapers cover the wall, reggae dub pounds from speakers and a whole bunch of cargo pants/sneaker-wearing students are milling about. Although it's 180 degrees from the thump thump techno bars I visited earlier in the night, the girls here are as beautiful as their heavily-made-up stiletto'd counterparts. I instantly befriend Andy, one of the loudest, most brusque and thoroughly entertaining Americans I've ever met. Born in Cluj, he moved to Chicago with his folks, and he's returned to study medicine because it's cheap here ($1500 a year!), not to mention a good life if you happen to be a foreigner fluent in Romanian. "Sometimes, you know, I don't want them to know I can speak Romanian," he tells me. "The girls here, they love foreigners." Maybe; in any case, I meet a whack of people, drink some ridiculously cheap booze, dance a little bit, play electronic darts and stare at impossibly good-looking girls. Everyone seems to speak good English, and apparently I'm the first South African to visit these parts. I happily stroll home at three a.m.; the rest of the guys roll in at five a.m., having ended up at Diesel, the city's most expensive (and, therefore, pretentious) club. We all had fun; we all enjoyed walking the fourteenth-century streets of Cluj-Napoca, eating great pizza and the largest chicken schnitzel you can imagine. There are just a smattering of tourists. It is quiet, it is peaceful and it is postcard Europe.

Much of the time, travel comes down to where the hell you happen to end up, and who the hell you happen to meet when you get there. The Hashers opened my eyes to a cultural phenomenon I have a feeling I'll continue to follow wherever I might find myself. Sally opened the door to rich traditional folklore and a rural life I've never encountered, and Andy, gloriously abrasive and unashamedly obnoxious, proudly showed me around his now-native Cluj-Napoca. As usual, I have barely scratched the surface, but Romania has proven to be so much more than vampires, dictators and gymnasts. Essentially, a country well worth sinking your teeth into.

The Hash House Harriers welcome Big Wanker

BEHIND THE SCENES IN ROMANIA

Like cockroaches, the Hash House Harriers hide in plain site. But lift up a rock and you'll probably find them everywhere. After doing my Hash story (and being forever branded the Big Wanker), I noticed HHH meets in Kiev, Vancouver, even Kingston, Jamaica. How I got my name is due to misfired research. I had read about Hash titles such as The Grandmaster, The Cash Hash and The Religious Advisor, and one of the names I came across was The Big Wanker. So when I asked who The Big Wanker was, and was answered with blank stares, I figured it might be a name specific to another club. Well, it turns out that I was reading something written by a hasher named Big Wanker, and since Hashers can share names, it made sense, after being floured and beered, that I would be christened Big Wanker. I would just like to point out that anyone who's ever met me can confirm I am not big at all.

Bucharest was steaming with heat, and the city was positively cranking in an economic boom. The meltdown that would burn the world financial markets was a few months away, and I wonder about the impact it has had on the boom in eastern European countries like Romania and Ukraine. Chances are, the people in the small village of Ture will keep on going like they always have. . The basis of my article, which ran in Associated Press, centred on Sally Corry, who runs a small Australian-based tour outfit called Carpathian Tours. Sally is a musician who fell in love with the music and culture of the ethnic Hungarian communities, and it's her hard work and effort that allows us, and her clients, to get an authentic glimpse into this world. There's so much more to Eastern Europe than old churches, squares and cobblestone. Although our stay was short, our hosts were gracious with their time and hospitality.

Outside of Ceausescu's House of the People in Bucharest, a
1100-room white elephant that was once the world's biggest building

A
farmer in the Transylvania village of Ture, where
life has changed little in centuries

Uncle Janos, in his 70's, teaches me how to dance with a twinkle in his eye. National Geographic online chose this as one of the top photos of the week.

Trying on the traditional threads of a Transylvanian bachelor for the Good Room

An ethnic Hungarian musician in Ture

The spires of Cluj Napoca

TURKEY

INTO THE OTHER HOLY LAND

Turkey will form a backdrop of biblical proportions, literally, to the 8th episode of *Word Travels'* second season. But let's begin in Bucharest with a taxi fiasco, commence our journey in Europe, head to the crossroads, and then over to the other side.

I'd read that the Gara De Nord in Bucharest is notorious for having the most sleazy, sketchy taxi drivers on the planet. We disembarked after a slow, cramped, ten-hour train ride from Transylvania, and I can confirm that everything I read is true. I won't go into details for fear my blood will boil over, let's just say the drivers took advantage of our confusion, and later, our wallets. Since this is a production expense and doesn't cost me anything personally, I don't know why it grates on my very being, but it does. Even with flights, meals and accommodation paid for, you can take the hostel out of the backpacker, but you can't take the backpacker out of the hostel. Meaning: Years of edge-of-the-budget travel has imprinted itself on my core. I still carry my own bags to my hotel room, because dealing with the awkwardness of tipping a porter, simply because I'm too lazy to carry a backpack, just isn't worth it.

An early morning pickup (fortunately through a driver service), and we're dropped off at the Bucharest airport, which has a small-town feel considering it's a major international terminal. We check in, with some slight confusion since our booking number isn't in the Turkish Airlines system. A three-euro cup of much-needed coffee later, we board; we fly. At the same time in Madrid, a passenger jet bursts into flames; 154 souls go to heaven. Strong onshore winds cause the landing in Istanbul to be one of the rockiest yet, like landing on the surface of the moon. Even frequent flyers sweat when metres from the ground the wings swing at a 45-degree angle.

Canadians have to pay an outrageous $60 visa fee on arrival, a full $40 more than people from any other country. I'm convinced an Ottawa diplomat hit on the Turkish ambassador's wife: there's just no explanation for the exorbitant fee. Production picks up the tab, of course, but again, it stokes the fire of my backpacker soul. It's worth noting that the fee is reciprocal, so Turks get the same treatment on arrival at Vancouver International. Bag retrieval is always a gamble. We've only had our luggage go astray once, in Colombia, on the first day of filming for the entire series. Since then, other than a missing boom pole, we've been fortunate, although my backpack has an annoying habit of *always* coming out last. This time there is a tear in the tripod bag, and the tripod's faceplate is severely damaged. A faceplate costs about $1000, so Sean is off to file a claim. He has Star Alliance Elite status, a fact he reminds us of constantly, but that doesn't get him to the front of the queue this time. Fortunately, he can still use the tripod, no doubt sparing our production assistant Chris a torrid first day in Istanbul.

With a crew of six people, I have come to appreciate the little man with a sign who greets us on arrival at every airport. Figuring out how to get into town is a painful task of modern travel, and lord knows I've done it more than anyone should ever have to, but on a tight schedule with a ton of gear, there's no time, energy or patience to deal with it. Hence the Bucharest train station fiasco, in which a $5 dollar cab ride ended up costing $50. Anyway, there's no man with a little sign waiting for us at Istanbul Atatürk Airport, and there should be. The only contact number we have is for a phone in the USA. We withdraw some local currency from the ATM, stress and moan our lament, when suddenly Ahmed appears, apologizing for being late; there was a bomb threat en route to the airport, and traffic is a mess. A good an excuse as any. Since we'd had to drop Georgia as our next destination, forgoing our plane tickets and hotel reservations because the Russians invaded, the threat of violence seems to follow us around like bad odour. As it no doubt does for just about everyone else. Yet the relief of having an air-conditioned van to shlepp us to our hotel in scorching Sultanahmet far outweighs anything as annoying as a bomb threat.

The last time I arrived in Istanbul I took the airport subway and met a friendly professor who showed me the way to my over-priced hostel by walking me through four steamy city blocks and the crowded bizarre in the upper 30C heat. This time, the van dropped us off at the far more civilized Hotel Arcadia, offering stellar views of the Hagia Sophia and the ever-spectacular Blue Mosque. There was much to reflect on, returning to Turkey after three years of non-stop adventure, during which my transformation from backpacker to travel writer has been complete. But first I'd have to finish up writing my articles about Romania, and upload my blog and photos, in a weekly ritual that cements the end of that particular journey. The discipline of writing and updating my website weekly has served me well since the very beginning of Modern Gonzo. It might be the very reason for my success. The sixth-century Hagia Sophia will have to wait, as it has done so across empires and invasions. First, I have work to do.

Around sunset, golden hour, the crew heads over to the spine that splits these two incredible ancient buildings. It is exactly as I remember it, although there appears to be busloads more tourists clutching guidebooks. We tend to visit some pretty unusual destinations with this show, so Istanbul in high season comes as something of a shock. People stare and take pictures of Julia and I as Sean knocks off writing and "establishing" shots, which will end up in fast-paced montage sequences. People see the big camera and reckon we must be famous. We have both gotten used to the staring. You have to, if you want to be on TV.

The golden setting sun is lighting up the Golden Arm, so we head back to the hotel rooftop terrace to film a time-lapse. A cold Efes beer is in order, but the hotel charges $6 for half a glass, while down on the street it is $2 for half a litre. Paul and I pop downstairs, buy some cold beers and bring them upstairs to the camera. The staff tell us this is forbidden, but we point to the camera and say we have to wait for it to finish. We get away with a lot this way. Sean's Golden Rule of Shooting: Get the shot, then ask for permission. Better to say sorry than to not get any shot at all.

Dining at an over-priced Sultanahmet patio restaurant, pencil shavings of nostalgia blow across my office space. It is liberating, in a sense, to see something familiar, yet be a changed person. Emotionally disorientating. I didn't think I would return to Istanbul so soon, if at all, but it looks the same as when I left it. It's been a long day with a country hop, so the exhausted crew heads back to the hotel. I pop into the Bauhaus, a hostel I stayed at before. I don't know what I was expecting on the rooftop bar, where I spent a couple of nights a few years and thousands of miles ago. It has been remodelled; a couple of young backpackers sit on pillows sucking on a *nargila,* listening to Jeff Buckley. I could join them, but I'm not a young backpacker anymore. Buckley hits his high notes, and I realize that I belong in a hotel, not here. Not now, while we're working. We have a mid-morning flight to Adiyaman, so there's no point in unpacking. A power shower paint-strips my skin; I notice my leather wristband (once my hat band) smells terrible so I soak it in a glass of shampoo, where I'll forget it the next morning. I'm sharing a room with Paul, which works great since we both don't snore – something that can't be said for other members of the crew. We see a promo for Nat Geo Adventure on TV. Turkey will see me on *Word Travels;* Turkey will see what my impressions of this visit will be. We flip the channel, watch some Olympics in Beijing and tune out.

At the domestic terminal, Sean's efforts to sneak everyone into the business class lounge are unsuccessful (sometimes it works, sometimes it doesn't), so I write up a story for MSN from the gate. I've got various deadlines looming, and more are added to the pile every week (I aim for three stories a week). Sometimes they just flow out; sometimes I have to hunt the words, laying traps, dangling carrots. Being online is essential for speedy research, but sometimes I just use the *Encyclopedia Britannica,* which I have loaded on my laptop. It doesn't mention anything about Mount Nemrut, my story/segment for this episode, which is an encouraging sign. The view from the spacious emergency exit row (again, sometimes we get it, sometimes we don't) shows stark, dry terrain melting in the sun. The pilot executes various turns and lands the small jet at speed, earning Sean's disapproval – you don't earn Elite status without doing a lot of flying, and Sean discusses flights the way a sommelier might discuss wine. The dry, hard heat is exquisite. The B-cam wants my reaction, and I rattle off a couple of lines – I feel like the roof of your mouth after you burn it with hot cheese. Or at least that's what I try to say. It comes out like: I feel like a… a… a cheese, hot cheese, on your mouth, inside, em… pizza. Like pizza." – demonstrating the challenge of being able to type the words, while not always being able to verbally express them. This happens to me quite a lot, and I'm often kicking myself when I see the final product. "Of all the things to say, Robin, you idiot…"

We're on a seven-night, seven-different-hotels streak. At twenty-one episodes in, this is a new record for us. Cluj-Napoca to Bucharest, to Istanbul, to Adiyaman, to Diyarbakir, to Mardin, to Sanliurfa. Even though I travel light, sometimes, when we arrive late and leave early, I don't even unpack my bag. Just brush my teeth, rinse in the shower, head on out. My story/segment is on Mount Nemrut, where ancient statues of the gods witness a spectacular sunrise until the sun crosses over a burial mound and a mirror image of the statues gazes upon the sunset. It's the kind of story where the photograph will sell it. Anyone seeing the golden light cast across the giant bust of Apollo is bound to say, "Where is that!?", and the same holds for the show. You'll see Robin bathed in light, energized by the history of this former temple. The breathtaking views of the surrounding desert... In the show, you'll see glimpses of my journey to get there, and hear me talk about my life as a travel writer and how it all began. It starts at midnight. I wake up early, a combination of nerves, energy and the tired residue of jetlag. Call time is two a.m., so I spend the next two hours finishing my MSN article, replying to email, doing some research and reading my book. The plan is for the crew to wake me up, as they have done so many times in previous episodes. This time I ambush them, stuffing my backpack and pillow under the sheet, hiding in the bathroom when they enter and jumping out just as they realize something is wrong. Sean is totally spooked, but, true professional that he is, he keeps on shooting. It still cracks me up to see the scene as an outtake in the episode's closing credits.

At 2:30 a.m., we take off for the two-hour drive to Nemrut. The energy that prevented me from sleeping vanishes now that I am awake. I daze and doze. I watch an awful movie on my laptop to keep me occupied as we drive into the dark early morning. We stop for tea, but I'm eager to move; there's still the hike up to the eastern terrace, where we'll need to grab our seats for the sunrise of a lifetime. We still need to film me getting out the car, walking along on the trail, with my thoughts, my expectations – the stuff of television that always takes longer than we think. I originally planned to hike the whole way, but 16km with a TV crew in plus 40C heat is a good enough reason to plan something else. It's only 500m from the car park to the terrace, and as I walk along the cracked stone path, the sky begins to brighten, announcing the arrival of a new day. Although we have left the busloads of cruise ship tourists behind, there are about fifty people already on the terrace, mostly Turks, wrapped in blankets to shield them from the cool mountain wind. Cameras are ready; all face east. Behind them are the gods built to honour King Antiochus I, ruler of the Commagene kingdom around 60 BC. Large 10m statues of the gods he worshipped, their stone heads decapitated but the rest mostly intact, face the sunrise. By placing his own statue with those of the gods, the king hoped to join their greatness, for the sun to rise below his feet. The statues are of an eagle, the Commagene messenger of the gods. Fortuna, the goddess of luck and fortune, still bearing her grapes and pomegranates, symbolizing fertility. We see the bust of Apollo, the God of light and reason, and the partly damaged face of Hercules, born to Zeus and a human mother. Of course, Zeus is here, too, the King of the Gods, as well as the lion Aslan, signifying greatness. Finally Antiochus himself, on the throne itself, an equal of the gods. The decapitated bodies sit against a tumult of broken stones, a fifty-metre-high pyramid painstakingly placed by human labour over the final resting place of the king. Behind them is a relief with ancient Greek inscriptions detailing the reason behind the statues: the final wishes of the King that people should have faith, worship the gods and enjoy their time atop the mountain. Mount Nemrut was rediscovered in 1881 by a German engineer, and the translation of the inscription was revealed some time later.

The sunrise lives up to its reputation, a perfect golden yolk cracked against the rim of mountains on the horizon. Wind muffles the fireworks-like oohs of the small crowd, who appear as transfixed by Sean's camera as the sunrise they've been waiting to see. I take dozens of photos of the busts in the blue pre-dawn light, but once the sun lights them up, I repeat every shot. Within a half hour the crowd has dispersed and we are the only people left on the terrace. Our guide for the week, the enthusiastic and energetic Sherif, tells us that the domestic tourism industry markets Nemrut's sunrise, not the statues. Westerners come for the history, Turks for the sunrise. Sean crosses a shaky chain fence to get a better shot, and a man appears with the usual "forbidden" tune. We sing our note from the Turkish authorities explaining our purpose, and the guard moves away, none too pleased that us foreigners can break the rules that no doubt anchor his life. It's amazing what we have to do sometimes to get the shots to make a place look incredible. We are shooting with very limited assistance from the Turkish Tourism Board, because they told us they were already supporting several TV productions this summer and had no more budget. They did give us a letter, though, which we've used several times already as over-keen officials pop out of nowhere ready to shut us down. Sherif disarms them and they fade away, somewhat annoyed. We're only trying to capture the best possible images we can.

By nine a.m., we are filming a time-lapse as the sun hits the statues on the western terrace, a duplicate of those on the eastern terrace. Here, the gods will watch the sun set beneath their feet. I scramble up some rocks, taking in the view around me. This is Mesopotamia, the land between two rivers: the mighty Euphrates and the Tigris. Geographically, it is an area that constitutes modern Iraq, southeastern Turkey, a salt-shake of Syria and a splash of Iran, too. This is the cradle of civilization, where biblical empires rose and modern humanity evolved. A spark of faith caught fire, and burned into the religions that shape much of our lives – Judaism, Islam, Christianity. Ancient ruins, caves, aqueducts, walls and bridges abound everywhere. No wonder Turkish tourists are down the mountain shortly after sunrise. Seeing 2000-year-old statues is not all that new for them. Considering the epic history here that gave rise to religion and modern civilization, stretching all the way back to 6000 BC, I expect the region to be lush and fertile, not dry and parched, baking in temperatures that crack 50C in the summer. The air feels like its blowing out of a hair dryer. Not for the first time, I wonder how people coped in the old days without air conditioning.

By ten a.m., we finish up and head back to the van, the cool mountain breeze at 2200m dissipating as we descend lower along the path. I've been up for ten hours already, but my attempts at sleep on the drive back to Adiyaman are futile. With the completion of the Atatürk Dam and Hydropower Plant, a vast project collectively known as the Southeastern Anatolia Project, the geography of the region has changed. Powered by the waters of the Tigris and Euphrates, cheap electricity and water for irrigation have been made widely available, and the heat notwithstanding, the region is on fire. Five years ago Adiyaman was a city of 80,000. Today it is closing on 200,000. Julia's *Lonely Planet*, although not the most recent version, does not even feature the city in the region. We pick her up and head over to a restaurant, where we feast on an eight-course meal that easily ranks amongst the most damn delicious I've ever had. Grilled chicken and lamb skewers, kofta, roasted eggplant, various traditional casseroles, fresh pita out the oven, various dips and sauces, and salads that taste like nothing found anywhere else. Turkish food, when done right, is in a class all its own. I gorge in an attempt to induce a food coma, for we've got a three-hour drive ahead of us before we reach Diyarbakir. Even with the air conditioning cranked and the back row to myself, I sweat, scrunched up, and suffer from no sleep. Finally we arrive in Turkey's hottest city. Diyarbakir has been conquered by the Hittites, the Assyrians, the Meds, the Persians, the Macedonians, the Seleukos, the Romans, the Byzantines, the Ilkhanide, the Akkoyunlu Seljuks and the Ottomans. It has a twelve-metre-high city wall built by the Romans that stretches 5.5km. I have been awake for twenty hours, encrusted with sweat, my eyes like drops of blood in the snow. I don't want to know about walls, or dinner for that matter, I just want to know about bed. By 10:30 p.m., I am asleep. We have an early eight a.m. departure to check out the ancient black basalt walls, and then head on to the next stop of Mardin.

By now, you're getting the picture. This isn't a holiday, although we do get some time off. This isn't a sightseeing trip, although we do see a lot of sites. This isn't work, because I do play a lot, and this isn't play, because I work pretty hard, too. In the end, all I can say is: This is Television.

A sand storm blows in from Syria when we pull into Sanliurfa. This is the final leg of our road trip: a town that oozes history. We head straight to the citadel, a complex of history where, from the roof a restaurant balcony, we can see a thirteenth-century mosque, a sixth-century church, a second-century ruin, a first-century castle wall and the cave where Abraham, founder of all three monotheistic religions, was supposedly born. So much history crammed into a natural amphitheatre. People in the street stop and ask: "Hello, where are you from?" – a typically Turkish greeting. Unlike touts in the west, they are not looking to lure me into a carpet shop. They just want to know where I am from. Sometimes I say Canada, and they always respond with an "Ooooh, Canyada!" Sometimes I say South Africa, which gets a puzzled, impressed response. Crowds circle around us when the camera gets a shot, and I'm not sure where they came from exactly, but suddenly we are escorted by three plainclothes policemen. They wave off abused street kids, who can be quite adamant in their curiosity, and help keep the bogeys (the word we use for people who wander into the shot) clear. Sherif and our ever-helpful driver Orhan get into the swing of things, too, two more vital members of the team.

Two days in one place is a luxury that allows me to explode my bag across the hotel floor (with Paul doing the same, it's one serious explosion). Punctuated by breaks for outstanding meals, we visit the sites – the Pool of Sacred Fish, the cave where Abraham was born, the beehive houses in the biblical town of Harran, located 40km away. The heat, dust and sweat cake everything, my sandals turning sepia, much like the dusty photos of Harran. A group of Israeli tourists arrive in Harran, and it seems like the serendipity I found in Sri Lanka continues to follow me. They form a great closing hook for my article, allowing me to bring all three major religions together, born out of the vision of the same prophet, born out of the same, damp cave.

We bid our farewells to Sherif and Orhan, kiss them on the cheek and catch the flight back to Istanbul. The sand storm shut down the airport the day before, but cleared up enough for us to take off. Back in Istanbul, the differences are immediately clear between the Turkey of the West and the Turkey of the East. The influence of Europe is everywhere: in the clothes, in the people, in the atmosphere. After a final night of feasting, we leave the gateway to the past, and step brightly into the future.

BEHIND THE SCENES IN TURKEY

Turkey is easily one of my favourite countries, and since this is where Julia and I met in 2005, there was a nice fit for our story about biblical tourism, knee-deep in our personal history.

My genesis as a travel writer began when I booked a round-the-world ticket to twenty-four countries, and disciplined myself to update my website weekly with writing, photos, reviews and interviews with all the people I had met. Many people keep travel blogs these days, but I took it to the extreme. It would take me about eight hours of work, once a week, holed up in a coffee shop or at some hostel. Since I didn't expect to travel much again, this would be my personal diary and a chance to share my adventures with anyone who cared to follow. My blog led to a column led to articles led to a TV show, and here was are.

Eastern Turkey is more conservative than the western part of the country, but no less friendlier or welcoming. The food is outstanding, and there is much to see. I found out about Mount Nemrut while doing research online, and the moment I saw pictures of it I knew I had found my story. It is officially my best sunrise, a book-end to Bolivia's Lake Titicaca sunset. Minutes after the sun had risen the dozens of Turkish tourists left, leaving us alone with the statue heads, soaking up the views of nearby Iraq. Modern civilization was spawned here thousands of years ago amongst the dry and scorching mountains, along with three of the world's major religions.

Julia and I first met on the other side of the country, in Koycegiz, a small lakeside town. She was tapping away on her keyboard and I was tapping away on mine, and some fellow backpackers made the connection that we were both travel writers. Three years later, neither of us could have expected we'd return to Turkey with a film crew: Sean, Michael, Chris and Paul, the guys you see dancing at the end of the episode. There's no point denying that they exist, the way some reality shows pretend there's nobody in the room (except for a TV crew). TV crews impact the way people react to us. As much as we try to ignore them, they define our experience and are part of the journey.

We did some long hours in the van in this episode. If you're going to be a travel writer, expect to do a lot of travelling. The dust storm that blew in from Syria created a spooky, sepia-toned atmosphere. *CSI Miami* uses software to boost their orange colours; we use desert storms. When the tour group first pulled into Harran I was convinced they must be Americans. Then I heard an accent and figured they were Germans. So it was a surprise to find Israelis - Jews - travelling in a Muslim country. Not only were they safe, they were welcomed, and had only positive words for their Turkish neighbours. This is why I love Turkey. For centuries, it has straddled the worlds of East and West, and somehow made it work. Sometimes things get rocky, and there is always pressure from radicals on both sides of the political and religious fence. But when Jews and Muslims can co-exist peacefully, surrounded by the ruins of their common ancient heritage, it's all the more inspiring.

A young boy sells *simit* bread on the streets of Sanilurfa

Balikligol, a sacred pool where Turks believe Abraham turned fire to fish

Face to face with the 2000 year-old statues of Greek gods on Mt Nemrut

Walking on the remains of an old Roman city wall in Diyarbakir

SLOVENIA
RUNNING WITH UNICORNS

We'll probably never know what possessed the president of Georgia to authorize an invasion into the largely Russia-supported breakaway region of South Ossettia, but a butterfly flaps its wings in the jungle, and the next thing you know you find yourself flying into Ljubljana, the capital of Slovenia. See, we were supposed to be filming an episode of *Word Travels* in a little-known Eastern European country called Georgia. So few people knew it existed I had to explain that we weren't flying back to the USA to film in Atlanta, but rather were scheduled to spend a week around Tbilisi, where I was to learn about Georgian martial arts (yes, they have their own martial art in Georgia) and traditional Georgian winemaking. Then Georgia picks a fight with Russia, and you know what they say about antagonizing bears… the Russians invade, and suddenly Georgia makes world headlines for two weeks as Europe sees war for the first time in years. Russian troops advance into the interior of the country amidst calls on both sides of genocide, while the Georgian president learns that having the USA as an ally doesn't mean shit when it comes to misguided and misinformed military posturing. Needless to say, Georgia is dropped from our itinerary just as quickly as the Georgian army dropped their weapons in the face of the Russian onslaught. So I'm looking at flights from Istanbul, since that is where we'd be the week before, and wouldn't you know it, there's a direct flight to Slovenia. "I've heard Slovenia is pretty beautiful," and a couple of phone calls and emails later our smashing production manager Leah tells us we've found our replacement country. Pack your bags, folks, we're going to the Eurozone.

I'll say this for Slovenia. It is beautiful. The natural assets of the small central European country are ideal for postcards: all green meadows, mountains and farmland. Since adopting the euro in 2007, it's also prosperous and entirely civilized. Excellent roads and infrastructure, towns and cities spit-polish clean. I didn't see a piece of trash on the streets of Ljubljana all week, human or otherwise. The capital city is quintessentially European – cobblestones, churches, squares, canals, outdoor cafes, parks, bicycle lanes – with a tiny dash of an alternative art scene and thousands of well-dressed students. Parts of the city, pronounced Yoobli-yana, remind me of St. Petersburg, Copenhagen, Stockholm and Budapest. While Slovenian history goes back way over a thousand years, it has always been considered an affluent region of whomever happened to be conquering it. Nobility from the Romans, the Austrians, the Croats, the Serbs, the Italians, the Germans and later the Communists all enjoyed the splendour and beauty of the country. In the former Yugoslavia, it was considered the pearl of the union until Tito kicked the bucket in Ljubljana and Slovenia pushed for independence in 1991. No crazy riots, no disappearances, no mass political turmoil. Instead, the very civilized, almost refrained population of 2 million shifted into the European Union with an almost uncanny ease. Today it is part of NATO, the Schengen, the Council of Europe, the Eurozone and all those other clubs that separate modern Europe from the so-called riff-raff. "We learned from the mistakes of other countries," explains my guide, Tillin, motoring through electronic tolls at alarming speed. Sure, prices went up with the euro, but Europe is expensive. This is not Eastern Europe, laced with corruption and volatile politics. This is not Western Europe, overrun with tourists and $19 cups of coffee. We're right in the centre, a few hours' drive from Italy, Germany, Austria, Hungary and Croatia. And while Slovenia might lack the edge of these countries, it certainly contains some of the best components of all of them.

Take Bled, for example. A medieval castle overlooks an azure freshwater lake. Mountains cradle the horizon, green forests and meandering roads lining the water. In the centre is an island with a church, the spire a striking symbol of tradition. A thousand years ago, Slavs worshipped the goddess of love and fertility here. By the eleventh century, the first church was built, the current steeple added in the sixteenth century. Today, wedding parties come from all over Europe for the spectacular setting, and for the groom to carry his bride up the 99 steps (if he can make it) and ring the bell three times for good fortune (easier said than done). On a sunny day, when the water has a crystal glow and traditional wooden rowboats ferry people to the island, it's so picturesque you'd think you'd stumbled into the airbrushed cover of a fantasy novel. Bled has been a holiday destination for centuries, mainly for European royalty and health-minded nobility. A famous sanatorium lined it shores, as did summer palaces, now mostly hotels and restaurants. Further up the road in Bohinj, I decided to see the surrounding Julian Alps the best way I know how – from the seat of a paraglider. I joined Borot from PAC Sports as we took a gondola and ski chair to our launch pad at Vogel.

Paragliding has become immensely popular the world over, partly because it allows us to fly, partly because it's relatively safe, and partly because it's easy to transport and set up a parachute on the edge of a mountain. A 25kg backpack contains my artificial wings, and my tandem instructor knows how to operate them. All I have to do is run until there's no more ground beneath my feet, sit back and take in the magnificent scenery. On a day like today, I see an emerald lake butted up against the mountains (including Triglav Mountain, the highest peak in the country). I see the land flattening out into green farmland manicured so smooth it could be a giant fairway. The early morning fog burns away, the colours of the landscape pop beneath a bright summer sky. Paragliding is as gentle as a shopping bag blowing in the wind, less a thrill sport than a chance for anyone of any age to float high among the mountains and get a bird's-eye view of the world below.

Back on solid ground, I headed over to Hostel Pod Voglom for a swing on their high ropes course. Connected to a safety harness, the goal is to navigate over a series of obstacles, all 8m above the ground. Balance, self-confidence, a chance to pretend I'm Bruce Willis in *Die Hard*, leaping off of edges and grappling for rope. The climax is a big swing, high enough to make you scream, and wonder mid-arc who decided that swings and slides in parks should only be for kids. High ropes courses are made for natural-born swingers like me.

In this part of the world, excellent pivo (beer) and thin-crust pizza are everywhere, an interesting meeting of Germanic and Italian tradition. Perhaps most closely related to Croatia in terms of culture, Slovenians are not to be confused with Slovakians, a completely different kettle of Slav. English is widely spoken, and the rich bounty of hikes, climbs, and rafting, kayaking, fishing and biking opportunities brings in mainly European tourists who want the best of Europe without having to deal with the crowds of summer.

My wild Slovenian ride continues south in Lipica, since 1580 the home of the famous Lipizzaner horses, the "cradle of the race." To be honest, I'd never heard about Lipizzaners, the Spanish Riding School in Vienna, or dressage until a few weeks ago. My experience with horses is limited to hopping on, hanging on and letting the beast do what it does best. There've been some unforgettable riding times on the plains of Mongolia, in the desert of Jordan's Petra and on the beaches of northern Brazil. And I'll never quite be able to get over the time when, as an 11-year-old on a school tour, my horse tried to mount the mare in front, which was being ridden by the prettiest blonde in the class. She fell off, or I fell off, or we both fell off, but either way Charmaine Diesel never quite looked at me the same way again.

To those who do know horses, Lipizzaners are the pinnacle, the cream of the equine crop. A product of centuries of careful breeding, Lipizzaners are noble and elegant, strong and intelligent, admired and royal. First bred in Lipica by Austrian-Hungarian nobility, the horses are recognizable by their white coats, although they are not technically white horses; they are grey (only albino horses can be considered true white horses). Stick a horn on its head and it's the closest thing you'll come to riding a unicorn. After a scary stint during World War II that almost wiped out the breed altogether (Lipizzaners taste like any other horse meat to starving soldiers), today there are about 3000 registered Lipizzaners worldwide, all related to the same six stallions from the sixteenth century.

With Lipica steeped in centuries of tradition, and the fact that classical horse riding is pretty much reserved for the elite, I felt like I was crashing a party at the country club, especially when I was assigned two beautiful trainers for a crash course in classical riding on a Lipizzaner. Fabrizia was from Italy (the border is just a few hundred metres away), and Monica from Slovenia, and both shook their heads universally as I tried my best to make Slovena, my unicorn, trot along the boards of the indoor training centre. Unlike in western riding, which is more befitting of my style, experience and Gonzo hat, classical riding is about form, posture, and physical nuances. Even the slightest movement will be interpreted by the horse, and by squeezing my legs and holding the reins I was telling my guy: "I have no idea what I'm doing; please don't buck and trample me to death; I saw what you did to Christopher Reeve, and if you can cripple Superman, you'll make mincemeat of Robin Esrock."

Lipica offers week-long courses, and after a short, uncontrollable stint outside, it was decided we should call it a day for the lessons in the interest of everyone's safety. I walked Slovena back to the stable, my ass numb from the trot, and decided it's probably best I stick to tourist horses with names like Jigsaw and Candy, and gallop on plains and beaches. Fab and Monica demonstrated for the camera how it should be done, by running their horses in the countryside, right over the unprotected border with Italy. Watching their Lipizzaners in stride was something to behold, although this was a just a taste of what was to come the following morning.

For Paul's birthday, our guide Tillin loaded us into the van for a drive to the Slovenian beach holiday town called Portoroz. A twenty-minute drive later we crossed the Italian border for the hell of it, skirting the port city of Trieste. Another hour and we could have been in Croatia. For Paul's birthday, we gave him a taste of Italy, some fine pizza and a vicious hangover the following morning.

Rising early, we set up on a field as the mares made their way to the pasture. About forty ghost-white Lipizzaner horses entered from the gate and broke out into a gallop, their hooves thundering past us, kicking up dust in the sunshine. It's not quite the migration of the wildebeest in the Serengeti, but as an animal encounter it was no less thrilling. Later, I approached the group of mares, walking slowly with confidence, trying to seduce them like a pickup artist horse whisperer. Their heads perked up and they formed a protective circle, but after some time they seemed to relax. A single large mare walked up to me and sniffed me out. I gently patted her nose and rubbed her ears, and after that, suitably accepted, I was allowed to roam amongst them. Without waxing on about connecting with the creatures we share the planet with, I will say I had a real touching moment out there, in the quiet meadow, surrounded by noble Lipizzaner femininity. When they cantered off, I ran with them, which in retrospect might have been a pretty stupid thing to do considering, as Chris reminded me later, I was sandwiched in by a ton of muscular animal. Fortunately we got it all on film, but as with so many other segments, the footage doesn't quite do the moment justice.

Although the Russians had promised to withdraw, there was still conflict and angry words being thrown about between NATO and Putin as we closed out the week in Ljubljana. Considering we were supposed to be in one of the world's political and military hotspots, the contrast of Slovenia's order and efficiency was stark. Boats on the canals, fresh gelato on the streets, stylish patio bars and bike rides in green parks, Slovenia could well be the most peaceful, civilized and beautiful country in Europe. I paraglided in the Alps, swam in an stunning crystal lake, swung from high ropes and wandered in a meadow of unicorns. More unforgettable moments in this ride of a lifetime we call *Word Travels*.

Crossing the lake to Bled Castle, originally built in the 8th century

BEHIND THE SCENES IN SLOVENIA

This beautiful Central European country was a happy accident. We were scheduled to film our episode in Georgia. Contacts were made, stories were researched, all was set, and then the Russians invaded. It was a country that few people had heard of the week before (and therefore great *Word Travels* fodder), and suddenly, it was headline news the world over. We thought it might blow over, this inconvenient and tragic war, and I honestly suggested we go ahead anyway, war and all. When the airport outside Tbilisi was bombed, we had to find fast alternatives. We looked at direct flights from Istanbul, and spotted Ljubljana. My only previous experience with Slovenia was a backpacker buddy swearing it was gorgeous. Journeys have been made for far less. Georgia, as it turned out, would come later.

After the heat and bustle of Turkey, Slovenia was like stepping into a cultural air conditioner. Everything was spotless, smooth, orderly, and very, very green. When I read about the Lipizzaner horses, I knew instantly I had my story. The way horse lovers reacted to the mere name (mare name?) alerted me, a horse novice, to their allure. I would not get to ride a Lipizzaner. It would allow me to ride it. My instructors were patient (not to mention photogenic), and I really wished I could spend more time getting to know the horses (not to mention the instructors!). In the stable, it took twenty-six takes before I could correctly pronounce Lipica. It sounds like "Lee's Pizza" in case you ever find yourself in a similar predicament. Anyway, I had a really profound moment walking in the meadow surrounded by dozens of grazing mares. Not many people get this kind of access, and not many people would be stupid enough to run at full tilt next to the horses, inches away from possibly being trampled. It was worth it, my moments with the unicorns.

The medieval Predjana Castle, which once belonged to a den of thieves

Nice day for paragliding in the stunning Julian Alps

Learning to ride a regal LIpizzaner at the cradle of the breed in Lipica

UKRAINE
FEELING THE CHERNOBYL GLOW

I've got my glow on in Chernobyl, where the Geiger counter is crackling over and I swear my feet are burning a hole right through my shoe. It's the final leg of Europe, if this can still be called Europe, which it is certainly not, according to the European Union. Ukraine, second-largest country on the continent, not to be confused with Russia, that other behemoth who likes their borscht. Moscow used to be a principality of the Rus, who governed out of Kiev, and I wonder if ancient Rus women wore high heels and painted-on jeans, too. From the uncanny civil order of Slovenia, we are met at the airport by a chain-smoking shark-eyed driver who speaks zero English. The airport is a picture of chaos, which is nothing compared to the lobby of the Hotel Ukraine. The location is smack dab in the perogy overlooking the main downtown drag of Independence Square, embellished with faded Soviet glory. The receptionist grunts, barks in harsh quasi-English commands, as welcoming as a pit bull covered in razor nails. Maybe she is related to the driver. There's a strip bar in the lobby and the key is with the attendant on the thirteenth floor. I hand her a paper and she points me to room 1305, which has the charming look, smell and décor of a Ukrainian matriarchal prison. A small single cot bed crammed against the wall, 70's chairs, an empty fridge, a TV set with a broken remote control, and a wide window offering a view fit for kings. Oh, and a rotary phone, which actually hurts the finger to dial out. I'm only in Ukraine for a week, and I've got so little time to get dialled in.

I am here to cover two stories: Chernobyl, site of the infamous nuclear disaster, and an ex-Soviet missile base that once housed intercontinental ballistic thermonuclear warheads, both well capable of ruining your day. This is some pretty heavy stuff, I admit, but there's no time to hit the beaches of the Black Sea and tourism is not exactly exploding in the country. My calls to the tourism office were met with a deep grunt and indifference. That being said, I hit a week of perfect weather, clear sunny days and warm, fragrant nights. The crowds are out, seemingly consisting of women dressed up for the runways of Milan. "Ukrainian girls, they are the best, no?" says Olga Number One, who resembles Cameron Diaz in a ballroom dress. Olga Number Two pulls out her iPhone to prove it, showing me a series of her modelling photos. "Actually, I'm more partial to Brazilian and Argentinean girls; their eyes are softer," I reply, just to piss them off. Incredible and abundant Ukrainian talent notwithstanding, the people-watching in this part of the world is exceptional. Fashions are slammed together like peanuts and gum (together at last), mullets and style, Eurotrash and money. After a disastrous start to its independence from the train wreck of the Soviet Union, the Ukrainian economy is enjoying its seventh straight year of solid growth. More new cars were bought in Ukraine than in another other country in Europe last year, and you can see them on the streets of Kiev. Preposterously prosperous vibes groove from the Buddha Bar, where a bottle of Heineken costs $12. In this part of the world, in nouveau riche clubs like this, they have dress code and face control. Restaurants offer burned or bland food at a cost far exceeding its value; the only consolation is in the beer, which is good and cheap the way good cheap eastern European beer should be. Although English is taught in schools, nobody seems to be able to speak it, and there's not a solitary sign to help out the few tourists wandering about. There are also no postcards to be found anywhere, ruining an unbeaten twenty-country run of collecting them. People are too busy making money, or, more accurately, looking at the few people who actually are.

Gotta love the People Chain. Jenja works at Ryders Eyewear, my sponsor, in Vancouver, and she was born in Kiev, so she gives me her cousin Vlad's number, and an email or two later I join Vlad and his friendly wife Anastasia for some beer and bunker chow. It's been a week in the country already, and they're the first young hip folks I've met with a brilliant command of language and a natural thirst for travel. "India wasn't too tough for us," says Anna. "We're used to overcrowded trains and buses, things not running on schedule, corruption…" If she can compare Ukraine to India in all seriousness, then so can I. But then you get the Buddha Bar and the horrifically overpriced Double Coffee and the department stores and the iPhones and the $400 handbags, and this ain't New Delhi, no sirree. Then read the cover story in the Kiev Post about the mayor selling large tracts of land to private parties for a fraction of their worth. Corruption runs so thick here, it would be rude not to try and pull a fast one. Politically, the president and prime minister are at each other's throats, and there's real concern about the Russian bear flashing its claws in Georgia. Putin apparently told Bush that Ukraine isn't a real country, conveniently forgetting history and sending blue and yellow nationalists into a tizzy. Still, I'm impressed with this country. They had the third-largest arsenal of nuclear warheads in the world, and you know what? They decided to dismantle every last damn one of them. A nuclear bomb would pretty much ensure their safety (and possible destruction), but they did it anyway, and to find out more I headed off to an ex-Soviet missile base.

About fifteen years ago, I would have received three-thousand volts of electric fence and seventy-two warning bullets in my chest for daring to visit this top-secret base. Guards were instructed to kill all intruders. Today the Strategic Missile Forces museum welcomes tourists wanting to visit a genuine nuclear missile silo complete with a twelve-level fifty-metre-deep underground command centre. Scrap the image of dozens of nerdy balding types in a massive room glowing with screens. The command silo is cramped, narrow, tight, frigid, sterile and soul crushing. Working six-hour shifts twenty-four hours a day, two officers would remain ready and alert, anticipating the phone call authorizing them to launch the missiles. Life is so far removed down here you'd want to destroy the planet just to relieve the boredom. And with enough equipment and resources to survive forty-eight days without coming to the surface (as well as carefully designed hydraulics designed to withstand a nuclear attack), you'd emerge as one of the few survivors left on a planet torn to shreds by atomics. A former colonel – one of the guys with the finger on the button in subterranean hell – was my guide. He looked like your average bloke, so it was hard to imagine he could have been responsible for millions of murders. But years below under that sort of pressure had taken its toll… he refused to sit in the co-pilot's chair for a photo. Any officer who showed the slightest bit of mental or moral issue was immediately transferred. Not everyone can follow orders knowing they'd literally end the world. Outside, my bones chilled from the sheer mechanical wickedness of the place, I come face to face with a massive black thermonuclear missile, disarmed of course, called the CC-18. NATO calls it Satan. Known as the world's most sophisticated and ruthless weapon, it can deliver a payload of ten warheads (each fifty times more powerful than the bomb that exploded over Hiroshima), and is practically indestructible. Built and still in use by the Russians, it can reach the USA within twenty-five minutes. Never have I felt such evil emanate from a lifeless machine. Walking beside it confirmed the very existence of hell. But there is hope, knowing that countries like Ukraine have disarmed their nukes and the remaining superpowers have reduced their warheads from the odd 70,000 they had during the cold war to the odd 10,000 they have today. There's also fear knowing that just a handful of them could wipe out every milestone humanity has achieved, indiscriminate of faith, gender or political view. Besides the Cuban Missile Crisis, there have been four other near-miss incidents, all caused by human or computer error. Somewhere in the US, China, Russia, France, India, Pakistan, Israel, Britain and North Korea, there are two men sitting in a bunker. They are bored, they are tired and they have their fingers twitching, inches away from the button.

Tourists have been visiting Chernobyl for years, so I wasn't exactly petrified at the prospect of exposing myself to radiation. Did you know that when you fly in a plane, you are having a couple of X-rays' worth of radiation?   Hundreds of people live in the very-freakily-named Zone of Alienation, the 30km fenced off radius that surrounds Reactor Number Four. Since the meltdown in April 1986, for reasons that are still hotly debated, the other six reactors have been shut down and the entire area is essentially the largest nuclear waste dump on the planet. Radiation has contaminated everything, which is why equipment had to be buried and nothing could be taken out. The nearby city of Pripyat, a model Soviet development with 50,000 citizens, was evacuated within two days and today lies abandoned. People could only pack a suitcase; everything else remains as is. The ghost city is the real reason tourists visit Chernobyl, a haunting, spooky movie set where tumbleweeds blow past deserted boulevards and time stopped in 1986. Hundreds of mouldy school books are scattered on the floor in schools, paint flaking, light fixtures rusting, cement cracking from the onslaught of nature. Blackened dolls gave me chills in the kindergarten, while a scream would echo amongst the empty apartment blocks. Our Geiger counter showed about 0.500, harmless if you don't stick around too long but still fifty times greater than it showed in Kiev, 100 kilometres away. In one hot zone, it cranked to 2.000, where the wind had scattered the radioactive dust. I go into more detail in an article, but it's safe to say the entire trip was so bizarre, so fascinating and so horrifying it's a stand-out travel experience.

I thought the article would sell like radioactive hotcakes, but it never did. Too hot for the travel section, perhaps.

When troops were trying to evacuate people in Pripyat, after dozens of firemen had battled the flames in the reactor and signed their death warrants, people needed to be convinced of the danger. Radiation is a silent killer, infecting your blood, targeting the weak. Yet nature has rebounded. Giant catfish swim in the toxic river, moose, deer and boar have proliferated in the forest, birds sing in the trees. We spend the night in a nameless hotel for firefighter guesrs, get drunk on cheap local vodka, try not to think about the air we're breathing. The food, brought in from outside the zone, barely scrapes by after emptying half a bottle of Tabasco on it. Intense Soviet iconography is everywhere, a snapshot of 1986, when the Cold War was particularly frosty. Propaganda flakes on the walls, portraits of Soviet leaders rot behind the theatre. Before we leave, we step into a Doctor Who machine that checks the levels of radiation on our bodies, clothes and shoes. It's kind of like an STD test. You know you're 100% OK, but still… The light is green, barely, and at last we drive out, the Geiger counter decreasing with each mile. I just finished reading Alan Weisman's *The World Without Us*, and in it he describes a world in which humanity disappears and our buildings, skyscrapers, prisons and schools sink back into the land. After visiting Chernobyl and Pripyat, I have seen that world with my own eyes.

We spend a night at a roadside motel. I mention this because it was owned and operated by a guy named Mikael Paplovsky, sort of what David Hasselhoff might become once he shrinks a few inches, becomes fat and corrupted. With a staff of pretty young girls, Paplovsky is a pop star who owns a chain of motels and restaurants, has appointed himself a cultural ambassador, produces high-quality bling videos, never married and surrounds himself with teenage girls and, more alarmingly, his babushka mother. His face is everywhere: on billboards, on screens in the restaurant, on the hotel walls, on the bottles of terrible vodka he produces. When he pulls up at the hotel the pretty young things I am talking to literally drop to their knees, hail to the king. He looks me over, shakes my hand and leaves. I go to the bathroom and wash my hands with soap. I mention this only because in Ukraine, people got a kick out of the fact that I met a kitschy, tacky cultural icon, and also because a night in a Ukrainian highway motel is worth remembering.

Four weeks in Europe have whizzed by, and as I write this on the plane from Amsterdam to Vancouver, I can't believe how much I've packed into the month. One week, one country, dozens of once-in-a-lifetimes, pressure, people, nature, fun. There are only a few days to rest before it's off to Central America, with the final three episodes of the shoot taking place in Jamaica, Belize and Mexico. The borscht is finished but the ride continues.

Standing next to Satan, the most advanced Soviet nuclear missile capable of unleasing hell on earth.

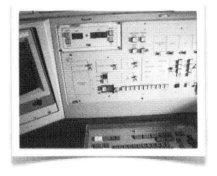

(l) The low-tech control panel that could have ended the world.

BEHIND THE SCENES IN UKRAINE

First off, it's Ukraine, not THE Ukraine. When people ask me what my favourite country during the summer shoot was, I answer Ukraine. Bear in mind it had, without a doubt, the WORST food, and the accommodation? Well, let's not talk about the accommodation. But the stories we uncovered there, Chernobyl and the missile base, had a profound impact on me. Nuclear disaster seems so… 80's these days, but feeling the cold cement of the missile silo, or the sinister silence at Pripyat, brought it all home.

I'm writing this on a plane (of course), and I just watched a movie I downloaded called *War Games*, made in 1983 starring a very young Matthew Broderick. I was nine years old when it came out, and I still remember learning the phrase "Global thermonuclear war."

It was chilling then, and it is chilling now, especially the scenes in a command centre, where two soldiers are commanded to initiate missile launch and realize they'll be destroying millions of lives. I felt that emotion in that Ukrainian missile bunker, decommissioned or not. I believe that energy leaves a resonance. You can feel the positive energy on a beautiful beach just as surely as you can feel the negative energy on a site of tragedy. In that bunker, the hairs on my arms were as sharp as pins, and the former general, the man who sat in that very chair with his finger on the button, made no bones about the severity of what had happened here.

I used my People Chain to connect with Vlad and Anastasia, young Ukrainians who are as addicted to travel as the rest of us. They took me to a beer garden festival, where I got the chance to mingle with the people, soak up the good cheap beer and take some local transport. Some parts of Kiev belonged in western Europe, others in eastern Europe. Rents are high, people struggle, but everyone loves their cell phone. The service industry leaves much to be desired, and it seemed like everyone was working too hard to make money to care much about the few tourists who bothered to visit. A few months later, when the economy collapsed, Ukraine was one of the first countries in Europe reaching for the IMF panic button. But you have to admire a country that feels constantly threatened by the growing might of its aggressive Russian neighbours, yet chooses to voluntarily disarm the world's third-largest nuclear arsenal.

Welcome to the Hotel Chernobyl. Plenty of vodka at the Hotel Chernobyl. Crank up the creepy factor here, especially when the Geiger counter rocked itself to 2.000 at one hot spot. Kiev was about 0.007. You hear about places like Chernobyl, but you never expect to find yourself walking in an abandoned city, the rust of Soviet iconography making it look like some cold war movie set. The food is all brought in from outside, not that that made it any more edible. Ukrainian vodka is amongst the finest, and in keeping with our ongoing tradition of watching new *Word Travels* rough edits in strange places, we gathered around my laptop in the sparse room of the sparse Hotel Chernobyl (or whatever its real name is) to watch an episode that had been FTP'd across to us. It's always an exhilarating experience to see how our team back home interprets the footage that gets sent to them.

Judging by the amount of people who live and work in the Zone of Alienation, I do not believe we were in harm's way in Chernobyl (although I can't say the same for anyone who ate the food that week). But I'm not about to go recommending the place as a must-visit for global tourists. Fascinating, unforgettable, bizarre and a story to tell the grandkids. Which pretty much sums up Ukraine in general.

Standing outside reactor 4 at Chernobyl

An abandoned doll in the derelict school of Prypiat, a scene from a horror movie

The forest retakes the city of Prypiat, a haunting legacy of nuclear meltdown

JAMAICA
THE OTHER SIDE OF THE TOURIST BROCHURE

There's a hardcover, glossy-paged and full-colour book called *Destination Jamaica* in my hotel room. It's the "official visitor magazine of the Jamaica Hotel and Tourist Association," and its pages are jammed with photos of people, mainly white, having the time of their lives. Between advertising for designer watches, jewellery, restaurants and resorts, there are plenty of tourist recommendations for honeymooners and cruise shippers, families and weekend get-me-aways. Most of the action centres on the north coast of the island – the resorts around Negril, Montego Bay and Ocho Rios – with a healthy section reserved for the capital, Kingston. I've spent a week in Jamaica surrounded by the warm blue waters of the Caribbean, but as I turn the pages of this book, it feels like I've visited another country altogether. Reflecting on Rasta villages in the Blue Mountains, dancehall parties in the streets or the community that embraced me outside Mandeville, I am trying to force the genuine circle of my experience into the airbrushed square of this promo book. Everybody comes to Jamaica, but it appears there's more to Jamaica than what everybody sees.

"Eve-rie-bo-die is in the ceme-te-ry, mon, so we say 'eve-rie-won!'" Typical Jamaican humour from Noah, his grey dreadlocks framing his face, creased with smiling. Jamaica, population 2.7 million, an island resort holiday destination. Blessed with tropical beaches and hallowed natural beauty, Columbus discovered it in 1494 and famously said, "Yeah mon!" Actually, he said something about this being the most beautiful land he'd seen, but I'm going to steer clear of traditional tourist propaganda. "Yeah mon" has entered my vocabulary, and I doubt it will ever truly leave. It can be said enthusiastically, and it can whispered sadly. Would you like another tasty chicken patty? – Yeah Mon! Were the Spanish responsible for the murder of every single last indigenous islander, the people known as the Arawaks? – Yeah mon. Did Jamaica win gold medals at the Olympics for the world's fastest men and women in the 100m sprint? – Yeah Mon! Did centuries of English and Spanish slaving burn tragedy into this island, scarring its descendants with the hard lashes of history? – Yeah mon. Nevertheless, for a small country forever at war with its unfortunate origins, the people of Jamaica have created their own distinct culture – language, food and music that have spread around the world. So we think Jamaica and we think Bob Marley, a prophet of peace and a musical genius. We think of jerk, the sweet, spicy marinade that has become a staple of Caribbean cuisine. We think of words like "irie," or "a little sumthin' sumthin'." Jamaican patois may be a colourful and creative stew of English, Spanish, slang and street, but the laugh that follows almost every sentence can be universally understood.

This is not the time or place for a Gonzo history lesson, although Jamaica's past does need some reflection. After the conquering Spanish found no gold, the island remained a trading post until war between English, French and Spanish armadas led to the rise of the buccaneers, the infamous pirates of the Caribbean. Sanctioned by various governments, ruthless men with loyalty for hire, like Blackbeard or Henry Morgan, pillaged for profit, based out of Port Royal. It's fun to think of swashbucklers and lusty wenches, but this was "the wickedest place in Christendom," a dog-eat-salty-dog world where murder, robbery, betrayal and disease ran through the veins of a population of human effluence, opportunists and backstabbers. As if on cue, an earthquake sunk this Sodom and a third of its population in 1692, and the town of Kingston was established in its wake. New masters of Europe, the English conquerors, found a lush and fertile land ready to be harvested, and the import of slaves began. By the seventeenth and eighteenth centuries, there were three times as many slaves as white population, human cargo brutally imported from the Niger and West Africa, treated worse than dogs, put to work in lucrative coffee and sugar plantations. One in three perished under atrocious conditions: replaced, raped, hung, whipped and subjugated in a time when concepts of enlightenment, freedom, liberty and equality were being debated in the royal parlours of Europe. Today, Jamaica's population, like those of many other islands in the region, are the descendants of these slaves, and while the rest of the world can only imagine the injustice, you can still taste it in the air, and the food; jerk cooking was invented by runaway slaves.

Nowadays there are understandable calls for reparations from Britain, which grew its wealthy empire on the scarred backs of its former Jamaican slaves. Yet, much like India and Sri Lanka, British influence can be found everywhere, from the national sport of cricket, education and parliamentary systems to the influx of English tourists. The irony today is that the descendents of slaves serve the descendents of masters in luxury resorts, restaurants and bars. Anyway, the moral repugnance of slavery was finally abolished by local parliament in 1834. Two centuries of political turbulence, massacres, and the violence of a power being transferred from former master to former slave later, Jamaica was able to finally gain independence in 1962. A flag of black, green and yellow flies all over the country, for these are a proud people, forever removed from their indigenous roots, forever bruised by the nightmare of their origins (be they slave, master or merchant), but determined to move forward as one people.

With my one shot to visit Jamaica, I'm keen to leave the resorts behind and, given my limited time, search out the other side of the island. If I were on holiday, or better yet a honeymoon, you'd have to clutch the pina colada from my sunburned fingers, but I'm here to discover a country and the people who live inside it. Without any single activity or destination in mind, finding my story would take a bit of travel, a bit of hunting and a bit of luck.

History has always interested me, but delving into the appalling world of the slave trade, however important, would fall beyond the scope of the traditionally more upbeat travel pages. Slicing away the truth of piracy with the cutlass of my pen intrigued me in Port Royal, but after earthquakes and ruin, there is not much to see or experience there that can't be gleaned from history books or websites. Since tourism dominated the country's economy, and most tourism centres around cruise ships and all-inclusive resorts, my angle would lie with the people of Jamaica itself.

My opening paragraph begins in the Blue Mountains, a range that overlooks the capital of Kingston, and which is home of the world-famous coffee bearing the same name. Travelling the narrow, braided, washed-out road towards Newcastle, along cliffs as steep and nerve-wracking as the best of them, my destination is the Temple Mount Zion Hill, an informal Rastafarian settlement.

Although Rastafarians and Jamaicans appear synonymous, only around 1% of the population subscribes to the religion, with the majority being Protestant and its various sub-denominations. Yet the mark of Rastas can be seen here, there, and the world over – every time you see someone with dreadlocks, listening to reggae or smoking pot. Not to say that everyone who does so is a Rastafarian, just that various aspects of the religion have been inhaled by popular culture. Its roots lie with nineteenth-century Jamaican and black Nationalist leader Marcus Garvey, who spoke proudly of North American black communities reorganizing and recognizing their heritage and their rights of status in an unjust world. Garvey, who died in relative obscurity but whose words inspired black leaders throughout the globe, wrote of the crowning of an African empire, a king of kings, signifying the coming of the Messiah. "Look to Africa, where a black king shall arise. This will be the day of your deliverance."

When Tafari Makonnen, traditionally named Ras Tafari, was crowned Haile Selassie, king of Ethiopia in 1932, Garvey's followers recognized the event as the fulfillment of Garvey's prophecy. Analyzing passages of the Bible that can be interpreted to suggest Jesus Christ was black, that marijuana is a sacred herb given to man by God and that the offspring of King Solomon and Queen Sheba have led to the descendents of the real chosen people, Rastafarians recognized in a somewhat bewildered Selassie that he was in fact the Messiah, chosen to save mankind from the evils of western technocracy, called Babylon, with a squadron of saucer-shaped flaming chariots. Before making any assumptions about the validity of such religious ideals, think of how an alien being might react to stories of virgin births, fiery talking bushes, an elephant-headed god or to women choosing to cover themselves head to toe in black robes. The Rasta colours of red (signifying blood to be shed on redemption), gold (signifying the wealth of Africa) and green (signifying the lands of the motherland) are known the world over as being symbolic of reggae, the Rasta-inspired music popularized by its most famous son, Bob Marley.

It's a slog up the slopes, and the thunderstorms of hurricane season are threatening. Mount Zion could technically be called a squatter's camp, as no taxes are paid and it was set up without permission.

From its ramshackle wooden shacks you can see a famous resort, the sprawl of Kingston and a nearby military base. A sign indicates I am on the right track to the Emperor Haile Selassie School of Vision, Bible Study, Prophecies and Sabbath Worship. Hundreds of people, including foreigners, have been baptized here, welcomed into the brethren of the Rastafari. I am greeted by Dermot Fagan, the dreadlocked priest and leader of the village. When he worked as a repairman in Miami, he tells me how clients used to expect a white Irish guy, not a black Rasta. A real "buffalo soldier," Dermot finished up at the army and found himself having a conversation with a Rasta in New York City. With the intensity and facial appearance of Samuel L. Jackson, he pulls out a King James bible and directs me to the passages that converted him to the religion.

The Messiah is black, as it reads in Song of Solomon, 1:5-6: "I am black, but comely, O ye daughters of Jerusalem." In Jeremiah 8:21, God's colour is revealed: "For the hurt of the daughter of my people I am hurt; I am black…" and in Revelation 1:14: "the hair of his head like pure wool…" "Feel my hair," says Dermot, his dreads indeed as thick as wool.

It is a cornerstone of our brilliance as reasoning beings, and our desire to interpret proof for our convictions, that the Bible can say just about anything to anybody. If a group of people feels it justifies constant marijuana smoking and the belief in an Ethiopian messiah, then all the power to them. Certainly an afternoon of conversation with Dermot is an afternoon of thoughtful and enthusiastic debate. This particular village, he tells me, has been set up specifically as a mission to prepare for the coming of the Beast. In a dream, the emperor, king of kings, appeared to Dermot and gave him the task of setting up a refuge off the grid, away from our impending doom – a doom with a remarkably technological twist.

I've heard of the RFID chip before. In the online documentary Zeitgeist, a friend of the modern-day Rockefeller family speaks out about the shadow government that twists and squeezes the world order through global finance, war and politics. When asked what the point of all this is, given the family has unlimited wealth and power already, a Rockefeller scion replies, "The ultimate goal is to get everybody in this world chipped with an RFID chip." Radio frequency identification (RFID) is a microchip inserted into pets, people and products, containing personal information that allows it, them or us to be tracked and monitored. If this sounds like batty conspiracy theory, think again. It is a very real technology offering very real threats to personal liberty, and is being promoted by various US government departments almost as heavily as it is being protested by various civil liberties organizations. Now Dermot has never seen Zeitgeist (he's never even been on a computer), but he's been told about the mark of the Beast, a tag that will allow Babylon to control our lives in every way. High in the mountains, his retreat will be an oasis from the madness, powered by nature (although they currently still use electricity), fed by the land. How this will happen within sight of a military base is not the point. "I am never leaving this mountain," he says sternly over a vegetarian lunch, and I believe him.

It is a fascinating village, and a glimpse into a different life, culture and religion. Dreadlocked men chain-smoke their spliffs as precocious Rasta kids run about. Colourful religious art praises the emperor inside and outside Dermot's house, which is adorned like a temple. Sun breaks from the storm clouds, vividly lighting up the red, green and yellow motifs. I donate some pencils and crayons to the schoolteacher, joking that all the other colours will go to waste.

At university, I made my own attempt at growing hipster dreadlocks, and there are more than a few people who smoke pot and listen to reggae. Yet here in this small community, high in the fields of the Blue Mountains, a Rastafarian sect is devoted to a way of life, a personal belief beyond fashion and lifestyle.

Haile Selassie died in 1975, and I ask Dermot how a messiah can die. "He is not dead, mon, he is alive, waiting to reveal himself, to deliver us from the rapture!"   I think about evangelical churches, Jehovah Witnesses, cargo cults and wiccans, and decide that whether or not you decide to grow your hair in natty dreadlocks, we all need to believe in whatever makes sense for us.

****

It's easy to meet Jamaicans outside the tourist zone. For over forty years, the Jamaica Tourist Board has been offering a program called Meet the People. Playing matchmaker between locals and tourists, they will happily introduce you to Jamaicans who share the same interests as you. Free of charge, for adults or children, the Tourist Board will make all the arrangements, ensuring a friendly, safe and authentic environment to connect you with locals. I've come across a similar private service in Amsterdam, where you pay a fee for the matchmaking, but this little-known, under-utilized service begged further investigation. My mandate was simple: I wanted to meet real Jamaicans in an interesting environment.

For a start, I'd head towards the south coast, not so much off the beaten track as under the radar. No traveller can claim to have seen everything unless they also stop travelling for awhile, and there's no doubt I'd miss not having seen the superb beaches and postcard views of Jamaica up north. But I've had my island paradises, bless me, and given its history and national spirit, I wanted something more out of Jamaica. Off the beaten track means a similar story is less likely to have been published elsewhere, and less likely to have been published elsewhere means a happier editor, and therefore, a happier bank account for me.

From Kingston, we drive under the 6 Mile Bridge along a toll road, and soon enough the highway is replaced by a tangled ball of concrete string. This season's hurricanes have taken their toll, washing out roads and felling trees and houses, and the cleanup crews are still at work. Two types of structures dominate all others: churches and pubs. Roadside shacks selling overproof rum lead us towards Mandeville, where I meet Diana McIntyre-Pike, a pioneer of community-based tourism in Jamaica. I'm not sure if it's because of our visit or her birthday, but we are greeted by a sing-along, and treated to a performance of local musicians, including a five-year-old boy on the drums. Julia and I sit and smile, coaxed into singing Marley's One Love – sure, let's get together and feel alright!   We are put into the very capable hands of Honey and his wife Angel, a descendant of Jamaican national hero Nanny of the Maroons. The Maroons were freed or escaped slaves who held their own against the British using guerrilla warfare in the mountains. We are joyously swept up into their world of countryside Jamaica, through a local outreach program called Countrystyle. Angel takes us to a roadside vegetable stall, and the house she grew up in, then introduces us to her mother, a Rastafarian who doesn't smoke pot (why would you burn something that is holy?).   At a roadside shack it takes hours to prepare a traditional meal of starches – yams, sweet potato, cornmeal dumplings, pumpkin. Since our arrival in the county, in which it took us over an hour to clear customs, we have learned that things move forward in Jamaica according to the slow hand on the watch – island time. What is the rush, mon?

Rain comes, rain goes, old drunk men stagger about yelling "one love," the kids have fun with a Frisbee. You might ask if this is preferable to chilling out on a beach, and to be honest that depends what you're looking for from your experience. Personally, getting my hands dirty washing yams gives me more of an understanding about Jamaica's way of life than ordering another pina colada would. Although I do love my pina coladas, and why should I be denied?

Jakes is a boutique hotel located on the south coast's Treasure Beach. Owned and operated by the same guys who own several glitzy high-profile resorts, it has the personal interest of company president Jason Henzell, since his mom started a small restaurant here in the 1990's and he just kind of ran with it. "Goldeneye [one of his six resorts] is for the famous people; Jakes is for people on their way up," he tells me over breakfast. Funky cabins and rooms face the beach; I swim under the stars in the warm Caribbean, which is paradise to me. Jakes holds a literary festival and a triathlon, and is a keystone in a community outreach project known as Breds, which supports the local fishing community with hurricane relief and medical and educational projects. I used one of the Breds' (slang for brethren) programs to connect with a local fisherman, Captain Ted. Sunrise is just breaking on the horizon when I meet the burly, surefooted Captain Ted and his quiet son Kallis on board a wooden boat powered with an onboard motor. Like most of the people I've met so far, he's all smiles, with an infectious laugh. "Every day is a fishing day, Robin Hood, but not every day is a catching day," he booms as we take off into the calm Caribbean to look for some traps. A few plastic bottles indicate a trap, and I use a sharp hook on the end of a stick to snag it. Pulling it up is hard work; I'm heaving as the slippery rope cuts into my hand. "It's hard work, mon, every day, sometimes up to sixty traps, mon. No fish, no food on the plate." Finally the mesh trap emerges, and inside, a solitary angelfish. Released into the boat, it flops about on the wood as we throw the trap overboard and head off to find the next one. This time, the rope is mottled with grime and sea slime, and a jellyfish manages to sting my elbow as we tug up the line. A snapper snaps about, big enough to satisfy one person's hungry soul, but not much of a catch considering the massive kingfish, tuna and jacks that swim beneath us. A coast guard boat appears, machine guns at the fore, and I'm not fluent enough in patois to know what went down, but they only left us when Captain Ted handed them the two fish. Tough life, this fishing business.

By the third trap, the sun is beginning to bake, my elbow is swollen red and my hands hurt. Captain Ted, commending me on my sea legs (probably because my director, Jordan, was throwing up in the shadowing crew boat), breaks out in a riddy, some impromptu reggae riffing…

"Holy Blessed from above,
Robin Hood, Kallis and Me, fishing in the sea,
No fish in the traps, oh mercy me
The policeman come and take away ma fish, now we left with empty dish
Oh mercy, in St. Elizabeth Parish…"

…and we float back towards Calabash Bay along a watery catwalk of sunlight.

****

It's about time I tried this bird-watching business, so further up the coast near Bluefields I meet Vaughn, who has helped a young local named Wolde Kristos set up Reliable Adventures, a grassroots eco-tour operator offering nature hikes, marine tours and bird watching. I've always wanted to get my head around the fact that people travel the world so they can spot endemic birds through binoculars. Boisterous Veda is my guide, and she's fizzing with excitement at the prospect of seeing her favourite Northern Patoo, one of the 28 endemic species on the island. We walk up a trail, and there it is! An owl, morphed into a branch. I confess I fail to share her enthusiasm, but as we walk quietly along the Belvedere forest trail, every chitter or movement produces a mild thrill, each named and recognized by Veda as a Sad Flycatcher or a Red-billed Streamertail hummingbird. Bird watching equates thrills with a bird name; the more obscure the name, the bigger the thrill.

They're all birds to me, but it's a fun enough game to play, hunting without any weapons. Filming the birds is tough work, since they don't stick around in any one place for too long, and we all have new appreciation for those birding documentaries, the ones where some poor schmuck spends three weeks waiting to get one shot. I reckon I'll slot bird watching into the "hobbies for later life" bin, along with golf, cruise ships and heroin addiction [winemaking].

****

Bent over, she gyrates her hips with a pulsating throb. Both hands around her tight pink shorts, he slams his groin into her. Spinning around, she mounts his crotch and continues to shake, moaning and sweating as he rotates and smashes her on the bar. There is dirty dancing, and then there are the dance crazes that sweep Kingston's dancehall parties, each more sexually overt and provocative than the next. Wednesday night is Weddy Weddy, and much later are the Passa Passa, the biggest parties of the week. By night, I mean early morning, since Weddy Weddy only gets going at around two a.m., and the larger open street party Passa Passa, after four a.m. Since we have an eight a.m. bus, and have already been working since eight the previous morning, we'd have to give Passa Passa a miss, but we head off to an open courtyard to find Weddy Weddy practically empty at midnight. Reggae is cut with dub, sliced with disco and peppered with pop booms from loud speakers, and large screens show the butts and breasts of the few girls gathering around the dance hall. By two a.m., there's a solid crowd, but still no one is dancing. As the hours click over, the music gets louder, the atmosphere tense, the crowd thicker. Something has got to give. The night is sponsored by not one but two energy drinks: Magnum and Bullet. I meet the marketing manager of Bullet and ask him why two drinks would sponsor one night, their promo booths directly opposite each other. "One, we call an energy wine; the other, an energy drink. The idea is that you mix them – load the Magnum with a Bullet. We call it a Lock 'n' Load." Rastafarian men are walking around selling huge stalks of pot and a cloud of green smoke sits over the courtyard. Interestingly, nobody is smoking cigarettes. The dance circle edges closer and closer together until two girls in hot pink shorts start flipping out in the middle. Some well-dressed Kingston guys, infamous Rude Boys, watch the action through their sunglasses, the light of the camera reflecting off the bling around the necks. One guy steps up, and it has begun. The Daggering is on.

From the socio-political beginnings of reggae music, Jamaican dancehall has evolved into a beat of bling, embracing hip-hop's fascination with wealth, sex and materialistic ambition. The old-timers prefer the purity of reggae as it was; the unemployed kids of Kingston, many living in slums torn apart by gang wars, can't get enough of the way it is. With the success of Sean Paul, Beenie Man and Shaggy, Jamaican music continues to find an audience worldwide, and here at Weddy Weddy is where the up and comers get their start.

Daggering is the latest dance craze, pushing the limit of whatever boundary protects dance from being public rape. Previous crazes had girls on all fours, shaking their heads violently to the point of neck injury. Daggering is as violent and passionate a sexual act as you can imagine, and the crowd screams their appreciation. But it's not as raw as it seems; dancers rehearse with their carefully selected partners, showing off their skills, thriving off the response. Some of the Rude Boys break out into choreographed moves worthy of a Broadway musical, unrefined, with the energy of the street. I've embarrassed myself countless times attempting local customs, but out here, if I attempted Daggering, well, I wouldn't be so much laughed at as taken out back and shot.

Kingston has a notorious reputation for violent crime, and our swell guide Carey is hesitant to let us stray too far. At Weddy Weddy, people weren't overly thrilled to see us, and the few white faces in the courtyard did what nervous minorities always do: gravitate towards each other with nods of reassuring acknowledgment. I got the feeling that dancehall parties are far more than just nightclubs full of locals having a good time. In the context of slums, gang wars and unemployment, they're a form of expression, release and personal identity. Perhaps I'm reading too much into it, but I felt I like I had notched up one more authentic rung on the ladder of Jamaican culture.

****

In the back pages of *Destination Jamaica*, I find a section devoted to the "real Jamaica," the off-the-beaten-path South Coast. There's a write-up about the community tourism projects in Mandeville and Treasure Beach, favourable reviews for Jakes and a mention for the Little Ochie Restaurant, where I used the Meet the People program to meet its owner, Blackie. Here, not only did I meet another friendly local, I got to feast at his fish shack, rated as one of the best in the Caribbean, and learn the secret behind his mouth-watering jerk sauce.

How does a small beachside shack selling breakfasts to fisherman on an obscure Jamaican coast grow into one of the most critically acclaimed and busiest fish restaurants in the Caribbean?
This was the question I posed to Little Ochie's owner, Evrol "Blackie" Christian. Arranged through the Meet the People program, Blackie and I were walking along the beach of Alligator Pond, as fishermen haggled over prices, transporting catches of massive lobsters, parrotfish and red snappers with wheelbarrows. The original shack has grown into a 400-seat restaurant, constantly busy with a mostly local clientele. Stilted wooden shacks, some in the shape of boats, contain tables with a breeze blowing in from the sea just a few feet away. Fishermen deliver their catch directly behind the restaurant; the spoils of the sea could not get any fresher.

Blackie, nicknamed by his mother, demonstrates how customers pick their meal, weigh it on scales and then choose from up to seventy different ways to cook it. Grilled, stewed, fried, escovitched – the secret ingredient of Blackie's success lies with the secret ingredients in his jerk recipe. After showing me around the hot grill and steamy kitchen, where up to forty dishes are prepared at the same time, I figure the secret must be sweat. Flipping the jerk parrotfish on the grill, the combination of hot oil and climate is almost overwhelming. The reward, in the form of perfectly grilled lobster, spiced large shrimp and the infamous jerk fish, is more than worth it. Blackie's version of the sweet and spicy jerk sauce – made with a combination of oil, shallots, garlic, onion, spices and hot Scotch Bonnet peppers – immediately answers my initial question. You want to share something this sensational with as many people as you can, and thus a breakfast shack becomes a famous seafood restaurant. A grinning Blackie tells me how visitors to the south coast find the local interaction more inspiring, and, no doubt, the food, more delicious. All of it makes for yet one more satisfied customer.

Everything I'd seen and done is available to any tourist, anyone looking for the other side of the tourist bubble, the grittier underside of a glossy full-colour promotional book. With my limited time, I helped myself to just a small taste of Jamaica – one bursting with music and faith and heartache and joy. I got my story. Now I deserve my pool, pina colada and palm tree.

When Bob Marley sings about a Rasta Man, this is the guy's he's referring to

BEHIND THE SCENES IN JAMAICA

Years ago I wrote about a service called Like a Local, based out of Amsterdam, that connects travellers with a diversity of locals. It's such a great idea, since the people you meet really make a trip memorable, and here's a little help if you really plan to get beyond bar talk. When I found out about the Meet the People program, I couldn't believe it was free and pretty much under-utilized by the tourists to the country. Sometimes I choose stories because they will sell; other times I choose stories because something great needs good press and I'm in the fortunate position to help.

So we leave behind the resorts and head to the south coast. First, though, we stop off at the Rasta village, which was totally authentic, run by an exuberant priest. Dealing with marijuana on TV is a tricky business; it's less so when we're writing. You can't exactly be subtle about it when it's literally in your face, growing everywhere you look. But as we hopefully show, this is a serious religion, and they're serious about their weed. Not featuring that aspect would be like visiting a church and pretending the crucifix doesn't exist. Since this was arranged for us by the Jamaican Tourism Board as part of the Meet the People program, we could only commend them on their trust that we wouldn't sensationalize our visit, condemn the herb, or, more realistically, overindulge in it ourselves.

Island time means nothing runs on time, but everywhere we went we were greeted with sincere smiles and genuine interest, something that comes through in the show. It didn't matter that I caught no fish, or saw just a handful of endemic birds. The fact was, I was meeting real people doing what they love. And the food? Jerk seasoning was created by escaped slaves to preserve food on the run, and today it's the signature sweet-spicy dish of Jamaica. The feast at Little Ochie's is the kind of meal you wish you'd never had, because no fish or lobster will ever taste as good again.

And those Scotch Bonnet peppers – well, one should never underestimate the power of the habanero.

We did stay at one resort: Jakes, in Treasure Beach, where you see us enjoying our pina coladas. It's funky and friendly, owned by the same guys who own a couple of mega-resorts, but with a far more chilled clientele and target market. In TV, and sometimes in writing, we paint with broad strokes to get an idea across quickly, but generalizing can bite you in the ass. There's nothing wrong with going to a resort in Jamaica – we were just trying to show another aspect of the country. If I had more time, I would have loved to look at the cricket culture, and investigate how Jamaicans won the gold medals for the 100m sprint at the next Olympics, both men and women.

This episode, Jordan Kawchuk rejoined us as director (we last saw him in Taiwan, eight countries ago) and we had a new production assistant on the team, too: Neil Maclean. Nothing brings a crew together like a long road trip, crates of cheap Red Stripe and the experience of seeing Daggering first hand. Hoo boy; we knew it was nuts, but we didn't know just how nuts it would be. We would love to have continued onwards that night to Passa Passa, but since these street parties only get going at three a.m., and our shooting days start early and end late, well, we'll just have to leave that for next time.

Daggering in Kingston   Rasta kids in the Blue Mountains

BELIZE

SWIMMING IN UNDERGROUND WATERFALLS

As published in the Globe and Mail

For millennia, our ancestors lived in dark, fire-blackened caves, which provided shelter from wild animals and the elements, a safe refuge for cooking meat and gathering water from underground springs. Perhaps this is what draws both tourists and adventurers to caves around the world. Why else would we willingly walk into a darkness so complete it burns the cornea, a silence so still it rings the ears? From South Africa to Slovenia, massive underground caverns lit up with coloured gels and traversed on damp wooden boardwalks pull in crowded tour buses. We marvel at the otherworldly shapes of stalactites and stalagmites, the limestone shaped by time into flowing marvels of geology. We imagine images in the rock, providing cute nicknames, like the Madonna, or the Elvis, or El Diablo.

On the other end of the scale, we find spelunkers, those who indulge in the more adventurous sport of caving. Using specialized equipment, ropes and harnesses, spelunkers seek out cave systems that run for dozens of kilometres, requiring contortionist techniques, rock climbing skill and the instincts of a navigator. At Belize's Caves Branch Jungle Lodge, I discovered I could hoist myself in the middle – a true cave adventure for the daring tourist.

Ian Anderson's Caves Branch Adventure Company & Jungle Lodge prides itself on being immersed in the jungle, a world away from the sanitized resorts on Belize's Caribbean coast. Sitting on an incredible 58,000 acres of property, it's a jungle heaven for bird watchers, nature lovers, and anyone who prefers a subterranean flavour to their adventures. Caves Branch rests on a foundation of soft limestone, and regular tropical rainfall creates the perfect conditions for the formation of hundreds of kilometres of caves and underground river systems. Archaeologists have discovered early Mayan pottery, carvings and relics deep within the caves, suggesting that man has used this system for thousands of years. From its luxurious suite and modern tree house accommodations,

Caves Branch offers multiple caving excursions tailored to meet different levels of physical skill, confidence and fitness. Guests can cave tube by sitting in the middle of doughnut-shaped rubber tubes and floating down underground rivers. The Black Hole drop rewards a jungle hike with a 200-foot abseil deep into a sinkhole, where you can camp overnight not far from the bones of Mayan sacrifices. Reading the activity list is like reading a menu of fun – hard to choose just one option. I settled for the Waterfall Cave Expedition, which combines the thrills of caving and canyoneering, a combo as natural as hamburgers and fries.

Torrential rain had swelled the river that runs alongside the lodge, so a heavy-duty farm tractor was needed to transport us to the mouth of the cave. All the Caves Branch guides are members of the Belize Search and Rescue Team, and with their decade of experience in the caves below, I knew I was in safe hands. Two guides accompany every group, and everyone is provided with a waterproof headlamp, hardhat and life vest. We drive through a beautiful orange grove offering wonderful views of the surrounding jungle and limestone ridges. Vultures fly above, their shadows sweeping the ground in circles. Crossing the river proves to be an adventure in itself, the tractor lurching over rocks, grinding to the other side of the riverbank. Twenty minutes later, it stops on a dirt track that borders the grove, and a thin path disappears into the dense jungle. We load up our gear and vanish into the green, the thicket vibrant with plants and insects, the humidity overwhelming. My guide Pablo points out a large camouflaged peanut bug, some fire ants and other wonders of the jungle. My back is wet with sweat, but I know that soon enough the strong heat and hard sun will disappear.

Trappers and hunters discovered the Waterfall Cave as early as the 1950's. Further exploration in the 1970's revealed that Mayans had used the system for centuries, their ancient artifacts found deep into the system. Although Caves Branch owns the land above and outside, the government owns all subterranean rights within the country. Still, you won't find any tour buses pulling up here.

After a quick picnic at the mouth, we gear up and slide into the cave. Immediately, I am acquainted with some of the extraordinary creatures that inhabit this world of dark. Harmless fruit bats dash above my head, using their sonar to avoid collisions with rock and human at the last possible moment. Pablo picks up a giant scorpion spider, possibly the most frightening insect I've ever encountered. About eight inches long, it has two sharp pincers that resemble those of a scorpion, a wide grey body and long hairy legs. Even though I know it is blind and harmless, it takes every ounce of my courage to let it cling to my T-shirt.

It is a one-hour hike to reach the waterfalls. We pass narrow, slippery channels, careful to avoid touching or breaking the thousands of impressive stalactites dripping from the ceiling, formed at the glacial pace of just one millimetre a year. At one point I crawl on my hands and knees, my hardhat scraping the low muddy ceiling. Fresh water runs from cracks in the rock above, forming deep puddles below our feet. Layered white limestone rock forms stunning natural formations, with water flowing from layer to layer like champagne over a glass pyramid. There are no cute names for these landmarks, no red lights painting a cavern as the "Devil's Kitchen." Here we are, deep in the planet, our headlamps providing the only comfort from the void. Wading across a pool, the ground gives way and I sink fast. Although I am soaked to the bone, the water is refreshingly cool, the dusty cave air a respite from the jungle heat outside.

Finally, we arrive at a series of seven waterfalls. I put on my life vest, leave my bag behind and dive headfirst into the pool below. Water gushes hard from the schism, so it takes some effort to heave myself up using holds in the rock to conquer this first challenge. The second will not be so easy.

Pablo climbs up ahead to secure the rope. In the ravines outside, a fast-flowing twenty-foot waterfall might not sound like much, but in the confined space of a cave, it is something to behold. It soaks up my strength just to swim against the current, the water crashing alongside me as I harness my carabineer hook to the rope as a precaution. This is canyoneering, the art of rock climbing up waterfalls. My hands struggle and slip to find grips, my feet clumsily seeking footholds as the gush of water bruises my thigh. I finally hoist myself up to the top, scream in triumph, drenched and utterly elated. The remaining waterfalls are not as high, nor as scary, but are just as fun. At the final pool, it is time to turn around.

While this particular cave system does have another mouth, the waterfall path is a one-way street. I descend each challenge until I arrive once again at the top of the twenty-foot falls. The only way down is to jump, arms together to avoid hitting the low rock ceiling. I steady myself on the edge, begin the countdown and take rock jumping to a whole new subterranean level.

An hour later, I emerge into the dark jungle. It takes some time to realize that night has fallen, and that dense thicket has replaced solid rock. Unlike the silence inside, the sounds of the jungle awaken my ears. As the tractor returns to the Caves Branch lodge, I gaze up at a clear night sky, pinpricks of brilliant stars brushed together in a stroke called the Milky Way. The warm air tastes sweet as firebugs dance amongst the oranges. Our ancestors may have lived in caves for thousands of years, and exploring their legacy is serious fun for the adventurous tourist. The real pleasure, however, comes from the re-emergence into the world in which belong.

Entering the cave mouth at Caves Branch

BEHIND THE SCENES IN BELIZE

Not many people know there is an English speaking country in Central America, or that tiny Belize has some of the best hot sauces you'll find anywhere. So good in fact, that every one in the crew loaded up with at least a couple bottles of Hot Mama's or Marie Sharp's - give me that grapefruit habanero goodness!

People expect me to have storage box full of exotic souvenirs, but the truth is I have collected very little in my travels. Artwork doesn't hold up too well when you're constantly moving, and the few items I do manage to bring home I usually give away as gifts. In fact, as I look around my apartment, all I see is this weird clock I picked up in Malaysia, with king scorpions embossed inside it. Of all the things I didn't lose!

I do not get tired of travelling, but to be honest, a tropical jungle is a tropical jungle, and by the time you've visited four of five of them, they do start to blend in together. Yet there's always something special in each one, be it creatures, ruins, or amazing adventures. Aside from the caving, which speaks for itself, I also had a blast on an airboat in the swamps off Lamanai, racing over reeds with the roar of the propeller against my back. I often find it ironic, and a little sad, that I get the opportunity to visit such incredible places, but sometimes lack the enthusiasm of say a history buff, or an geologist, or someone who would kill a small colony of lepers for the chance to see the ruins or jungles on offer. Lamanai holds many secrets and mysteries, but my head was already underground in the limestone caves of Caves Branch, or thinking about the airboat. Good travel writers have insatiable curiosity, but also need energy and short attention spans to pack in *so* much information and variety in such a small amount of time. The moment we become absorbed in just one subject, is maybe the moment we stop travelling to seek something new.

Our crocodile story was a wash out, and to illustrate this, we decided to stand in the tropical storm doing our best impersonations of lightning rods. We foolishly tried to sit out the storm in hopes of going out on an open-roof boat to find the crocs. It belted heavy rain for days. The amazing staff at Lamanai Lodge took care of us though, with excellent food and some inspired cocktails. The Mennonites came to the rescue, adding an unusual story beat and a quirky alternative to picking up crocodiles.

As for the scorpion spider, let me just say that it scared the bejeezez out of me. It is one ugly mofo, but completely harmless. I reference my mom in the show because only she knows how petrified I was of insects growing up. And spiders. And scorpions. When people ask me if travelling around the world has changed me, I say yes: I can now hold an insect, and not just any insect. I can hold the meanest, baddest insect on the planet.

Our crew does a great job capturing our experience on film, but sometimes, it's technically difficult to project the image of a memory. Rock jumping inside a cave was a new level of thrill, but when I saw the footage, it looks kind of easy. It wasn't. There was a small gap to put your head otherwise you would crack your skull against the rock. I jumped with the camera a couple times to try and capture it, but that's like looking for details on a passing bullet. I'm going to make a sandwich now, and crack my 12th bottle of Marie Sharps habanero. It's so good it inspired a column about the best condiments in the world.

The still ruins and waters of Lamanai

MEXICO
UNMASKING LUCHA LIBRE

As published in the Globe and Mail

MEXICO CITY – Metalium has tied me into a human pretzel. He's pinned one arm behind my neck, looped my leg behind my back, and has me in a lock designed to separate one's shoulder from one's body. In an unfortunate case of lost in translation, this big, boisterous wrestling student mistook "travel writer wants to learn" for "wrestler wants to fight." The moment I entered the practice ring I was thrown against the hard ropes, picked up, slammed down, flung about, T-boned, elbowed, body kicked, rolled over and clamped tight. I'm slapping the floor with my one free palm, the frantic wave of submission, writhing in equal parts pain and shock at my latest predicament (the TV crew capturing all of this are laughing too hard to know how to stop the carnage). Serves me right for putting on a mask so I could throw myself into the story.

In Mexico, Lucha Libre refers to the high-flying world of professional wrestling. Much like its WWE counterpart in North America, Lucha Libre involves colourful characters, theatrical violence, multi-team tournaments and rabid fans of all ages. Yet Lucha Libre (literally, "free wrestling") is also known for its breathtaking acrobatics, the tradition of its masks, and as one of the best nights out for any tourist to Mexico City.

It's Friday night, and Mexico City is throbbing. The world's biggest city is renowned for its pockets of culture and art, sport and music, all connected along choking lines of traffic. Outside the Arena Mexico, the sidewalks are choked, too, as vendors sell masks, toys, T-shirts, food and all manner of wrestling paraphernalia. It takes a few moments before I become accustomed to the grown men wearing the masks of their favourite Luchadore – they look more like flamboyant bank robbers. The kids are out in force, too, for despite the violence to come, wrestling has always been fun for the whole family.

Lucha Libre was born in Mexico in the 1930's, but really took off with the advent of television in the 1950's. The rules are simple: Opponents lose if they are pinned to the mat for three seconds, removed from the ring for twenty, or disqualified for illegal holds, groin strikes or the removal of a Luchadore's mask. It is the mask that gives each wrestler his mythical allure, his character and personality. Ever since El Santo, the most famous Luchadore of all time, stepped into the ring with his silver mask, the public has been fascinated with these heroes of the ring. The mask does more than just conceal the true identity of the wrestler (who will never be named or seen without it in public); it becomes their honour, to be protected at all cost. Battles take place between arch-rivals for the right to remove the mask, and it is not uncommon for a Luchadore to lose his mask and continue wrestling, but never replace it. Others may retire a mask for a new one, allowing them to switch characters between the good "*tecnicos*" and the bad "*rudos*". I had yet to decide if I was a hero or a villain when I stepped into the ring wearing a customized mask with ESROCK glued across the top in red sequins. Metalium didn't give me a chance. Under the eyes of his watchful trainer, he was hungry to show off his skills, and the Mighty Esrock proved easy fodder. Soon enough, Metalium will be ready to enter the ring, but it will still take some time before he can earn the right to wear his own mask. Dating back to the time of the Aztecs, symbolic colours have made way for designs of beasts, angels and gods, and choosing the right mask to resonate with the buying public can make or break careers.

The announcer hypes up the crowd with his deep voice; beautiful girls in bikinis line up behind the ring. We're not so much ready to rumble as we are to marvel at the acrobatics. The hard ropes of the ring are designed to provide extra spring for the Luchadores, who are regarded as amongst the most agile and versatile of all wrestlers. Their somersaults and leaps add all the excitement of a Cirque du Soliel performance. In the practice ring, I'm not about to do a backflip off the ropes just yet, but as Metalium shows me how to roll, I ask him just how fake the fights are. He explains that moves, holds and blocks are taught so opponents know how to absorb the blows, land safely and avoid getting hurt. Which moves they use can either be rehearsed, or decided on the spot. Having thought I was a wrestler myself (Luchadores come from the US, Canada, even Japan), he assumed I would know how to block his high-flying kick to my chest. I assumed my ribs were only bruised, not broken.

Teams are battling each other in the 16,000-seat stadium, and it's pretty easy to determine the crowd favourites. The good guys play by the rules, receive their acclaim with honour and always seem to come back after receiving a horrific beating at the hands of the *rudos*. A midget in a white mask seems destined for punishment until he pulls off the most incredible manoeuvres, spinning around the heads of his opponents and throwing them out of the ring altogether. Kids are screaming their approval, the atmosphere is electric, and while the contest seems to have shifted from camp to the bizarre, the entertainment value is top notch. The best of three rounds always goes to the wire, the bad guys always threatening to remove the mask of the *tecnicos*, and in one case they actually do in what appears to be a wardrobe malfunction. The unmasked Luchadore clutches his face wildly and is led out the ring before his true identity is revealed to the masses. For unlawful unmasking, the villain is disqualified and justice is served.

Lucha Libre is a form of physical theatre designed to steam up our emotions, wow our senses and provide dazzling entertainment. With its free-wheeling high-flying moves and lack of commercialized pretension, weekly tournaments in Mexico City are guaranteed to thrill the adventurous tourist. Just don't step into the ring before you've earned your mask.

BEHIND THE SCENES IN MEXICO

OK, here is the truth behind my adventure in a Mexican wrestling ring. The plan was to meet some professional Luchadores to learn more about what they do, and maybe try a couple of the less hardcore moves. I came up with the idea of the mask and cape mainly as a sight gag for the crew, and because I'm generally an idiot. So we arrive at the stadium post-fight, but there's nobody there. It's a public holiday, and even though things had been set up weeks in advance, suddenly a key component of my story was non-existent. So our guide scours the parking lot and finds this young kid with his trainer, who agrees to show me the ropes.

Now, there might have been some language issues, a possible miscommunication or two, but whatever it was, our young, buff wrestler thought I was a wrestler myself, and wanted to play around a bit. I mean, look at my biceps; it's obvious I'm a wrestler!   Luchadores know how to take the blows, how to fall, how make it look like it hurts without it actually hurting. I didn't know shit. I climbed in the ring, goofing off as is my custom, when Metallio unleashed himself and proceeded to beat the living crap out of me. At first, I just went along with it. Then he did a flying kick that almost certainly bruised a rib. Then he tied me up and showed me what my ass looks like in red tights. The crew were crying, they thought it was so funny (there's a great shot of Paul and Neil peeing themselves), and finally I managed to communicate that I was actually getting squashed and might not survive if he continued in such a manner. At this point, the communication was cleared up and I carried on with the sequence, even though I was in utter pain and discomfort. Sometimes, when the camera is rolling, I just go for it and deal with the consequences later. You see such consequences in the credits, which makes me hurt just watching it.

The pain did go away, with the help of tequila, and lots of it. After our visit to Jose Cuervo, I have come to appreciate the finer aspects of tequila. To Mexicans, the idea of shooting back good tequila is the equivalent of the French shooting back a fine Bordeaux. It was a great story, but the very real hangover you see the next morning was actually the result of a very big night out in Guadalajara, where I ended up on stage at a live band karaoke thing singing Radiohead's Creep. Only I substituted the words to: "I'm a creeeeeeep... I'm a GRINGOOOOOO... What the hell am I doing here? I don't belong here." To which, it has to be said, I received a standing ovation, many a tequila, and the hell-on-earth hangover the following morning, which you can see in the show.

This was the last country we filmed in for the season, and we had a blast. On my day off (while Julia was out getting her spell on), I ended up getting a new tattoo (to mark yet one more unlikely adventure around the world) and going to a Manu Chao concert in a rainstorm with 30,000 people.

Ismael Gama, a jimador in the agave fields of Jose Cuervo

Colonial and surprisingly beautiful Guadalajara

Season Three

ALBERTA
COW FISTING AND HELI-YOGA

I've seen and done more than I could have ever imagined, and things have to get seriously Gonzo to surprise me these days. As Gonzo as, say, a pregnant cow with my arm shoved inside its vagina, all the way to my shoulder. One can imagine all manner of adventures, destinations and people, but what does it feel like to penetrate a cow, and why would anyone want to?   Well, it feels warm and soft and strangely pleasant once you get over the shock, and the reason behind it is, I'm on a ranch in Alberta's Porcupine Hills and I'm learning how to be a real-as-sin honest-to-goodness down-home tobacco-chewing cowboy.

Season 3 of *Word Travels* kicks into gear as we start our adventures (to 13 new countries over the summer) with a short flight from my base in Vancouver to Calgary. Cow Town. Home to a million-plus folks who can wear cowboy hats with no irony whatsoever. They take their steaks rare, their trucks big, their roads straight and their mountain ranges high. Alberta is to Canada what Texas is to the United States, only colder, smaller and seriously into ice hockey. Its oil sands (also known as tar sands) are the largest in the world, although the resulting crude is more expensive to extract than regular black gold. Canada is the largest crude oil supplier to the US, and that's a lot of goop making its way south, and a lot of money making its way back north. Fortunes are shaky with the current economic climate, but Alberta is by far the richest province in Canada, and that wealth extends into its traditions of cattle, rodeo and pioneering spirit.

My lesson this week is to learn the ways of the cowboy. The school is Skyline Ranch, a family-owned cattle ranch a ninety-minute drive south from Calgary. My teacher is Bill Moynihan, owner of the ranch and a genuine one-of-a-kind outdoorsman. His voice is like polished gravel, his hands leathered and tough, and his moustache a proud army protecting his upper lip. Bill is a former

Royal Canadian Mountie, a boxer, a bush pilot, a mountain guide, a hunter and an award-winning rodeo cowboy. At 71 years of age, he's hauling heavy blocks of hay, galloping on his horse, roping up steer and branding cattle. He chews Jack Palance and spits out Sam Elliott.

The cowboy commands admiration and respect the world over because the cowboy is the essence of masculinity. Man at his finest: tough, resourceful, honest, and in synch with land and beast. I enjoy my westerns, but I was about to find out, as I often do, that Hollywood and reality operate according to different cosmic dimensions.

Cowboys and City Slickers

The word cowboy dates back to 1725, the English translation of the Spanish *vaquero*, or cow herder. They're also known as buckaroos, but don't be calling them cowpokes – that describes the lowly person who prodded cows in cattle cars. According to a nineteenth-century US census, about 15% of all working cowboys were black, and around 15% were Mexican – a fact you don't see represented much in the movies. Low on the social ladder, cowboys earned a pittance as they participated in huge cattle drives across the emerging western United States, steering the meat to the market. The lifestyle demanded men be men, whatever their sexual preference. Their duties were many: rounding up, branding, protecting, securing, breaking in and birthing cows and horses. Cattle herds averaged around 3000 head, rounded up by just ten cowboys with three horses each. It was a tough life in a tough, unforgiving land, and this is where the image of the cowboy was born, the hard men of the west. It is interesting to note that, despite Hollywood, there were few battles with Native Americans. Cattle drives usually paid off chiefs to let the cows cross their land. The cowboys and Indians myth is exactly that – adventurous and romantic fiction written to appeal to urban dwellers hearing the call of the Wild West. By the mid-twentieth century, the introduction of a rail network, ranch fences and new farming techniques all but ended the need for cattle drives, and the heyday of the roaming cowboy came to a close. Modern cowboys, like Bill and his son Reid, work hard on the ranch and display their skills at competitive rodeo shows. The Calgary Stampede, founded in 1912, is the richest and biggest rodeo in the world, a celebration of the traditions and abilities of cowboys, and cowgirls too. Reid competes as a bareback rider, cow milker and wild horse racer, while Bill's daughter Erin was the 1993 Stampede Queen, winning several other titles, too. All this is to show that if this city slicker was going to earn his new hat, he was with the right folk to do it.

Esrock Changes Hats

The Gonzo Hat. It's been with me to 53 countries, warped and disfigured, scarred with acid rain and Chernobyl dust. I lost it in Bangkok in an airport taxi, and somehow it found its way home. I forgot it on a bus in Mexico, but managed to retrieve it just as the bus pulled off into the unknown. I left it on a train in Croatia, but made a dashing recovery, exiting the train while it was already in motion. Figuring I could keep it going for another trip around the world, I walked into Vancouver's only cowboy shop hoping they could breathe some life into the old boy. Buddy takes one look at it and says: "Let it go, man; it's over."   Finding a new travel hat is no easy feat. I went with a new white paper crushable fedora. A new look for an old traveller.   However, I hadn't counted on Albertan hospitality. No sooner was off the plane than I was presented with a new hat, albeit one that didn't fit. Exchanging it at the airport hat shop (like I said, this is Hat Country), I stumble upon a substitute Gonzo Hat, similar to the old one, also a Baileys pure wool foldable. It's in black, though, and so I am Back in Black, so to speak, ready to get shook all night long, and hit the Highway to Hell. Wearing it, you'll be happy to know, is the same Gonzo idiot. We shall learn in the coming months whether it is the hat that makes the Gonzo, or the Gonzo that makes the hat.

Back at the Ranch

We arrive at Skyline, a modest 120-acre ranch in a valley surrounded by smooth yellow hills, grazed by 300 head of fat Angus cows. Pine trees pierce the sky, hence the name Porcupine Hills, and the snow-capped Rockies frame the western horizon. Bill hands me a pair of leather chaps, I choose a smooth white stallion named Barry, and we mount up for my first adventure, rounding up the cattle. Skyline has been offering ranching vacations for some thirty years, whereby guests can participate in a number of activities, from simple horse riding treks to full-on down-and-dirty farm jobs. Reed and Erin join us, along with Katie, the happiest dog

I've ever seen, and we corral the cows forward. Weighing up 1200 lbs, the size of these cows can be intimidating. Bill tells me how a neighbour was beat up pretty good by an over-anxious cow, and a stampede would flatten anything in its path. "Do you ride much?" asks Erin, a champion cutting horse rider (cutting horses are trained to round up cattle by turning, stopping and running quicker than normal horses).

"Well, I've galloped on the plains of Mongolia, on the Jordanian desert alongside the ancient city of Petra, and in the Slovenian countryside on pure-bred Lipizzaners, but no, not really," I reply. We both pause to dwell on the absurdity of such a statement.

It takes us a while to film the action, as it always does, and Sean almost loses his $100,000 camera when the horse he's riding goes for an impromptu gallop. That he's filming on a horse in the first place is pretty nuts, but I haven't seen him this spooked since that guy threw a cobra at him in Taipei. We've travelled to 24 countries together, and conversations often run like this:

"This kind of reminds me when we were driving through that war-torn area in Sri Lanka," or "That landing was bumpier than the time we landed in Bogota." I'm sure it intrigues the hell out of eavesdroppers.

Tagging Vegetarians

It's not branding season, but I do get the chance to tag a new-born calf. Things can get pretty tricky, because mom is the size of a buffalo and protective of her three-day-old baby. Tagging is done to keep track of the cattle, as they can roam for weeks before they are herded up again. With mountain lions, wolves and bears in the area, it's not uncommon for some to go missing. Even bald eagles can swoop in and carry away young calves. Fortunately, mother cow doesn't attack as I punch a tag into the ear of the baby, number 64. It's a strange feeling to be so up close and personal (although things would get more personal still) with cows. I enjoy my meat, and somehow we've divorced the concept of beef and animal. As human beings, it's a case of us breeding new life specifically to end it. Vegetarians will no doubt be skipping this entire chapter. I certainly wouldn't want to go to the processing plant where these cattle will end up, boxed in and fattened up before being "processed" into Grade AAA Alberta beef. I wouldn't do that to myself, or to you. After all, ignorance can be delicious.

Rope burn on the Eyeball

It is playoff season in the National Hockey League, and Canada all but shuts down when a game is on. Certainly the *Word Travels* crew heads to the nearest TV when the Vancouver Canucks and the Calgary Flames are playing their US counterparts. While Sean, who films NHL games when he's in Vancouver, rejoices in an early Canucks lead, Erin teaches me the art of the lasso outside. The rope is tough and hard, wiry and not nearly as flexible as I imagined. We set up a practice steer and I learn to swing and release, roping the plastic horns before pulling back to engage the noose. Lucky brand beers are flowing, and before long, things get silly. On camera, we decide to have Bill lassoing Julia and I. If we were cows, we'd be locked in instantly, but I react like a nervous human, and step out at the last moment, the rope smashing against my face, the coarse material slicing my eyeball. It's painful and begins to swell, a cosmetic injury that will be with me for the rest of the week. Fortunately we got it on camera, so we'll be able to explain to viewers where the shiner comes from, without them thinking I must have been hitting on Reid's wife.

"When the stars are out, you can see every one of them," explains Reid as we sit around a large campfire late in the evening. This time of year it could be blizzarding in Alberta, but we were really lucky with the weather, or as our Calgary-based director Michael puts it, "we threaded the needle." We spend the night in the Victorian-styled ranch B&B, tastefully assembled by Bill's late wife. For all the cows, horses, dogs and wildlife, it is as quiet and still as a cave.

Intimate Moments with a Cow

There are more tasks to perform in the early morning hours. A pot of hot coffee fuels us up for a ride into the countryside, where we check fences that might have blown over from strong winds or wayward elk. The movie *Brokeback Mountain* was filmed in these parts (Reid even had a small part), and if you've seen the film, you'll know the beauty of the rolling hills and valleys that jut up against the Albertan Rockies. The wind is icy, and in summer temperatures can still plummet, but the valley is also blessed with the Chinook, the warm front that blows off the Pacific Ocean in

British Columbia. Things heat up when I feed the heifers from a trough and take out the tractor to feed the cows in the fields. Moving hay, shovelling shit, feeding the animals: farm life is physically tough and yet satisfyingly simple. You know what has to be done, and you do it. I had no idea what I was in for when I was called into the barn to find Bill holding a red plastic "arm condom," and the backside of a very pregnant cow. These are the moments that make great television. The goal is to make sure the calf is positioned correctly for birth, it's head between its hooves. Mama cow is restrained in a gate-like contraption to prevent her from crushing everyone the moment my hand enters her holy of holies. OK, so here goes – first the fingers, then the hand.

"You need to get in there," says Bill as I hesitantly push harder into the moist, warm void. Mama rocks her giant body, startling me as I go deeper.

"Can you feel the head, the hooves?" asks Bill.

I can, and all is in order. I gently extract my arm, greased with uterus goo, go outside, and for some reason, feel like a cigarette.

The word "dude" technically refers to someone who doesn't know cowboy culture, but pretends otherwise. You can also say that a dude is "all hat and no cattle." A dude like, say, me. Still, the hospitality from these earthy folks was wonderfully warm and genuine, the values of the modern-day cowboy alive and well. Reid might work up in the tar sands over the winter, and Skyline might earn its keep through the flow of tourists, but ranch life remains as real and alluring as the myth that promotes it.

I take Barry out on a hilltop, ponder life as a cowboy and stare out into the distance at the majesty and dramatic beauty of the Canadian Rockies. High up in those snow-capped peaks, my next adventure awaits.

Part Two: Heli-Yeah!

Take any activity, and add the word "heli" in front of it. Doesn't it sound just hella-cool! Heli-hiking. Heli-dating. Heli-flossing. Heli-ping pong. You just can't go wrong. With the help of a company called Icefield Helicopter Tours, I was about to get my heli on, and one of the best places in the world for any heli-action has got to be the Albertan Rockies.

Driving west on long, straight roads, we pass small towns and dozens of pump jacks extracting the oil that drives the province's economy. Almost running out of fuel, we stop in a small town where a beef jerky shop has 27 flavours of processed, dried meat. Once we arrive at the foothills of the Rockies, I am awestruck at the massive icing-sugar-tipped mountains. We'd be spending the night at the famous Chateau Lake Louise, one of Canada's oldest and most famous hotels, which looks out over one of Canada's most beautiful vistas. In summer, the turquoise glacial colour of Lake Louise makes it the perfect postcard photo, while the hotel, originally built by the Canadian Pacific Railway in the early 1900's, is a flagship of the luxurious Fairmont hotel chain. Surrounding Lake Louise is the UNESCO World Heritage Site, Banff National Park. Simply put, the emerald lakes, mountains and forests make this one of the most beautiful and pristine places on our planet.

Heli-Namaste

I'm driving our 15-seat passenger van, hauling ass along a valley road. Not one car passes us in over an hour, and the slight bends and long straights seem built for the super sports cars I'll soon be driving in Italy. We threaded the needle again, a clear, partly cloudy day that will allow us to truly experience, and show off, the might of the Rockies. The following day, we'd be caught in a whiteout snow blizzard, but not this day. This is my heli-day. To anchor this story we found an activity that will have people scratching their heads (and hopefully editors champing at the bit). Heli-yoga. Hell yeah!

Our heli-yoga instructor is Martha McCallum, a certified hiking guide, wildlife biologist, wellness coach and hatha yoga teacher. She vibrates with the sort of serenity I find in most yoga teachers, a calm steady voice laced with refreshing hints of optimism. Martha is aware of the fact that combining jet-fuel-powered machinery with earthy, spiritual exercise is a dichotomy of sorts, but rejoices in the fact that Icefield's helicopters are bringing people closer to nature, literally. Not only can you access the most remote of areas, the helis come and go leaving not a trace of their visit. We sign our waivers, plan out a shooting schedule of sorts, get briefed on the basics of heli-safety (see, even safety sounds cool), and climb in the back of a Jet Ranger. No jumping out the door ("or it will be the last time you jump out of anything"). Keep strapped in until Martha "invites" us out, keep low, make sure there's nothing loose around to blow into the rotors. Ralph Sliger is the sharp quick-with-a-quip owner and operator of Icefields, our guide in the air just as Martha is our guide on the land.

I heart helicopters. This is only the third time I've had the opportunity to ride in one, and each time I love it more. Even though the wind was blowing us around a fair bit, the flexibility in the air and the sight lines make you feel like you really are floating. We fly over Banff National Park, which prohibits landing, and after some sensational whirlybird's-eye views of the scenery, land gently on a spot called the Wedding Knoll. If you wanted a heli-wedding, this is where Ralph would take you. It's also the perfect spot for a bit of yoga, a clearing surrounded by snow, 2700m high, completely embedded in nature. Martha leads the yoga class while Sean leans out the second heli, harnessed in of course, to get some aerials. It's the first time we've ever used a helicopter on the show and I'm hoping the results are amazing. The wind gusts as I pull a downward dog, a warrior pose, a tree pose, and while I've done plenty of yoga before, for the first time I seriously enjoy the stretches. It's medicine for my tired and stiff ex-cowboy muscles.

We have to improvise when it comes to the heli-snowshoeing activity, since the snow is melting and we still sink to our waist. We hike up a small peak where the wind is so intense I can fully lean back without falling. It's as if we're hot pizza and the mountain is blowing on us. Exhilarating stuff, the cold, fresh win, blasting the magic of nature right through me. Neil snapped a lucky shot of me jumping in the wind, and the photo captures everything.

It's a real shame that helis are so expensive to fly and maintain, because otherwise it would be my ideal choice of travel. We hit a few more spots in the canyon, including a thrilling low-altitude meander up the river, straight out of the 80's TV show *Airwolf*. I couldn't get enough of it. By dusk, we're eating Alberta's other gift to Canada – perfectly grilled steak – and enjoying the views at the nearby McKenzie's Ranch. Laurie McKenzie, who hosts tourists throughout the year, tells me she loves the living out here, even if the population is about eight.

Even though I had never visited the Rockies before, I confess Alberta wasn't my first choice for our third and final Canadian-based episode. It just seemed too accessible, an adventure I could do one day when I'm tired of all the hectic travel. *Word Travels* gives me the incredible gift of sponsoring my journeys, and I know there's no way I would have enjoyed the Rockies the way I have in the last week without an audience of both readers and viewers to impress. In one week, I've packed in a cowboy adventure, stayed in fine hotels, and soared in the mountains. I've also met some terrific folk in a land where everyone seems to own their own Gonzo Hat. I know I'll be back, and when I do, you might want to lock up your pregnant cows.

Posing like warriors on top of the world

BEHIND THE SCENES IN ALBERTA

I've lived in Vancouver the past ten years, and, relatively speaking, the Albertan Rockies are in my backyard. Canada is the second-largest country on the planet, so "backyard" is relative, but I'd been waiting to see the Rockies for years. *Word Travels* has not only helped me find great stories, but also helped me tick something off my bucket list. Originally I had planned to go heli-skiing, which I've heard is as amazing as it sounds. But in spring, the only place we could do that was across the provincial border in British Columbia, which wouldn't do for an episode based in Alberta. So we looked around for heli-activities, and found heli-yoga. Every time I tell people about it, their jaws drop. Taking a helicopter into the mountains to find the perfect place to do yoga? It's excessive, incredible, beautiful, thrilling – all adjectives for the life of travel writing. We were staying at the gorgeous Fairmont Lake Louise, and I remember waking up that morning praying for a good weather day. With our crazy schedule, we only had one shot for the heli-story, and we needed a clear sky. As would happen most times this season, the weather played ball (perhaps to make up for the last season, where it caused a bit of havoc). Our instructor Martha was fantastic, as were the folks at Icefields Heli. Once we were done, we joined them for a beer in their quarters to watch an ice hockey game, rounding off a quintessential day in Canada.

I described Skyline Ranch's Bill Moynihan as a guy who chews Jack Palance and spits out Sam Elliott. I'm a born-and-bred city boy, and here I would be asked to spend two days with a cowboy legend, a true outdoorsman. There was no point pretending I could do half the things he could (like when he picked up two bricks of hay and I could barely hoist one), but as always, I tried to throw myself into the story and do my best. Our director of photography, Sean Cable, throws himself into his job, too, hanging out of helicopters (which you can see in the show), standing on boats and bikes. He got a little more than he bargained for when he mounted a horse for a-point-of view shot of me rustling up the cattle. Sean can ride, and he's filmed atop horses before. He just didn't expect his horse to take off on him while he was barely clutching the reins, his big expensive camera on his shoulder. To this day, I believe it's the closest he's come to losing his gear, and he has a newfound respect for horses, too. I never learned to ride horses properly, so it always amazes me that I manage to stay on. Considering horses were featured in Jordan, in Slovenia, in Alberta and later in Barbados, I think I've become pretty good at not falling off.

So the sun is setting and spirits are high. That's when you get shots like the one of Julia and I throwing our hats into the purple sky. We don't plan or script these things; they just happen. We'd had a more than a couple of cans of Lucky Beer, and I challenged Bill to lasso me up like a steer. Now, these ropes are not soft. I take off a little quicker than I should have, and Bill flicks the rope, which somehow manages to graze my eyeball. Yes, graze my eyeball. It swelled up big and red, and I wore it like a badge of cowboy honour.

I had such a great time in Alberta I went back a few months later for the Calgary Stampede, the biggest rodeo on earth. It gave me further, valuable insight into cowboy culture, and a great deal more respect, too.

Sean films me having a cow

Neil captured this epic jump shot of me at the top of a knoll

Beam Me Up! At the Star Trek museum in the town of Vulcan

With my heli-yoga instructor Martha high in the Rockies

NICARAGUA

SANDBOARDING BETWEEN HOPE AND HELL

I'd been harbouring the idea of buying some beach property in Nicaragua since I'd visited the country during that in-between year I call 2006. Central America's largest country had a distinct feeling of being just under the radar, one of the few places of beauty left where even a lowly-paid travel writer could buy a little slice of paradise before the Euros and Ameros invade with their real estate agents, buy up the country, drive up the prices and rob yet another affordable destination from us, the working-class enslaved.

Considering it is the second-poorest country in the western hemisphere, still scarred from the civil war that ravaged it through the end of the twentieth century, you would think the window of opportunity would be open for some time. After all, Nicaragua still sounds terrifically scary, stretched like the large, untracked arm on the dangerous and drug-ravaged body of Central America. Backpackers don't mind this one bit: travel junkies calling up our dealers, ordering a few more hits of Nicaragua, where waivers don't exist and anything is possible. Backpackers: The canaries in the coalmine of modern travel.

Last night I was hanging out at Bigfoot Hostel in Leon after spending the afternoon boarding down an active volcano. *As one does.* The hostel was a smorgasbord of backpackers engaged in a multitude of activities, creating the most utopian travel environment I've seen in a long time. The Dutch were reading magazines, the Americans were flirting, the Swedes were pounding a piñata, the Australians were playing pool, the English cooking dinner – a few scattered nationalities making their claim, and amongst them all a TV crew rewarding themselves for a hard day's work. Ounces of sweat lost racing up the rocky cone of Cerro Negro were being replenished by bottles of excellent seven-year-old Flor de Caña, Nicaragua's much-loved rum. A playlist of eclectic music was pushing tunes from behind the bar, where a beer costs less than a dollar and a fresh-made mojito just a little more. Spirits, to abuse the pun, were high, and the attractive gender ratio was an almost perfect split. If you press your ear to this page, you can overhear snippets of conversation:

"I was in Costa Rica, and everyone was telling me about Nicaragua."

"We only came to Leon for a few days, and we've been here over a week."

"So, there's no other country in the world where you can sandboard a volcano?"

"Have you been to the north? It's incredible!"

"Have you been to the south? It's incredible!"

"Usually we feel nervous travelling as girls, alone, but it's been fine here."

"Dos cervesas, por favor."

"You guys have the best job in the world."

Fast forward to the scene tonight, as I type these very words. I am in a hotel located in the hills of Matagalpa, coffee and cocoa country. The hotel is basic by North American standards, but it's the finest hotel in the city. In the lobby, where wireless Internet is available, there is not a single soul around, unless you count the occasional unidentifiable insect crawling across the tiled floor. The ground floor L-shapes into the restaurant-bar, and by 9:30 p.m., it is empty, too. It rains up here in coffee country, and the air feels as sticky as the floor in my hotel room, where the sheets are sticky, too, but I'd rather not think about that. The crew are off in the countryside filming a home stay for Julia's segment of the show, and here I am, feeling very much like a blind assassin in a Mango Republic. Or perhaps a consultant for an unfair-trade coffee multi-national battling with ethical demons. This is not to say this small town isn't salsa dancing away with the rest of Nicaragua on this sticky night. I'm sure the local bars and hostels are busy, but they're about a half hour's walk away down a washed-out hill as steep and slippery as the ethics behind modern genetics. In Nicaragua, hotels cater to business, politics and charities, while the real fun rests on the backs of the backpackers. However, I don't expect this will last very long.

Eco-tourism has boomed in Costa Rica, and you can hear the shockwaves all the way here in its northern neighbour of Nicaragua. It also has jungles and surfing, fresh lakes, hills and adventurous volcanoes. The country doesn't begin to approach Costa Rica's tourist infrastructure, but it's starting to make a concerted effort, and it certainly has the eco-goods to back it up. In Leon, I do not encounter a single McDonald's or Starbucks, or any other western chain known for chasing western crowds. Walk in any direction from Central America's largest cathedral and you'll find tiny shops selling local goods at local prices (even if by local I mean cell phones and cheap clothes and plastic toys). Young gringos are plentiful, safely roaming around, taking photos, returning from Spanish class. On my first visit, I was charmed, and now I am charmed again.

I was also surprised by Managua, the capital city. Expecting massive crowds, noise and pollution, instead I discovered a leafy sprawled-out city where the traffic runs smooth, the horn is only used in emergencies and heaving crowds were nowhere to be found. While I noticed plenty of security guards, barbed wire and high walls, I didn't notice much in the way of the elements they are designed to subdue. Even when we headed directly into the largest garbage dump in Central America.

NGO's are often all that stands between poverty-stricken people and total social collapse. Their work is important, but other than the surge in voluntourism, not the usual fodder for a perky newspaper travel section. For the 28th episode of *Word Travels*, however, we headed to La Chureca to find out about an organization that has been established to help the kids who literally live in the country's filth. An estimated 175 families live in this open-air garbage dump, earning $1 to $2 a day by sorting through the garbage to recycle plastic and glass containers brought in by a seemingly endless supply of overflowing garbage trucks. Welcome to the other side of environmentalism. Disease is rampant. Glue sniffing is prevalent. Barefoot men, women and children comb hills of trash, sifting through used condoms, dead animals, rotting food and other waste for anything that can be salvaged or sold. Burning piles of stench create a low-lying muddy cloud, a mist that browns the skin and reddens the eyes. It is the closest version of hell I have seen on my travels, so what the hell am I doing here?

Nica HOPE is one of several NGO's that have been set up to help educate and support the growing number of children living in such conditions. It is spearheaded by Deanna Ford, a young American with a seemingly unlimited supply of hope and compassion. Her acts of kindness and sacrifice give me hope for humanity in general. Yet the cynic in me looks for the catch, the reason why anyone would want to slave away in the oppressive heat of Managua to help strangers buried in the rubble beneath the bottom rung of the lowest social ladder. It makes me feel terrible, which I suppose is the point. Nica HOPE, founded by Deanna in 2007, is clearly the brainchild of someone who knows they can make a difference, and has the education and experience to go about doing it. We meet at Nica HOPE's centre, where a few-dozen kids are busy making jewellery. The organization takes them out the dumps, puts them into schools and teaches them skills, hygiene and that life exists beyond the glue addiction and garbage. Simple but creative bracelets, necklaces and earrings are sold around the country, and the money supports the kids and their families. Deanna acknowledges the fact that children, mostly under the age of 10, are indeed working on the premises, but at least it's on their own terms, for their own benefit and away from the diseases, drugs, prostitution and abuse in La Chureca. Nica HOPE is not into child labour. Nica HOPE is into child saviour.

You can see the brown, acidic fumes of La Chureca hanging over the city from the hills, where the old presidential palace was destroyed along with much of Managua in the earthquake of 1972. Over seventy fault lines run through Lake Managua, and the city is sporadically pockmarked from the last big quake, which killed over 5000 people and redesigned the city map. We drive a few blocks from the Nica HOPE centre, following beastly garbage trucks with young boys hanging off the end. On a potholed, dusty dirt road, our van edges into the City of Trash. Trash, piled thirty feet high, stretching as far as the eye can see. Burning piles of plastic and rotten food create fires of oil, the gray dust caking the people, animals and shacks found within cleared mounds and tin shacks. We visit a family not far into the dump, the kids barefoot and covered in grime. A baby pig struggles in a puddle of mud, a few bony horses, dogs and cows walk by. One kid is high on glue, his eyes like a pinball, his face alternating between helplessness and a threatening violent sneer. Four young girls under the age of ten walk by with a collection of salvaged garbage. I see a dead bird in a bag, strips of plastic, the odd condom wrapper and syringe. And the trucks keep coming in, one by one, delivering a new round of cast-off misery.

Several Managua tour operators now offer La Chureca drive-ins, where tourists enter, take some photos and leave in sorrow but with a good story to tell. Call it Poverty Tourism. You can find it in the townships of Soweto or in the *favelas* of Rio. The attraction of seeing the pitiful extent of wretchedness lies on many levels. Some tourists want to see the reality, not just sugarcoated tourist attractions. Some want to understand the poverty, and help in any way they can. Others merely want to feel better about their own lot in life, because no matter how bad it seems, it's infinitely more pleasant than watching teenage girls whore themselves in a garbage dump. Others seek out photos and fodder for dinner parties. As a travel writer, I'm at odds as to how to approach this. The line between exploitation and discovery, fun and experience, is often too thin to walk on. I talk about this with Deanna. How can I write about this and profit from the result? How can I write without being sensationalist? How can I contrast this segment in our TV show with the next one, a thrilling adventure involving carefree backpackers sandboarding off an active volcano? These thoughts swilled in my head like ice cubes in a strong drink, until I finally make peace with a few compromises of my own.

1. Any money I make from this story, if I make any at all, will be added to my donation to Nica HOPE. $30 a month sponsors a child, providing education, clothing, food and, most of all, a future (I ended up donating $250 to NICA Hope from the sale of the story).

2. If I expose the misery of Managua without the beauty of Leon, I'd be treating Nicaragua as different, and that's all Deanna wants us to do: treat these poor kids like they are human beings, and the country like it belongs.

I don't do well with human zoos, and having visited ugliness the world over, I would and could just as easily visit beauty. The Red Cross, Doctors Without Borders, NGO's like Nica HOPE... we cast our lots and choose our path. I look around this dumpsite, and just as its inhabitants scour the filth in the hope of finding value, I scour the despair and pull out the optimism and positive actions of Deanna and her friends. In La Chureca the inhabitants sift through commercial waste in search of the means to sustain their survival. In La Chureca, Nica HOPE sifts through human waste in search of potential and the means to sustain our compassionate humanity.

Phil and Gemma have taken over Bigfoot Hostel in Leon, and they've got their system down, their smiles up and their shit sorted. En route from Managua to Leon, they reckon the best place to wash off the gloom of grime is in a fresh, clean and clear volcanic lake at the Laguna De Apoyo. Crater's Edge is run by Vancouverites who have carved out their slice of paradise with a property overlooking the stunning crater lake. I like places that pay attention to details, and they've done a bang-up job. The contrast between the morning's encounter with poverty, leaving a coffee-stained ring of despair around the circles of our eyes, and the sheer beauty and atmosphere of Crater Lake was stark. Under bright stars, we dine, drink and dance, swimming to a wooden jetty, screaming like banshees into the night. Well, at least I did, and when I couldn't see a moon, I decided to give the night one. Off go the bathing suits. Says Ann, just after dinner:
"Make yourself at home. The water is 27C, clean, with nothing that can hurt you whatsoever. Have fun!" And, oh boy, we did.

Hell returns the following morning in the form of a rum hangover. Good, cheap coffee helps (50c for an espresso, anyone?), but I still see stars when I close my eyes. We stop off to visit Angel Miguel in the town of San Juan de Oriente, which is trying to revert its name to the original Mud Plates, where Nicaraguan pottery was founded. We watch Miguel take a lump of clay and effortlessly mould it into a ceramic bowl, pot or vase. As with many villages in the country, small houses are brightly painted, walling along narrow streets with low-hanging trees. Two little girls smile at me from the doorway of the local church. A teenage couple flirt against an orange wall, oblivious to my observations. That they are so unselfconscious feels like a gift. Miguel demonstrates his craft and I take my seat at the low-spinning wheel, attempting to make art when we all know I'm going to make one hell of a mess. It doesn't take long before I've got a clay facial, mud all over my clothes and a cow patty, which, with some quick thinking, gets called an ashtray.

Darryn, the crazy Aussie who figured out exactly how to sandboard down Cerro Negro without killing oneself, sold his hostel and operation to Phillip of Barbados, and tours continue to leave Bigfoot daily loaded with backpackers eager to enjoy the latest, greatest activity on the Central American gringo trail. Due for eruption, Cerro Negro is a perfect cone of hard, sharp black granite, sitting as just one pearl in a necklace of volcanoes surrounding Leon. Darryn tried fridge doors and mattresses before settling on strips of wood affixed with metal and plastic stabilizers and a design that allows you to sit, hold on tight and hope you don't tumble down the rocks. Although you wear protective orange overalls and plastic goggles, more than one sled has tipped, depositing its rider into the granite, resulting in cuts, bruises and the occasional gash. Not that anyone really minds; they're having too much fun.

It's a forty-five-minute drive out of Leon at the back of an open-top 4x4, exposed to the blazing sun and tales of traveller ribaldry. Cerro Negro, the youngest volcano in Central America, lies within a national park, and I take the opportunity to cuddle a couple of iguanas at the entrance, protected and bred to be released into the wild. Later, I would see men peddling iguanas on the side of the highway, a key ingredient in a local soup. I'm sure they taste like chicken.

We grab our boards and begin a strenuous climb around the back of the volcano. It doesn't take long before we crest along the lip, where the wind is cranked and we can barely hear each other speak. Gas and fumes rise ominously from the crater below, and you can see the lava flow from the last eruption in August 1999, which covered Leon in ash and destroyed the surrounding scrub. It looks like a large tin of black paint tipped over, smothering the bush in inky goo, hardened in the unforgiving sun. If the volcano were to erupt today, everyone would be instantly incinerated. Says Kim from Sydney: "I can see it already, in a newspaper: a story about backpackers killed on some volcano in Nicaragua, and everyone thinking, 'Well, of course. What the hell were they doing there in the first place, the idiots?!'"

Cerro Negro will erupt one day, but not this day. We make it to the launch pad just in time to catch another perfect sunset. There's no time to run into the crater as I did last time, but plenty time to experience wind so strong it creates new hairstyles. Last week I got the icy blast in the Rockies; this week, a hot blast in the bush. As a force of nature, wind can be truly exhilarating.

Arms straight, back up, use your feet to stabilize. Sean gives me the OK. We're the first TV crew to film this properly, and we're going to do it right. The countdown, and I'm off. Black sand, stone and rocks fly into my face, scratching my knuckles, grinding against the wood and metal. I'm wired for sound but can't speak or I'll be eating granite. A large bump almost sends me flying, but somehow I stay on, a backpacker cowboy at a wild volcano rodeo. A speed gun is a new addition, and someone clocked 72 km/hr yesterday. I'm nowhere near that speed, but I don't need to be going fast to enjoy this descent. We've timed it with the last spike of sunshine, and no sooner do I hit the bottom than the sky turns the shade of a glowing blueberry. Michael runs up for a reaction, and all I can do is drop the F-Bomb, lean back and scream. Cold beers are presented; wounds are called for (nobody tumbled on this day). We look like we've just emerged from a coal mine. On the drive home I hop aboard the roof, watch the stars pop from the sky and wave at young boys riding bareback on skinny horses. I called this the hottest edge of adventure tourism a few years ago. It still is.

Back at the hostel, enjoying the best pizza in the city, a couple of *mojitos* and whatnot, I realize that nothing has changed much in Leon these past few years, and hopefully nothing will. Politically and economically, Nicaragua appears to be at the mercy of its populist president, Daniel Ortega. Corruption and poverty are rampant, and Gemma reminds me that visiting any country as a tourist, as opposed to actually living there, are two very different beasts. The Internet is down for a couple of days, roads are in disrepair, service is slow and bribes must be paid. These and other aspects might keep Nicaragua from becoming Costa Rica, at least for the meantime. And for the meantime, we the canaries don't seem to mind.

BEHIND THE SCENES IN NICARAGUA

This would be my second visit to Nicaragua, and I couldn't pass off the opportunity to once again sandboard down an active volcano. When I first did it, a few years ago, I couldn't believe such a thing still existed. No waivers, no crazy safety equipment, just a bunch of backpackers doing what they do – having fun on the edge. It became one of my biggest-selling stories, and I felt flattered to find a printout from my Chicago Tribune feature stapled to the activity board outside Bigfoot Hostel. Now I was returning with a TV crew, and I wanted to show the world, visually, what I experienced a few years back. Leon is a great city to visit, and held fond memories. As for Bigfoot, it's the definition of a well-run hostel, crammed with travellers from dozens of countries, good music and cheap booze, and in a city like Leon it's the kind of place you can easily get stuck in. Now walking up the volcano with an awkward wooden board is one thing; try carrying a camera and heavy tripod. Whenever I find myself bitching about anything on this series, I always think about the other guys you don't see, working in the background, dealing with their gear and the task of making me look good. I think Neil grew a new shoulder that day on the volcano. When I got back home, I asked my mom to make a tripod shoulder pad to help in the future. She did, and it did.

I had a very real concern about doing the volcano boarding story in the same episode that would feature poverty tourism. One is fun, one is serious, but how do I do both without coming across as being insensitive? How do we transition from backpacker party to people living in abject squalor?   La Curecha is as shocking as it looks, a little piece of hell right here on earth. I've done tours in Soweto outside Johannesburg, and a few months before, a *favela* tour in Rio de Janeiro. It fascinates me that tourists want to see the other side of the beaches. I want to see it, too, but it's a fine line between cultural exchange and exploitation. I was trying to figure out an angle, eventually settling for a story that examined the trend itself, using my experiences as a platform. I donated my payment for this story to Nica HOPE, which is doing important work in La Curecha.

The scene where I wake up on a beautiful crater lake was shot the day after La Curecha. Sometimes you drink to celebrate, and sometimes you drink to forget. It was a case of both that night – celebrating our luck and good fortune in living where and how we do, and trying to forget those tragic and disturbing images of kids surviving in garbage. Not that we ever would.

Getting ready to launch myself off an active volcano, an adventure that I discovered backpacking in 2006

An episode of contrasts: Kids in La Chureca pushing garbage

GEORGIA
THE ONE IN EUROPE

Admit it, you've heard the name Georgia in the news but don't know much about it. Where it is (even more or less), what language they speak, what they're famous for, what religion they follow. OK, then I'll admit it. When news reports first surfaced that Russia had invaded Georgia in August 2008, it was no surprise that residents of Atlanta choked the emergency lines, clogged the freeway and loaded up on ammunition. This small country in the Caucasus region of Eurasia has remained mostly under the radar since its 1991 independence from the collapsed Soviet Union. Suddenly, it found its radars being bombed by Russian jets, and it's wiki page bombed by millions of confused Americans.

The August War of 2008 dominated headlines for a few weeks as Russia and Georgia sparred over an ethnic enclave called South Ossetia. It's the kind of remote yet geo-sensitive conflict that would make a great post-Cold-War spy movie starring Clive Owen. As it happened, I was just weeks away from landing in the capital of Tbilisi, ready to film an episode for the second season of *Word Travels*. The fighting was mostly north, and it seemed we still might have had a chance, until bombs landed around Tbilisi itself and we diverted to Slovenia, instead. A year later, we once again reached out to our contacts, and after a long thirty-two-hour transit from Vancouver via Amsterdam, then via Istanbul, we arrived in Georgia.

Georgian script, called Mkhedruli, has deep historical influences, which somehow invoke memories of Thailand. Georgian itself flows off the tongue and sounds unlike any language I've come across. *Gamarjoba* means "hello," *gmalobt* means "thanks," and *vxvdebi rasac gulisxmob* means "I know what you mean," which, of course, I don't. Rounding off the facts, there are some 4.7 million people living in Georgia, surrounded by Russia, Turkey, Armenia, Azerbaijan and the Black Sea. The currency is the *lari*, 82% of the country are Orthodox Christians, they're close to joining NATO and have a crazy history stretching back thousands of years across snowcapped mountains and lush green plains. They also drive like lunatics, feast like there's no tomorrow and are friendly as hell. In other words, the kind of Eastern European country everyone should visit, but very few people do.

Tbilisi is overlooked by the impressive fourth-century Narikala fortress, spiked with gold church domes that sparkle in the sun while frenetic traffic hauls ass along streets blessed with surprising and excellent public art. The Kura River meanders alongside old churches and tree-lined boulevards. The exhaust smog can parch the throat, but there's plenty of historical juice to quench it. Sacked by everyone from the Mongols to the Persians, Turks, Byzantiums and Arabs, and Russians, too, I walk across the landmark Metekhi Bridge and learn how hundreds of thousands of Georgians were beheaded by the Persians, right here, for refusing to walk over their Christian icons. Georgians are a ferociously brave lot, boldly outspoken, steeped in nationalist pride. They couldn't wait to declare independence from the USSR (called the Rose Revolution), but also found themselves in a civil war shortly afterwards, mired in an ongoing battle with separatists in regions like South Ossetia and Abkhazia. These and other newly acquired facts were helping me to focus on anything other than the fact that I was sprawled out naked on a marble slab with a man walking on my back.

You can spot the Abanotubani bathhouse district by its upside-down brick teacup domes. Built in the seventeenth and eighteenth centuries, royalty and locals have long enjoyed the healing qualities of the natural, hot, stinky sulphur springs that feed the mosaic pools in the traditional bathhouses. Writers, too, like Dumas and Pushkin, and now myself, butt-naked for the cameras and sweating from the heat even as my body sits submerged in water. I've waited a long time for my first full Turkish-like bath experience, so I have no idea what to expect when I am summoned to an adjoining marble room. A man tells me to lie on my stomach, and the moment I do, he proceeds to scrub the living crap out of me. After dousing me in hot water, he walks up and down my back before taking a coarse rope to exfoliate my inner organs. I turn over, and he proceeds to scrub my chest so hard my nipples barely hold their grip. I have to clutch my crotch in a protective manner, an action that my future children should be grateful for. Another bucket follows of hot sulphur water over my head, stinging fresh, raw skin. I recently read a book called *The Dirt on Clean*, learning about the fascinating history of hygiene. Did you know Romans never used soap, preferring to scrape the skin with an instrument called the strigil?   Did you know that Americans considered warm or hot baths effeminate for men, or that seventeenth-century royalty bathed just a handful of times in their entire lives?   Public bathhouses have been popular since the Romans, a central meeting point open to everyone along the social ladder. When the plague hit Europe, medical geniuses at the time shut down the bathhouses to stop the spread of the infection. In fact, it might well have helped rid people of the fleas carrying the problem in the first place. Still, Georgia's position as a crossroads on the Silk Road, infusing European, Asian and Islamic customs, ensured that bathhouses continue to exist today.

My washing continues with a soapy foam that gets deeply massaged into my body (and my mouth), before I get rinsed once more and the ordeal is over. Never have I felt so clean, so utterly devoid of dirt. As I leave the Erekle Bathhouse, a Georgian rugby team are waiting in the dark, musky foyer. A dozen huge sweaty men, ready to strip naked and soak their battered skin in the same pool from which I had just emerged. Timing, my friends, is everything.

For this episode, we're investigating stories of Georgia's past, present and future. The night we arrive, local rock bands put on a show for us as Julia opens a journalistic guitar case on something called Brutal Death Metal. Not just Death, mind you, but Brutal Death. The ponytailed musicians look more like computer technicians than the tattooed killers I was expecting, but along with the promoters Givi and Giorgi, they're trying to deal with the power failure that has relegated their gig to darkness. After spending thirty-two hours in transit, and having been practically flayed alive, the prospect of audible torture is confirmed when the lights flick on at eleven p.m., and the first band takes to the stage. I opt out of this one, head back to the Hotel Tiflis and lie awake on my single bed, buzzing from overstimulation. Given my hopscotch on three continents today, I can't help but feel very far away from everything I know, and everyone I love.

Pity the Information Warrior who pleads for respite, for a sharpened battleaxe waits to tear him limb from limb. Here's one for you: Did you know that there is a medieval martial art in Europe? As fast, deadly and intricate as practitioners of karate, kung-fu, taekwondo or judo, Georgian mountain warriors developed systems of self defence that gave them a reputation as being the finest fighters in Christendom, systems encompassing holds, grips, wrestling, boxing and a variety of vicious weapons. Under Soviet rule, in which cultural traditions were prohibited and repressed, Georgian martial arts were all but forgotten, barely kept alive by a handful of old men in the mountains. Since the early 1990's, guys like Lasha Kobakhidze have worked hard to revive these traditions, founding a federation, opening training schools, and incorporating the various systems into a complete martial art they've named Khridoli. The name comes from ceremonial wrestling tournaments in which Georgians would fight with one hand tied behind the back. Even with this disadvantage, limb breaking and serious injury were common, but I was happy to learn that today's Khridoli keeps the carnage to a minimum. Instead, it's about re-establishing a national treasure, and honing mind and body. In a country that still walks the precipice of war, there's something to be said for reintroducing an ancient custom that once made mincemeat of enemies.

I meet Lasha at an old Soviet military gym. Fading cement walls remind me of my visit to the abandoned city of Prypiat outside Chernobyl. The legacy of Soviet times are everywhere, from the battered Lada cars on the road to old hammer and sickle statues, engravings of Lenin on buildings and ugly squat cement apartment buildings. In this bleak gym, twenty young men have gathered to kick, punch, stab and wrestle that era to the loser mat of history. I am handed a traditional warrior outfit, heavy and woollen, the rough wool scratching my recently polished skin. It is 200 years old, and was procured from a family for around $2500. The men stand in a line before training, crossing themselves in prayer to the Virgin Mother, honouring the past. Warm-ups in the boxing ring involve jumping over two, three, four men, landing on both hands in a fluid somersault. I join the group, landing awkwardly on my left foot, still smarting from a motorbike that fell on it a few months ago. I show no pain, and some of the men turn to each other, nodding their approval. I am one of the few outsiders who have been exposed to this ancient form of defence, and surrounded by its most fervent practitioners, it's best I take things seriously.

Archil, my translator, explains the thought behind each system as Lasha prepares me to wrestle. Both hands behind the back, using nudges, shoulder and head butts, trips and feints to fell the opponent. Lasha is smaller than me, but I feel like I'm barging into a brick wall. "If you can beat your opponent with both hands behind your back," says Archill, "imagine what you can do with them in the front."   Body positioning is key. I try to lift Lasha up and find it impossible. I join five guys trying to push over just one, who somehow resists our thrusts. During another wrestling exercise, involving one hand behind the back, the other in a handshake, my arm socket is almost wrenched out, my wrist almost snapped clean. There's all manner of painful Georgian goodness that can be unleashed on your opponent in such an encounter, even if they were practiced for mostly folk festivals. Next up, Archil explains how to bend your body into a blow so that you can absorb punches. A lean, shirtless bald man with eyes that would intimidate a cobra stands opposite Lasha. Apparently this guy killed a three-year-old bull with a punch, or maybe it was just his stare. They begin punching each other in the face, hard enough for the clap to echo in the gym. Lasha asks me to hit him in the face. I prod, I push, but I just cannot bring myself to punch a guy surrounded by heavily armed buddies. They laugh. "Hit him harder! Don't worry; be strong!"   It's like standing on the edge of a mountain connected to a harness. You can lean back, it's safe, but your brain won't let you. I could punch Lasha in the face as hard as I could, but my brain just refuses. That credit I earned in the warm-up fast evaporates.
"When you punch a man, it must be like you want to go right through him," says Lasha, and for the next half hour I watch the group train by beating on each other, absorbing the blows, including five men on one. I join in the thrashing, and the victim bulldozes me with a shoulder charge, sending me flying. As punishment for this act of defending himself against the gringo, the others raise their game, kicking and punching with a little more force. All I can think about is the unlucky Turk or Persian or Arab who faced a Georgian warrior one on one. My imagination can hear their bones crack.

I discovered Khridoli through clips I found on YouTube, and our visit has caught the attention of local media. When foreigners are filming a Georgian tradition that many Georgians don't know much about, it must mean something. A TV crew from a national public station are in the gym filming our film crew filming me. I am also interviewed by a local newspaper, and another TV crew, too. They are curious as to why we'd flown halfway around the world to focus on a forgotten tradition and something as underground as brutal death metal. Simply put: That's how we roll.

We move on to the Narikala Fortress, a spectacular setting for a public display of Khridoli. En route, a blown tire gives the opportunity to amble along to an old Soviet housing estate. Locals look at us like we've arrived from another planet, but the atmosphere is more one of curiosity than of threat. Automobilic relics sit like skeletons in the grass. We eventually decide to take a taxi, and I notice that just about every car that passes us has some form of damage. A BMW chugs past, half the car crushed from several rolls in the not-too-recent past. Windows are smashed. Bumpers absent. Georgians seem to drive whatever will move, and drive it however they feel the need to.

Narikala is as impressive as Edinburgh Castle, yet casts a more authentic and medieval shadow on the city. Roadwork necessitates a detour, as does a large demonstration that has been calling for the resignation of the current president for weeks. We pass a striking modern glass building with a helipad, and learn that it is the residence of a billionaire Russian oligarch. Old buildings are crammed together, their roofs perfect for Clive Owen to race across chasing a frightened informant (I watched *The International* on the plane, and the final scene in Istanbul might as well have been filmed here). A TV tower is in the distance, and at night it's lit up like a disco, adding an impressive element of eye candy. There are few tourists. Some guys from Greece. Switzerland. Belgium. I meet some Israelis who are here on business. This is not tour bus country. An Armenian wedding crowds the central square near Shardeni Street, a part of the Old Town enjoying a renaissance with its trendy outdoor cafes and bars. The US rapper Ja Rule is performing in a club this weekend, which is kind of weird, and I see signs advertising kosher food for the 10,000 Jews who live in the city, one of the oldest-surviving Jewish communities in the world, dating back as far as the sixth century BC. Tbilisi has prided itself on its religious tolerance for centuries, and while there's no shortage of churches, nearly 10% of the city is Muslim. A functioning mosque, synagogue and eastern and oriental church are all located within 500m of each other in the Old Town. My guide Nica points out that both Sunni and Shiite Muslims worship in the same mosque, proving the point.

In my old medieval warrior treads, I learn how to use various weapons. Swords, shields, whips, knuckle spikes, archery – my favourite is the *tabari*, a large and heavy axe. The trick is to follow the trajectory of the movement, spinning as I slice and dice the invading army. Everyone takes several steps back, no doubt thinking of the headline: Travel Writer Decapitates Film Crew in Freak Medieval Weapon Accident. Regardless, a *Lord of the Rings* fanboy like myself is in heaven. It's much harder getting the bow to release the arrow, and I struggle to flick the whip and generate a gunshot crack. Demonstration fights on the old fort's walls appear straight out of a movie, the swords clanging while the entire city is sprawled out beneath them. Not for the first time, hopefully not for the last, I surge with travel buzz as Sean films me on the old wall, practising with two swords, the late-afternoon sun breaking through the storm clouds behind me. I had a vivid imagination as a child. I could turn a candle into a Jedi light sabre, a coat hanger into a six-shooter, and battle my way through epic fight scenes where my aim would always be true. I'm 34 years old. Standing on that castle wall, clad like an ancient warrior, it occurs to me that not much has changed.

There are only about 500 people practicing Khridoli in Georgia, and there's nobody practicing this elaborate martial art outside the country. I ask Lasha why it's not practised in the military as a form of defence and source of national pride. "Now, we have American military instructors; before, we had Russians," he shrugs. The Georgian Martial Arts Federation is, however, growing, and their performances at festivals around the country are drawing attention. It drew mine.

Traditional Georgian cuisine consists of the following:
1. Roasted eggplant stuffed with a walnut-garlic-herb mix
2. Dumplings (*khinkali*) stuffed with mixed meats

3. Cheese bread (*khachapuri*) – the smellier the cheese, the better
4. Mushrooms fried in garlic and herbs
5. BBQ'd pork, chicken, veal or lamb
6. Tomato and cucumber salad; various strong cheeses
7. Salted and herbed nugget potatoes, roasted to perfection
8. A spicy tomato and savoury herb sauce for the meat
9. Kern-baked bread shaped like long triangles
10. Stuffed roasted red peppers with walnut-garlic-herb mix
11. Heart, lung and liver mashed into a starter
12. Flavoured nuclear-coloured lemonade (tarragon, vanilla, pear)
13. Copious quantities of sweet red and white wine

This has been the menu for the last week, and I have come to know these dishes very well: what combinations work, when to subtly remove the cheese bread because you can't see the table from the water pouring out of your eyes. It is far more delicious than I expected, and different from other cuisines I've had the good fortune to consume, although slugging back sweet wine does take some getting used to.

Georgians don't know which came first: the wine, or the people to drink it. There are some 200 endemic species of grape here, and the growing, making, preserving and drinking of wine is a cherished national custom. Wine in Georgia?   Believe it, and in such varieties and quantities you cannot imagine. The sweet nectar of the white Rkatsiteli or red Saperavi grape is coaxed into countless homemade wineries using centuries-old underground clay barrels. Visiting villages in Kakheti, the wine-growing region, is far removed from your average slick western wine tour. We enter damp, dark cellars, a local family pulling out their most treasured homemade elixir with a customary display of Georgian hospitality. The wine is… complicated, young on the nose, sweet on the palate. It's also high in sugar and alcohol, and is the oil that lubricates traditional social feasts. Tbilisi had faded into green plains covered in vineyards. Abandoned but restored castles add a different touch, as do old men and women sitting on the side of the road watching life and traffic go by. Historical buildings and churches in Georgia are unpretentious, medieval, and seemingly everywhere. Our destination is Signagi, a small, scenic town that hosts many of the country's festivals and which looks over a vast valley to the snow-capped "Caucasian" mountains in the distance.

<Note> On the word Caucasian. It has come to denote people of the white race, but its origins are controversial and somewhat distasteful. The word has subsequently been abandoned in scientific circles. From what I can gather, it was coined by a German anthropologist in 1775 who discovered skulls around the Caucuses Mountains belonging to ancestors of the fair-skinned people in the region. From this, all fair-skinned people were therefore said to have origins in the Caucuses, although he conveniently ignored the fact that there were dark-skinned people living in the region, too. Praising this beautiful race of men, the smug anthropologist made no bones about stressing that dark-skinned people were degenerate, which is why race groups in the US have gone to the Supreme Court to rid English of the word. So the next time you hear a TV cop say "Caucasian, six feet two, carrying a large gun," he's using a discredited term more suited for loser asshole supremacists. </Note>

Back to Signagi, heavily restored and promoted as a centre for Georgia's fledgling tourism industry: views of the old, sun-baked church steeples and the long medieval city wall will make any camera smile. Tonight, I am partaking in Supra, the ritual of traditional Georgian feasting. A long table has been set, crowded with all the above-mentioned menu items, and I sit next to the *tamada*, the toastmaster. It is his responsibility to propose toasts, blessings and designations. The fun part is that each toast necessitates the emptying of a full wine glass. Beer drinkers might want to know that Georgians toast their friends with wine, their enemies with beer. The first toast is made, Nick translating the ceremonial language, and we slug back the wine. Since grapes and their skins are not separated, the sweet white wine has the colour of whiskey and is served in a constantly refilled clay jar. The four men at the head of the table bust out into a traditional polyphonic Georgian folk song, their harmonies perfect, the volume pure. No sooner has the glass been filled than another toast is called, this time using a horn that, once drained, is filled up and passed around for each member to make a toast too. You can see where this is going.

Several glasses in the gut, I'm standing up and using the finest flowery language I can muster to praise Georgian hospitality,

Georgian food, Georgian language, Georgian wine. I draw attention to its unfortunate challenges in the political and economic sphere, but assure my esteemed guests there is no doubt Georgia will triumph and take its rightful place as one of the most vibrant and distinct nations in the world. I praise my film crew, who have spent the last week capturing my experience and joy. I praise my co-host, my production team, our guides, and the sun, moon and stars. "Georgians have a rich tradition of being warriors, and it's people like Nick and his tourism company who are the new Georgian warriors of a new age, the Information Warriors spreading your traditions to lands far and near!" As Nick translates, he cannot help adding, "You're good at this." I slug back the horn, and soon enough I'm standing and singing at the top of my lungs. It is clear that these men are not performing; they're living, breathing and drinking their cultural tradition in a way that strongly makes me want to reconnect with my own.

Next morning, I strongly want to reconnect with whatever's left of my skull. Naturally, the evening spilled over onto the cobblestones of Signagi, and I'm thankful I managed to escape before four more jugs made their appearance, even if my director Peter did somehow manage to get into a drunken knife fight. Some guys get all the luck. For the first time in twenty-eight episodes, I'm forced to stop the bus, on the winding steep road out of Signagi, and run for the bushes. Ian Mackenzie, editor of *Brave New Traveler* and the newest member of the *Word Travels* team, helms the Puke Cam, my Brave New Breakfast splashing against the nettle bushes. The drive back in our pimping van is fraught with overtaking on blind corners and hills, but maybe a head-on collision would make the pain stop. I'm interviewed later that evening by a journalist from *Georgia Today* who explains that Georgians can hold their wine like no one else. Certainly better than me.

This week, I learned a lot about a splendid little country that far exceeded my expectations in every shape and form. From the bathhouses to the toast-making, the heavy metal show to the training gym, I'm reminded that the best travel comes from authentic encounters, when locals involve you in their normal way of life and treat you more like a friend than a tourist. They realized, as we do, that this was an opportunity to introduce "the other Georgia" to a curious, oft-confused world.

BEHIND THE SCENES IN GEORGIA

Sometimes I have expectations, and sometimes I really have no idea what to expect. When I told friends we were going to film an episode in Georgia, I had to distinguish that this was not Georgia the US state (something we do in the episode, too). We were actually supposed to film there last year. Everything had been set up and arranged, and then the Russians invaded. Initially we had thought it was one of those skirmishes that wouldn't impact our filming in Tbilisi until bombs started dropping on the runway of the international airport. So we ended up in Slovenia instead, but, fortunately, had another opportunity to visit this year. What we found was an interesting country filled with friendly people and unusual stories. The war was still on people's minds, but it didn't stop them from hosting us with superb food, sweet wine, and plenty of laughs. We decided in this episode to incorporate both myself and Julia into each other's stories, just to see what would happen. The results were pretty funny, as Julia voices her very real concern that I might lop off her head with that big medieval axe (my favourite line: "Travel writer decapitates travel writer in freak medieval weapon accident."). Wearing ancient warrior clothing and playing with a variety of weapons was right up my alley, of course. In that old Soviet brick of a gym, I felt like I was Bruce Lee in *Game of Death*. These guys practice by actually kicking and punching each other. And I suppose I should apologize for the nude scenes in the bathhouse – I didn't know what I was getting into, and kudos to Paul for taking on camera duties while I got my skin scrubbed off. Nudity does not worry me nearly as much as, say, injury, and when that guy jumped on my back, that was a very real concern. You can just make out my shaking hands at the end, trying to both hold a pen and drink a cup of sweet tea.

In every country, we usually have a guide or fixer, someone on the ground to help get us from A to B, communicate with locals and get permissions and whatnot. We also have drivers, when we're lucky. I mention this because the driving is insane in Georgia, and I retain the image of the crew looking nervously at each other as our driver blitzed on the highway back to Tbilisi. As Julia often says: "I refuse to die making a travel show!"

The toasting was a lot of fun, and to this day I'm still standing up and saluting the table, Georgian style. You should try it. As for the wine, well, it's closer to dessert wine – thick and sweet. Drink too much and you'll find yourself like I did in the credit roll, throwing up in the bushes.

Medieval monastery

Toasting with a polyphonic chant

Filming in the wild vineyards

Fighting on the walls of Narikala Fortress

Travel writer kills pet cat with wayward arrow

Scenes from the countryside

ITALY
FAST CARS AND GOOD VINEGAR

Nobody indulges the five senses quite like the Italians. Taste, obviously, with their cooking, seeped in tomato and cheese, wine, and olive oil. Touch, with their sensual fashion, a drop of sexy summer sweat, the texture of expensive leather. Smell the aroma, the thick espresso, the scent of garlic swirling in the wind along with the glittering dust of Roman history. Hear the roar of a sports car, a heated argument about politics, the vines rustling in the slow, aging breeze. And see it all through my eyes, this week, as I head north to Modena, to race Lamborghinis and Ferraris, eat the finest cheese, slurp inky-black Balsamic bliss and bake in the shadow of the Coliseum.

It's been nearly eighteen years since I was last in Italy, a post-high-school European trip with my two best friends. We were introduced to boozing and women and toga parties, and looked much like the thousands of tourists I encounter at Rome Airport, camera case slung around the shoulder, shorts and sandals, ready to spend the next two weeks in high season lineups. I asked my mom to stitch a large black biker patch on the back of my bright blue anorak. It had a skull and said: "Lawless Rebel." I was an idiot then, but no more than anyone else new to travel, like a grape that has yet to ripen. I have avoided Western Europe these past five years because of the exorbitant cost, the tour buses, the fact that I'd seen all the sights before and have had little desire to see them since. Paris, Rome and London in summer are circuses for psychopaths – a tourist mob foaming at the mouth with swelled, star-struck craziness in their wine-stained eyes. After a two-hour debacle to rent a car, surrounded by elastic family units stretched to their breaking point (Daddy, when we can leave the airport, Daddy?) we finally escaped inside a tiny blue Peugeot 107, bolting out of Rome north on the 130 km/hr autostrade. The road to Bologna is immaculate, the farmland manicured like a bowling green. Cheap pizza at road stops somehow tops the best pizza back home, as if some sort of Italian magic is added to the dough, a magic wand waved across the cheese. A few hours of effortless driving, give or take a stop for directions, and we arrive in Modena, the yellow glow of the late afternoon bouncing off the cobblestone of the downtown piazza. Park at the Hotel Estresse, take three breaths and let the brain catch up to the body that left Georgia via Istanbul at two the previous morning.

If you look at any bottle of balsamic vinegar, you'll see it comes from Modena. Like champagne, it can only be called balsamic if it comes from a particular region, but unlike champagne, there's a vast difference between real balsamic vinegar and the stuff you have in your kitchen. Who doesn't salivate at the prospect of dipping warm bread into a plate of extra-virgin olive oil dribbled with the oil black sweet-sour vinegar?   It's been produced in this region since the Middle Ages using a technique that incorporates a daisy chain of wood barrels, a complicated process of cooking grape must, and, most of all, time. It's not exactly vinegar, either, but more like a sweet, thick grapey goop that can be sipped neat or poured over ice cream. And you'll know the stuff you have is "industrial" because, chances are, you didn't pay $100 for a 100ml bottle, as you would for certified Aceto Balsamico Tradizionale di Modena.

In an old farmhouse that has been making balsamic for centuries, the matriarch simply cannot *believe* I am a Virgino Balsamico. I have never had the good fortune to sample the real stuff, the ridiculously expensive stuff. She leaks some 25 year old family recipe goodness onto a small plastic spoon. My tongue touches the liquid; my palate explodes. It tastes like everything good in the world. It tastes like the finest wine enjoyed at a perfect sunset. It tastes like rich chocolate when you're needing a sugar boost. It tastes like peace in a war zone. She refills the spoon and I suck it back, willing the memory of the vinegar from the polished plastic. Upstairs in the attic, where balsamic is usually aged, she explains how it is made (to enhance and flavour the meat of a future article). Downstairs there is a feast of Italian cooking: a brick of soft Gorgonzola, fresh olive bread, a variety of meats and cheeses, blood-red cherry tomatoes, eggs and two bottles of expensive Balsamic Tradicionale, to be dribbled over it all. You never cook with it, you never waste it and you can eat it with just about everything. Industrial balsamic is wine vinegar with colourant, caramel and flavouring, and is certainly an able substitute for the real thing. Unless you happen to know anyone who enjoys spending $100 on their salad dressing.

Ferraris, Maseratis and Lamborghinis all come from the region surrounding Modena, a Golden Circle, the Cradle of the Engine, the Engine of Italy. Each manufacturer has a legend, with loyal followers, collectors, heroes and naysayers. Super cars are more than just toys for rich boys. They're the manifestation of speed, status and power. The fact that I drive a rusted twenty- year-old Honda Civic might not make me the appropriate authority to investigate a story about Italian super cars, but since I've got the opportunity to visit the Lamborghini factory, the world's largest collection of Maseratis and the Ferrari Gallery, I'd be a fool not to buckle up and hit the gas. It starts with the Maseratis, rescued from a closing factory by the Panini family, local businessmen who made a fortune designing and distributing trading cards. Although Maserati is now owned by Ferrari, they're not nearly as flashy as other Italian sports cars. Powerful, stylish, expensive, but more of an understated flaunt for the rich and powerful who want to impress those in the know. The collection is located on the Panini's Hombre dairy farm, which manufactures fine, creamy organic Parmigiano-Reggiano, along with various other products. In a chilled room, I walk amongst 8000 wheels of cheese that fetch around $800 each. The smell is rich, and indeed, the cheese tastes like money.

Inside a large warehouse just metres away sit two dozen vintage Maseratis, including racing cars driven by legends such as Sterling Moss, and dozens of motorbikes and bicycles. When I ask Matteo Panini how much the collection is worth, he skittishly replies it is worth as much as anyone would pay for it. Considering some of these models are one of a kind in the world of car collectors, I would guess it is worth more than a few dairy farms.

The collection is a suitable warm up for the half hour drive, just over the Bologna city line, to the Lamborghini factory. The legend goes like this: The self-made tractor and business magnate Ferrucio Lamborghini loved collecting cars, and was particularly fond of his Ferraris. But the clutch kept sticking, so he eventually contacted Enzo Ferrari, the ferociously driven founder of the world's most famous racing brand. Now, Enzo had a famous disdain for his road car customers, because they were simply a means to an end. That is, financing his race cars. Ferrari tells Lamborghini that a tractor maker has no business commenting on his sports cars, to which Lamborghini responds by setting up his own company to prove that he did. There would be no Joker were it not for Batman, and there would be no Lamborghini were it not for Ferrari. Focusing solely on road cars, Lamborghini hired the best engineers, and it didn't take long before his cars, designed specifically to race into the heart of the wealthy enthusiast, became a true competitor to Ferrari. Even though Fiat owns 90% of Ferrari today, and Audi owns 100% of Lamborghini, there's no love lost between the powerful offspring of these two famous Italians, famed for their love of cars. All this was the focus of my feature for the South China Morning Post.

Clearing Lamborghini security and accompanied by a press officer, I get a tour of the factory, watching how the Batmobile-esque Murciélago is handcrafted on a spotless assembly line. Every 190 minutes, the cars move forward and a small team installs the interior, electronics, engine, wheels and custom components. Lamborghini keeps no stock. Cars are made to order, and the waiting list is long. Only two to three Murciélagos are produced each day, by a young staff working with the finest Austrian leather, latest technology and most powerful engines. When the engine gets switched on for the very first time and the beast roars to life, it induces goosebumps, like being privy to a secret, or granted special access to a birth canal. Lamborghini has recently opened up factory tours to the paying public, so I'm not alone in all this: smelling the leather (it takes five cows to fit out one car), hearing the machinery, seeing the dream.

I had a mounted poster of a blue Lamborghini Countach on my wall as a teenager, because it's the closest thing I knew to a rocket ship on earth. It had always been my dream to drive one, although justifying the price tag will always fall outside my middle-class sensibilities. In the gallery, I walk amongst the company's most fantastic creations, from the vintage classics to the jaw-dropping concept cars. The design of Lamborghinis seems more inspired than those of Porsches or Ferraris, as if there are no limits to the creativity, no ceiling too high to reach (or given its low, sleek chassis, no tarmac too close to touch). The growl of an engine announces that one more dream is about to be fulfilled, one more "one day I'm going to," one more item to be ticked off on the bucket list. One of the company's most experienced test drivers, Valentino, has just pulled up in a silver Gallardo LP 560-4 Spyder. We're going for a drive in the countryside, which will involve a lot of power, incredible speed, and my taking the wheel of my long-awaited fantasy.

Of course, I sign a waiver to assume responsibility should something go wrong. Not long ago a Top Gear presenter crashed a vintage Ferrari while filming the show, and if I lose control or drive beyond my talent level, I could be paying for this experience for the rest of my life. There's always risk when it comes to these kind of things, so I sign the dotted line, slide into the red interior, and Valentino pulls out into traffic. Valentino controls the car the way an artist might control a paintbrush. He knows the dimensions, the capabilities, just how far and how fast he can push it. No hesitation whatsoever regarding oncoming traffic or tight corners. For the passenger, it's like being on a rollercoaster, attacked with constant jabs of G-force, and smooth, but sudden, braking. The sun beats down on us as the crew set up a couple of shots, the temperature in the cockpit cracking 50C. I can feel the heat radiating off the blacktop, but pay careful attention to the paddle shifting. Valentino reassures me I can do no wrong – the car will compensate if it needs to down- or up-shift – and then he slides over so I can take the wheel. I press the R button on the left of the wheel, do a three-point turn and carefully pull off. Under my control is a 560 horsepower super car that can go from 0–100 km/hr in 3.9 seconds, with a top speed of 324 km/hr. Next to me, one of the most experienced Lamborghini drivers in the world. Before me, a meandering country road with sporadic traffic. And a TV crew, ready to capture the memory. What the hell would you do?

Zoom Zoom Zoom.

I'm sweating a sweet smile when Valentino graciously allows me to drive back to the factory, with Sean in the passenger seat to capture some in-car reactions. While my drive is something of a blur, burned in my memory is one incident. We are stuck behind a truck, travelling at about 40 km/hr on a two-lane road. This is no place to be in a super car. Approaching traffic prevents overtaking, and I'm becoming frustrated. Finally, I sense a gap. There is no way in hell I'd attempt this in any other vehicle, but I know, and I've seen, what this Gallardo can do. So I floor it, swerve out and overtake in a manoeuvre so fast and smooth it's like shaving with a nine-blade razor. Sean looks at me with real fear in his eyes, something I have seen only once or twice in thirty countries. Valentino, and certainly the spirit of Ferruccio Lamborghini, might have nodded his approval.

We deposit the Spyder, skip our lunch in the new staff canteen and beeline it for Maranello, where I am scheduled to get in the cockpit of a Ferrari 430 Scuderia. Enzo Ferrari relocated his factory from Modena, after it was bombed in WWII, to the country village of Maranello. Today, Maranello is best described as Ferrari Land. The prancing horse logo is everywhere: on restaurants, hotels, shops, as public art, on flags that wave over the Ferrari factory. The difference in size between the two companies is immediately obvious. Ferrari is not so much a car as a religion for the enthusiasts making their pilgrimage to the source, bowing down at the F1 cars on display in the Ferrari Galleria. My test driver Gabriel is waiting with the metallic blue Scuderia 430, two silver racing stripes splitting the middle. It's getting late, so I strap into the fighter jet seatbelts and the car booms to life. Compared to the Lamborghini, the Scuderia screams business, and by business, I mean racing. The Gallardo's lush interior has been replaced by steel foot plates for grip around bends, and a basic control panel to ensure you don't blow the engine when you hit the top speed of 320 km/hr. Gabriel reckons this is the best Ferrari he's driven, because this particular model, launched by Michael Schumacher at the Frankfurt Auto Show in 2007, is all about racing. There are other models for flash, but this is for speed. We are not passengers. We are two men strapped to a 510-horsepower engine, being blasted into the countryside. The engine sounds like the grunt of some primal monster, a dragon coughing up hellfire. I literally scream around the bends, taken at such speed my sunglasses go flying off my face. It feels as if we are lions hunting on the plains of Automobile. We head back to the Galleria, caught up in surprisingly busy rush hour traffic, and inching along is painful as I watch the Scuderia's racing potential squandered. For all the speed and power, in Vancouver rush-hour traffic, this tiger would be stuck in the same boat as my crotchety old Honda Civic.

Ferrari's gallery highlights the importance of racing, with a recreated pit stop and several of the F1 World Championship cars on display. Upstairs are the classic road cars, the F40, the 308GTS made famous by Tom Selleck in Magnum, the Testarossa, and an Enzo Ferrari, named after the founder and the world's only street-legal F1 sports car. All are racing red, in the famous Ferrari tradition, the colour assigned to Italy by racing officials in the 1920's. Blue for French, green for English, white for German (later changed to silver). In a special showcase sits a black Ferrari, a 1957 Testarossa race car. It was auctioned in May 2009 for a staggering $12.1 million, at the time the most expensive car ever put on the block. It doesn't have headlights.

I'm in post-dream awe when I climb back into the tiny Peugeot 107. The sudden lack of power is a reality check. Our dreams drive us forward, but what happens when you wake up? What happens when you reach the end of your bucket list?   I suppose you pull out a pen and make a new one. I put the gear into first and head back to the hotel. The contrast between my blue bubble and the dream machines I'd spent the day in is enough to give me emotional whiplash.

We take a train back to Rome, arriving at the central station, an ant colony of chaos, with ponytailed taxi drivers perched like vultures swooping down on a fresh battleground. The heat has followed us, the upper 30's, as has the food – fresh pizza and pasta – and good, cheap wine. In the shadow of the Coliseum I do some promo for Nat Geo Adventure, the satellite channel that broadcasts *Word Travels* in Italy, swapping up film crews for a few hours, hacking away at scripted Italian. I avoid umbrella-carrying group tours and overpay for water, all part of the ambience of being at one of the world's most popular tourist destinations, in high season. Rome itself is a magical place, every block seemingly holding some ancient building or monument that would be the showcase of any other city. Our hotel is close to the Vatican, and as Sean shoots a sunset time-lapse just over the fence (or he'd risk having the tape confiscated), a Contiki bus pulls up. Out pour the perky passengers, 18–35 years old, stretching their legs, taking a few photos and piling back on. Eighteen years ago I was on that bus. Today, I'm on a different sort of bus. Life seems to have a way of racing us around in circles.

BEHIND THE SCENES IN ITALY

Sometimes I push it a little too far. I really had no business visiting Lamborghini and Ferrari on the same day. Typically, a journalist might spend a few days doing this story, not one. But since it was possible to do so, why not? When else am I going to get the chance to test drive two of the world's fastest super cars? First, we had to get there. We thought it would be cute (and affordable) to rent a tiny rental car and drive from Rome. After the chaos at the airport, we discovered it was so small we barely managed to get our luggage in. Our director Peter somehow crammed himself in the back of that blue tin can to record some conversation. It led to musings about life, the universe and everything at 130 km/hr, as road trips invariably do.

We were joined on this leg by the founder of BraveNewTraveler.com, one of the best travel mags on the web. Ian Mackenzie has become a good friend these past few years, and his humour and enthusiasm often reminded me of the millions of people who wish they could do what we do. In between the jet lag and crazy schedules, it's important to go into each country with a fresh heart and open mind.

When we arrived at Lamborghini, the company had no intention of letting me actually drive a super car. One needs credentials, and I, for one, didn't have them. So there was a tense few minutes as my childhood dream (and story) hovered on the edge, until the PR team helped us out, for which I'll always be grateful. After touring the plant, I got my chance to race a rocket ship under the tutelage of Valentino, a test driver since the 1960's. What you don't see on camera is how hot it was that day. The temperature in the cockpit reached a mind-melting 50C degrees! After a couple of twists and turns, I almost hurled right all over that expensive leather.

Julia and I did a promo for Nat Geo Adventure, the channel that broadcasts us in Italy. For a few hours we adopted another crew, and filmed around the Coliseum. Our show is called *Autoro del Viaggio* in Italy, and I recited an Italian script for the spot promo. "Sono Robin Esrock e Julia Dimon" etc., etc... for some reason, I put on an Italian accent, too. Meanwhile, Paul and Sean, our sound and camera, were indulging in pasta, wine and pizza as only the Italians can make it. We all bought a bottle of authentic balsamic vinegar, too, which I insist that anyone who visits my apartment sample. Discovering just how amazing it tastes is one thing; sharing it with my friends and watching their reaction is another. I've found the best experiences are the ones I can share. Good thing I have a TV show.

The Good Stuff: wheels of Parmasan cheese and barrels of Balsamic vinegar

A boy loves his toys: The Lamborghini Galliardo Spyder that I took for a wee blast in the countryside (above) followed by the rocketship Ferrari 430 Scuderia.

PORTUGAL
THE BULLS AND THE BLIND

For a moment, the Bull stops to weigh his options. There are people everywhere, taunting him, laughing, showing no respect whatsoever. There are rock walls and wooden barricades, and more people on those walls and barricades, exuding a cacophony of celebration. Around the Bull's neck is a thick rope, held many yards back by several men dressed in white. They're supposed to limit his movement, but the Bull knows, and they know, it's more of a nuisance than anything else. A nuisance like the young men who dare to step forward, threatening him with movement from jackets or blankets or by hypnotically twirling red umbrellas. The impetuousness! To dare to challenge such a beast, one so strong and muscled that cows shudder their udders at the sight of him. A young man crosses the imaginary line and the Bull springs forward, horns primed, an unstoppable tank of nature. But the man sidesteps, deftly turning in a circle, and while the Bull is fast and the Bull is big, the Bull does not have power steering. For a moment, it looks almost comical, like a cat chasing its tail. They play this game, closely bonded, man and beast, until the man skips away to the applause of the crowd. The Bull has choices. Should he charge into the crowd to send them scattering? Should he make an unexpected leap over a low wall to a place where many others stand, mistaking it for safety? Should he trample the man holding a notebook, with his baseball T-shirt and distinctly un-Portuguese appearance? The Bull turns his thick neck towards me, and in the black orbs of his eyes I see him weighing his options.

I'm in the Azores, and the Azores lie in the middle of the North Atlantic Ocean. Nine islands straddling the intercontinental plates, 950 miles from Europe, 2400 miles from North America. An important trading post going back as far as the 1400's, the archipelago is part of Portugal, has a population of around 240,000, and is blessed with fertile land, diverse scenery and its own unique culture. Think of the Azores as Europe's Hawaii. I'm on the island of Terceira, which has a long and storied history and a checkered green countryside that easily recalls Ireland or Newfoundland. It's summer, and the annual festivities are in full swing, with glittering coloured streamers over the streets, lanterns, bright flags and flashy fairs. Each island in the Azores has its own appeal or attraction this time of year, and in Terceira the biggest drawing card is *touradas à corda* – the Bullfight on a Rope. Not one, mind you, but hundreds, taking place throughout the summer, attracting visitors from the mainland and beyond. The bullfights can take several forms and differ from other bullfights you may have encountered in Spain or Mexico. For one, it is illegal to kill bulls in a Portuguese bullfight. While it's up to you to decide how heavily this all sits on your personal scale of ethics, organizers stress how well the festival bulls are treated, prepared, rested and fed for the occasion.

My first encounter with the *touradas* was on the beach of Angra do Heroísmo, Terceira's main city, with its UNESCO World Heritage Site Old Town. I expected a small baby bull for the kid's bullfight, but arrived under an overcast sky to find a chest-high baby bull capable of causing bodily harm to child and adult. Two men held a long rope attached to the bull's neck while teenage boys ran up and taunted the bull. The bull would charge them right into the sea, where they could swim just a few metres to safety. The baby bull didn't charge everyone on the beach, but rather seemed content to go after only those who dared to challenge him. Kids under ten were on the sand, with plenty of distance to run to safety should the bull move in their direction. Confirmed by the hysterical laughter of the kids, it all seemed like harmless fun, providing the bull didn't get too close. After a while I got a little braver, walking closer to the action and seeing how the braver teens kept still until the last moment, when they would dart in circles. I was taking some photos, when suddenly the bull took off in the direction of the shelf on a wall, where the majority of spectators were watching the action, including our crew. It was at this critical juncture that we all learned something else about bulls. They can jump. The bull tore up the ledge, sending everyone scattering up stairs or spilling onto the beach. Somehow, of all the places to run on this wide-open beach, the bull managed to get tangled in Paul's wholly expensive sound gear. I can't exactly describe why it's so funny to see a baby bull roped in electronic equipment, with a sound guy from Whistler charging the *bull* down in a sudden act of bravura. As I was to learn later, Paul was unexpectedly demonstrating some key aspects of bullfighting – machismo, testosterone, the public demonstration that man can stand up to the mighty beast. With the bull seemingly intent on mounting Paul's fur-covered boom microphone, and the crowd tearing up in hysterics, it also proves the age-old truth about show business. Never work with children, never work with animals, and, for God's sake, never work with children and animals at the same time.

Terceira's landscape has been divided up by ancient stone walls into neat squares which run right up to Angra do Heroísmo, the oldest city in all the Azores, dating back to 1534. Monte Brasil, a lush hill and all that's left of the volcano that once gave birth to the island, overlooks the city, along with an old castle named São Filipe. Its 4km rock wall, blackened by time and the elements, looks more like it belongs in Angkor Wat. Considering Angra's rich history of pirates and buccaneers, imperial warfare, trade and relocated royalty, it's odd to find everything so clean and fresh-coated. Blue and orange-painted churches seem almost new, while the facades of buildings along the narrow, snaking cobblestone are polished and decorated with flowers. The last major earthquake, a bastard that struck on New Year's Day, 1980, damaged up to 80% of the city and 60% of the island's settlements (the agricultural stone walls survived intact, as they have throughout the centuries). Angra was carefully rebuilt using photographs to resemble all that was lost, giving the city its old, yet polished, appearance. Cuisine is all fried fish, or steak with rice and potatoes, with Azorean-made passion fruit soda and good cheap wine. Sodium freaks will enjoy the salty meals, along with the local recipe for peri-peri, the chili sauce you'll find throughout Portugal, mixed here with more salt than usual. I dived into the sea to find it warmer than the Hotel Caracol's pool. When the sun finally came out, the land sparkled like emeralds, the sea like sapphires.

The Spanish matadors were dressed in skin-tight traditional costumes, as if their fans might need confirmation of the size of their balls. If they hadn't been getting in the ring with a raging bull, I might have made a comment about the pink socks. I've never been to a bullfight before, and I know they split the travel community. Many are disgusted by the spectacle of taunting and torturing a bull and spearing it repeatedly until it's stabbed to death to the cheers of those in the arena (although in Portugal, as previously mentioned, bulls are spared this fate). Many are thrilled by the cultural impact, the excitement, the tension, the art of the matador, the thrill of the sport. My jury was out when I first entered Angra's bullfighting arena for a more traditional bullfight. A brass band blasts out their anthems, and the all-ages crowd, paying around 30 euros a ticket, anxiously awaits the first of several encounters. Behind me is Frankie, the same taxi driver who picked us up at the airport (it's a small island), and who explains to me what's going on in the American accent he's picked up from the US soldiers stationed on Terceira. The bulls, he explains, are bred and raised specifically for the bullfights. They are fed the best food, get the best treatment, are trained, and are rested before the fight. Local breeders are honoured and renowned for the quality of their bullfighting bulls. The first event has a local kid performing *cavaleiro* on his white horse, an excellent display of classical riding that I can recognize and appreciate after my visit to Slovenia's Lipica. Tame enough, until they let a 450 kg bull into the ring. For the next fifteen minutes, the bull charges the specially trained horse, which brings the rider up close enough for him to stab decorated spears of varying lengths into the rump of the bull. As the spears get shorter, so it becomes more dangerous, and at one point the bull seems to connect with the horse, which remains calmly under the rider's control at all times (as opposed to, say, panicking and freaking out). It is overcast, and I don't really see much in the way of violence until the sun breaks in the late afternoon sky, reflecting off a sheet of blood on the bull's side. I finally understand why bullfights are so bloody. At the last spear, the young rider gets a heavy applause for his efforts.

"Watch these next guys; they're the suicide squad," says Frankie, and what follows is easily in my top three of The Craziest Things I Have Ever Seen Anyone Do, Anywhere.

The Suicide Squad, or *pega*, consists of eight men dressed in traditional garb who enter the ring with the same bull, by now way pissed off, what with all the spears in his back. Their role – one unique to Portugal – is literally to grab the bull by the horns. They line up in single file, with a young kid no older than eighteen right up front, about ten metres ahead of the rest. The crowd hushes. I can hear the ashes on the cigarette being sucked back by someone in front of me. The boy, carrying no capes or weapons, yells something and takes a step forward. The others duplicate his step. Another yell, another step. The bull is now facing him head on, stamping his front foot like something you'd see in a cartoon.

"That kid is going to get killed," I say.

"Just watch," replies Frankie, who has been attending these events his whole life.

Boy Suicide is getting closer and closer to the bull, the others behind him carefully making sure that all the bull can see is the kid up front. Any second, there's going to be a charge down. Dead silence in the arena. I notice that I haven't breathed much in the last minute. Suddenly, the bull explodes forward and the boy lets out one last scream. He's got seconds to move or get crushed, but instead of darting to the side, he crouches low. You can hear the WHUMP of impact as the bull crashes into the chest of the boy, who jumped at the just the right time to wrap his arms around the neck of the bull. Within a second the other guys rush forward to absorb the speed and blow of the bull, ensuring the bull cannot smash his head down. The bull has just run headfirst into a wall of men, and the men have prevailed, calming the bull down, blinding any further movement that might antagonize him. Somehow, they extract themselves, and the crowd erupts into cheers. His face smeared with the bull's blood, the boy becomes a man, and the man becomes a hero. The bull is coerced back into his pen and the rider and the hero give a victory walk around the stadium. A teenage boy stands down an angry 450kg charging wounded bull. The line between bravery and stupidity has never looked so thin, or so impressive.

Next up: the Matador, who faces an even bigger beast (480kg), this time with no horse, although he does have two assistants in the ring to occupy the bull's attention. Flown in from Spain, the Matador uses deft feints, distractions, sidesteps and his red cape to confuse the bull. The crowd is once again respectfully quiet. I hear the strange yelps of the Matador, the stamping of the bull's hooves. The poses and facial expressions are almost comical, a kind of traditional dance used just prior to a ritualistic slaying. The Matador gets within a hair's length of the bull at full charge. His prancing and bows to the audience seem arrogant, like a boxer demanding respect even though his opponent is blind. Bulls have been known to maim and kill matadors, but it becomes pretty obvious that the Matador knows the bull's weaknesses (manoeuvrability, confusion in sight and movement) and teases these weaknesses for the audience. As a further show of pride, he turns his back on the bull, a strut to demonstrate his compete lack of fear for the beast. It's more challenging when, like the horse rider, he has to spear the bull with different-sized spears. A couple of times his assistants jump into the fray to prevent the bull from getting too close. You can hear the slam of the bull into the wooden fence where the assistants take shelter. The Matador lands his blows until, finally, he holds nothing but a long sword.

"In Spain, this is when he'd kill the bull," explains Frankie.

In Portugal, where killing the bull is illegal, the Matador instead places one more spear, a symbol to show that he could slay the bull if he wished, and the crowd applauds his efforts.

There's no Suicide Squad this time; instead, five brown cows with bells around their necks are released into the arena, and the hurt and horny bull chases them back into the pen. Some of these bulls will shortly face the butcher's blade. Others will receive veterinary care, return to the fields, and may or may not take part in next year's bullfights.

The jury is in. There is such diversity of culture around the world, and time and time again it has proven folly to force the moral values of one culture on another. In Saudi Arabia, women are not allowed to drive. In parts of China, cats are on the menu. In tribal Africa, girls are married off as young as twelve to men who have a dozen wives already. I enjoy a good steak, and the fact is, steak comes from bulls and cows. If I wanted to become a vegetarian, I would visit the nearest abattoir, because part of the joy of eating meat is in the bloody ignorance that comes with it. It is upsetting to see any living thing hurt, much less killed, and yet we could have this argument over a burger. Vegetarians, I strongly suggest you stay away from such ethical bullfights. Bullfighting in Portugal aims to spare the bull's life (inside the arena, anyway), but you're witnessing an important and cherished cultural tradition for the local people. Agree with it or not, but every traveller has a duty to respect it. There is no bullfighting in Canada, and that's just one more reason why I live there. Condemn the people of Terceira for their bullfights on the other hand, and you may as well start condemning everyone and everything that doesn't agree with you, in which case you'd be too busy to read stories like these, or enjoy travel shows on TV. Meanwhile, I'll continue to root for the bull, and continue to enjoy my steak medium rare.

Unless the bull is staring *me* down, in which case I'll root for myself, thanks. The next day's bullfight on a rope takes place on a street in Angra lined with shipping containers for spectators to sit on. This time, it's the grown-up version, and the stakes are much higher. Two days ago, a local slipped and was trampled to death by the bull. It's crazy enough for me to be on the dance floor with this monster; I don't have to do the tango with it. As 6:30 p.m. approaches, the street becomes filled with men, many clutching small brown mini-bottles of Bock beer. There are plenty of women on the containers and patios, but none on the road itself. A loud firecracker explodes, announcing that the bull has been released on the street. I am a hundred metres from the bull's pen, but feel an immediate pulse, as if the entire street just stuck its fingers in a plug socket. People further down start running back, causing a ripple up the street. Eventually I see the bull, at eye level, a terrifying site that forces a hard swallow. Attached to its neck is a long rope, but the bull moves freely, pounding up the street, turning to attack the men who would dare get close enough to touch it. As the bull gets closer, adrenaline surges and I sprint further up the street to safety. At the top are two white lines, and it is the job of the men holding the ropes to ensure that the bull does not cross it. As a sign of confidence in their ability, a half-dozen caravans sell beer just metres from the line, and hundreds of people have congregated there to watch the action. There will be four bullfights on a rope this evening, and the first bullfight is uneventful. I keep my distance, taking photos, daring myself to move closer, but always quick to bolt back or eye a fence to jump over. Frankie had warned me that the really dangerous part is not so much being near the bull, but tripping over people as you run, or tripping over the rope. As long as you can run, you can make it to safety. Frankie also points out that when it comes to this type of bullfighting, it's people who get hurt, not bulls. It's not going to satisfy PETA, but it's a long way from the animal gore you'll find in traditional bullfights in Spain and Latin America. After twenty minutes, the bull is slowly pulled back towards its container, with the crowd moving forward, a human wall closing in. Two firecrackers signal the bull is off the streets, and immediately it fills up with families and revellers. Stands have been set up a bit further down, and it is here that most of the crazy stuff happens, where feats are pulled for applause. I happened to see the TV news that morning, which showed the highlights from the arena fight, and also the guy slipping on the beach and being trampled to death. One local actually makes his living filming the bullfights and then compiling DVD's of guys getting trampled. Kind of like those "World's Best Sports Disasters" shows, only with bulls and people. After watching just a few minutes of one on a TV inside a beer caravan, I'm more than happy to leave the horn grabbing to the professionals.

Bull number two distinguishes himself by launching over a low wall that hundreds of people mistook for a safety barrier. Talk about crowd dispersion. Sean had set up his camera on this side, and I hadn't seen him move that fast since that guy threw a live cobra at him in Taiwan.

Bull number three trashed the glass beer bottles accumulated in a badly placed garbage bin, much to the delight of the crowd. For the fourth and final bull, I decided I knew enough to stand with the inner circle of lunatics closest to the bull. Branded on his muscular black hide, I did not know the organizers had saved the best till last – the meanest, fastest, biggest bull of all. There are plenty of exciting moments being that close. The bull can change directions at any moment, and a couple of times I had to really hoof it or risk being trapped by the containers. Sure, things could have turned sour, like the time he charged me and I jumped over a hastily assembled wooden fence. The bull smashed it with his ceremonially padded horns, and I had to help some guy literally prop up the wood, otherwise the bull might have jumped into the small courtyard where women and children were watching. Fortunately, no fodder for the DVD guy that day, but I still shake my head in disbelief when I think about it.

Bullfighting in Terceira dates back to the sixteenth century, and bullfighting-on-a-rope, which takes place all over the island, has evolved to include beaches and boats, umbrellas and kids' versions. I felt a little sorry for the bulls, which looked bewildered, like high school bullies being showed up by a horde of nerds. Aside from tradition, perhaps the reason the men of Terceira ridicule the bull is as a means of ridiculing nature, exerting some human control over the powerful and mysterious. Bulls have certainly been prominent for thousands of years across multiple civilizations. They were the symbol for idolism in the Biblical tale of the Golden Calf. Theseus battled the Minotaur, a man with the head of a bull, in Greek mythology. Shiva rode a bull, Egyptians were known to worship and mummify certain bulls, Celts had a bull deity and some Christians believe there was an ox or bull present at the birth of Jesus. Taurus is one of the astronomical star signs, which reminds me: one week I'm racing a Lamborghini with the logo of a bull, the next week I'm running with them on the streets of Portugal. When the stock market is performing, as hopefully it will again one day, it's described as a bull market. Bulls, the symbol of strength, virility and raw power. Face up to a bull, as a kid on a beach, a Matador in a ring or a travel writer on a street, and maybe a little bit of bullish energy will rub off on you. Hopefully, it won't trample you to death.

About 250 fights take place over the summer, and every year there are at least a couple of casualties. Far tamer was the parade for the Festival of St. John, the patron saint of Portuguese nobility, which takes place down the main street in Angra and involves thousands of costumed dancers. One section was set aside for kids, and with the colours and fairs and ice creams, I made a note to add Terceira to my list of great family destinations. Kids can even see a bullfight, without anyone, man or bull, getting hurt. With just a few days remaining on my European leg, which has seen me clash swords in Georgia and race Lamborghinis in Italy, I'm a little exhausted and completely over-stimulated. Boarding the plane for Lisbon, I hope that my next adventure will help with that.

****

PART TWO: THE BLIND

Lisbon is known as the San Francisco of Europe, and it's easy to see why. From atop the old walls of the Castle of Saint George I see street trams beneath tiled rooftops spanning across a hilly terrain all the way to the blue Tagus River, which flows under a familiar-looking red suspension bridge. The 25 April Bridge could be a twin for the Golden Gate, although San Francisco doesn't have statues and squares that date back hundreds of years, or a history so vast that when Julius Caesar named it a Roman municipality in 205 BC, Lisbon had already been occupied for over a thousand years. While the Portuguese capital runs on the euro, it's a lot cheaper and less trafficked than some of its western European counterparts. Food is great, wine is cheap, but I've only got one day to see the city and I want to make that day count. There are so many ways to explore a city these days, and tour operators are becoming increasingly creative. In Berlin, I drove an old Trabant. There's geo-caching, ghost tours, the ever-present open-top bus tours. I was looking for something different, and ironically, San Francisco came up with the initial burst of inspiration.

Invented in California, it's called a Go Car, and it looks kind of silly and kind of fun, which is the point. A bright yellow low-seated three-wheeler with motorbike-like handlebars, the Go-Car has a built-in GPS that speaks with a sexy voice and questionable wit. The goal is to allow tourists to take control of their sightseeing, explore a city at their own pace, learn from the GPS guide about what they're looking at and navigate in normal traffic to the curious stares of bystanders and motorists. It purports to be relaxing, which it might be if you don't drive on one of Lisbon's main roads during rush hour, and don't have a passenger like Ms. Julia Dimon, who insists that Go Cars can ruin friendships, relationships and marriages in the time it takes you to complete a city tour. The two-stroke engine creates a solid growl, and maxing out at around 50 km/hr you do get some go with the Go Car. The GPS blasts you with information in a loud ooh-la-la voice, which is great because then you can't hear the horns as you hold up traffic. The fibreglass body swings from side to side with each turn, the back tire can get stuck in the tram lines and the looks of fellow motorists are priceless. All this to conclude, then: the Go Car is an absolute blast of a way to see a city. It originated in San Francisco by two tech-heads who knew their way around a motorbike and the potential for using GPS. They built the cars, programmed the tours, and have rolled out Go Cars in San Francisco, Miami, San Diego, Barcelona and Lisbon. Incredibly, the Lisbon operation tell me they've had no accidents, which speaks volumes about the abilities of Lisbon drivers as they avoid smashing into wayward, arguing and defiantly confused tourists in Go Cars. Julia and I chose the Belem tour, which would take us along the banks of the Tagus River to the early sixteenth-century Belem Tower, built in honour of Portuguese seafaring discoverers and later used as a prison and trading post. We pass Lisbon sites such as the impressive Monument to the Discoverers, Commerce Square, drive through the tram-obstacle streets of Baixa (downtown) and past Jerónimos Monastery – all the classic sights and sounds of the city in a few hours, at our own pace. Well, technically not, because we also had to film all this at the pace of our camera Go Car and our director Go Car, which convoyed along like the minis in *The Italian Job*. While motorists were giving us wolf whistles, the cops seemed slightly annoyed. We returned the Go Cars late, but safe, to find a young female backpacker taking the wheel by herself, pushed into the busy rush-hour traffic, with the white of fear in her eyes. I'm sure she had the time of her life.

Back in Baixa, we head up to the historic Santa Justa elevator to find a lucky charm left behind by our show transcriber, who visited Lisbon a couple of months ago. Given the high traffic to this tourist site, incredibly it's still there, a good luck charm called a *figa*, which has a thumb pressed between the second and third fingers of a fist. In South Africa, its known as a fig sign, which is used in far less flattering circumstances. Good luck, then, that I find a guy offering Segway tours, which gives me the opportunity to roll amongst the crowds on a pedestrian boulevard and come up with terrible lines involving a pun on the word "segway". When they were first unveiled by inventor Dean Kamen, he promised the Segway would revolutionize mankind. Buddy tells me they cost over 7000 euros each, which might revolutionize the lives of lazy and rich people, but few others. There was not enough time to see the sights by Segway because I was off to my next alternative tour, which would have me seeing no sites at all.

Sensorial Lisbon is a walking tour unique to Lisbon, but hopefully not for much longer. Designed by Hugo, Pedro and Rita at their creative design company Cabrecega, the idea is to blindfold tourists for walking tours through Alfama, Lisbon's labyrinthine old town, led by a blind guide. The goal, explains Hugo, is to open up our senses, experience the world without sight and learn about the practicalities and challenges of being blind. They were inspired by the Dark Restaurant in Berlin, where blind servers serve patrons in complete darkness. I tried to eat there a few years back but it was booked up, now that it's a hip favourite of celebs like Leo diCaprio. Hugo tells me they were having a drink one day next door to ACAPO, the Association for the Portuguese Blind, and were discussing how dependant we are on sight. As my sensorial guide Carlos Silveria explains, sight sends the most signals to the brain. Blind since he was a baby, Carlos adds: "Sight annihilates the other senses." Operated by Lisbon Walker, a specialized tour operator that offers a variety of walking tours in Lisbon, Sensorial Lisbon is still somewhat experimental, but absolutely outstanding. With proceeds donated to ACAPO, blind associations around the world should take note. All you need are some volunteers, a couple of blindfolds, a cool neighbourhood and the desire for a unique experience.

Walkers are paired up together and led by a seeing volunteer. We hold Hugo's elbow as we are led forward, and he informs us about any obstacles. Jose from Lisbon Walker translates that we must trust our guide more than 100%, and that the ground won't move beneath our feet, unless, of course, there's an earthquake. I Velcro the comfortable blindfold on and close my eyes. Keeping them open would allow my eyes to constantly search out any source of light, so it's better to just keep them shut. Immediately, I am overwhelmed with a sense of vulnerability. Without my lifeline to Hugo's elbow I would probably panic. It takes a while to get comfortable, and in the beginning my steps are nervous with caution. Alfama is the oldest district of Lisbon, which through the years has been built like a maze of alleys and squares, lined with small shops and cafes. It's the perfect location to awaken the other senses: full of people, sounds, smells and texture. We walk down a street, and in my imagination I am constantly conjuring up my surroundings. A castle wall? A large hall? A busy market? Within seconds, it feels like I could be anywhere in the world, save for the far-off murmur of Portuguese. Carlos explains at various stops things about his life: how he knows what clothes he is wearing, what he imagines colour to look like. Modern technology has enabled the blind to lead more independent lives, a fact that Carlos gratefully acknowledges. After a half hour I notice my hearing becomes more acute. I am aware of birdsong and footsteps, and also feel the heat on my face as I walk in and out of shadow. Jose asks us to guess where we are, and in my mind's eye I see a tunnel (it was a corridor), I see a viewpoint (it was a square). We feel different types of trees and leaves, stopping in at a grocer to touch various types of fruit. If a car comes too close, Hugo patiently and calmly repositions us to safety. I simply cannot imagine being like this all day, all my life, and yet millions of people are. In an old communal washing room, Jose explains some of the history of Alfama and I find myself clinging onto his words (as opposed to drifting off to whatever eye candy I can normally find).

After an hour I have become a little more accustomed to Hugo's nudge, which indicates an obstacle, and walk a little faster and more surefooted. It is time to remove the blindfold, which we are advised to do in the shade, and slowly. Every night, my eyes are shut as I sleep. Today, this is the longest I've ever been awake, aware and concentrating on a constantly changing sensory landscape, with my eyes closed. I hear the rip of the Velcro and light floods in, stabbing my optic nerve, a dull pain that appears and then quickly vanishes. Colours explode, and the information sent to my brain requires me to take a few seconds to compose myself. Carlos is smoking a cigarette. Instead of pupils, he has an off-white sheen beneath his lids. He can't just remove a blindfold. I wonder what it must feel like for him to hear the relief when the walkers regain their sight, but don't feel like asking him.

For my week in Portugal, I gave up attempts to grasp the nature of Portuguese culture or history. There's never enough time, and there's always too much to see. Instead I focused on each experience as if they were different ingredients in a single meal, to be enjoyed as a whole. Bullfighting, blind tours, chessboard fields and bright yellow cars – spicy, bitter, sweet and salty – a meal for the senses, perfect for the appetite of a traveller.

Ole! Hola? A bullfighter in the ring during the annual Festival of St John

That's me in the baseball shirt getting closer and closer to the bull, which looks bigger and angrier on the ground, trust me

Terceira is the epitome of pastoral countryside, and the cows think so too

BEHIND THE SCENES IN PORTUGAL

It's all about the bulls, and the bulls gave us a behind-the-scenes moment so great we had to include it in the show itself. The bullfight on the beach was our first encounter with the beasts, and even though the bull was a teenager he was still pretty big and angry. A few days later we would see the big guys, and maybe if the schedule was reversed I would have been braver on that beach. But baby bull or papa bull, I wasn't going to stand in the way of that thing for anything. Nor would the crew, or so they thought. Joined by our senior producer, Deb, they were perched on ledge out of harm's way. Or so they thought. The bull wouldn't be able to jump up on that ledge. Well, baby bull launched himself up the ledge, charging anything in sight. Ian protected himself with the tripod, an able defence, but the bull became entangled in Paul's sound gear. Locals had warned us about bringing our gear onto the beach, so you should have heard them laugh when the bull started trashing the control unit. Next thing, Paul is facing down the animal, clearly demonstrating that his health is worth less than the value of his sound gear. It was a tense stand-off, especially once the bull began making love to the furry boom mic. A hilarious moment, and since the equipment (not to mention Paul) somehow survived, it was not a serious one. And thus great moments of production are born.

The weather boned us in the Azores, which really is more beautiful than we could show under those dull, gray skies. That's just the way it goes sometimes, but I always regret it. Especially when you have a once-in-a-lifetime opportunity to film a TV show.

As for the main bullfight on a rope? I saw a guy get killed on the TV news that week. He was taunting the bull, holding its head and running in circles. He slipped, and the bull crushed him to a pulp. Any thoughts I had about being too brave were quickly crushed, too, although I did become more confident as the bullfighting went on. I did have one moment where, if the bull had decided to charge at that moment, I would have been in big trouble. It didn't, another calculated risk that worked in my favour.

The blindfolded walking tour was sensational, and the Go Car was fun, even if Julia wanted to strangle me a half-dozen times. We lost the crew pretty quickly, but did manage to actually see the sights of Lisbon, to the curious stares of locals still adjusting to the sight of Go Cars zipping about.

I'd been learning Portuguese for a few months, and was curious to see how it would help me in Portugal. It didn't. People are always amazed to discover I speak only English (although I am fluent in drunkenese and bullshit). If you would have heard me trying to communicate with locals in their native tongue, you'd understand why.

I hustled a Segway jaunt in Lisbon, because I knew the shot would work.

Seeing the sights of Lisbon from the seat of a bright yellow Go Car

FINLAND

LIFE IS A ROLLERCOASTER

It's been ten years to the day since I was last in Scandinavia, driving up from Denmark, crossing the ferry at Malmo into Sweden, motoring north into an endless countryside of forest and lake, crossing the Arctic Circle into Norway, bowled over by the fjords and snow-capped mountains. I wanted to add Finland to the top tier of my Scandinavian trophy case. Mis-named Iceland (which is largely green) and Greenland (which is largely ice) will have to wait for next time.

Perhaps it is fitting that my goal this week is to try a little experiment called couch surfing. For at least one night, anyway. The realities of filming a TV show like *Word Travels*, when schedules and budgets are tight and a crew of six must be accommodated, means that returning to my broke and backpacker travel roots can only be alluded to. The formerly broke and formerly backpacking Robin, the same guy who ten years ago slept in a cheap shared rental car or camped on the side of the Swedish highway, is greeted at the airport by a sixteen-seat passenger van, along with smiling representatives of the Helsinki tourism board, and shepherded to the stylishly modern Hotel Klauske. Bottles of in-room mineral water cost $10. The Finns, who are regarded in some blogs as being shy and somewhat cold to foreigners, warm up to us with almost motherly care (especially when they see me swaying in my restaurant chair, the result of too little sleep, too much schnapps and way too much smoke sauna).

Sauna, my first story, is so intrinsically Finnish that the ceremony of sweating borders on the religious. Inside the sauna's hot, wooden walls, Finn's meditate, make lively debate, or to catch up with family and friends. The Finnish sauna — or, more accurately, the saunas in Finland — have little to do with getting sweaty or feeling sexy. Finns sauna naked because that's how a sauna should be enjoyed, and I pity the fool who walks into a large public sauna wearing his Speedo. In fact, in some parts of Europe nudity is strictly enforced. Here, it is understood that the body in sweat is not the body in heat. Which is how I come to find myself lying butt naked in a public sauna, stuck to a wet plastic mattress, watching a jolly rotund young woman scrub the bejezus out of me. But more on that later.

Sandwiched by Helsinki's fish stalls and ferries, I see a T-shirt in a market that read Good Girls go to Heaven, Bad Girls go to Lapland. To answer whether bad boys go there too, we hop on a one-hour Finnair flight to Rovaniemi, the capital of Lapland. North to the Arctic Circle, to the land of the midnight sun.

66° 33′ 39″ north of the equator runs another imaginary, but just as important, line in the world of latitude. The Arctic Circle receives at least one day of twenty-four-hour sun, when the sun does not rise above the horizon at all. While midnight gloom benefits few save clever vampires (as illustrated in the excellent graphic novel and less excellent movie *30 Days of Night*), the midnight sun is a boon for Lapland tourism. Over the summer months of never-ending daylight, the landscape melts into beautiful forests, rivers and lakes. Rovaniemi, with a population of around 60,000, is located just a few miles from the mythical line itself, and markets itself with summer and winter dog-sledding safaris, cross country skiing, camping, hiking and canoeing. Most successfully, it has marketed that Santa Claus actually exists and resides in Lapland, and you can visit him, free of charge, at his village right on the Arctic Circle. The post office here has received over 13 million letters from 197 countries, addressed to Mr. Claus. Over Christmas in 2008, he received some 600,000 letters alone. Along with most of the world, the Finns have adopted the long-bearded, red and white Santa invented by Coca-Cola in the 1930's, the so-called Coca-Cola Santa. Good marketing begats good marketing, and so today tour buses pull into Santa's Village, depositing thousands of Japanese and German and other tourists into the waiting arms of Santa and his elves, who do a roaring trade in Santa Village postmarked postcards, souvenirs, and other ho ho ho paraphernalia. North Americans, of course, believe that Santa lives in the North Pole, not Lapland, but that doesn't stop millions of letters from arriving from the good ol' USA anyway. Dear Santa, this Christmas I wish for everyone to stop buying into the crass, commercial holiday that has evolved from a once-thoughtful pagan ritual to celebrate the movement of the stars. I also wish they'd refrain from carpet bombing retail stores and public spaces with those awful Xmas songs *in October*. I also want a new red motorbike and a couple of strips of delicious reindeer jerky.

At midnight, the sky is dusky, caught in the nowhere land beneath sunset and sunrise. We drink some champagne, swatting away mosquitoes the size of flamingos. Like vampires in the winter, mosquitoes are the legendary local bloodsuckers that thrive throughout summer. They don't bite, these bastards; they stab you, hoovering your blood with their sharp snouts. We come prepared with a variety of all-natural and DEET repellents, and after some in-the-field product testing, I confirm that the all-natural citronella stuff works just fine, although you do end up smelling of crushed orange peel, much to the annoyance of anyone standing within twenty-five feet of you. I visit a reindeer farm where a local tourist shaman, calling up traditions from a long time ago (and a little bit further away), rubs two streaks of ash onto my forehead, symbolizing the horns of a reindeer to help ward off evil Lapland spirits. The reindeers themselves are soft to the touch and friendly to play with, so long as I have a mound of food pellets in my hand. I'm reading Michael Pollan's excellent *Omnivore's Dilemma* right now, which is making me hyper-aware of what I eat, especially meat. In this important book about how we choose what we eat, Pollan makes strong connections between the actual animals and the meat on our plates. Here, I am petting the sensitive, velvety horns of reindeer, horns that will harden to bone over the course of the season before they fall off, and the reindeer grows new ones. Like snowflakes, no two reindeer horns are the same. They spiral and twist as ornaments of beauty, and yet before the day is out I will enjoy dried reindeer meat sprinkled with blue cheese placed over a mouth-watering medium-rare steak. An existential dilemma indeed – perhaps I'd become a vegetarian if I didn't find meat so damn delicious.

From the reindeers, it am off to the dog kennels – the huskies, malamutes and mutts that work the dog-sledding circuit during those long, dark winter months. I'd learned much about the dog-sledding world when I was in the Yukon, and didn't need to be reminded that these are just about the happiest, well-cared-for dogs you'll find anywhere. Strong as oxen, too, as I discover racing along the dusty, narrow practice track. Ten dogs, harnessed and working as a team, pulled a modified six-seater ATV with ease, the driver using her brakes to maintain the speed, barking orders for left or right. It's what these doggies are bred to do, it's what they love to do, and only after a few laps did they begin to tire and settle down. I thank my dog mobile, one panting engine at a time, and climb back into our blinged-out Mercedes van. While the weird midget stripper pole at the back of the van does give the van some character, its pistons don't drool their appreciation for the chance to run in the countryside.

It is time for a traditional log wood smoke sauna, a living tradition practiced for centuries. Wood is fed into a stove for six to eight hours, heating stones and smoking up a dark room with no chimneys. When the heat is at a suitable level (around 80C), the smoke is cleared through the door and several small shutters, and the sauna is ready for use. In Finland, the heat in a sauna is like a spirit, a character who shares the experience with you. Finns call this the "löyly," respecting it, discussing its quality, offering to adjust it if it is too hot or, more often, too cold. After a short river canoe trip and a walk in the woods at the Vaattunki Lodge Estate – a government-owned but privately operated nature park – the smoke sauna was ready for us to enjoy. I've seen Sean's Sony XD camera take on all the elements during *Word Travels*, but was still impressed that he could leave it for a half hour in a scorching hot box to acclimatize for our in-sauna scene. The camera records digitally to a DVD-like disc. As Sean explains, tape would never be able to survive the heat, nor the -40C temperatures we encountered up in the Yukon.

I strip to a towel, Julia to a bikini (nudity, she informs me, does not extend to work colleagues), and it doesn't take long before rivers of sweat run out my body. Unlike electrical-heated saunas, the heat allows us to stay in for longer periods of time, a soft heat, strangely devoid of smell or the thick black smoke that filled the room. Another sauna tradition is taking birch tree branches and whipping the body, stimulating the blood cells, rejuvenating the skin. We handpicked these just moments before entering the sauna, and the earthy smell of birch adds a welcome fragrance to the mix. It is not quite as intense as my similar *banya* experience in Siberia a few years back, where the whipping heat took my breath away, but I think Julia enjoyed her chance to finally flog me on camera. After the sauna, we cool off in the adjacent brown river, clean but rich in iron, where I let the waters wash away my worries, and the current carry me away.

Rovaniemi has one of the best museums I've encountered anywhere: the Arktikum. The museum has an exhibit all about the history of the Lapland (including how the Nazis destroyed just about everything they could before the Finnish and Russian armies could get rid of them), along with exhibits about its animals, culture and landscape. The other side of the museum is all about life in the Arctic Circle, including the four million people who live within it. Interactive, colourful, animated and creative, this typical routine museum stop surprises us all, although by now we know that no museums don't make the final cut. Neither do the practical tube baths in the Clarion Hotel Santa Claus, or the superb Lapland food: fresh salmon, smoked fish, and crisp salads.

Back to Helsinki, population 600,000, with more than a few busfulls of tourists enjoying its long, hot summer days. The sauna experience would not be complete without a visit to the old, gritty Kotiharjun Sauna, the only remaining public wood-burning sauna in the city. Finns say the body only looks its best after thirty minutes in a sauna, and the sight of a half-dozen men – naked save for a towel – cooling off with a beer outside the sauna entrance might prove a decent counter-argument. Most Finnish apartments and houses have their own saunas, but for people who don't, or for those who prefer to engage the community soaked in puddles of sweat, there are community saunas that still serve the same function as they have for centuries. Women and men are separated, so while Julia grilled a local sauna expert named Ulla-Maija Rouhianen in the sauna upstairs, I disrobe downstairs with naked old men reading newspapers amongst the smell of time, wood and sweat. The large sauna gets packed on weekends and holidays, but today there are only a dozen or so men, of all ages, engaged in conversation in that distinctive Finnish tongue. Related to Estonian and Hungarian, it is one of the few non-Indo-European languages in Europe, and therefore completely impossible to understand on any level. There are a couple of tourists, too, since the sauna is mentioned as a must-do in the *Lonely Planet*. Picture the scene: I'm in a large sauna with a group of about a dozen naked men, the temperature scorching around 110C. Sean's camera has acclimatized, but an old-timer objects to the fact that he's wearing shorts. It's also too dark to film, so a bright spotlight is attached to the camera. So now Sean is naked, too, a big bald naked pink man with a monster black camera, filming everyone in the spotlight as they make wisecracks, while I play the host and attempt to describe what's going on. Three words: Hi.Lari.Ous. These guys can handle their heat. It's quite possible the old-timer was born in a sauna, since Finnish women were known to give birth in saunas up until the 1930's. When bathing went out of fashion and smells were masked with perfume, the Finns were the cleanest people in Europe, bathing after a sauna weekly, if not daily. An old-timer invites me to the small top-most level, just centimetres above where everyone else is sitting. The heat is so intense I become lightheaded, my ears literally burning in pain. The Finns have a word, "sisu," which is basically translated as a combination of: strength, spirit, man up, do what must be done, show courage, don't be a pussy. All the "sisu" in the world couldn't keep me on that upper level for more than a minute, the temperature easily over 120C. The löyly is especially sizzling, since bravado is in full force, and local men take turns adding bursts of water to the furnace, increasing the steam and the likelihood of a tourist fainting. Cooling off outside with a gin drink in a particularly strong rain storm, I can't leave without the "real treatment," i.e.. being scrubbed-down by an attendant. And so, for the second time this season, I find myself being hand-scrubbed on camera, although fortunately, unlike the Georgian bath attendant, my scrubber doesn't practice the salsa standing on my back. We worked particularly hard to film the public sauna, and yet not a frame made it into the final episode.

Outside the sauna, suitably free of toxins and dirt, a young English traveller is telling me about his couch-surfing experience in Russia. Using the increasingly popular social network that aims to connect travellers with locals, he found someone who was prepared to put him up for a couple of days, for free. There's no such thing as a free lunch; is there such a thing as a free couch? Buddy soon found himself being held ransom, forced to buy all manner of things for his host at the threat of physical violence. It's one of the few bad stories I've heard about couch surfing, although I'm sure there are plenty more of them out there. Either way, it would play perfectly into my story research. I was asked to write about cities that are kind to the traveller's wallet, and wanted to demonstrate that it's possible to visit a city like Helsinki – one of the most expensive in

Europe – on as little as twenty euro a day. A formidable challenge, but entirely doable, even if it was just for a day or two. First up, I had to find free accommodation. Couchsurfing.com has 1488 registered members in Helsinki, and I'm sure more than a few would be willing to accommodate me for a night, but of the dozen or so I contacted, none got back to me. I've tried couchsurfing.com a couple of times, and always had the same result. It seems you have to get lucky to get a bite, and then be lucky that the bite doesn't take a chunk out of you, like in the case of my unlucky English friend. I remembered a similar service I'd come across a few years ago called Global Freeloaders, and so tried that. After a couple of days, I got a nibble from a guy named Juuso, who said he'd be happy to host me on his couch in his one-bedroom ground-floor apartment. Further, he'd be on a work holiday, and so could show me around the city a bit. Now it's one thing to take a risk and crash at a stranger's apartment, and it's another to show up with a TV crew to capture the experience. It was fitting, as I buzz Juuso's number at his apartment block, that I have absolutely no clue who this guy is, or what kind of couch I could expect.

20 euros a day (at the time a little over a $30 bucks) is not going to get me far. It cost two euros for a ticket on Helsinki's excellent tram network to get to Juuso's apartment, so now I was down to just 18 euros. Juuso greets me outside his door. He's a 21-year-old Euro dude who works for a bank and lives in a spotlessly polished modern furnished apartment owned by his family. The motif is all black and white, with various works of art, a version of my trendy hotel room. I am picturing something more studenty, a little bit trashy, a couple of Bob Marley posters. Juuso explains to me the few rules he has: no smoking, that sort of thing. Is there any kind of person he wouldn't allow to crash over? Hippies, naturally; the man does not like hippies. It's been over a dozen years since I cut my long natty hair and silently chucked out my tie-dye shirts, so I am safe. The couch, meanwhile, is as close to a five star hotel as you could get in the world of couch surfing. Extra long, extra wide, L-shaped, soft with a neat fabric. I can also crash on the mattress in this weird slit in the wall, another option for the various guests that Juuso entertains. I had done my homework on activities to explore without spending money, and Helsinki is blessed with beaches and parks, squares and markets that will be just fine to hang out at all day. Like in any northern hemisphere city experiencing a fine

sunny day, those that hadn't made off to their country cottages were enjoying themselves. We catch the tram (with a little bit of practicality van action for the crew) to the beach, where an Ultimate Frisbee tournament is taking place. I wear my Vancouver Canucks hockey shirt (the Finns can appreciate ice hockey) while Juuso is dressed up in black with leather shoes, as unlikely a pairing as you could find, which is the beauty of the travel social networks. You really do get to meet people from all walks of life. After we check out some more sights it is time for lunch. We visit a supermarket, where I buy one protein milkshake (1.50), an apple (33c), a few slices of excellent traditional bread (67c) and a packaged salad dish comprised of cubed cheese marinated with olive and oil and sundried tomatoes (1.25). Total cost came to 3.75; delicious, except for the protein shake, which I chuck after one unfortunately yucky sip. That leaves me with 12.25, natch! Like other cities, Helsinki offers free CityBikes, which can be used with a two-euro deposit. And also like in other cities, it is impossible to find them, since it isn't rocket science that two euros for a bike is a pretty good deal. There was a news report recently saying that a private company took over Paris's Vélib' bike-share program but gave it up months later for its being completely uneconomical. The cost of maintaining and replacing damaged and lost bikes is a budget breaker. That being said, it's still a wonderful idea, and kudos to those cities that keep trying. The ace up my sleeve is a contact at Helsinki Tourism, and my TV story needs the bike, so a quick call later there is a bike waiting for me. If only life worked like a TV show! The bike is heavy, with no gears, a flat front tire and back-pedal brakes. Still, it is super fun to ride. I check out Helsinki landmarks like the Helsinki Cathedral, the bustling downtown arteries, the art museums and the port market – all at no cost. I made plans to meet Juuso and his friend Doti at the Linnanmäki Amusement park. It's free to get in. Previously inside the public sauna, I had heard about this crazy old wooden rollercoaster that has a brake operated manually by a guy standing in the last car. The park also has a free ride built for the 1950 Helsinki Olympics, a rotating glass elevator that will give me a view of the entire city. Too good to pass up, especially with only 12 euros in my pocket. Juuso and Doti (easy to spot with her shock of pink hair) are waiting outside with a cold beer, which made it even better.

TV Land took over, arranging a permit for us to film anywhere and everywhere in the park, which had some pretty wild rides, each at a cost of about 6 euros a ticket. If my host wants to treat me to something, technically that falls within the rules, so we beelined it to Vuoristorata, the infamous wooden rollercoaster – or, in Finnish, mountain track. The last time I rollercoastered was with a Norwegian pop star named Sondre Lerche at the Six Flags in New Jersey. Quiet and timid, he went nuts at the six mega-coasters in the park, riding one after the other. By the fourth coaster, I was green and swallowing my own puke. The dirty little secret of Modern Gonzo: I get intense motion sickness, quite easily. Save me from the pirate ship pendulum, and as for the spinning things – back, back, I say, you spawn of industrial Satan! But Vuoristorata is the most popular ride in Finland, one of only two remaining rollercoasters operating as it does (the other is in Denmark), built in 1951 and still using the original cars on tracks that have fortunately been replaced over the years. The driver, a harnessed manual operator who stands during the ride, can choose just how scary to make the ride, such as upping the speed or slamming into corners. TV Land means that we'd have to get multiple shots from multiple angles, and that the operator would do his best to freak us out. Although it looks pretty tame, like most of the old rickety rollercoasters still in operation it is absolutely thrilling. I am almost ejected out of my seat a couple of times on each run, and poor Juuso is on the side that I slam into at every sharp corner. In the front car, able to board before general admission, we end up riding that son-of-a-bitch NINE times, the crew taking turns, too. Those in the lineup shoot daggers at us with their eyes for constantly taking the front car, but being good Finns, keep their feelings pent up and to themselves. It is just the kind of Gonzo action I am craving – something unusual, out of the ordinary, unexpected; a rollercoaster of fun. As much fun as we had on the rollercoaster (nine times!), the thrill didn't translate well on camera, and the entire segment was cut.

Dinner is an excellent flat crust pizza in a Turkish pizza-kebab shop, the daily special (tuna and pineapple) for just 4.90. That leaves me enough to catch one more tram and get myself a beer at a cheap student watering hole. Here I meet some more of Juuso's friends, and at midnight, my experiment over, I can afford to buy a round of shots. We continue drinking back at Juuso's place, and I crash out on his large couch, as promised, as comfortable a sleep as the crew had back at the hotel.   And there you have it: a day of fun, sights, people and places in Helsinki, one of the most expensive cities in the world, on just 20 euros.

Compared to trips to South America, Asia or Eastern Europe, a visit to the northern countries of Scandinavia can be a quiet affair. Everything works, the streets are spotless, the trams run on time and the potential for unforeseen chaos is minimal. You can drink the water, eat the street food and converse with just about anyone, since most of the country speaks good English. Add friendly hosts who seem delighted to show me a good time – from the Arctic Circle to the fabulous meals throughout – and in the end it was as easy an episode as we've ever had filming, and as easy a week as I've ever had travelling. It wasn't the first time I'd met huskies or reindeer, or walked beneath the midnight sun. But it was the first time I'd done it as a working travel professional, snacking on expensive bear salami (yes, they eat bear salami), staying in nice hotels and focusing on what I do best: travel and writing. If I want chaos and a little bit of madness, I don't have to wait too long. Just a few hours' train ride away I will be returning into the big paws of the great bear herself, Mother Russia.

Mosquitoes get quite large in Lapland

BEHIND THE SCENES IN FINLAND

It's been over a decade since I drove across Denmark, Sweden and Norway, and I was looking forward to returning to Scandinavia. It's beautiful, and just so remarkably civilized. It's also crazy bad-ass expensive. The recession hit travel writers, too. Newspapers folding, cheques bouncing, freelance budgets slashed. We wanted to acknowledge that times were tough, although hopefully this show will be broadcast when times are gravy, too. So I gave myself a challenge. Helsinki, one of Europe's most expensive cities, on just 20 euros a day, including accommodation, food and entertainment. With social travel networks like Couchsurfing.com, Air Bnb and Global Freeloaders, you can save huge cash by finding friendly locals to put you up for the night. I had no idea what to expect when Juuso answered my request on Global Freeloaders (I was not having much luck on Couchsurfing.com, even though there are hundreds of members in Helsinki). These websites are terrific in that users review their peers. If there's a knife-wielding maniac trying to trap you on their couch, you'll know about it from user reviews and warnings. With its self-regulated system, you can generally avoid the whackos. Juuso worked at a bank and knew we were coming with a TV crew, which is why his place probably looked so immaculate. We hadn't actually spoken until we met on camera, and when I saw his couch I was pretty happy. Lord knows I've slept on some spring-coiled nightmares. Public transport soaked up a lot of my skimpy budget, like the salad oil soaked up my cheap supermarket bread. I figured I wasn't contravening any rules if Juuso bought me a beer because, hey, people buy me beers all the time. When I was backpacking on $40 a day a few years back I sometimes ate the leftovers of strangers, which is a tad distasteful, but frugal. No need this time; there were deals to be had.

Meanwhile, up north, the mosquitoes were not as bad as I was expecting, although they were none too pleasant, either. Fortunately, Julia attracts them, so travelling with her is like having your own permanent mosquito repellent. Word Travels took us to both the equator and Arctic Circle within a matter of weeks. There's got to be a prize for something like that. Sean, our director of photography, was getting married in a couple of weeks and his fiancée joined us for a couple of days in Finland before heading off to Sweden to visit family. After three years, she could finally see what life was actually like on the road.

(left) We spent hours filming this old, hand-braked rollercoaster, which never made the cut

(right) Julia gets a couple years of frustration out in a traditional smoke sauna

(above) Santa's address outside of Rovaniemi, receives 600,000 letters a year

(right) Only in TV Land: Juuso shows me a conveniently placed city bike in Helsinki.

(left) Pounds of sweat lost shooting in this public sauna that never made the show. (right) Sean Cable's fiance Kris joined us, a rare chance to see family on the road.

(left) Crossing the Arctic Circle. (right) A writing shot at the Suomenlinna Sea Fortress outside Helsinki.

RUSSIA
SPACESHIPS AND SUBWAYS

Let's not beat around the borsht. Travelling in Russia is a challenging affair. For a start, you need permission: visas, obtained at significant cost, and with significant hassle. Russians will argue that visa arrangements are reciprocal, that they have to jump through just as many hoops to visit your country, and they're right, of course.

Russians are pragmatic and tough, because Russians have to be. It has ensured their survival since medieval times, in the face of foreign invasions, insane dictators and truly lousy weather. For things to work here, there is a way, and should you not conform to that way, you pay. Permits are required if you are media, and paperwork must be filed, in triplicate, if you plan on filming outside any public space. If you plan on filming inside, there's more paperwork (in triplicate). Customer service is practically non-existent, and you'll be hard pressed to find a smile from a restaurant server, much less assistance from, say, a police officer.

And then you have the language. It's like waking up one morning to find that the alphabet you know has been sabotaged by dolphins. Suddenly, an R becomes a P and a C becomes an S, and while you might recognize certain characters, they don't sound like anything you recognize at all. The fact that there are no English signposts, no help for the wayward visitors even in a tourist hotspot like Moscow's Red Square, can lead you on a treasure hunt for directions. That's hampered further by the fact that, in all likelihood, the person you ask for help doesn't speak English, and even if they did, they wouldn't want to help you anyway. Yes, Russia can be dour, and the steely-eyed glares of locals can be unnerving. Until you get used to it, and realize that you're in the world's biggest country, occupying one full eighth of all land on Earth. Stretching across eleven time zones, Russia is not some quirky backward country good for a laugh (like, say, Albania). Rather, this is the *other* country that has shaped our modern world, through revolutionary ideas and the revolutions that they subsequently spawned. Through writers and artists and scientists and soldiers. During the era of the Soviet Union, the paws of the great Russian bear were extended so far it eventually had to drop its arms under the sheer strain. Now, after a turbulent hibernation, the bear is rustling from its sleep, opening its eyes, and ready to emerge once more at the top of the food chain. It is eager to claw and fight its way out, prepared to roar in anger at other predators who might threaten its goals (USA, China). Its current leader is famously ruthless, its people ambitious and determined, and tourism… tourism… well, that's simply not as important as mining for gas and oil in the Caucuses. You won't find glossy government tourist brochures with models having the time of their lives in Moscow. You won't see bright billboard advertising, or sweeping television commercials exclaiming: Visit Russia; it's like No Place Else on Earth!   And yet it is. Like no place else on earth. And that's why 4 years after an epic journey on the Trans-Siberia Railway, I have returned.

White nights in St. Petersburg, when the sun stays high late into the summer evening. Nevsky Prospekt is jammed with pedestrians, the souvenir markets are booming with cruise ship and tour bus tourists. In the centre of the city, you can gaze down just about any street and see something of interest: a golden-domed church, a Venice-like canal, a building propped with statues, or perhaps the symbols the once-great, now-kitschy Soviet iconography. It is, without doubt, one of the most beautiful cities to walk around in, or, better yet, to cruise along the narrow canals. Less than two hours off the train from Helsinki, I'm doing exactly that, sprawled out on the roof of a river boat, basking in the early evening sunshine, taking in the sights. At this time of year, it only gets dark around eleven p.m., so there's plenty of time to putter along, ducking under the low-hanging bridges, stopping off at statues, waving to mismatched couples drinking on the riverbanks. Mismatched – for the slim, young women are dressed for ballrooms and the balding beer-gut men are dressed in tracksuits, or suits too large. Together, the fashion can be mind boggling. I spot a woman wearing a shirt with leopard print, zebra print, polka dots, and stripes, glitter and paisley – all at the same time. There's not a stain it couldn't hide, which is perhaps the point. The clack of stiletto heels on cobblestone, the dull thud of stiletto heels on a hiking path. Neon colours, a variation of mullets, and the shoes. Oh, my God, the shoes… there are few countries where the simple act of people watching can yield so much entertainment.

I see Saint Isaac's, the third-largest domed cathedral in the world, its huge golden crown sparkling in the sun. The Church of Spilled Blood is my personal favourite, a true marvel of architecture formerly used by the communists to store potatoes. Topped by gem-stoned, ice-cream-swirl onion bulbs, adorned with murals, paintings and detailed sculpture, resting on a narrow canal. It rests on the site where a czar was assassinated, blown up into bloody bits, hence its gruesome name. Several bridal parties are taking photos, fulfilling a tradition for St. Petersburg newlyweds, to include the city's sights in their memories. One group jumps in the air for a photo before a muzzled baby brown bear is passed to the groom for an awkward photo op. The souvenir market has thousands of Russian Matryoshka dolls (invented in Japan, made in China), including newly minted Barack Obama eggheads. There's even Osama Bin Laden, housing Saddam Hussein, housing Yasser Arafat, housing Mussolini – and at the core of evil, Hitler himself. Obama houses the four previous Democrat presidents. Putin is as popular as ever. There's even a Vancouver Canucks ice hockey doll, but the Chinese manufacturers cannot keep up to date with the constant player trades, and the names of players are out of date. Shady shysters peddle dubious cans of black caviar, which is illegal to sell outside of strict government regulations designed to protect the sturgeon from extinction. If someone tries to sell you a can of fish eggs for $50 bucks, marked down from $400, you can bet they're fake, and still taste like salty goo. We rock a time-lapse on St. Pete's main drag – Nevsky Prospekt – and I try solicit a smile from the hundreds of people who walk past. It would have been easier to get the concrete sidewalk to crack a grin. Young girls have no shame about sizing me up, using their distinctly Russian manner of staring right into my eyeball, attacking with lust and certain danger. It is said that when a Russian woman gets her hooks into you, she'll use them to tear your skin off while you smile. Meanwhile, there are the plenty of the usual hipsters and yuppies, the aging beauties and teen pop tarts you'll find in any major city. Just with a lot more edge.

Our guides this week are courtesy Intrepid Travel, and they've had their work cut out for them organizing the necessary permits and getting the stamped documents (in triplicate) needed to help us promote the country. A beaming Maria is all warmth and helpfulness and eagerness to please, proving the folly of my generalizations. She's so damn proud of her country that I have to wonder what might happen if the government were ever to support its fledgling tourism industry. Oh, there are plenty of tourists in Russia, alright, because there is big money to be made, and plenty of clever Russians (and foreigners) to go about making it. Maria shows us around, taking us up to the rusted roof of an old artist's loft to watch the sunset. We dine at one a.m., but as the team heads back to the Hotel Pio, Caroline (making peace with the tripod as a first-time production assistant) and I join Maria and her friend for some champagne at the raising of the bridges. It's two a.m., thousands of people are out on the streets, spirits are high, and here is another side of Russia, the side that is less about baring its claws than about giving you a jolly old bear hug. The night is warm. A statue of St. Peter dating back to the 1780's is spit-polished and immaculately lit. Since prime minister and de facto king Vladimir Putin is a proud St. Pete's boy, the city is in a state of constant restoration, and whoever calls the shots is making sure those shots are being fired. We pass some street work outside our hotel and joke that the long deep trench will probably be ready just in time for Armageddon. The next day, we are surprised to find it fully repaired. You notice change in the most unlikely places. At the Hotel Pio, a little bit of Italy in the heart of Russia (it's exterior is grim and blackened; it's interior is light and warm), the stern-faced cleaner/cook notices I am about to leave the hotel in my crinkled blue collared shirt. She insists on ironing it for me, tut-tutting like a disapproving mother. When I try and tip her before we leave – for the cleaning, the cooking, the ironing –   she flat-out rejects my pittance of appreciation. These are the sweeteners I add to my overall experience, especially when I am served up a mug of that famous Russian scowl. Which is not to say that people here don't care, or won't help a stranger in need. But unless you can magically decipher the Cyrillic alphabet and speak their language, it sometimes feels that way. On the other hand, our driver Yuri seems hell-bent on bending over backwards to help us. On the other hand, Yuri is from Finland.

A few years ago, I took the train from Moscow to St. Petersburg. This time, I took the plane from St. Petersburg to Moscow. Last time it was rainy and grey when I visited Red Square. This time, the sun was glowing orange, boosting the colour of St. Basil's. Built in the 1550's, the cathedral (often mistaken for the Kremlin) is so beautiful, rumour has it the czar had the architect blinded so he could never repeat its glory. Red Square gets its name from the old Russian word for "beautiful," which later became the word for "red". Coincidentally, much blood was spilled on its cobblestones in the form of public executions, and the Soviets marched their nuclear missiles and parades here, too, incorporating Red Square as a symbol of their Red Power. We are warned beforehand by our local fixer Peter not to bring in our big camera, or even our tripod. The police in Red Square are notorious for being little more than sanctioned street thugs, targeting tourists with passport and permit scams. Hunting in packs, they single out the weakest of the herd – the tourist, a poor bewildered beast – and sniff out roubles like chum in shark water. Without the proper permit, itself a grander form of extortion, they would tear us to shreds. The last time Michael was here, directing an episode of *Thirsty Traveller*, he was shut down, taken to a police station and locked down for the day as he tried to bargain for his freedom and not bust his budget. Heeding his advice, we moved in with our new "C" cam, a tiny HD Panasonic, and filmed away. Cops circled, but never moved in for the kill, although I'm sure others were not so lucky. We emerged from Red Square elated that we had somehow managed to visit the most famous attraction in Russia without being shut down, hassled or having to pay bribes. One day, perhaps the Bear will learn the benefits of not treating visitors like walking dinner.

D.E.N.I.E.D. As someone who has a job that requires access, it is a humbling experience. I initially wanted to write a story about ballet dancing in St. Petersburg. After months of letters back and forth, our request for permission was denied. I next tried to get into circus school; I even tried to blow up shit with a variety of weapons. D.E.N.I.E.D. It's possible to fly in a MiG jet, but that costs around $16,000. Actually, I got the feeling it was possible to do just about anything, providing you paid off the right people. In Moscow, there's a tram restaurant that lets you eat and see the city. We thought it would make a great beat for the show, and it would have if the owners didn't want 10,000 roubles just to let us on board. The long-term benefits of public relations have yet to seduce the Bear's short-term hunger. D.E.N.I.E.D. So I was thrilled, nigh on elated, that we had been given permission to film at the Yuri Gagarin State

Scientific Research-and-Testing Cosmonaut Training Center in the even-cooler-sounding Star City. Well, by permission, I mean a price that we could actually afford and one that seemed reasonable. A barrier guarded by two soldiers was being raised. Access permitted. I was heading straight into the heart of the Russian Federal Space Agency. Sort of.

One of the better known space tourists is Guy Laliberté, the founder of Cirque du Soleil. He is a very rich man with the money to afford a very expensive dream, namely to be blasted off into orbit for a ten-day stint aboard the International Space Station. Like the half-dozen other space tourists before him (or "pioneers of commercial space travel", as they'd rather be known), Laliberté was trained in Star City at the Cosmonaut Training Centre. This is where Yuri Gagarin, the first man in space, was prepped for the 1961 mission that fired the starting gun of the space race, and this remains the largest of three cosmonaut training centres. Here you'll find life-size replicas and simulators, including a twenty-ton pool for spacewalking, rocket modules and all sorts of equipment and knobs and buttons and switches that power the cutting-edge world of rocket science. You're probably imagining something akin to a Star Trek movie. Because that's what I was imagining as our van pulled up to the parking lot, cracked with weeds and neglect. It's been a tough couple of years for the Russian Space Agency. Originally funded at whatever cost by the Russian military, the end of the cold war coinciding with the end of the Soviet Union dramatically shifted the priorities from outer space to here on earth. Slashed budgets necessitated the innovative idea of space tourism, along with highly productive cooperation between all the world's space agencies. Recently, funding for the Russian Space Agency has been transferred out of the military budgets and into the public sector. It costs around $400 million to deliver a rocket with a suitable payload into space. When it comes down to it, the $30 million you'd pay for the ticket of a lifetime barely covers the cost of the seat. With this in mind, it's a little easier to do away with the flashing neon lights, sterile hallways and space-age uniforms. Instead, picture a town of 8000 people supporting and developing some of the boldest scientific experiments on earth, with a basic budget and dated facilities. Far from the space centre of my imagination, this cosmonaut training facility brought my expectations very much down to earth.

It's the weekend, and things are understandably quiet. After walking down a long corridor lined with the photos of previous space heroes, I emerge in a big gymnasium. In front of me is a full-size replica of a real Russian rocket ship, the Soyuz, large enough to deliver three cosmonauts into space. Forget *Star Wars*. Built in the 1960's, this seven-metre-tall cubicle is still the most reliable and efficient means of blasting three people safely into orbit, even if it lacks automatic doors or a talking computer. It reminds me very much of the nuclear missile silo I visited in Ukraine. Lots of manual switches, a tight squeeze, a drab interior. It is here where I realize the enormous gap between actual space science and science fiction. Science fiction has no room for duct tape.

Another simulator is further down the hall, manned by a couple of PC's, with a couple of couches beneath it. To remind everyone which planet we're on, a dozen or so green plants separates the two simulators. There's a far more futuristic third vessel in white, but that one was off limits. It is here that our guide Marina begins to explain what cosmonauts (literally translated: star sailors) have to endure for their ordeal. Besides the fact that they're being strapped onto forty tons of rocket fuel and blasted at 28,000 km/hr into the sky, the pressure, G-force, gravitational spin and sheer physical stress requires intense training and preparation. Cosmonauts train for a full year before their liftoff. "As for astronauts, they take pills," says Marina, a trace of space race competitiveness still in her voice.

Space tourists like Laliberté have to endure full-time training, in such marvellous pieces of equipment as the vomit comet, a zero-gravity training aircraft and the world's largest, fastest and most powerful centrifuge. This enormous machine is an absolute jaw-dropper. While the human body can handle a maximum of 12 G's (acceleration relative to free fall), the design of the centrifuge can get you to 30G, enough to literally crush a man to pieces. Unfortunately, it was not possible to look inside, or even see it move (it requires a large number of staff, at considerable cost, to operate it). Even so, tourists can take the ultimate theme park ride for a spin at a mere $1000 a pop. The water pool uses twelve tons of liquid to mimic the motions of outer space. Taking a look from the hot and humid observation deck made me long to just jump in. As

Marina points out the space suits, mentions the practicalities involved in eating, and talks facts and figures, I can sense her pride, and at the same time, her practiced acceptance that visitors expect… something more. Something like in the movies. The stakes are high, the cost mind-boggling, and the technology, well, it requires the brightest minds of the smartest rocket scientists. But it also requires the engineering of simple nuts and bolts, like the ones holding a life-size replica of the retired Mir Space Station. Assembled in modules and occupied for a period of over twelve years, Mir held a crew of three, which conducted experiments and did maintenance in its labyrinthine structure. Star sailors (astro, cosmo, taika and other 'nauts) from thirteen countries visited Mir before it was retired and crashed into the Pacific Ocean. Here at the training facility, the Mir replica is not only a valuable training ground, it is also a living museum of one of humanity's earliest and most successful attempts to live above the clouds.

Space tourism has proven to be somewhat controversial. Some credit it with saving scientific research by drawing valuable public attention to the topic and generating much-needed funds. Others think it is an excessive playground for the excessively rich, putting something as universal as space beyond the grasp of the rest of us. Mark Shuttleworth, the South African space tourist, objects to the word tourist, since they are trained like cosmonauts, and in some cases participate and conduct experiments just like scientists. Then you have the Ansari XPRIZE, which was a $10,000,000 award given to the first non-governmental organization capable of manufacturing a reusable commercially operational spacecraft. The money was just for show – the eventual winner spent ten times as much in research and development. There's no ceiling when it comes to the potential for space tourism. Groups like Hilton have bid on moon hotels, Virgin Galactic is taking Richard Branson to the stars, and while this might seem like science fiction, once you find yourself standing in a real-life rocket ship it begins to feel awfully real indeed. Even if the ship is over forty years old.

Things change. In the 1960's, Star City was a heavily guarded top-secret facility. Today, it is open to visitors and film crews, though some maps still don't acknowledge its existence. Those interested in visiting the Cosmonaut Training Centre can apply for permission through the official website (www.gctc.ru), or through a Russian tour agency. Throw around some dough, and you can get thrown around in the centrifuge, or even the vomit comet, if you so desire. Yet one would be mistaken for thinking this is some sort of expensive theme park. The air is serious, the tone sombre and the mission, critical. There is so little we know, and so much we need to. I'd like to think that visiting Star City was like visiting the first Ford Model T factory: one marvels at the mechanics but wonders if these strange, clunky machines will ever actually take us anywhere. They will. No doubt, to infinity, and beyond.

****

After Tokyo, the Moscow Metro is the second-most heavily used transit system in the world: it has 12 lines and 177 stations, stretches nearly 300kms and transports an average of more than seven million passengers each day. Aside from its efficiency, there is no other rapid transit system that comes close to the design, architecture and legacy of Moscow's stations. Grand, opulent ballrooms largely devoid of tacky advertising, Moscow's Metro stations have chandeliers, mosaics and iconic Soviet statues. It was Stalin's dream for the Metro to mirror all that was great about the Soviet Empire, and to be palaces for the people.

The best and brightest architects of the day were invited to design the stations, to create living museums trafficked by millions. There are 65.4km of escalators, some 10,000 train runs a day, nearly 35,000 employees and not a scrap of litter anywhere. There's even a new art car that allows passengers to enjoy watercolours underground. For the show, I took the cameras to three of the most famous stations. Ploshchad Revolyutsii Station sits adjacent to and below Red Square. Bronze figures are crouched, glorifying the socialist revolution. When Stalin first heard about them, he was ready to scrap the lot, since Russian heroes should never be on their knees. When he saw them, however – their proud lifelike faces, noble spirit, simple farm clothing – he changed his mind. During World War II, the statues were evacuated to the Urals, while the Metro served as a safe haven from the bombs above. Some of the statues have dogs, and students have created a tradition that involves rubbing their noses for luck. Decades of rubbing have polished their noses, and watching tourists and locals come together in this strange custom reminded me that we're not all that different, the

Russians and us. "I hope the Russians love their children, too," sang Sting in his pleading and earnest Cold War song.

Novokuznetskaya, lit up by old, shadowy lamps, honours Soviet war heroes. You could be in a spy novel, or a period romance. Impressive overhead mosaics sit atop crowds as they hurry to their next appointments. Mayakovskaya is the true ballroom, the majestic station you might see in photos or travel shows. It's one of the largest and busiest stations on the network, lit by giant chandeliers and framed by giant archways and chrome columns. We have permission to shoot down here, but it doesn't stop overweight guards in too-small uniforms from circling us like vultures, eager to shut us down and poach a decent bribe. One guard sports a black eye. I can practically smell his corrupt soul. He grabs Paul's arm and shoves us to make us stop until his superior grunts that we have been approved. With one piece of paper patiently arranged by Caroline over several months beforehand, it feels like we have just pulled a bazooka on a knife-wielding mugger. Further along I landed in Sretensky Bulvar, opened in 2007 and the newest station in the Metro system. The contrast between the grand old Soviet style and Modern Russia is stark. The halls are sterile, adorned in mixed media art, cold and urban. The angles are sharp and functional, the grunge polished. An attractive wedding party take photographs. Their smiles and laughs echo off the walls.

The sun is setting behind one of the Seven Sisters – the seven mammoth gothic buildings commissioned by Stalin to show that the Soviets' buildings could compete with American skyscrapers. Today, they look like something out *Blade Runner*, even if they have been converted into hotels, offices and universities. Muscovites are gathered by the old 90m Olympic ski jump, checking out a view of the city that gave birth to what would later evolve into Russia. Some breakdancers do the windmill; bikers compare their choppers; students drink beer. There's the usual clickity-clop of high heels, the neck-twisting miniskirts. I can just make out the spires of St. Basil, but dominating the skyline are several skyscrapers under construction, the result of Russia's status as an energy superpower. Like the concentration of its political capital, its economic wealth lies famously with the oligarchs, the right men at the right place and time to carve up the remnants of a former global superpower. Sean reckons he's never seen so many luxury cars all in one city before. Moscow is one of the world's most expensive cities for expats. Meaning if you go to a decent restaurant, rent a decent apartment or buy a decent pair of shoes, you're going to pay more for it here than anywhere else. Most tourists seem to congregate at Hotel Izmaylovo, the old Olympic Village, where four Vegas-size hotels hold over 8000 beds. Together they make the largest hotel in the city, but apart do not feature on any lists. Our rooms on the 27th floor of the Gamma block are nice enough, even if the lobby has the strange scent of Play-Doh. Our meals are costing us around $20 a hit, until we discover the best and most unlikely shawarma joint in the world, a tiny hot-as-hell room where one man crafts the perfect $3 meal in a wrap.

When you travel, it takes a few days before you can play the system, and until then, the system is designed to play you.

On Arbat Street, shortly before a legendary storm hits that will flood streets and crack the whip of earth-shaking thunder, Julia and I are recognized by a couple from Toronto. They're big fans of the show, and have used it as inspiration and advice in their own long-term travel plans. They can't believe they've actually bumped into us, just four days into their own magnificent journey, and their first question is: Are we married? We reply with our running joke: Well, we fight a lot and don't have sex, so technically, you could say we are. Later, I bump into them again, staying at the same hotel (small world, I know). I dish out the vital things I have learned on my own journey:

1. It's the people you meet who create the paradise you find.
2. Wherever you are is where you're meant to be.
3. Learn to listen to, appreciate and trust your gut.
4. Smile, even when things get tough.

I bid them good luck, feeling a little foolish for playing the travel guru I'd thought I'd never be. I feel drained from the pace, exhausted from the pressure, dizzy from the Cyrillic, and miss my girlfriend back home. Five years ago I never would have thought I'd end up Moscow and St. Petersburg. Now, I've visited twice. At this rate, I may as well set my sights on being the first travel writer in space. Esrocket Man, burning up his fuel up here, alone.

BEHIND THE SCENES IN RUSSIA

It was never going to be easy to organize the appropriate permits for Russia. That's because I'm not sure the appropriate permissions exist. Given the incredible history, size and scale of the country, it's surprising to find they have no tourist board, no concerted government effort to attract tourists and the foreign income that comes with them. We work with tourism boards because they play a key factor in our jobs as travel writers, and they help facilitate things for the travel show, like taking a camera crew into public spaces in a manner that benefits everyone involved. With Russia, we worked with a great company called Intrepid Travel, which provided us with an experienced on-the-ground fixer to help us get around and avoid the infamous bribe hunt. She's the one who warned us about taking cameras into Red Square, and without the documentation she secured for me in the Metro, I'm sure that one cop (with the black eye) would have taken me to a jail cell and beaten the rubles out of me. Ah, Russia! But then look at those fabulous shots of us cruising the canals of St. Pete's, soaking up one of the world's most beautiful cities! Russia has all sorts of things to do that don't fly anywhere else, because in Russia one gets the feeling that anything has a price. Fly a MiG fighter jet? Drive a tank? Train with the Moscow State Circus? These were all story ideas that crashed due to outrageous costs, scheduling, or the fact that media promotion there is in its infancy. So I headed into the Metro, and I would love to have shown you some of the other amazing stations, but we lacked the permits. If they exist.

Star City was bittersweet in that we were at ground zero of modern space tourism but were not allowed to perform any training exercises. I've always been a hands-on kind of guy, so to show me the world's biggest, most gnarly centrifuge and not let me see it in action? Well, it's kind of like saying "Walkies!" to a dog, and then locking it up. Nevertheless, my tail was wagging to walk around the Mir Space Station replica, or step into the humid underwater training facility. The founder of Cirque du Soleil was scheduled to blast into space a few weeks later, having paid $20 million for the ticket. He'd been in Star City for six months training, and I can only imagine what they must have put him through. The first travel writer in space? If only.

Souvenirs from Russia: A Barack Obama Russian egg. A Beatles Russian egg (with Lennon on the outside). A warm fuzzy hat for the winter. My first-ever ballet – Russian Hamlet. And the memory of the best shawarma ever, located in a sweaty little hut just outside the mammoth hotel that we stayed in. The Bear has always captured the imagination of travellers, and hopefully this episode gives some idea why.

Church of Spilled Blood in St Petersburg where Tsar Alexander II was murdered

Built in the 1550's, Moscow's St Basils is the most famous building in Russia.

Standing alongside the world's largest centrifuge in Star City

Mayakovskaya Station in the Moscow Metro looks like a ballroom

CHILE

SNOWCATS IN THE ANDES

As published in the Globe & Mail

Three hours drive from the Chilean capital of Santiago is a ski resort without any shops, malls, or promenades. There are no restaurants, bars or hotels either. There's not even a ski lift. Yet it still attracts clients from around the world, and for good reason. Ski Arpa is the dream of a lifelong ski instructor who scrapped and saved over three decades to open a mountain for anyone in love with stunning views, and untracked snow. Here, two Pisten Bully Snowcats shepherd up to 22 skiers to the top of the mountain, where they have mind-boggling access to 4000 acres of skiable terrain.

74-year old Toni Sponar, a veteran ski-instructor of Aspen, Banff, and number of South American ski resorts, bought 5000 acres of land back in 1983. At just $5000, it was a bargain even for a ski instructor. The location was ideal. From atop the peak of Alto del Arpa you can see the Pacific Ocean to the west, and Mount Aconagua, the tallest mountain outside the Himalayas, to the east. The south facing slopes receive plenty of sun, protected from harsh winds, with chutes forming in natural abundance. Surrounding you is the Andes mountain range in all its glory - so different from the view in the Rockies, or the Alps.

A year after his dream purchase, Toni installed a ski lift and set to work creating an 8km switchback road to the base lodge. Then disaster struck. A massive storm dumped metres of snow, causing an avalanche that wiped out the lift, the lodge, and all of Toni's savings in the process. He would still visit his mountain with friends over the years, but it would take another 20 years before he could resurrect his dream of a skier's ski resort. He purchased two Snowcats, aligned with booking and marketing agents, and finally created the most rewarding catskiing operation on the continent. Clients visit from around the world for the powder, the sweeping vista, and the unlimited fresh tracks.

As we slowly make our way up the switchbacks, the van abruptly stops and one of my fellow passengers throws up. It's a rough road, which Toni maintains himself, zig-zagging 600m up the valley. I'm feeling a little queasy from the altitude, but the excitement seems to settle my stomach. I only discovered the joy of snow when I moved to Canada in my twenties. When I was 6 years old, a once-a-century freak snowstorm hit Johannesburg. My schoolteacher, having never seen snow, made the class hide under our desks. She thought it was nuclear fall out.

I was retelling the story in the van as the switchbacks became ever steeper. Finally, our Swiss driver announces we have arrived. Next to the parking clearing is a humble, rustic building, built deliberately into the hill to avoid being wiped out by an avalanche like its predecessor. I am blessed with perfect conditions – the sky is clear and blue, and a 20cm of snow fell overnight. I sign a waiver, and get handed an avalanche transmitter by Anton, Toni's son and partner in the operation. There are a dozen clients today, made up of Americans from Colorado, some French, some German. This is not Whistler or St Moritz or Aspen. We have all packed our own lunch, and accept the simplicity of the amenities. We have come for the snow, not the glitz.

It takes 45 minutes for the powerful snowcat to make its way up the mountain. I am standing at the back of the outdoor passenger area, watching Toni and another skier being towed behind us. The snowcat eats the steepest of inclines, charging like a tank up towards the peak. The air gets thinner and colder, and suddenly, the full might of the Andes appear on the horizon, a true alpine wonderland. After a final push from the powerful cat, my back against its protective rails at a near 45-degree angle, we arrive on the peak and dismount. The groups split up respectively, choosing a wild multitude of lines. Mount Aconagua, nearly 7000m high and dividing the Argentinean and Chilean border, beckons me forward. I let out a Wilhelm Scream, for if you can't scream at the top of the world, where can you? Within seconds, I begin carving this mountain like a Thanksgiving turkey.

A full day with Ski Arpa includes four runs with a guide. By my third run, I am feeling braver, dropping into a gully to attempt an unsuccessful launch through a chute. It takes a while to dig myself out. Toni joins me on the next run, rocketing down his mountain, enjoying the start of another stellar season in Chile. He whips down so gracefully I find it hard to believe he's old enough to be my grandfather. Meanwhile his clients are bonding over fat smiles and white powder. Warming up in the sun outside the base hut, we all agree: Who needs malls and promenades when you have a 1000m vertical descent on some of the best powder in the world? Especially when you have it all to yourself.

Gut-busting switchbacks on the road to Ski Alpa

Taking a break on the Snow Cat

Posing for a hero shot with Mount Aconagua, the tallest peak in the Andes, behind me.

BEHIND THE SCENES IN CHILE

Anyone who snowboards will quickly see I'm not exactly a pro. It was my first time on a mountain in almost a year and my initial launch, gratefully left on the cutting room floor, had me wiping out on my ass. But fresh tracks on an empty mountain has been a dream ever since I first picked up a snowboard six years ago. The freedom of virgin powder! And to top it off, we got the only blue-sky day in a week of filming, a pure bluebird day amidst overcast days of gray. That was a first for me, too. Together with the helicopter day in Alberta and the water sport day in Barbados, I needed a blue sky more than ever. After this, I couldn't complain about the weather for the rest of the season.

I'd been pushing for a snowboarding story ever since Season One because our talented director of photography, Sean Cable, and sound/B-cam guy Paul Vance, happen to be two of the best snow production crew members anywhere. When not filming *Word Travels*, they work on ski slopes all the time, and are capable of hauling themselves up and down a mountain with their heavy gear intact. I knew they'd manage to make my pitiful attempts at carving look epic, and they did. Watching Sean ski backwards with his large camera resting on his shoulder is something to see. And even these guys were stoked to find Ski Arpa, which is off the beaten track – a big find for ski bums looking for something different.

Then to the desert, the Atacama. For me, it will always be one of the most magical places on earth. Last time here I was backpacking on a crazy budget and spent a few nights in a room the size of a closet. This time 'round we stayed in one of the most stunning hotels I've ever seen. So there was much to reflect about in the driest place on earth. That crystal lagoon was freezing; it may be the coldest body of water I've ever dipped in (and I've swum in Siberia and in Norwegian glacier lakes!). Santiago was cold, Valparaíso was mild, the desert was hot: Chile is like a four-season pizza.

Julia's childhood injury brings home the dangers of all this adventure stuff I get up to, and how lucky I've been to come out unscathed after five years of heavy travel. Another visiting travel writer was not so lucky. The reason why we lacked the permission to film the flamingos was that our tourism board fixer had to rush the journalist to hospital with a broken leg. I was happy to get off the mountain in one piece, see the Atacama for a second time and inhale the meaty, eggy goodness of the J. M. Cruz Social Club *chorrillana*!

The otherworldly beauty of Atacama. We swam in the freezing, mineral lake.

(l) Alta Atacama, embedded into the desert hills of San Pedro
(r) Watching the pink sunset over Atacama's Valley of the Moon

ECUADOR

SHAMANS AND GUINEA PIGS

It is folly trying to experience Ecuador in just seven short days. The country has four wholly distinct ecosystems:
- The coast, famed for beaches, surfing and diving,
- The Andes, famed for mythical volcanoes and indigenous culture
- The Amazon, famed for unparalleled bio-diversity
- The Galapagos, perhaps the last unspoiled natural wonder left on earth.

There are more animals and plants per square kilometre in Ecuador than anywhere else. It has the world's second-largest number of endemic vertebrates, third-largest for amphibians, fourth for birds, fifth for butterflies. Over 10% of all vertebrate animals on the planet, 35% of all hummingbirds and 10% of all plant species are all slammed together in just 0.19% of the earth's surface. All this, and we haven't even gotten to the country's indigenous people, Spanish colonial history, colourful markets and taste for guinea pig. Pure folly, then, but what the hell, I'll give it a go anyway.

Ecuador is the last major South American country for me to visit, a gaping Latino hole to plug in my global itinerary. The opportunity presented itself while filming *Word Travels*. Just Guyana and Suriname are left. Everyone dreams of visiting the Galapagos, but not everyone has to contend with outrageously expensive film permits, or balls to the wall production schedules. Instead, I would focus on the people of the Highlands, the history and haciendas, the myths and mystery, with a little coastal action thrown in for good measure.

I only have a few hours to acclimatize to Quito, 2850m above sea level, where walking up a flight of stairs at Old Town's Hotel Patio Andaluz left me searching for breath. The hotel, like Old Town itself, is a carefully preserved testimony to Spanish colonialism, which is why UNESCO declared Quito's Old Town a World Heritage Site in 1978, the first such classification of its kind. A few hours of sleep and we hit the ground running with an early departure for Otavalo – a town in the central highlands, leaving the sprawling city behind. As we grind up steep switchbacks and over mountains brushed with shrubbery, the city sprawl thinned out, along with the traffic. Flipping through my US dollars, which replaced the local *sucre* as official currency in 2000, I was thinking about what makes Ecuador distinct, a nation apart from its neighbours, the former Gran Colombia dreamed up by South America's liberator, Simon Bolivar. Gran Colombia included most of modern Venezuela, Colombia, Panama and Ecuador, before Bolivar was dethroned and his generals sliced and diced their territories into the counties we know today. Ecuador shares Andean and indigenous roots with neighbours Peru and Colombia, along with simmering border disputes. I was thinking about the Galapagos Islands, Darwin's playground located some 1000km west into the warm Pacific Ocean. Much to chew on, and I was about to chew on a whole lot more.

I did a television interview recently about the world's most exotic foods – insects, bull's balls, fertilized duck eggs, ox penis soup – and in the end they ambushed me on air with slimy buttered Brussels sprouts, the one vegetable I really struggle with. My list should have included *cuy*, which we know as that mis-named cuddly rodent, the guinea pig. The last time I had the opportunity to taste this Andean delicacy, four years ago in Peru, I quietly retreated from the table. Much has happened since, and this time I was determined to shine a spotlight on the little critters, cuddly as they may be. Now *cuy* is not some light snack to accompany the local *futbol* game. It is a revered meal eaten mostly on special occasions, and at considerable expense. US$9 might not sound like much, but when nearly 40% of the population live below the breadline, the cost of the four-legged furry entrée becomes significant. Traditionally, the rodent (no relation to the pig whatsoever; nobody is quite sure why it got its name) runs freely in village huts, sharing the abode and keeping away the rats and bugs. I got to see this in action in Quiroga Village, where three withered old ladies lived in a dark, smoky cement shack. Scurrying around the dirt floor are guinea pigs, about a foot in size each, in brown, black or cow-print-coloured fur. The ladies, hunched over by time, seem delighted to have a TV crew invade. Outside the hut, in the high and hot equatorial sun, I am quickly reminded why I love South America so much. Everywhere you look is a photo opportunity, and for all its problems you sure do see a lot of smiling people. Another old lady walks down the road, a "cartoon character," as my director Jordan likes to call them. I call them postcard people. She sticks out her hand for money, but before I can sigh with the resign of disappointment (forever scarred by Ethiopia's *ferengi frenzy*), she snaps back her hand and erupts into a high-pitched cackle. Jordan and I laugh at the absurdity of the moment, the good humour of it, and there in a small village we all enjoy a tiny fleeting moment of human connection across the widest of socio-economic and cultural gaps. It lasted but a second, but these are the kind of nuggets that make my travel treasury so rich. These are the kinds of experiences that make South America my favourite continent.

In Cotachi there are a dozen or so restaurants that serve up their specialty: deep fried crispy guinea pig, served spread-eagled on a plate of potatoes and salad. Local farms breed the rodents to maintain a commercially demanded supply, and while Julia and the crew went to check one out, I wandered down the dusty road under signposts advertising restaurants specializing in *cuy* feasts, crossing a tumbleweed-quiet plaza to one such establishment, called La Hornilla. Given the time of day (noon), the time of week (Wednesday), and the time of tourist season (off), the restaurant is empty save for one man tucking into a guinea pig, and the kitchen staff sitting up front watching a World Cup qualifier between Ecuador and Bolivia. As with every other country on the continent, when there's a game on, everything stops. I ordered fried chicken, waiting for the crew before braving a taste of *cuy*. Ecuador scored three times by the time a golden brown furless guinea pig was served up as a taster. Deep fried in three separate pots, its tiny claws gnarled, eyes burned, serrated sharp teeth blackened, it appears as appetizing as a fried rat. Of course, culture determines what we find acceptable, and should anyone be starving to death, they would not turn down a fried rat, guinea pig, or platypus, for that matter. There's not much meat on the bone, that's for sure, and together with the crew we cautiously pick away at the white stringy meat, forking it into our mouths, torn between the thought that we are eating actual food and the thought that we are eating a childhood pet hamster. My hamster's name was Harold. The little tyke roamed freely in our digs at university; was adopted, named and abandoned by a gay German traveller named Jens; and once went missing in my car for two solid weeks before he resurfaced on my dashboard. But I digress. So what does guinea pig taste like? Chicken, of course; white meat with a dash of rabbit. The brown crispy skin, on the other hand, is gamey and almost sour, which made me realize that I am chewing on rodent. And since I'm not exactly starving to death, I race to the bathroom to spit it out. Household pets, then, an acquired taste I hope never to acquire.

Simon Bolivar was crucial to the establishment of independence in Ecuador, Peru, Colombia, Bolivia, Panama and Venezuela (which today is officially known as the Bolivarian Republic of Venezuela). He also bathed with six beautiful women in Room 1, at least according to the manager of the 300-year-old Hacienda Pinsaqui, owned for generations by members of the Ecuadorian elite. Here, it's easy to get a sense of the colonial past; Spanish masters worked their indigenous slaves in fields, farms and textile factories like the one at Pinsaqui. The gardens are vast, the dining room fireplace huge and blackened with time, the rooms spacious, each with their own pig-iron fireplace. Horse-jumping trophies sit on the wooden shelves of the oldest part of the Hacienda (now a bar); a peacock struts around a fountain up front. Haciendas belonged to the nobility of a bygone feudal system, the farmhouses, villas and lodgings of the elite. It feels as if we have turned off the busy Pan American highway, lined with cheap eateries and vegetable stands, and entered the decadent past. "The father of the current owner, he was the ambassador to Chile, and also Panama, and also Mexico," says the enthusiastic manager. A black-and-white photo of the above-mentioned sir sitting with a rather bored-looking Frida Kahlo sits on the walls, along with paintings of the ladies, gentlemen and horses of the aristocracy. After a fine dinner I return to my room, stoke the fire and climb beneath thick blankets to find a waiting hot water bottle. I need to get all the rest I can; tomorrow I'm meeting the shaman.

I cottoned onto the idea of exploring indigenous shamanism after reading Graham Hancock's book *Supernatural*. He's my favourite real-life controversial archeo-anthro-astrono-journalist, even if his writing is a little too dedicated (i.e. long winded) in proving his point. After reading his exhaustive research, you can't fault his ideas, though, even as the mainstream scientific community writes them off as sensationalist. About fifteen years ago Hancock inspired me to go travelling to South America with his book *Fingerprints of the Gods*, and now he was inspiring me to look into the world of shamanism. Among his theories: Cave paintings made over the last 70,000 years were not random graffiti, but rather the visions of shamans, men and women who used dance, psychotropic plants and meditation to connect with the spirit world, a world we can all connect to through our own meditation, psychedelic drugs or a visit to a shaman. Shamans, in effect, connect us to the very essence of humanity, a line that stretches to the beginnings of time. There's a full chapter about the word shaman itself, and how it has repeatedly been misused and misunderstood in our modern age. For our purposes, let's just say that our excellent fixer Juan-Diego had secured a visit with Jose Maria Cordoba, a respected elderly shaman within a nearby mountain community. Visiting a shaman is common in Ecuador, a surefire method to ward off evil spirits. Finding the authentic experience, however, requires someone with the excellent local knowledge and connections of Juan-Diego. It is touch and go all the way, especially when we show up with cameras in tow. After a short negotiation, the long-haired shaman agreed to a consultation. Normally, he gets paid with chickens, corn, favours. But given the times, even shamans won't turn down a fistful of dollars. Shaman Jose tells me his father was a shaman, but he only found his calling when he was fourteen years old, when he entered a trance-like state for two days, discovering the spirit world. Everyone thought he was dead. During this time, the spirits told him to heal others, and he has been doing so ever since. I ask him his age, and he thumbs through some identity documents because he isn't sure. We discover he was born in 1948, making Jose – his hair fine, black and long, his smooth skin carved with angular lines – an incredible 61 years old. (That being said, we gave a ride to an indigenous girl who looked no more than 16; later, she told us she was 24. For the rest of the week, every time we saw a kid we wondered how many children they might have themselves). I enter the shaman's hut to find an assortment of chairs, herbs, pots and pans, old photos, bags and a colourful poster of Jesus. I ask how Christianity fits in with shamanic tradition, and the answer is that the world will always have good and evil, God and the Devil. The Spanish cleverly incorporated local superstition into their invading religion, a tool to control the masses, gods replaced by saints. Like other countries in South America, Ecuador today is 95% Roman Catholic, even as millions consult their shamans for help with the spirit world. I watch a variety of beans and herbs being added to water, which will be boiled to create a protective tincture. Then my shirt is removed and the shaman uses a candle to measure my spiritual well being. He waves the lit candle around me like a wand, then stands over it, mumbles and chants. Juan-Diego translates the diagnoses: I am well. I am healthy. I am walking in the middle of a wide road into the sun. All this is very positive, and despite my natural skepticism, I breathe a sigh of relief. Next, he picks up two eggs and shakes them around my body. Immediately, his demeanour shifts. Something is not right. No, something is not right at all. He barks some orders to his wife, who appears quickly at the entrance to the hut. "This is not good," says Juan-Diego. "Someone is wishing you bad wind." Someone is cursing me, sending bad energy my way, and only the shaman can help stop that evil, at least for a short while. I have no doubt that he is concerned. While the initial consultation felt cursory, a performance for the gringo, perhaps, once the eggs speak, everything kicks into a very high, very serious gear. Burning incense is brought in, smoking the shack with a rich cloud that leaves my eyes watering. Swigging from a bottle of sugarcane rum, the shaman blows and spits on my head, asking me to rub the energy over my face. He repeats this blowing/spitting on my chest, my arms, my legs and my back. A quick consultation with the eggs tells him more is needed. This time, he inhales a cigarette and exhales the smoke all over my body. Next, he makes me squat over another burning mixture of wood and herbs, the thick, sweet blue smoke enveloping me. Some more blowing/spitting, a technique that all shamans must master, and then come the branches; the leaves of this plant are whipped all over my body. Juan-Diego warns me that this plant has poisonous qualities that will cause intense itching and get the blood circulating. After a few moments of whipping, my skin explodes into fire, the itch becoming an unstoppable bush fire closing in on the city of my sanity. There's the smoke, the spitting, the chanting, the slashing of plants, the fire on my skin... and then, just as suddenly, the pain dissipates. The shaman is physically exhausted, beads of sweat on his smooth forehead. He shakes some eggs, and the curse is gone. He tells me to put my shirt back on and, filling his mouth with a sweet lemon-scented oil, he blows it on my head, my chest and my arms for extra protection. He has battled my demons, and he has won.

I am strongly advised to bathe in red and white carnations, or the curse might return. The shaman will also enter my dreams this evening to search for more information about this source of evil. I thank him for his consultation and enter the hot sun with no doubt that something incredible has just happened. I'm not sure what it was, exactly, but it was undeniably… something. I buy some red and white carnations at a local Cotachi market set amidst food shacks displaying fully roasted pigs. Juan-Diego suggests bathing in a crater lake, although the water will be a frosty 10C. When was the last time you felt so alive you could feel your skin dancing on your nerves?   For me, it was when I jumped into the freezing waters of the crater lake, surrounded by carnations, the spit and rum and smoke and sweat of my shamanic purification ritual washing away into the frigid waters of the dead volcano.

I purchase some gifts at the Otavalo market that afternoon, bargaining from 50% of the first price, as advised. But my mind is elsewhere, curious as ever to enter the dream world, to see if the shaman appears as he said he would. There's a cold, dark and definite spooky atmosphere around the Hacienda after dark, and I sleep fitfully, dreaming of being chased by an Apache helicopter, and, for some reason, being in a downhill snowboarding race. Checking my email (even 300-year-old mountain haciendas offer wireless Internet, albeit very slow wireless Internet), there is a piece of hate mail, an UPPERCASE rant from some nutcase (@aol.com) about how he read my World's Most Beautiful Women column and wants to kill me, poke out my eyeballs, destroy my stupid hat, etc., etc. The last time I received hate mail, I found it hilarious. This time, I find it kind of weird that it came the very morning after a shaman warned me that someone was cursing me. There was no time to dwell on it, however, for I had an early morning transfer to the Quito Airport, and a quick flight later I land in Ecuador's biggest city, Guayaquil.

Ecuador is named after the equator on which it lies, the imaginary line that is equidistant from the North and South pole and which divides the globe into its northern and southern hemispheres. There is a definite thrill in visiting the equator just a few months after visiting the Arctic Circle in Finland. A few tourist sites capitalize on those, like myself, who'll get a buzz out of visiting the exact middle of the earth, where the planet is at its most flat. At one of these, a couple of experiments had been set up amongst gift shops and snack bars. The first proves that, yes, in the northern hemisphere water flushes counter-clockwise, and in the southern hemisphere, clockwise. This is the result of the Coriolis forces that sweep around us as a result of the planet spinning on its axis. We fill a basin with water, and just a few steps north of the line of the equator we watch in fascination as small leaves spin clockwise before emptying into a bucket below. Counter-clockwise, a few steps to the south. And in the middle, on the exact line of the equator? The water gushes out with no rotational spin whatsoever. Physically discovering that forces are at work beyond our ability to perceive them is surprisingly powerful, which is why visiting science museums is so much fun. The second experiment involves balancing an egg on a nail head, which is apparently a lot easier to do on the equator, although to be honest, I've never tried doing it anywhere else.

Guayaquil is Ecuador's largest and most populous city, home to over two million people across a sprawling delta. It's loud and noisy, but is reaping the benefits of its last two mayors – who "have balls," according to our guide Roberto – and who initiated a series of urban renewal projects that are cleaning up the streets, parks and neighbourhoods. It's Juan-Diego's birthday, so we head out to a bar, where we get ripped off for a bottle of rum before heading off to an eardrum-busting salsa club. We are joined by Grace, from thee local tourism office, and her boyfriend. The crew fades after a particularly long day (we had woken up at a mountainside hacienda, driven two hours, taken a flight and climbed a lookout hill that day), but Paul and I join the couple for a house party with some friends. As fun as it is to get paid to travel, something gets lost on a tight production schedule, and that's the people you meet when you travel on your own dime. In a ground-level apartment doubling as an office during the day, we meet Grace's friends, pick up a crate of beer for ridiculously low non-gringo prices and sit around a big screen watching salsa music blaring into a smoky room. "Two things you'll notice about Ecuadorians," says one of the group, whose name escapes me. "They might not have much, but they will have a big TV and a big speaker system." The beers flow, along with beats on a conga drum, in perfect rhythm to the music on the TV. A place is as much about its people as it is about its natural beauty.

I'm a little hungover when we drive the following morning into the countryside to explore a cocoa plantation, where Guayaquil's elite have gathered for a charity horse ride along with a luncheon of paella, crepes and mojitos. I learn something about chocolate: how 400 cocoa beans make one pound of chocolate, and how to crack open a cocoa pod by splitting the heavy, red football-shaped shell in the middle. We follow the process – the drying in the sun, the chocolate-making machines – as the hacienda owner explains how he's hoping to make exclusive organic destination chocolate. We buy huge slabs of chocolate, 55% cocoa, the perfect gift for chocoholics. An hour later I'm bodysurfing with Sean in the warm Pacific, the setting sun casting a cool shadow over the beach. It's time to call the shaman and find out what he saw in his dreams, and in mine. Over Juan-Diego's Blackberry, he explains that the curse has lifted. He saw that it was from a couple: that a man and women had bid me ill because of my job. It's a pretty acute reading, given that the shaman does not really know what my job is, that many people are envious about said job, and that envy seldom breeds goodwill.

Another great meal of ceviche, another early morning flight and we arrive back in Quito, where we head straight off to a football game and bake in the high-altitude sun, the sky a clear blue. We last as long as we can before heading back to the Hotel Patio Andaluz, for a few hours of much needed rest. I can't remember the last time we went this hard. Julia locks herself in her hotel room and refuses to come out for our final segment, infuriating the crew who all wish they could do the same. So I channel one more burst of energy for the Chiva Bus, a brightly lit party bus with a full horn band on the roof, a great way to see Quito and party in the process. I pull in strangers from the street, gringos and locals, the horns blaring, passersby clapping, traffic trailing behind us. I hop aboard the roof, grab some giant cymbals from a young musician and bang away, like some sort of King of Quito. I half-heartedly suggest we head to the Gringo District, so that the backpacker who discovered South America four years ago can ride atop a party-mobile in triumph: Ecuador, at last, with a TV crew at the fore and a suitcase back at the fancy hotel. Except, with all this amazing country has to offer, all I could manage was a plate of guinea pig, a visit to a shaman, some iguanas at Guayaquil's Bolivar Park, cocoa, football, ceviche, a house party, a bus party, a swim in a volcano crater and the warm

Pacific Ocean. Not bad for seven days, mind you, but, as always, I'm cursed to keep moving forward, to discover the next exotic destination.

Jose, the traditional shaman who discovered my curse

The old Hacienda where Simon Bolivar (and Frieda Khalo) once played

Almost didn't see the young girl sleeping in her mother's market stall

BEHIND THE SCENES IN ECUADOR

No matter how much I travel, and no matter how many countries I manage to visit, people I meet have a knack for asking me if I've visited the places I've never been. No, I've never been to Bermuda, or Vietnam, or Morocco. And although I've been just about everywhere else in South America, I had never been to Ecuador. Naturally, this is the first South American country people ask me about, so I was happy to finally cross it off the list. When I say Ecuador, people assume the Galapagos, and the fact is there's a helluva lot more to the country than those remarkable islands. And while I am the action-adventure guy, fans of the show know my interests extend to culture, food and human-interest stories, too. I'd been reading a book called *Supernatural* by Graham Hancock, a terrific non-fiction author and travel writer. It delves into the roots of shamanism, including the use of trance states to tap into a world that has remarkably similar properties across continents and cultures. So my story was to meet a real shaman, not a tourist gimmick, and learn more about what he does and how he works. I toyed with the idea of taking ayahuasca on camera, but was told that psychedelic drugs on camera is verboten. A wise decision in retrospect.

Crucial to finding the real deal, and the entire episode, was our guide Juan-Diego, who seemed to know exactly what we needed even when we didn't.

I really liked Ecuador. They eat a lot of ceviche, which is my favourite fishy dish. They have a vast and diverse country. They also love football (we went to a game, which didn't make the cut), can vibe with 150 iguanas in a city park (which didn't make the cut), offer beautiful historical haciendas (which didn't make the cut) and have some terrific beaches (which didn't make the cut). A lot of unnecessary travel and hard work for nothing, but the experiences were interesting. What I did cut was the *cuy,* the guinea pig delicacy. I was there with Julia, and I tasted it, too, although, unlike Ms. Iron Guts, I beelined it to the bathroom because I thought I was going to hurl. Taste like chicken, looks like rat.

The local delicacy: *cuy*, also known as deep fried guinea pig

Somehow mustering the energy for the party bus on the chilly streets of Quito.

Just a few weeks after the Arctic Circle, I stand on the Equator.

BARBADOS
YES, PLEASE!

It says much about Barbadians, or Bajans as they're known, that their be-all and end-all answer to a question, a statement, a polite request or a loud proclamation is, "Yes, please."   And compared to other islands in the Caribbean, Barbados is pleased to say yes to many things, including the highest standard of living in the West Indies. This might have something to do with the island's strong British influence, its magnetic appeal to the mega-rich, or simply that it isn't in the Caribbean at all, but rather floats in the western Atlantic Ocean. However you look at the island nation, it shouldn't be confused with the other B's – Bermuda, and the Bahamas. Sure, they're all tropical islands blessed with the turquoise water of dreams and powdery white beaches (although Bajans will certainly argue their water is that much brighter, their beaches that much finer), but unlike the other Bees, Barbados has a history stretching back to the 1550's, and a proud culture – one that has developed through the constant movement of people tossed together like the soup a surfer might find inside the big waves of Bathsheba. Slavery and religion, colonialism and uprisings, cricket and roundabouts. A bountiful sea crashing against some of the world's most exclusive resorts alongside luxurious villas built for the rich and famous. Further inland I discover wooden chattel houses recalling eras of sugarcane fields and slavery, parishes and rum shacks, all in a climate that hovers between perfectly hot and just perfect. One week is all I had, but, as usual, it would be a busy one.

Unpacking a suitcase: what simple pleasures a cupboard shelf can offer the weary traveller! For only the second time filming in thirty-five countries, the *Word Travels* crew would be staying in one place for the entire week. Sometimes, we can find ourselves in a different bed every night. During Season Two, we clocked ten hotels in twelve days. Here, at the 1980's-pink-hued Bougainvillia Beach Resort, we were each gifted our own suites, which included a small kitchenette, a living room and a balcony with an ocean view. After fourteen hours of travel, Quito via Miami to Bridgetown, I found late-night reserves to be able to unpack my case, hang up my crushed and creased collared shirts, spread out my toiletries and move the bloody hell in. Next evening, Paul, a sound guy/foodie who apprenticed as a chef, relished the opportunity to cook for us using two electric stovetops to whip up an excellent risotto, pan seared pink-red tuna, shrimps in a fine tomato sauce and a fresh baguette with Ruffina cheese (a starting cheese for those who want to get into cheese but don't know where to start, he assures me). For my part, I whipped up a chicken stir-fry in a honey cilantro sauce, although we couldn't find any cilantro on the island itself, maybe because Bajans call it shadowbunny. That's why my homemade hand-picked-at-Oisten's fish market barracuda ceviche fulfilled only 85% of its potential for greatness. I substituted basil for cilantro, gazed upon the ceviche, and lo, it was fine. Point being, on an island famed for its restaurants, the weary traveller finds comfort in home cooking, and, always, in good company.

It's summer, and it's the off season. Although the temperature remains pretty constant throughout the year, winter months equate to less rain, and therefore fewer storm clouds in paradise. For our stories to work we needed the good weather. Maybe it was karmic payback for the miserable grey rain in the Azores earlier this year, but we were blessed with unseasonably clear skies, a deep rich blue. Perfect conditions for my first adventure, a day of water sport action with a *genyouwine* Bajan hero. Having Brian Talma teach me how to windsurf was like having Tiger Woods teach me how to swing a golf club. The shaggy haired, bright eyed, deeply tanned Talma is a Barbadian national hero, a world champion windsurfer, an Olympian and an Island legend. Everyone I met over the course of the week, of various social classes, cracked a smile when I mentioned his name. And every time he smiles, which is just about all the time, Brian's teeth twinkle like piano keys in a smoky New Orleans jazz bar. Over the course of his twenty- year career, Talma has been profiled countless times, sponsored up the yin yang, hosted a travel show, recorded a hit album, been a mainstay on the worldwide pro circuit and a regular go-to character for anyone delving into beach culture. When he's at home in Barbados, he operates De-Action, a colourful little surf shop offering rentals, lessons or just a sweet place to catch the action on Silver Beach. "Action!" It's his key word, his mantra, because, as he explains, "We should always choose a life of action, man." Since I qualify, to some degree, I decided that the best way to attack the island's wealth of water sports would be to learn from a living legend, get swept up in his wave of irie euphoria, and maybe kitesurf it down the beach a little. When I tell him that I hope to learn how to windsurf (never tried), kitesurf (never tried) and stand-up paddle (never tried) ALL IN THE SAME DAY, all he can do is jam a toothy tune with those ivories and belly laugh. Action, indeed.

Full disclosure: I had been on a windsurfer before. I was five years old, and I would stand between my dad's legs on a long board at Wemmer Pan, a dam in central Johannesburg. My dad was among the first wave of windsurfers, and there we would go, every weekend. My shock of blond hair would be flapping in the wind as I lay down at the back of the board, a true windsurfer child. Shortly afterwards, my ear troubles started and my dad moved onto the next fad, cycling. The windsurfer gathered dust in the garage. It had been almost thirty years since I'd been on a board, and since I was but an ankle-snapper then, I've never tried to actually windsurf by myself. Brian shows me the ropes on a training board (imagine Tiger, showing you how to grip a putter... Talma windsurfed the big waves of Jaws in Hawaii, for Chrissake!), and I get up the first time, the wind stiff enough to blow me towards Saint Lucia, with Brian swimming after me. Easy enough, and good enough to cross off the list. The next challenge would be kitesurfing, the craze sweeping the world. It involves a large stunt kite capable of launching you thirty, maybe forty feet into the air. All you need is a board, a power kite, waves and a certain amount of lunacy. I know three people into kitesurfing. They've all injured themselves horribly. And they all continue to love it.

Silver Beach is the IT beach for kitesurfers, and people come from all over the world for two-week vacays to learn how to control and harness the wind, direct their kite, hoist it from a crash and launch themselves over waves. I had two hours and a camera crew to capture my uselessness. Brian explains the appeal: "You can do anything you want, man; there's no limit when it comes to kitesurfing. Action!" He starts me off on a small stunt kite, showing me how to swing it in a figure eight to get power, how to keep it at twelve o'clock to steady, sort of like neutral in a car. I start to get the hang of it even as the mid-day sun, sweat and cheap sunblock sting my retinas, my skin roasting from the reflection of the white sand beneath me. Factor thirty lasted minutes. We don't have much time so we bring out the big kite. I slip into a solid harness and watch as

Brian gets dragged across the beach, the big kite powerful enough to blow him into Bridgetown. At $1500 for the kite alone, it's plenty expensive enough for me to worry about. He hooks me in, the cameras roll and within seconds… I crash it hard into the beach, feeling the bone-cringing slam of material on sand. We launch it again and I crash it again. It's disheartening to be so uncool next to the coolest cat on the island. When I do finally get the kite under control, the moment I try a figure eight and begin to feel the awesome power I'm playing with, I panic. I'm an ant holding onto dental floss in a hurricane. The Wind is into some serious flossing, although, unfortunately, not serious enough. Brian tries to demonstrate the sport in the water, an act that involves more strength and mental concentration than my tired body can muster, but the wind dissipates and he's unable to launch. Wrong time of year. Off season, low wind. No Action! In all probability this saved me from a power kite ripping my knees in half and towing my feeble remains far over the reef into shark-infested waters. Bummer. Paddle boarding, in the hands of a beach man like Brian, involves standing on a long customized surfboard, oar in hand, riding the current, cresting the waves. Brian looks relaxed, his back straight, shoulders square, as comfortable on swells as he is walking on tarmac. Here's me, bent over like I've taken a blow to the gut, slipping and sliding off the board every few seconds, wobbling and wiping, much to the amusement of all who care to witness. It's fair enough to say that no one in their right mind should ever attempt to learn three water sports in one day, much less ones that require hours of practice just to reach beginner level. But then that wouldn't be very Modern Gonzo now, would it?   For all the effort, however, spending the day playing in the sea with a living legend like Brian Talma, one of the best characters I have met anywhere, was well worth a couple of sore muscles and my red Robin sunburn.

Far more civilized is the Atlantis submarine, a tubular white vessel that can take forty-eight passengers 150ft below the sea in pressurized, air-conditioned bliss. The submarine was invented in Vancouver, a marvel of soft adventure, perfect for anyone who wants to go unda da sea without actually getting wet. We caught a boat out to the reef and waited for Atlantis III to surface from the depths like a graceful beluga whale. We climb aboard, bobbing with the swells, a peaceful blue atmosphere below courtesy of the portal viewing windows. Lock. Check. Dive! Dive! Dive! The captain sits up front staring out a bubble, surrounded by an impressive array of buttons and knobs. We are told that the sub can submerge to much greater depths than 150ft, but that is all that insurance can handle. Watching a digital altimeter, I learn how light is filtered the deeper you go, so that some colours change or disappear altogether. We pass a shipwreck, an old barge rusted and dead yet teeming with all manner of marine life. A turtle glides effortlessly in front of us, padding up some rocks, unbothered by the aquatic spaceship in its wake. We are all mesmerized: the sound of water, the shades of blue, the hallucinogenic fish. I close my eyes and sink away into the soporific depths of the sea. A great rabbi once said that everyone should try to find fifteen minutes each day to spend time with their God, whether it's a deity, a spirit, a messiah, an energy or just a feeling. For a full half hour, somewhere beneath the waters of the deep blue sea, I know exactly what the Rabbi was talking about. Chilled out in absolute wonder. I see schools of red snapper, parrotfish and other species on the handy fish guide next to the windows. Did you know there's something called a Jew Fish?

I wondered if it was celebrating Rosh Hashanah, the Jewish New Year, as I would be, in a small Bridgetown synagogue, the following day. Happy 5770, we say. Shana Tova, little fishy.

A couple of years ago, on tiny Turtle Island off the coast of Malaysian Borneo, I had the privilege of witnessing a mature sea turtle waddle onto the beach where it was born, and lay dozens of white ping pong ball eggs. Watching the mother turtle – herself a miracle of survival, since only one in a thousand turtles born ever reach maturity – nest on the beach, depositing her eggs before sliding back into the sea exhausted, is something to experience. This night, as part of Julia's segment for the show, I stood with the crew and some turtle conservationists as a momma Hawksbill turtle continued the cycle of life. Besides the usual on-shore predators like dogs, cats, lizards and birds, some locals have taken to stealing eggs to sell. The conservationists cover up the mother's tracks, but do not remove the eggs. They hide the nest (even though momma does a great job herself, camouflaging her eggs beneath sand and plants) and return when the eggs hatch. Turtles navigate by the light of the moon, and we're not really sure how the few female survivors will know to return to this exact beach when they mature in twenty-five years, except they do; another miracle of nature. Earlier we had helped dozens of hatchlings make their way into the sea, careful to avoid shining any light they might confuse with the moon. Covering our camera and headlight lamps with red gels makes us completely, like a sorcerer's cloak allowing us to observe the world around us. It was a clear, warm night, the moon high, the stars bright. Another fifteen minutes with God, perhaps. Maybe I'm just getting old and sentimental, but I only seem to find time for this heavenly consultation when I travel, which is probably the reason why everyone should travel in the first place.

By the time the weekend blows in, the resort pool bar is crowded with Brits on holiday, like pink cherries floating in a blue cocktail. Barbados is a massively popular destination with the UK. Its capital, Bridgetown, was one of only four destinations with regular non-stop scheduled flights on the Concorde. Because of this fact, one of the decommissioned Concordes sits in a hangar museum adjacent to Grantley Adams International. We took a peek, getting a tour on the supersonic luxury jet was so ahead of its time and so prohibitively expensive to run. 26,000 gallons of fuel burned on a single flight and it had four hours, max, flying time. Inside the skinny cabin, which had a small hold at the back for luggage (there was only one level on the Concorde, and strict weight allowances), I can barely see out the tiny windows that were capable of handling the stratospheric pressure at Mach 2. I sit on narrow designer leather chairs and learn that the cheapest bottle of wine onboard cost around $800 and was served complimentary, with lobster and truffles. No seat-back screens, but there was a defunct promotional video about passengers bumping into rock stars, royalty and people who could spend $10,000 per ticket. The museum hangar is a great way to kill an hour or two, and hey, now I can say I've been on the Concorde. So what if it was grounded? It's the closest thing to a rocket ship. Oh wait, I went inside a real rocket ship at the Space Centre outside Moscow. You know what? This job is getting kind of ridiculous.

Friday night at the Oistins fish market is THE night out in Barbados, as thousands of locals and tourists gather to eat fresh flying fish with mac and pie chased with a cold Banks beer and perhaps a few drops of excellent yellow Scotch Bonnet pepper hot sauce. There're dozens of fish shacks; some have long lineups, some don't, but you can't really go wrong. There's a stage pumping groovy reggae tunes and a large crowd has gathered around it, although nobody's really dancing yet. Since all the world's a stage, I get up on it and shake my booty, to general disapproval. I try to pull some locals up since Sean is filming all of this, of course, and am told, in no polite terms, "No, Please!" Further up there's a small square with more mature local couples dancing to country music. It's a hot night, swarms of horny English girls chatting up smooth-talking local guys in dreads, and I wish I had the energy to follow them to that place where the music gets louder and the drinks get stronger, but I don't. It's been a busy couple of weeks, nineteen days of hectic travel, and besides, my ass still smarts from the polo.

If you want to feel the wealth and power that congregates in Barbados, it makes sense to investigate the Sport of Kings. I'm writing an article called Confessions of a Polo Virgin for a beautiful glossy magazine called *The Polo Magazine*. In it, I confess that until I arrived at the stunning Waterhall polo field at the Apes Hill Club, I couldn't tell a mallet from a hockey stick, a chakka from the All Black haka. Briefly, then: Polo is played on horses galloping at high speed, whereby teams consisting of four riders each use mallets to knock a white ball through posts to score a goal. The field is 300 yards in length, and arena matches consist of four six-minute periods called chukkas. Right, then. White pants on, polo shirt tucked in, boots strapped, on the horse, chase the ball, shwhack it, there's a good lad! My instructors were two incredibly patient professional players, the brothers Jamie and Neil Dickenson, who made me feel as though I have potential with this sport. The way a kid playing with toy cars has the potential to be a Formula 1 driver. Shwack! Jolly good! Surrounding us is an immaculate virgin golf course lined with $2 million villas that reek of money, taste and the kind of high class one does not acquire. You're either born into it, marry it, steal it or trip over it. All at the same time. For the purposes of the show I am wearing an Apes Hill polo team shirt. The team recently won the Queen's Cup, a clean sweep. If one applies the Six Degrees of Kevin Bacon principle to garments, I am exactly one degree away from the Queen of England. This does not help me shwack the ball any better, but I give it a jolly good go all the same. If I close my eyes, which I tend to do every time a horse breaks into a canter and I have no idea how to stop it, I can hear the clink of crystal champagne glasses, the muffled laughter of high court ladies, the thump-thump of hooves, refrained clapping and the occasional tasteful cheer. Although most polo matches are open to the public in Barbados, it remains an elite, highly exclusive sport. The confession of a polo virgin?   I'm a working class hack with a filthy mouth and cynical regard for elitism. And boy, I think I love this sport! Find me some kings to sponsor a horse, will you?

A full, hot day of polo filming and none of it made the show. I felt bad for everyone who went out of their way for us, but story editing was out of my control. Meanwhile, my polo story ran in a high-end polo magazine, although I never got paid for it. Maybe it was revenge for the segment being cut.

We closed out the episode on a catamaran, a treat of a half-day trip around the east and west coasts, with an open bar, reggae, lunch-time feast and a final lucky break in the weather. The Tall Ships Tiami Catamaran Cruise company is one of several operators who take tourists out into the waters, supplying snorkels and masks to dive around the reef, a shipwreck, or a well-known sea turtle hotspot. The captain has deadpan one liners that actually work, even if they largely fall flat on the all-English clientele, most of whom will return home pink and flabby. My shark phobia disappeared after watching a documentary called *Sharkwater*, which I nowadays prescribe as the Jaws antidote. Coincidentally, it stars, and is directed and produced by, the nephew of Gail Stewart, our amazing and tireless host for the week. Watching it allowed me to swim under the stars on our arrival without a second thought for what lies beneath the inky depths. It allowed me to dive head first into the sea to swim amongst graceful turtles and gliding stingrays. Spectacular stuff. If I could insert a photo of that experience here, I would. Fortunately, we captured some of it on video for the show. Viewers are going to shit a turtle shell when they see just how magical that moment was. At least I hope so.

We pack a lot into these weeks of filming, and I get to see and do more than most people ever should. A submarine and supersonic jet, horses and turtles, kitesurfers and water sports – there's no rush; it's all here waiting for you. Easily in my top three most romantic destinations, will I be coming back to Barbados? Yes, Please!

BEHIND THE SCENES IN BARBADOS

On the road, we live out of a suitcase and often crash in five different hotels over seven days. By the time we got to Barbados, we'd had one of those runs in which you end up wearing the same clothes each day because there's no time to unpack and see what the hell you brought with you anyway. Then we get to Barbados, and each crew member is shown to their own beachfront apartment in the beautiful Bougainvillia Beach Resort, where we'll stay for seven consecutive nights. That's enough time to unpack, to figure out where the light switches are, to memorize your room number and to cook a meal or two. Paul (our sound guy/B-camera) is also a foodie capable of cooking stupendous meals. After twenty-two countries, this was his first opportunity, and he wasted no time. A perfect risotto, pan-seared tuna, some good wine and better Bajan rum – you have no idea how good a home-cooked meal tastes when you're on the road. I believe food tastes only as good as the intention of the chef, and Paul's intentions were to treat us royally. Meanwhile, outside in the parking lot, mini-vans would camp out during the day and sell delicious island cuisine out the back, a bargain for those of us working in paradise.

Brian Talma is easily one of the best characters I've met anywhere, tasked with the impossible task of showing me three water sports in a couple of hours. Any other person would probably have killed me, but Brian gave us a wide island smile and went along with everything. It didn't matter what I was doing, in the end, because here I was hanging out with the nicest bloke on the island, and a real surfing legend. I was lucky the wind died down with the kite surfing because I would have been blown half way to Tahiti if it had kept on blustering, and I doubt Brian would have been able to swim after me (although anything is possible). He lives by the mantra of "Action!", and there was plenty to be had that scorcher of a day. You can see my sun-roasted forehead at the night market shortly afterwards. After our first miserable rainy day, the famous sun of Barbados came out to play and we took full advantage. It lit up the water like an underwater disco, to be enjoyed by submarine or snorkel. Unfortunately , there was no room for my introduction to polo (which led to a hilarious article called Confessions of a Polo Virgin) or even our quick visit to the Concorde, retired to a hangar adjacent to the airport. But there was enough time to hit the Oistins fish market to pick up some fresh barracuda and make my first Ecuador-inspired ceviche. It tasted delicious, but then again, I think everything does on an island as beautiful as Barbados.

Stand-up paddleboarding, polo, kitesurfing with Brian Talma - all in a Bajan day's work.

EGYPT
HEAT, DUST AND DIRT BIKES

Sean and I drain a couple of bottles of Stella beer, staring over the River Nile from my balcony of room 709 in the 150-year-old Shepheard Hotel. It's three a.m., but the Cairo traffic remains intense, as it has the entire day, the entire week. Traffic flows like the muddy waters of the Nile, the world's longest river and the lifeblood of a country comprised mostly of desert. Most of its 83 million inhabitants live near the riverbank. That's 99% of Egypt's population concentrated in a mere 5% of its land. It explains the crowd, the chaos, the 24/7 rush hour.

Cairo shouldn't work, and yet somehow it does. There're just too many people crammed into too tight of a space. Too many cars on the road blaring their horns and spewing leaded fumes into an atmosphere laced with smog so thick you'd swear it leaves splinters in your throat. Constant jostling on the sidewalks, Frogger in the cross streets, people tripping over each other in metro stations, clothing shops, bazaars and tea shops. It hasn't rained in ten months and everything is caked in a safari-yellow dust blown in from the desert that encroaches upon the city limits. From atop a viewpoint, sucking on an apple-flavoured hookah, I see the sun set like a deep orange egg yolk being lowered on a string, disappearing too high behind an impenetrable black cloud of gases. It is hoped rain will wash the pollution away one day, like a shower clearing away a ring of muck around the bath tub. But in one of the world's most polluted cities, where two million cars choke the potholed roads and fires burn sugar cane for fuel, it will take more than just a thunder shower. I savour the Stella, the Egyptian beer brewed since the late 1800's, as it washes down the soot in my throat. And the traffic slugs forward.

I last visited Cairo in 1993 with a group of fellow kibbutz volunteers made up of Swedish, Danish and German travellers, and a duo of South Africans. I remember being mobbed by Bedouin touts at the mighty pyramids, the line-ups at the Egyptian Museum to see the royal mummies, the horror of seeing a polar bear in a cage and two chained-up elephants in the zoo. I don't remember why we went to the zoo, but Michaela from Sweden swore she would write to the

World Wildlife Fund, and maybe she did. My return, filming the 37th episode of *Word Travels*, would be under the auspices of the Egyptian Tourism Authority, who seemed adamant on flexing their authority as to what we could depict. As a writer and as filmmakers, we do our best when granted the freedom to observe and report. When we first visited Khan el-Khalili, Cairo's biggest market and a famous tourist trap, we were prohibited from filming. An endless stream of police in coffee-stained white uniforms constantly demanded papers, as if we had dared to cross the line of their pencil-thin moustaches. It is said that bureaucracy was invented in ancient Egypt. One would think that after thousands of years of paperwork they would have perfected the system, but to make that assumption I would need to get permission, in triplicate, and kick back some baksheesh to an officer from the Ministry of Information, who might make it difficult for us to leave at the airport, just so we know. After visiting over thirty countries as a travel writer with a film crew, in the middle of a seven-week, seven-country slog, there's little patience for chauvinist Egyptian control freaks.

Did you know Egyptian men belly dance? I didn't, which is why I was keen to meet Aleya, an American belly dancer who transplanted herself in Cairo to learn from the masters in the Home of Belly Dancing. The only problem being that the Birthplace of Belly Dancing no longer welcomes belly dancing, unless it's for tourists on the brightly lit Nile dinner cruises, or in seedy underground cabaret bars. It's a tough time to be a belly dancer in a nation slipping deeper into religious conservatism. Once the pride of the harem and the pinnacle of sexuality, the largely tame belly dancers are regarded nowadays as whores and harlots, entertainment to be tolerated for tourists. Its traditions and beauty, art and skill, are slowly being sunk to the bottom of the Nile. In a city where women are advised to cover their heads, and where many cover their entire bodies save the slit of their eyes, there's no room for bellies and sequined brassieres. Aleya, a busty and boisterous Latino, waves off insults and dirty leers the way you'd wave off flies in the bush. "Haram alayik, emshee!" Shame on you; go away! She accompanies us to Khan Al-Khalili to get kitted out. Here we find four floors of brightly coloured sequined dresses, a virtual belly dancing megastore hidden in an alley, decidedly low key. Men typically wear robes, but for the sake of quality entertainment I picked out purple pants flecked in gold sequins, with a red fez hat for effect. Julia selects a gold ensemble, and we head to a dance studio to learn some basic moves. It's quite the workout, involving a lot of core exercises, hip shakes and stomach pulls. By the end it's easy to see why belly dancing has taken off as a gym alternative and why dancers like Aleya feel it's addictive. We are joined by a small man with a large drum, and shake, rattle and roll our bellies to the amusement of kids waiting for their ballet lesson. Later that night we eat dinner on a Nile cruise with dozens of other tourists, watching traditional musicians soundtrack a whirling dervish – a man who gently spun in a circle for a half hour without stopping once. The main act was an Argentinean belly dancer who wooed and wowed the Chinese, shaking her belly evocatively, rattling the pillars of Islam. The boat cruised along Cairo's riverbank, hushed by the din of traffic, a fog of pollution protecting the stars above. This is a city of secrets. It would take months, if not years, to try to figure them out. It's better for tourists to just hit the museums and the pyramids, the cruises and souvenir markets. It's perfectly safe to pop the bubble (I enjoyed a great haircut and barber shave in a smoky salon), but the heat, dust and noise quickly take their toll.

Sean, Paul and I leave the hotel in search of local food, eventually finding a chicken kebab shop where we hope the burning coals kill whatever might be partying on the *poulet*. We cross Garden City alongside the heavily fortified American embassy (while a well-armed army protects the large US compound, I note that the Canadian embassy is protected by only one guard and several bushes), walking along a main road rowdy with old Peugeots and backfiring buses. Men sit on the sidewalk smoking hookahs and drinking small glasses of sweet tea. Hole-in-the-wall eateries are flypaper sticky with grime as we pass a liquor store of sorts, marked as a den of iniquity. Few people smile, although we get some curious stares. I could count on one hand the few smiles I'd seen in Egypt all week, and it left the subtle impression that life there is hard and times are tough. Just a few years later, the political turmoil would make things even worse.

Later we attempt to cross the street to visit the Egyptian Museum, shadowing locals who dart in between the cars. The museum closes in two hours so most tourists have left, and Neil (our field assistant), Cathy (our director) and I wander the impressively large halls gazing at an overwhelming amount of history. Mummies, papyrus scripts, jewellery, ancient art and the golden sarcophagus of King Tut – I walk from one humid room to another, reading the faded typewritten card descriptions, wondering how much this would be worth to a collector, and how much we understand about one of history's greatest civilizations. The museum looks like it hasn't been upgraded, painted or appended for decades, the low lights creating a dusty, spooky ambiance. Shouts echo down the hall; somewhere a guard hums a traditional song. Outside, Cairo is exploding in early evening action. Inside, the Mummies remain frozen in time.

Cairo's pace is frenetic and chaotic, its traffic almost certainly dangerous, but it's just the way things are here. I see one man splattered on the side of the street, and just about every car is dented, covered in the October dust. The city feels impenetrable, its rhythm, erratic. Yet seventeen million inhabitants in the Arab world's largest city dance to the beat of Cairo. Tourists drink their tea, take their pictures and beeline for Giza.

I remember, from the last time I was at the pyramids, the heat, the pushy Bedouins selling camel rides and the dark, humid narrow tunnel inside the Pyramid. This time I'll remember eating beef sandwiches in the shade of ancient rubble, the stress of filming beneath a punishing mid-day sun, the "official" kickbacks for "official" permission to shoot and the atmosphere of being at one of the world's most recognizable tourist attractions. It's surprising just how close the Giza complex is to the city, a part of its western skyline if you could see through the smog. I watched *The Spy Who Loved Me* recently, whereby James Bond walked into Giza, crossed a path and emerged in Luxor (a long ways away). Better than *Transformers 2*, though, where the pyramids are shown to be in the middle of the desert and a stone's throw away from Jordan's Petra – clearly the director was too busy looking at Megan Fox's butt to consult a map. I've read quite a few books concerning the pyramids since my previous visit, and believe there's more than meets the eye when it comes to their creation. There's just too much going on here – the way they line up with the stars, their exact dimensions, their appearance on the American dollar bill – no wonder conspiracy theorists have a field day with them. My own suspicions arise from hearing author Graham Hancock discuss the corrupt dealings of Egyptologist icon Zahi Hawass. There's so much that can be discovered, but so much is held back, and Hawass seems to hold the key. You can google all this stuff; in the meantime, I'll take a camel ride, replace an old pyramid photo with a funkier digital one and create a personal photo collage of me at all the "new" Seven Wonders of the World, ancient and otherwise.

It was not until the plane took off for Sharm el-Sheikh that my shoulders loosened, the air cleared and the sun could sparkle in a clear blue sky. Much has changed since I last visited the blue, salty Red Sea sixteen years ago. The backwoods backpacker haven of Dahab is now a resort town, and the granddaddy resort town of them all is Sharm el-Sheikh. Just about every major hotel chain is represented, offering five-star service for visiting Brits, Italians and, most of all, Russians. It's a world away from the bustle of Cairo. I see tourists in bikinis crossing the wide, dusty main road, and alcohol is freely available. As a tourism powerhouse, vital for Egypt's economy, nobody's going to deny a tourist a cold beer, or even topless sunbathing. And tourists come in droves, around 130,000 a week, on direct flights from Moscow and Warsaw and England and Rome. Sharm's tourism magnet also attracted fundamentalist terrorists, resulting in a series of suicide bombs in 2005. 88 people were killed, mostly Egyptians, but dozens of international tourists were, too. Security is tight: roadblocks, checkpoints, metal detectors at all hotel entrances. Tourism has recovered, although it sickens me that there are terrorists cowardly enough to attack a bus tour. Sharm is back because of the quality of its hotels, the colour of the sea water, the diversity of the Red Sea's marine life and the terrific day-in, day-out weather. We stayed at the Savoy, a resort sprawling onto both sides of the desert highway, with a half dozen restaurants, three overflowing pools, tasteful design, a shopping mall and water sports. Once you walk out on the plastic blue jetty, which gets you over the sharp coral and directly into fishy wonderland, you can see similar jetties stretching into the aquamarine Red Sea, tentacles of the Holiday Octopus. Snorkeling and diving here are famous for a reason. Of all the places we've snorkeled the last couple of years – the Philippines, Maldives, Barbados – the Red Sea delivers the brightest fish with the clearest visibility. I haven't seen anything like it since I snorkeled off the Blue Hole in Dahab, here in the Sinai, all those years back. On the beach, meanwhile, it feels like I'm in Russia: there's a wild assortment of mullets and *nouveau riche* bling, not to mention hot bikinis. Swimming in the buoyant waters at sunset, breathing in the fresh desert winds, I feel the heavy memories of Cairo fading like tea swept off a marble cabinet.

According to the Bible, the Israelites spent forty years wandering the desert before Moses presented the Ten Commandments atop Mount Sinai. Getting to that mountain would take more time than we had, but the desert was calling me. Egypt is the size of Texas and California combined, twice the size of Spain, big enough to accommodate the whole of Central America. Most of that is bone-dry desert. While the Hebrews discovered the world's moral code amongst the sand and dust, I was just looking to have a little fun. The company's name is Ciro & Felice, and they "made me" a great price to take an ATV, dune buggy and dirt bike for a triumvirate of motorized fun. Of course, this would all have to take place before ten a.m., when the sun can get hot enough to melt a helmet. I awaken at five a.m., freshen up and head out to their compound to find two dozen other ATV's ready for adventure. Besides eating, drinking, swimming and lazing by the beach, cranking an ATV in the desert is a must for visitors to Sharm. Our driver wraps my green sarong around my head in the traditional Bedouin style, protecting me from the dust and heat. Once we get into the desert, we split from the group to go it alone. The unique beauty of the desert opened her heart. Throttling the ATV, I pass Bedouin shepherds tending their camels, brown rocky outcrops littering the expanse of sand. If the Hebrews were riding ATV's they would have reached Mount Sinai in no time. Next up was a four-seater dune buggy, a loud engine at the rear, a crash bar overhead. I had the chance to rock this mode of transport a few years back in Dubai and it's still the most fun driving I've ever had. The buggy growls and roars, its stick shift adding extra juice over hills and thick sand. I'm deliberately sliding all over the place, the whiff of the rally car driving thrill. With a low centre of gravity, flipping it is almost impossible. The only thing I have to worry about is stalling, but fortunately we have a mechanic on hand. When it was time for me to mount the dirt bike, he knew he was about to get busy.

I got my motorbike licence a few months ago, and I can count on one finger the hours I've spent on the road. As for a dirt bike, crossing knee-high sand and slippery gravel, this will be a first. The chances of injury are high, but the last time I got injured on a bike it led to my global adventure, so that, at least, was reassuring. With no helmet or padding, what's the worst that could happen, anyway? I hop on the dirt bike, steady it into first gear, give it a little gas, and in my crowning moment of television glory, stall it 50m from the crew. How does James Bond know how to fly, drive or ride every vehicle ever imagined? Because he's a fictional character, and I'm just a schmuck who likes to try things. As I found out earlier in the week with belly dancing, most of the time I don't do very well at the things I try.

Catch a sunset boat ride, pack the bags, shuttle, road block, shuttle, security x 4, welcome back to Cairo and a marvellous view over the River Nile. No time for Aswan, or Luxor, or a cruise down the Nile; the next country awaits. I came, I saw, I biked, I belly danced.

Paul and I take a break in the bazar. Hurry up and wait is the nature of the beast

Aleya shows us how to belly dance. Yes, I am wearing a red fez, for no particular reason.

BEHIND THE SCENES IN EGYPT

Note: We visited Egypt shortly before the Arab Spring, the fall of Mubarak and the onset of chaos that would cripple Egypt's tourism industry for many years.

Men can belly dance; who knew? I didn't, so was as surprised as anyone to find myself crunching my hips, wearing a red fez hat. The costume, incidentally, was entirely of my own creation and is not what male belly dancers wear. I didn't really know how silly it all looked until I saw the footage, but after the crazy traffic of Cairo, I would have let loose dressed up as a penguin. The city is so frenetic and heated and mad and alive it can be overwhelming. A challenge for Sean, who found himself being shut down every time he pointed the camera out the car window. Some societies are so open and giving, and some like to conceal themselves behind a veil.

Our belly dancer, Aleya, was in fact from the USA but had come to Cairo to get to the source of the art. Most dancers in Cairo these days are not Egyptian, and belly dancing has now become something almost strictly for tourists. Of which there was no shortage at the pyramids, where I found out my story didn't really exist. Every once in a while I like to remind myself that you can't believe what you read on the Internet.

Coming from the veils and *hijabs* of Cairo, my first impression of Sharm el-Sheikh was of two girls in bikinis crossing the road. Russians are the biggest tourism market, and in Sharm there's no shortage of beautiful Russian girls running about, a little borscht bubble in the Sinai desert. We stayed at one of the massive five-star resorts that line the coast, safely away from the roads, which are heavily patrolled. But my story was in the desert, and I was lucky enough to set up my adventure with the help of a local operator. With a low centre of gravity and such a vast expanse of space to work with, there's a particular thrill racing about on a variety of boy toys. I had just gotten my motorbike license a few months previously, and fortunately, you don't see me stall the bike just metres after setting off. Or wiping out and piling into a camel, for that matter.

Suitably proud of myself for hustling a fun story in the Sinai Desert.

(r) Two Giza guards on camel back overlooking the city.(l) A spectacular October sunset over the Nile, as seen from my room at the Shepeard Hotel.

KENYA
FLYING DOCTORS AND THE GREAT MIGRATION

Now:

From the window of the Cessna Caravan, I can see the red soil of East Africa bleeding. Cracks in the Great Rift Valley run like veins across the barren land, crumbling under the weight of one of the worst droughts in decades. Small circular settlements lie below, thatch huts surrounded by rings of scrub, isolated from tracks or roads. The plane is rattling with turbulence, wings shaking, doing rollercoaster dips. A lake appears, reflecting the sun, and even from 7000ft I can see orbs on its riverbanks, the bulk of hippos. We bank left and descend suddenly onto a bracken, dirt runway. There will be time to admire hippos and crocs later. It's time for the Flying Doctors to get to work.

Earlier:

They looked like long, dented tin cigar holders. When the first one rolled by, as I stood in the hallways of Kenyatta General Hospital in Nairobi, I thought it might be food prepared from the kitchen. It couldn't be…. could it? The second one confirmed it, and the third, with the unmistakable shape of feet discernible just inside the lid, removed any doubt: dead bodies being wheeled along between patients, visitors and a TV crew. The hospital smelled like a moral stain, an overcrowded urban nightmare, a rose made of rusty blades. Upstairs, I had just been introduced to Longopito, a 14-year-old boy who had survived a tribal massacre, walking 10km with a bullet wound to the shoulder and his jaw blown off by an AK-47. His parents were not so lucky. The Flying Doctors had rescued him, saved his life. This was a routine follow up, a personal visit in a clinical system. I shook the boy's hand, looked into his eyes and felt his courage, his confusion, his sadness, his hope. This is Africa, and his future is Africa's future.

Later:

The alarm goes off at five a.m.. Time to get up for a sunrise safari in Masai Mara National Park. From my luxury four-poster bed, inside my opulent five-star tent, I can see a dull flashlight of morning sun over the savannah and make out dozens of grazing wildebeest sprinkled across the landscape like poppy seeds on the top of a toasted bagel. The animals have survived a tense night amidst their predators and will now continue their great migration south to the Serengeti, across the border into Tanzania. For a brief part of their journey I'll follow them, secure in the back of a Land Rover, clutching a delicate Pimms cocktail, stuffed on some of the best food I've tasted anywhere in the world. I'm living the safari cliché in the wildest style imaginable: a butler, a chef, an infinity swimming pool overflowing into the veldt, metres away from huge buffalo, a string of elephants in the distance. This is Africa, too, the Africa of dreams.

****

It's been too long to be away from Africa. Even though I'm thousands of miles from my birthplace in South Africa, I'm still homesick. Here in Nairobi, there's MNET on TV, Steers and Woolworths at the local mall, names that probably mean little to you, but which are South African stalwarts – a TV station, a burger chain, a clothing brand – that cradled my upbringing. Nairobi felt just like Johannesburg, or Bloemfontein or any other dry South African city with horrendous traffic and well overdue for a spring cleaning. Speaking to locals, I hear a familiar tune: the crime is horrendous, the corruption ridiculous, the economy stagnant and… and it's the best place to live, and they love it. It doesn't make sense, but then neither does Africa, blessed with unmatched natural resources, an overabundance of labour and a growing middle class. Looted by colonial powers over centuries, scarred by tribal warfare, disastrous autocratic leadership: Africa, forever tarred as the Dark Continent, scares the crap out of people in the developed countries, who seem content to write it all off as a safari wonderland surrounded by AIDS, violence and babies beset by flies. And yet anyone who has ever visited Mother Africa will tell you of the strange way she pulls you to her bosom. There is something in her red earth, which connects us to millions of years of evolution still evident in our DNA; something about her people, capable of such incredible acts of horror, yet also capable of such incredible acts of hope. Her music, her hot sun, her beauties and her beasts. It is my first time in Kenya, although I have been to Ethiopia in the north and Tanzania in the south. I've got one week and an extraordinary opportunity to give my readers, and viewers of *Word Travels* a taste of all this, a difficult challenge at the best of times. I've visited eleven countries in the past five months alone and fatigue is setting in. Can't I just sit back on safari, slurp Chef Joseph's incredible chili-lime soup and toast the savannah at sunset?

My published travel writing typically focuses on adventurous activities and sweeping landscapes. The World's Best Beaches, or The World's Highest Bungee Jump, or The Magic of Laos. But there's another side of the coin in any country, and to get a good look at Kenya's, I needed to look at it from above. This I managed to do through the window of a small plane and the eyes of the Flying Doctors.

The African Medical and Research Foundation (AMREF) Flying Doctors is the largest air ambulance service on the continent, operating a fleet of aircraft equipped with medical systems and capable of evacuating or transporting patients around Africa and beyond. As the for-profit arm of an NGO, its business model is best described as Robin Hood with wings. Generating income from third-party insurance companies and private membership fees, it uses these funds to support vital community outreach programs, charity evacuation services and volunteer medical programs. While the Flying Doctors has received extensive coverage in media, and was even the subject of a film in the 1960's directed by Werner Herzog, I first heard about it when I met Scott Griffin on his book tour to Vancouver. A former CEO and chairman of large manufacturing companies, Griffin and his wife flew by Cessna to Nairobi, where he volunteered his small plane and time to shepherd doctors into the most remote parts of East Africa. His book, My Heart is Africa, recounts their story, and over dinner with friends in Vancouver I was fortunate to hear some of them first hand. Pilots landing on tiny airstrips, doctors treating patients under the shade of a wing, a mix of wealthy tourists needing evacuation to private hospitals and tribes who have no access to medical attention whatsoever. I contacted the organization and arranged to bring the crew along to Wilson Airport in Nairobi to discover more. If only I had arrived a day earlier.

"If only you had arrived a day earlier," says Sean Culligan, the grizzled man at the helm of the operation. With Ginsu-sharp wit and a sense of humour drier than a camel's tongue, Culligan explained that yesterday would have been the best opportunity to film the outfit in action. A car accident in the Serengeti required two Cessna Caravans, flying over the heads of animals at sunset, to evacuate the patients back to Nairobi. Nobody was too badly injured, and there would have been enough space to fit our crew. As for today, we would have to wait and see. In the meantime, he showed me around the modest headquarters, its control room, manned 24 hours a day by trained medical personnel, the visitors centre and private hangar. Three former RAF pilots who wanted to contribute the tools and knowledge at their disposal founded AMREF in 1957. Today, the organization has several aircraft capable of operating in a wide range of conditions, evacuating patients from Nairobi and places as far away as Europe or South Africa. Culligan, himself a former RAF pilot, is a man with a healthy obsession for his job. Almost every day he has to weigh up the information coming in to the control centre. Does the patient need to be evacuated? Can the plane land in that area? Is the evacuation financially viable? How is the patient going to get home after the evacuation? Life and death decisions, with the knowledge that every day his organization is saving lives, building communities, giving hope. Well worth getting up for in the morning.

I meet Bettina Vadera, the German medical director who has been in Nairobi for fourteen years, a former volunteer who found her calling. She agrees with my comment that Africa's magnetism is hard to resist. Even with the traffic. Even with the chaos. From the volunteer program that Bettina coordinates, doctors get unparalleled medical experience and the chance to give something back. 34-year-old Dr. Dan Deckelbaum of Montreal is a second-generation Flying Doctor following in his father's footsteps. His father was a volunteer in the early 1970's. Dr. Dan is an emergency trauma surgeon – picture the real-life ER – who has taken a few months of unpaid leave to work in Kenya. Once he leaves, other volunteer physicians follow, gaining experience in the field and the opportunity to contribute to communities that need their skills the most. I ask Dr. Dan why he doesn't just go on a beach vacation like a normal person. He explains that seeing the gratitude in the eyes of a patient, someone who's never even been to a doctor before, is better than any vacation. To understand what he means, we hopped in the back of an ambulance for a traffic-choked drive to Kenyatta Hospital. Visiting any hospital, in any country, is never about entertainment. Yet here we are, an entertainment-focused TV crew, walking bloodstained hallways, feeling the eyes of the curious on us and knowing full well that everyone we pass has something bigger to worry about. Dr. Dan tells me about the particular challenges of the medical system in Kenya, where public health insurance is negligible, staff are underpaid and overworked and conditions are appalling. Injury, he explains, is one of the leading causes of death in Africa. Meaning, if you were in a bad car accident in Europe, you'd be patched up. In Africa, you'd probably die. Millions of people, dying without need every year, simply because they don't have proper access to healthcare. Of course, for those with money (like Kenya's upper class and most of its 30,000 remaining white inhabitants), excellent clinics do exist. The Flying Doctors offer standby medical coverage for as little as $50 a year, and in a few days I would see first-hand just how much that small amount buys you. But in a country where the average person earns as little as $830 a year, emergency medical evacuation insurance is low on the list of priorities. As we walk along the corridors, passing a broken elevator and hallways needing light bulbs, Dr. Dan tells me of some of his trauma room experience in Miami ("You wouldn't believe the violence we see!") and the fact that most medical TV dramas are the product of overzealous imaginations. Finally, we reach the children's ward, and are ushered in to find a skinny boy clad in green hospital pajamas, a tube running into his nose and his still-developing bony limbs resting above the sheets. Knowing his story – the massacre that killed his parents, the gunshots that blew off half his face – it's a heartbreaking moment when we meet Longopito. He seems relieved to see Dr. Dan, the mysterious man who flew in from the clouds to save his life. With the linguistic help of Kizito, one of the FD's medical practitioners, Dr. Dan asks Longopito how he's feeling. As I watch the interaction, I can barely keep it together. We've met many people and filmed in many places these past three years, but I know the crew are feeling it, too. Drool drips from Longopito's mouth as he does his best to speak through a jaw that Dr. Dan stitched together. He somehow manages to smile a couple of times – if not with his mouth, than with his eyes. Dr. Dan is impressed with his progress. "You should have seen him before," he says with a grin. "He had no life left in his eyes." Even after all he had been through, Longopito wants to live, and I could feel it. My eyes holding back tears, I tell Longopito that he is a very brave boy, and we will show his bravery to the world so that other children can be brave, too. I wondered about his future. Orphaned, with a deformed jaw, Longopito would most likely end up as an outcast. His challenges were only just beginning. Sean Culligan had explained this to Leah back in the office, and *Word Travels* kindly agreed to donate $400 for reconstructive surgery. Our visit, at least for one skinny kid with big eyes, will hopefully have lasting and positive consequences.

We all head up to the adult wards to find them crowded – around twenty men in a room built for eight. Here, two other survivors of the massacre are recuperating, two more patients rescued by Dr. Dan. Bullets had blasted legs and shoulders, and now these men were holed up in a rank-smelling room, pinned and wired up with metal and rope, surrounded by other maimed and sick men reading Bibles beneath sheets caked with dry blood. For all the action movies I watch (and I watch a lot of them), I've never come face to face with the reality of gun violence – the truth behind a bullet wound. It is unforgettable and horrifying and something that will haunt me always. In real life, you don't get shot, continue to fight the bad guys and get the girl. If you're lucky, you'll experience only months of extreme pain and discomfort, a permanent physical disability and a vicious scar. Sean Culligan points this out in graphic detail, showing me where an AK-47 bullet obliterated his anklebone during a violent home attack in Nairobi a few years back. Real, mindless violence is not cartoon violence. When I saw it firsthand, it stabbed me in the worst place of all: my belief in my own invincibility; my delusion that I can "Bruce Willis" a violent attack and come out a hero. Culligan is a real-life hero. In real life, you're lucky to walk away with just nightmares and a metal rod holding your leg together.

On the way back from the hospital, numb from the experience, haunted by the sight of tin coffins being wheeled past us in the corridors, the traffic is backed up. In all my travels, I never saw as many accidents as I did in Nairobi. It's like drivers and passengers here should wear helmets. Our ambulance turns on its siren, but there's no give in the chain of cars ahead. Dr. Dan and Kizito jump out to see if they can be of assistance, and I chase through the cars with them, my heart pumping, nervous of what I might see. One car has collapsed into a deep trench on the side of the road, a mini-van is shattered and another car is on its side, crushed. Glass is everywhere. Fortunately, the victims had already been taken to the nearby hospital, probably in private cars, since ambulances are few and far between, and fortunately the FD's were not needed. It would take hours for the wrecks to be cleared, and traffic was snailing past, curious onlookers wondering how anyone could have survived the crash, if they did at all. Tomorrow, Dr. Dan would be taking off for two months of volunteer work in a rural hospital. Then he would be returning to Canada as the assistant professor of surgery in the trauma unit of McGill University. He has too much experience to be fazed by the blood and guts of what he does, but way too much heart to be a cold and clinical physician. I bid him safe travels, and walk away hopeful... knowing there are people like him out there in the world, and that somehow they are blessed with the strength to keep doing what they do. Would I?   Would you?

On returning to Wilson Airport and the Flying Doctors' HQ, we found out we had just missed Robin Hood in action. A wealthy, obese American trophy hunter had taken ill and was evacuated. When the plane arrived the staff had trouble fitting the guy through the door. The hunter, through his insurance company, had paid the Flying Doctors for their service. In turn, part of that money would be used for charity cases such as the one involving Longopito's evacuation. Culligan is proud of what his service does and how it operates. Earlier, I had passed a busload of school kids getting a tour of Wilson Airport. He hopes they'll be inspired by aviation, by medicine and by the fact that they live in a city with the continent's largest medical aviation service. Maybe the school tours of AMREF's hangar will create a few more Robin Hoods.

I had placed myself on twenty-four-hour standby in the event of a medical evacuation in the hope that I'd be able to hop on a plane and witness the FD's in action. Sunday morning, I got the call. There were two incidents: a car accident and a less-severe evacuation. The planes wouldn't wait for me, but if I could get to the airport in time there might be space. I grabbed my camera, raced down the stairs of the Fairmont Norfolk hotel and hailed a cab. Nairobi's traffic can be horrendous, and the last thing I wanted to do was get stuck in a traffic jam.
"Wilson Airport, please. It's a medical emergency!"
Just saying that got the blood pumping, never mind the fact that

the taxi driver took the task to heart and sped around the chaotic roundabouts. Considering we'd seen about three or four accidents in Nairobi each day, I wondered if the medical emergency might end up being myself. The car pulls into Wilson, I pay the cab, rush into the control room and get the details. It turns out the car accident might be too hectic to shoot but there is plenty of space on an air ambulance heading out to Lake Baringo, where an elderly man had collapsed. As a paying member of the FD's insurance arm, I would get to see the third and final component of the organization in action. Just then, I hear Sean bellowing from below. The crew had been on their way to a giraffe rehabilitation centre and just happened to be passing the airport. On the off-chance I might still be around, they'd popped in, and since the flight to Lake Baringo was not scheduled to leave for another couple of hours, Sean could join me to film the events. It never ceases to amaze me that in our wonderful fly-by-the-seat-of-your-pants (ahem) travel series, things always work out. The evacuation only required a nurse, so we loaded up with Kizito and two pilots and took off into the wind. Pilots are not told what each case is about, although they do assist with loading patients and help out in other ways. Dan and Marcus, the pilots, were as cool as a pair of aviator sunglasses.

"When we get into the Rift Valley, it's going to be bumpy," warns Marcus.

We fly over Kibera, East Africa's largest slum, home to over a million people living in an area about the size of Central Park. Then, above the wealthier suburbs, and, finally, across the deep, rich earth of Africa. It is a beautiful flight, the views of the Rift Valley serene and otherworldly. The plane shakes from the turbulence and I regret having drained a bottle of vodka the night before with Sean and Paul in an attempt to drown the intensity of our hospital experience. After an hour, the plane arrives on the dirt track and is met by two 4x4's. The patient, possibly having suffered a stroke, had fallen and cracked his head pretty badly. I assist the pilots and the nurse in loading him from a stretcher into the plane. His partner graciously allows us to film the whole thing.

"I was evacuated from Ethiopia after a car accident a dozen years ago. This service is just wonderful," she says.

The tour operator on the ground agrees. As he signs an appearance waiver, he says, "Anything we can do to help these guys, we will. Their role is vital for Africa."

The plane takes off, Kizito doting on the patient, wiring him up, inserting a drip. The patient's partner is relieved and calm. Her man is in safe, gentle hands.

From the air, I can just make out the forms of hippos in Lake Baringo before the plane returns to Nairobi, landing a tense hour later to be greeted by a waiting Flying Doctors ambulance outside the hangar. Door to door service; he will be taken to a clinic. Another job well done. Kizito might be involved in one or two evacuations a day. As a nurse, he's been with the Flying Doctors for two years, a mild-mannered, calming presence in the face of frantic emergency.

"You never know what is going to happen," he explains over the roar of the slowing propeller. "Today, I was at home preparing to go to church when the call came."

The entire team is on 24/7 standby; the phone could ring anytime.

"You should hear Bettina's stories about the suicide bombings in Nairobi and Dar Es Salaam," says Culligan. The carnage. The hopelessness. The importance of having – and the morale boost gotten from just knowing that there is – someone to call.

I leave Wilson Airport feeling privileged to have witnessed the Flying Doctors in action, to have met its characters and feel its heart. It beats hope into the entire continent. But that was not the last time I would visit Wilson Airport. Early the next morning, I would return for a charter flight that took us to the other Africa, the land of fairytales and travel dreams. Less than twelve hours after participating in a dramatic medical evacuation I was on my way to Masai Mara National Park, and the Migration of the Wildebeest.

****

It's tough to imagine the amount of space, and even tougher to imagine the numbers: The Masai Mara is 1530 km^2, part of a protected ecosystem, the Masai-Serengeti, that covers an incredible 25,000 km^2. The abundant wildlife that call it home include lions, zebras, giraffes, hippos, antelope, gazelles, hyenas and, most of all, wildebeest – well over a million of the shaggy-faced, skinny-legged beasts. Their annual migration in search of food – north from the Serengeti, and later south from the Mara – is the largest single movement of animals on the planet. As our private charter flight approached the dirt runway of the Mara's Kichwa Tembo camp, I could see wildebeest scattered all over the savannah, an invasion of ants on a never-ending carrot cake. Warthogs were grunting on the runway, their aerial-like tails facing Allah, causing our pilot to brake hard and bounce the Cessna Caravan to a stop. *Word Travels* has been my ticket to a lifetime of experiences, and now it presented an opportunity to safari in one of the world's most luxurious lodges. The guide company &Beyond's Bateleur Camp in the Masai Mara recalls another era. Overlooking a vast plain, it offers five star tented accommodation, butler service, an all inclusive never-ending flow of fresh cocktails, and incredible gourmet food. Large leather sofas and fireplaces offer a perfect refuge for reading classic National Geographic magazines from the 60's and 70's, while the dining is set just metres from a low electrified fence that keeps buffalo, elephants, hippos and the occasional lion from wandering into camp. Two swimming pools allow you to swim and view wildlife at the same time, while the tents themselves have four-poster beds, wooden desks and leather seats on a patio facing the savannah. It's not the first time I've stayed in a $1000-a-night hotel, but it's the first time I've received such warm and welcoming service in such a stunning and sweeping landscape. The staff remembered our names before we'd had time to finish our first Pimms cocktail, the ginger ale frothy with fresh cucumber. They'd tie themselves in a knot if it would make us happy, their smiles so wide I'd swear it would make them happy, too. Paul and I shared a tent, splitting the bed, another case of my enjoying the most romantic place on the earth outside the confines of romance. While I grew up visiting game reserves in South Africa, this would be Paul, Sean, Cathy and Neil's first safari experience. It was great to share their enthusiasm for finally being able to see animals in the wild. The tone was set on the runway, with champagne and snacks and the sighting of giraffes, zebras, wildebeest, buffalo, antelope *and* a pride of lions on our first drive to the lodge. The Mara has been home to the Masai people for centuries (or forever, according to their legends), but it's still odd to see tall, lanky figures herding their cattle, unprotected, just a few kilometres from lions resting under a tree. Animals and Masai share this space, and while we are told they respect each other's place, research suggests that animal numbers are dwindling as Masai communities continue to grow and develop. Research also points to the drastic decrease in cheetah numbers, primarily due to the disruption tourism causes in their habitat. But while the drought continues to ravage the country further up north, the Mara is doing noticeably better and both animals and people appear well fed. I ask Joseph, our safari guide, why the lions don't attack the Masai or their cattle. He points to the thousands of wildebeest – the sheer abundance of easy food available. Warthog: Lion sausage. Wildebeest: Lion Takeout.

Being Masai himself, he is able to discuss the fear lions have of the Masai warriors, and the fact that for generations young Masai boys would come of age by killing a lion. Lions have been trained to fear them. That being said, we are advised to only walk around the camp at night with an armed guard, and Masai villages are protected by a circular defence of thorny scrub. The famous Big Five are all found in the park: Leopard, Lion, Elephant, Buffalo and Rhino. They got their famed moniker from English colonial hunters, not fans of modern wildlife photography. After lunch (pumpkin and coriander soup, herbed chicken, roasted vegetables), accompanied with South African wine, prepared and proudly detailed by our chef Joseph (not just another Joe in the kitchen, I can assure you), we head out for our late afternoon game drive. Within an hour we've seen three of the big five, and by the next day the crew see the final two. A night safari yields dozens of hippos, 7km from the river, roaming the dark like ominous tanks. Hippos kill more people than any other mammal in Africa, save humans. We also get up close and personal with an elusive aardwolf, a thrill for Joseph, who has only seen one in all the years he has lived in the Mara. We almost catch a kill when the wildebeest roam a little too close to a pride of lions, but the moment is lost when a dozen Land Cruisers pull up, complete with obnoxious tourists yelling with excitement. There's a lot of traffic in the Mara, and our camp is by no means the only luxury lodge around. The guides do share their information, but it's not difficult for the cars to spook the animals. A large, muscular lioness walks right past our open-air lodge, just feet away from my legs. As long as you stay inside the vehicle, the animals do not pose a threat. The second you leave, as I tried to do with some giraffe, the animals will see your form and will either flee or attack. As the lioness pads by, she gazes directly into my eyes. It's hard not to think just how easy it would be for her to leap up and have us all for lunch.

The wildebeest are being stalked, and they know it. Instinctively they group together, the largest adults on the rim. This is a waiting game, and after an hour we have waited more than our bladders can stand. We cruise off for an anxious pee in the bush. We do see one teenage lion stalk a warthog, which deftly hightails it before the lion can pounce. Joseph tells us these predators are teenagers learning how to hunt, not capable of pulling off a real kill just yet. With a never-ending conveyer belt of prey – over two million animals – the predators can bide their time, pick up a takeaway and leave plenty of scraps for the hyenas, vultures and other scavengers. We see dozens of skeletons to prove as such. In nature, nothing goes to waste.

A Masai village has been set up for visiting tourists, offering the usual song and dance – a craft market. I learned about their art of jumping, and how the man who can jump the highest is the most attractive to potential wives. Masai are polygamous, and after jumping together with a group of men I joke that I'd surely be the only single guy in the village. The Masai diet consists of blood and milk, and considering their high cheekbones and slender builds, I expect it might one day extend to the runways of Paris and Milan. It takes some time for me to get some kids to relax, but when they do I snap some fantastic photos and have a little moment in time in which to connect with two young brothers while Julia learns of the village's domestic routines. We giggle and snicker and play hide and seek, and it's these ten minutes I'll treasure above all else in the years to come. A simple moment whereby three little boys could communicate with smiles and mischief. OK, one, not so little.

Each meal surpasses the last, the presentation immaculate, our butler Eunice answering any request with a smiley "Yes, please" or a "Sama sama." Pimms, a great accompaniment to the hot African sun, flows like a waterfall. We drink vodka and honey as the stars pop above us, the harmonies of red-robed Masai men chanting around the fire. It feels like a dream, this Africa. A dream everyone should experience at least once in their life. We return to Nairobi, Eunice and her cute-as-hell baby Tuffee hitching a ride, and as we approach Wilson Airport, descending over Kibera, the other side of Africa emerges once more – the chaotic, the desperate, the overcrowded, the polluted. A few years back, former South African president Thabo Mbeki spoke of an African Renaissance. Then he watched Robert Mugabwe take Zimbabwe to hell with him: the slaughter of hundreds of thousands in Darfur, the corruption-fuelled oil disasters in Nigeria, the squandering and misappropriation of charity and aid. What do I think? You can throw money at Africa all you want, forgive its debts, air drop cheap medicine – but you may as well just throw it all down a bottomless black hole. Africa has been pillaged by the developing world, and as it continues to be it operates according to principles the developing world will never understand. The plague of corruption exists because Africans have learned from us. There is plenty of food, yet mismanagement causes famine and drought. There are plenty of minerals, but the profits are being channelled into dubious Swiss bank accounts while the majority of people live in squalor. Still, new generations bring new hope. And hope in Africa manifests like nowhere else on earth.

For the Masai, jumping high is a sign of virility

BEHIND THE SCENES IN KENYA

I was homesick in Nairobi, and I'm not even from Kenya. It was something about Africa – perhaps the strong South African influence in the chain stores and fast food franchises (which nonetheless never came close to meeting the expectations created by my memories), and even the TV channels. From the wonderful Fairmont Norfolk I even called my grandmother in Johannesburg, since for once we were in the same time zone. It's hard to explain why someone in Nairobi will complain about the crime or traffic or corruption and yet quickly explain they'd never live anywhere else. That's just Africa. My Flying Doctors story worked out through luck and circumstance, and I was fortunate to meet and have been inspired by some incredible people. With our crazy schedule, sometimes I feel like we are in somewhat of a bubble, but every once in a while we can pop it and truly discover some extraordinary. Such was the case with the Flying Doctors. We donated $400 to pay for facial reconstruction for Longopito, who was shot in the jaw by an AK-47. I emailed everyone in production and told them the story, because through our efforts we had touched one life and hopefully changed it for the better. I extend that thanks and gratitude to you, the viewer. Without you, we wouldn't have visited Kenyatta General Hospital, and a 14-year-old boy would forever be disfigured, denied the most basic opportunities in life.

I grew up going on safari, which is a common getaway for kids growing up in South Africa. But I'd never seen anything like the &Beyond camp, or the migration of the wildebeest. Being able to watch animals crossing the savannah from my bed at sunrise was unforgettable, never mind watching buffalo and elephants from the lip of a swimming pool. We saw all of the Big 5 – lions, elephants, buffalo, rhinos and the elusive leopard – along with hippos, hyenas, giraffes, zebras, gazelles and, of course, the never-ending stream of wildebeest. All the while we stayed in absolute comfort, were treated to incredible service and had our meals lovingly prepared by the best chef I've ever met (the memory of those soups will stay with me forever).

My friends back home tell me that I keep forgetting stuff. My theory is that I've packed in so much experience in such a short time that there's no room left in my brain to reflect and process the information. Within that one week in Kenya, I had seen so much, and of such a high intensity, that I still haven't quite comprehended stepping over dried blood at the hospital or coming face to face with a lion prowling a kill. I don't know if I ever will.

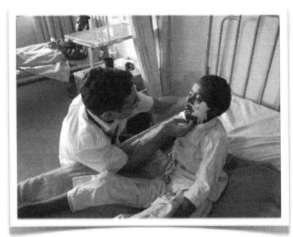

At Nairobi Hospital, Dr Dan Deckelbaum examines a boy he evacuated after a village massacre. The boy was shot in the face

Under the shade of a wing, the Flying Doctors treat a patient on the strip

It took a while for me to coax this curious Masai boy outside the hut

(l) A young lion perches up following a massive herd of migrating wildebeest

(r) My en-suite luxury tent overlooking the savannah. Safari in luxury

TUNISIA
A SLIGHT CASE OF "EXPERIENCE FATIGUE"

Note: These events took place before the Tunisian Revolution in December 2010 that led to the ouster of president Zine El Abidine Ben Ali.

I looked Tunisia in the eyes and said, "It's not you; it's me."

A wise man once said, "The fastest way to ruin something you love is to turn it into a job." I don't know who that was, exactly, but this week I understand better than ever what he meant. See, I love travelling. Always have, and always will. The reasons include the obvious (new cultures, beautiful scenery, wonderful people) and the not so obvious (the thrill of impermanence, the adventure I find outside of my comfort zone, the Modern Gonzo). But what happens when travel truly and indeed-ly becomes a job? What if you are told exactly where you can be, what you can do, who you can meet and even when you can eat? What if the bus to Good Times heads south but your ticket is for the bus heading north? Is this still travel? Perhaps travelling without moving? I was asked this week, in an interview, what the biggest myth is in travel writing. My answer, as I have come to learn, is that people believe travel writers are perpetually on holiday. Join me this week in Tunisia. It's a beautiful country in North Africa, with friendly people and a long history stretching back thousands of years. We'll visit ancient ruins, labyrinthine funky old medinas, colourful ports and comic-book characters. We'll also visit the reality of being a travel writer at the end of the largest, biggest and most mind-blowing granddaddy assignment of them all. It's the end of the road for *Word Travels*, episode forty out of forty. And all of those many roads, flights, trains, boats and buses have led to Tunisia.

First, some facts:
1. We were supposed to go to Syria, but that country proved to be a Banana Republic slap bang in the Middle East. I was thrilled to learn just a few days prior to the visit that we had been diverted to Tunisia. It's a country I've wanted to see for years.
2. I write articles for newspapers, magazines and online portals. Over the years I have become something approaching an adventure

writer, meaning I chase adventure, I write adventure and I live for adventure.

3. Television, let someone finally confess, is not real life. Television crews require permits, time, equipment and schedules. Writers do not abide by the same rules that apply to television hosts. Television hosts must be engaging, honest, communicative and fun. Like "The Dude" Lebowski, writers might or might not abide by these rules.

4. It's worth pointing out that there is plenty of adventure to be had in Tunisia, mostly down south, in the fine, dusty sands of the Sahara. But I rocked the desert just two weeks ago for our Egypt episode, and besides, we are locked into a schedule created by the Tunisian Tourism Board, focusing on the north, and the archaeological circuit containing Roman ruins, and yet more Roman ruins. Show me the Gonzo. The Edge. The… OK, fine, yes, yes, yes, I'll get back on the bus; When, did you say? Fifth-century BC? Wow, that's old….

Forty episodes and thirty-eight weeks of filming spanning three years, six continents and thirty-six countries. I remember my first press trip: meeting a large group of jaded middle-aged writers, travel veterans who had seen it all before, twice, and were just going through the motions. I was only a few months back from backpacking, still sleeping on couches, many physical and mental years younger and happy just to have a hotel room to myself. I simply could not believe that anyone could become jaded with travelling for a living. And yet I read the last few paragraphs and realize, painfully, how it must look. Here is a guy getting paid to see the world, and he's *bitching* about… well, something. I'm not sure what. A hotel room has become a hotel room and my life, lived out of a suitcase, has become as crumpled and untidy as the shirts packed within it. Today we're looking at second-century Roman ruins; tomorrow, a UNESCO World Heritage site. Take some photos; get back on the bus; off we go.

"But Mr. Mohsan [our boisterously enthusiastic, highly educated guide, bright-eyed and bushy-moustached], I need to find some adventure; these ruins are great; I got some awesome photos but I can't write about them; they're just not…not…not Gonzo!"

"Hmmm. OK. OK… Let's visit some more ruins."

My hotel room is on the twenty-first floor of the Hotel Africa, the tallest building in all of Tunis. It has a lounge, two bathrooms and a gorgeous view over a hodgepodge of beige buildings and wide boulevards. It is, to be honest, far above my station, and as isolating as Rapunzel's chamber. Walking on the way back from the Metro station – having ditched our bus in the pretty blue-white suburb of Sidi Bou Said to take a train and actually do what real people in Tunis do – I see two young backpackers in front of me.

"How're you doing, guys? Having fun in Tunis?" I ask.

"We just got here, mate, and we're staying in the worst place ever – a real rat hole by the station. Oh, man, it's awful!"

"Ouch," I nod, knowing what they are experiencing and matching it to many I have had in the past. I don't mention that I am staying in the city's best hotel and that I have a king-size bed to myself. In fact, in some sort of weird way, I'm embarrassed by it. As if I've betrayed my roots. Violated some sort of backpacking credo. Sold myself out. Sure, their room sucks. But they'll move on and they'll meet other travellers, and they'll find themselves in places they never expected to be, doing things they never expected to do. In my day bag is a printed schedule with a daily breakdown of my activities, my lunch appointments and my transit times. I know everything before I even get there, and I since I've been doing this for a couple of years, I can visualize exactly how the week will go, right up to the part when I say goodbye to our guide and driver – an awkward moment of tips and hugs – and walk into the airport without looking back.

My dear Mr. Esrock, is this what you signed up for? Is this travel? Is this your job?

It's my job, friends and travellers, to see the world and report back on what I discover. It's a cruel, crazy, beautiful World (with a bow to singer Johnny Clegg). I have come to love it dearly. I have learned that the World is not nearly as scary as the media reports. Not nearly as hostile, violent, sick or evil. The World is a romance, a tragedy, a comedy and a musical all at once. The biggest picture of all time. The ultimate blockbuster. The World holds all the Oscars, the Grammys, the Michelin stars, the accolades and the People's Choice awards. It has also been lambasted by critics, spat on, kicked, violated and polluted, and yet shows up every day in the hope that today will be different: the poles will spin positive and something remarkable will happen. Just last week I met a young boy with a bullet in the face and an inspiring determination to live. Just last week I saw thousands of animals on their great migration in search of food. Perhaps I am still shuddering with the aftershock of Kenya. Perhaps I am not ready to embrace the hustle of a medina, the smoky coffee shops or the views from the casbah. I'm sorry, Tunisia. It's not you; it's me. It's the sign of someone growing up.

I turned 35 this week on a day spent driving from one point to the next before being deposited at a large, modern and faceless resort for a night of rest... only to hit the road again. 35!   That's… that's five years older than the oldest guy in the hostel, which I already was five years ago! That's an age to accept some responsibility and to recognize that I have transitioned my passion into my work, and that work means getting up early, visiting ruins and staying in large, cookie-cutter resorts. Is this the start of my becoming the *Accidental Tourist*, the grey-suited, blank, monotone traveller depicted by William Hurt in the movie of the same name?   If it is, it would mean retiring, hanging up the backpack and quitting while I'm ahead. Is this the end of my Modern Gonzo?

Fat. Effing. Chance.
Tunisia is far from the straw that breaks the camel's back. It's the kind of vast and sweeping country that encourages deep thought, the discovery of hidden truths, and ultimate redemption. And, of course, I found it in the unlikeliest of places, such as:

* Stopping off on the side of the highway to help an old, leathery-skinned shepherd tend his flock of sheep. He asked me no questions and seemed unperturbed by the fact that a funny-looking gringo just popped out of nowhere; he was ready to stroll along, clucking directions at wayward animals.

* Stopping off on the side of the highway to ride donkeys so healthy and fit they could be pin-ups. The two old men volunteered their donkeys for a cute shot and an even cuter experience, one so quick if you'd blinked, you'd miss it, and yet one so authentic and real, with a connection between three people of different ages, nationalities and cultures.

* Stopping off on the side of a highway (see a theme?) to eat fresh-baked baguettes and delicious, fat, juicy rotisserie chicken stuffed with hand-picked rosemary. We're sitting on newspaper; cars are whizzing by; the ground is hard and dry. After so many long, stuffy meals in restaurants, the least-comfortable setting becomes the one with the best meal of all.

* Meeting the head of tourism for Bizerte, a gorgeous town with a rich history, and watching the joy he has for his job, his home and his country. This is no government wonk. This is a man delighted to be playing host. And then there is our guide Mohsan, a certified cartoon character, so proud of his nation he'd drive you crazy.

* A heavy storm is washing away our chance to see Dougga, the best-preserved Roman ruins in Tunisia. Sean insists we wait for it to blow over, and when it does we are the only tourists left, overwhelmed by the sheer size of it: the magic of ancient stone glowing in the pink post-storm late-afternoon sun. The ghosts blow icy winds down my neck; I am awash in travel buzz.

* Atop the casbah of El Kef, the highest point in the town, school children are walking amongst whitewashed walls with bright blue windows. The smell in the air is distinctive, with faint whiffs of olive and subtle hints of blossom.

* It's my birthday, and Paul and I are the only people in the casino. Only foreigners can gamble, and we are outnumbered eight to one by the staff. They give us a free drink for my birthday and watch as we win $50 playing blackjack (the dealer advising our play. Successfully, as it turns out). We tip them well and leave them to the empty room and the games they cannot play.

* We're arguing over the strength of the beer on top of the tenth floor of El-Hana hotel, the Bar Jamaica, hidden from the street and lit by neon light. The beer is light and expensive, but locals are drinking it comfortably, up here and in smoky card bars below. Like Turkey, Tunisia offers a middle way – an Islam that seems more accessible to the West. Nobody is saying Muslims must drink beer, but it's swell, and appreciated, when they allow others to do so.

* On a subway train, I'm watching a group of shy young boys flick

glances at a group of shy young girls, their eyes daring an exchange. This is courtship at its most humble and innocent, and so far removed from a bar or nightclub.

*A room party in a humble hotel room in El Kef, shared with Neil because my actual room smelled like the mouth of a chain smoker. I'm mixing cocktails. We're listening to music on my laptop. There's something sentimental in the air – the knowledge that the end is nigh.

*On a pier in Bizerte, I am fishing with two locals, which is the closest thing we could find to a physical adventure, given the circumstances. I don't catch anything, and I hadn't expected to, but I do realize that as far as finding a story for the show goes, sometimes the search for a story is the story itself.

* Finally, the last night in Tunis, and the last night of *Word Travels*. We decide to order in pizza (a disaster, with egg and mussels – together at last!) and celebrate with the last remaining bottle of duty-free vodka. Julia is so relieved to have survived three seasons physically intact that she's in tears. Sean looks at us and says, "This is it, you know; this is the end." I've travelled with him to thirty-six countries, and every incredible experience I've had these past three years has been recorded through his lens. Through his eyes. I suddenly realize that I'm going to miss him, and, looking around the room, everyone else, too. I realize that I'm going to miss all of it.

We set out in August 2007 to film a show called *Word Travels*. It would show the truth behind the byline; a glimpse into the lives of real travel writers. Sometimes we nailed it; sometimes we didn't, but nobody could have expected or anticipated the challenges and adventures we had, both professionally and personally. Most of the moments described above, the moments I'll cherish and hold dear when I hear the word "Tunisia," were not recorded on film. Some of them were. Sometimes travelling is a job. And sometimes it's not. Sometimes we love our jobs, and sometimes we don't. But never, for one moment, would I trade it for anything in the world. A wise man once said: The best way to appreciate your job is to imagine your life without one. Another: Choose a job you love, and you will never work another day in your life. Perhaps one or two, Confucius, but let me tell you – it's all worth it.

BEHIND THE SCENES IN TUNISIA

We'd reached the end of the road — the final episode of our forty-part series. Sentimentality settled in, slowly, along with the realization that this beautiful North African country would be the final stop on an incredible adventure. Julia, Sean and I had been there from the very beginning. Neil had been with us in a half-dozen countries, Paul, for 26, and Catharine, our director, was on her third trip. Among the ruins of empires past we began to reflect on some of the stories — the more challenging moments, and the fun ones, too. Tunisia turned into one of our most difficult episodes ever, in that we were originally scheduled to visit Syria but changed plans just weeks before due to government permit issues. So here we were in Tunisia, knowing that most of the adventurous stuff was in the south, but that after Egypt and Dubai and Petra, we'd pretty much milked the desert. So we headed inland and north, on the archaeological circuit, discovering the ancient ruins of Rome and Carthage. Our itinerary included long drives and many activities. It was one final reminder that a media assignment, a holiday, a business trip and a TV production are all very different beasts. Our attempts to put them all together were not always successful, and sometimes we lost patience trying to keep all the balls in the air. I spent my thirty-fifth birthday in a big, empty hotel lobby talking to my girlfriend, friends and family via Skype on a dodgy Internet connection. I looked up and saw each crew member huddled over their MacBooks, the blue monitor glow reflecting off their faces. And this is what life on the road becomes, my friends — six people sitting on six couches trying to keep in touch with the world they know and love, even as they discover a new world with each waking day. This is the truth behind the byline, and the truth behind a travel TV show, too.

We live hard and we play hard, but in the end, when all is said and done, everyone needs a home. This is certainly not the end of my travelling, my writing or my insatiable curiosity about the world. But after thirty-six countries, I think I deserve a well-earned rest and the chance to look back on the stories, the photographs and the episodes of *Word Travels* themselves. A chance to let it all sink in.

(above) Fishing boats on the bright
waters of Bizerte.

(r) Inside the Medina of Tunis

(l) Lunch in the
courtyard of an
18th century
house in Tunis

(r) View from my hotel room in
Tunis

Dougga, one of the world's best preserved Roman cities

(above) All that is left of the great city of Carthage

(r) Paul, Sean and I enjoying the scale of the mosaic art at the Bardo Museum in Tunis

APPENDIX: HOW I GOT THE DREAM JOB

I wrote the following timeline story for a Reel West cover story halfway filming our second season. It sheds some light on how the show was created, and how it was made.

May, 2003

The day before I am to be sworn in as a Canadian citizen, a car rips through a stop sign on Alberni Street in Vancouver and crashes into my scooter. I execute a swan dive over my handlebars, but instead of a medal, my bike is mangled and my left kneecap is broken. Subsequently, I am scootered off to the hospital, piled up on painkillers, and return to my job in Artist Development at music powerhouse SL Feldman & Associates. A friend of mine hires a street violinist to perform in my office; woe is me. A few years later, I would come to see these seemingly tragic events as the best day of my life.

December, 2003

With the aid of a lawyer, I receive a $20,000 insurance settlement from ICBC. After six weeks of incredible pain, my knee had healed perfectly.

October, 2004

Having spent much of the year promoting music and charity events, that chunk of change in my bank account continues to bore a hole through my dreams. Should I buy a car? Should I put a deposit down on an apartment? Should I finally cash it in and do the unthinkably cool – take a year off to see the world? On my 30th birthday, I walk into a travel agent and book a 12-month return round-the-world ticket. The moment I hand over my credit card, providence takes over and my Trip of Dreams is unstoppable.

February, 2005

What I don't sell, I put into storage. I dust off my old backpack and depart for Peru, the first leg of a year of madness I christen Modern Gonzo. My ambition to see so much in so little time, with so little preparation, has a definite gonzo flair to it. Having built a website for my friends and family to keep up to date with my progress, I pitch a regular column to the Vancouver Sun. My first column, also called Modern Gonzo, runs the day I leave for South America, and a few days after Hunter S Thompson kills himself. Suddenly there are a lot more people following my progress. I'm determined to upload writing, pictures, and more to my site every week, as much for my own diary records as for others to live vicariously through my adventures.

February, 2006

I return to Vancouver a year to the day. My travels took me to Peru, Bolivia, Argentina, Brazil, Czech Republic, Poland, Slovakia, Croatia, Albania, Greece, Hungary, Turkey, Dubai, India, Thailand, Cambodia, Laos, Malaysia, Japan, Australia, New Zealand and Fiji. I spent every penny, and then some. During this year, Modern Gonzo builds a cult online following, my column becomes a weekly, and I pitch other newspapers around the world, selling stories in major newspapers in the US, Hong Kong and South Africa. Coincidentally, I also meet another young Canadian travel writer named Julia Dimon in a small village in Turkey. She is also writing a round-the-world column for the Toronto Star, travelling in the opposite direction. We discuss the unique pressures and joys of being a travel writer, and decide to keep in touch.

May, 2006

The explosion of YouTube allows me to stitch together some of my video footage in Final Cut Pro (incidentally shot on a point-and-shoot 5-megapixel Canon) and upload it online. Suddenly I can share more than just writing and photos with the world.

August, 2006

Sleeping on couches and house sitting for friends and strangers, I persevere with the travel writing and begin to sell enough stories to get some industry attention. I score an assignment on the Trans-Siberia Railway, and another to Borneo. The absurd reality that I am broke and homeless, yet able to jet set around the world on thrilling adventures, underscores the misconception around the glamour of travel writing. After 18 months on the road, enough people tell me my life should be a TV show that I start to believe them. But who is lucky enough to get a travel TV show? I ask a friend who works in the television industry and get the names of two production companies who might consider a pitch; one in Toronto, one in Vancouver. Although I'd no experience in such matters, I work on a one-page idea for a half-hour TV show, adding *Metro News'* Julia Dimon as a co-host to make the package more dynamic. Neither of us could have imagined what happens next.

September, 2006

I cold email Omni Film in Vancouver. Considering I spend a great deal of time unsuccessfully pitching stories, I don't expect any reply. I'm seriously considering moving to Buenos Aires and opting out of the grid. Within a week, however, Omni VP Brian Hamilton replies and sets up a meeting with TV vet Heather Hawthorn-Doyle, who has just recently been asked to head up a newly established Omni Lifestyle division. Heather checks out my YouTube and sees immediate potential. Our first meeting goes great – Heather is a fireball of creative energy and enthusiasm. I work with her and her fantastic team to revise the one page and cut a demo to be pitched at Reel Screen TV conference in Washington, DC in January. Meanwhile, I take off to Central America on another two-month backpacking assignment. Omni's interest is encouraging, but I'm told it can take years to get a TV show off the ground, so I try and keep my excitement in check.

February, 2007

Travel CUTS sponsor me on a well-received 10-city national speaking tour, and I meet Julia in Toronto, for the first time since Turkey. I'm jumping from one house-sit to another, still living out of the same backpack for two years running, when I get the call from Heather. Although my original show concept included an interactive element, the network OLN have a bit of a variation.

Would Julia and I be interested in a show about our lives as travel writers? I have to seriously think about this… for about 0.4 of a second. Plenty of fist pumping, screaming and jumping ensues. We rework our concept, one-page and demo, and *Word Travels*, a new title coined by OLN, is born. Within a few weeks, OLN order 13 episodes, and we have a TV show, set to begin filming in the summer. When I tell my family I will be hosting a travel TV show, it takes some time before they actually believe me.

May, 2007

Pre-production begins. Julia flies up to Vancouver for crew interviews, as we all recognize the team has to gel personally for such a strenuous assignment. To bond, we hire a karaoke room on Robson Street. If we can survive that, maybe we can survive 13 weeks of hard travel. Our senior producer is Gemini winner (and double Ph.D.) Deb Wainwright. Production Manager is Leah Merrell, who has backpacked enough on her own to know the pressures ahead. Our director of photography is Sean Cable, a big man with a great eye, well up for the physical challenge. Multi-tasker Zach Williams is on sound, and we have a production assistant/jack of all trades, too; first Katherine Di Marino and later Chris Mennell. Lifestyle vet Mary Frymire signs on as director.

I'll never forget my first day in the office, when Leah and I looked at each other and realized how much work there was to do. Neither of us had worked on anything like this, and it's not like you can buy a book that tells you how to produce a travel show. There was only one place to start: Google.

June, 2007

Julia and I choose the countries we'd like to go to, and together with Leah and Deb we thrash out the logistic and budget possibilities. We spend hours researching in the library, calling tourism contacts and emailing leads. Immediately we learn that some countries are more set up to accommodate TV crews than others, but Julia and I are both attracted to offbeat countries, where the stories will be more unusual and rewarding. Leah and I walk into a travel agent and buy plane tickets for the first 3-week leg to South America. She is the same travel agent at Travel Cuts from whom I bought my first round-the-world ticket over two years ago. My transformation from office worker to backpacker to TV host surprises her as much as anyone.

August, 2007

Principal photography begins on *Word Travels*. Heather, Deb and Leah are our support and brains back in Vancouver. We arrive in Bogota, Colombia for episode one. Our luggage doesn't. This is the first time my luggage has ever been lost! We begin filming anyway and stumble upon a vibrant street carnival that happens to be taking place that day. This is the first of what will be many, many serendipitous events during the course of filming the series. With Sean's trademark time-lapses, multiple set-up shots and all things TV production, it finally sinks in that I am not only a bona fide travel writer, I'm on my way to becoming an on-air TV personality, too.

In our first 3-week, 3-episode sting, we fish and swim with piranhas, soak in a mud volcano, shop for emeralds, bike the world's most dangerous road, eat giant worms, sleep in hammocks, get travel sickness, swim with dolphins, run into political roadblocks, get caught in tropical storms, sail on Lake Titicaca, island hop in the Caribbean, get stung by wasps, abseil over waterfalls and fire machine guns into bullet-proof vests. We battle mosquitoes and taxi drivers, both of which suck your blood. We can only spend one hectic week in each country, and then we take off to the next destination. Each episode is designed to be stand-alone, so we make no reference to where we were, and where next we are going - jet lag and 18-hour transits be damned to hell!

September – November, 2007

After a two-week break, the crew embarks on a staggering nine-week shoot that sees us travel to eight countries on four continents. The show's description of "follow the lives of two travel writers, under pressure and under deadline" applies to the crew, too. Every week we have to ship tape back to Vancouver to slot into the editing schedule. With OLN planning to broadcast the show in January, there's little room for delays, and every day counts. Julia and I continue to write articles every week on the road. Her *Metro* columns and my online blog correspond with the week's events.

Back in Vancouver, editors Peter Steele and Jessica McKee begin work at Omni Post on scripts and stories assembled by Deb Wainwright. While we are out filming, it is no easy task to set the style, tone and shape of a new TV show. With my background in music, I always wanted it to be loaded with tunes and have a music-video-style edge, a notion supported by Heather and Deb, who used a similar format on their previous show, the Gemini-winning *Make Some Noise*. With the help of production coordinator Caroline Manuel (who would soon join our crew full time), we mine our indie contacts and manage to pull in some incredible artists, given the budget we have. Vancouver artist Max Serpentini signs on to create our theme song and other original compositions.

Nine weeks in eight countries is full of incredible adventure, and, subsequently, incredible television. The camera wakes me up in the morning, invades the nightclubs, even follows Julia into the bushes for a pee break in Ethiopia! Depending on the support we receive or the focus of the particular show, accommodation varies from bush tents and youth hostels to five-star hotels. In a hostel in Riga, Latvia, we gather in the common room to watch the first FedExed rough cut episode of *Word Travels*. A bunch of backpackers join in the excitement – it's not every day you get to see your first appearance on TV. Much as I originally imagined when I put together the first one page, the Venezuela episode is cut fast, action-packed and loaded with cool independent music. We love it, especially when we see Julia in the jungle, opening wide for a mouthful of fresh worm guts. This begins an ongoing tradition for the show, watching rough cuts in unusual places. In Hong Kong, the only TV we could find was in a narrow alley covered in porno. With a little persuasion, they ejected the porn and allowed us to watch the Bolivia rough cut. Most recently, we watched a rough cut inside the Zone of Alienation in Chernobyl!

We were not the only ones getting excited by the results of our insane race through the world. OLN loved the direction of the show and subsequently green lit another 27 episodes. As I gleaned information from the experienced crew around me, I realized that not only had I chanced upon a remarkable executive producer in a great company, not only had I found myself surrounded by an incredibly talented production team, not only is it "unheard of" for a cold call to turn into a TV show within six months, but I had also landed the most helpful, understanding and supportive broadcasters anyone had ever worked with. OLN's Patrice Baillargeon and Heather Eustace have been behind us 100% from the beginning.

January, 2008

After post-production, script assemblies, publicity, web development and voice-over work with the ever-helpful Larry Baker at Headroom Studios in North Vancouver, we gathered at the Regal Beagle in Vancouver for the on-air premiere of *Word Travels*. Surrounded by friends and family, my adventures around the world were about to be exposed to a lot more people. Julia and I had just completed a bunch of media, being interviewed on CTV, City, and the CBC, among others, and the show had already received rave reviews in the *Globe and Mail*, *National Post* and other Canwest papers. At 7 p.m. on Wednesday, the cold opening kicks in with a montage of images. I hear my voice: "My job is to go out there and find things that are going to inspire people to live their lives, and want to see the world." Adds Julia: "We get to travel, we get to meet all kinds of people, make a little bit of money, but we also get to change people's perceptions. It's really the ultimate job!"

March, 2008

Heather calls with more exciting news. Nat Geo Adventure, a new offshoot of National Geographic International, has picked up both seasons of *Word Travels*. Viewers from over 50 countries will now see our adventures, read our stories, learn about the world and become inspired. Back in Canada, I begin writing a regular column for MSN (Canada's most-trafficked website), *Chill Magazine*, and *Outpost Magazine*. Julia continues writing her weekly Travel Junkie column in *Metro* on Wednesdays. I continue to sell stories to newspapers around the world. A TV show about travel writers delivers great bang for the promotional buck, as the stories we write about on the road slowly leak with every episode of the show. Pre-production begins on season two of *Word Travels*. With Caroline and Leah rocking in the office and a successful season under our belt, tourism boards and operators are far more receptive to our requests. The challenge is to keep the experience authentic, so that we remain travel writers, under pressure, under deadline. Once a week when the crew put their tools down, Julia and I at our laptops, frantically writing away to keep our heads above water, filing stories for both our editors and readers, and for the production team back home. For season two destinations, we settle on South Korea, Sri Lanka, Taiwan, Maldives, Philippines, Romania, Ukraine, Turkey, Georgia, Jamaica, Belize and Mexico.

Switching up directors and crew, I work with and learn from terrific new travel partners; Jordan Kawchuk, Michael Bodnarchuk and Peter Steele direct, while Paul Vance (surely a contender for Whistler's Ambassador-at-Large) takes on sound and Chris Mennell and Neil Maclean rotate on PA and camera duties. Sean Cable, surely one of the best shooters going, continues to film the action.

May – September, 2008

Filming begins for our second season, shot in three regional legs, with a stand-alone Vancouver Island episode filmed "in our backyard." In Taiwan, I encounter a doctor who sets me on fire as a form of healing. In Sri Lanka, Julia and I witness an incredible ritual in which holy men insert knives into their skulls in a crazy ceremony. In the Maldives, we enjoy life at one of the world's most exclusive island resorts. In Turkey, we follow the footsteps of the Bible just miles from the Iraqi border, and in Ukraine we watch the Geiger counter tick over as we stand outside Chernobyl's reactor number four. Our plans to visit a little-known country named Georgia are derailed when the Russian military invades, giving us just a couple of weeks to scramble a replacement destination in Slovenia (it turns out to be a fantastic episode!). In the Maldives, Julia and I watch ourselves on *National Geographic*, a golden rectangle above our heads, a surreal moment for both of us. Neither of us could ever have imagined…

Is this the dream job? In life, so much is relative. When your job is to travel, you'll find yourself facing all sorts of nightmares you never think about when you're on holiday. Yet every day, I stop, take a deep breath, and realize that somehow, I've managed to create a lifestyle where I do indeed get paid to see the world.

By far, the most inspirational aspect of all this is the opportunity to share these adventures with readers and viewers around the world. In some way, I feel like my job is a quest, a mission to learn about this cruel, crazy, beautiful world on behalf of so many people who want to know more. People, I suppose, exactly like you.

Word Travels was later picked up by Travel Channel International and dubbed into 21 languages, and broadcast in over 100 countries. Years after production wrapped, the series continues to air around the world.

APPENDIX: CLIPPINGS

In 2011, I wrote a weekly column for the Globe & Mail, Canada's largest national paper, where many *Word Travels* stories found a home.

Clippings from Dubai's Gulf News. I wrote a regular column
until their financial bubble burst

Clippings from Outpost Magazine. I wrote a column called Thrillseeker for years

Articles researched during Word Travels also appeared in: The Chicago Tribune, South China Morning Post, Dallas Morning News, The Guardian, The Toronto Star, The Vancouver Sun, The National Post, The Gulf News Dubai, The Sunday Mail, MX Australia, The New Zealand Herald, Australian Associated Press, Chill Magazine, Mabuhay Magazine, She Magazine, Mango Magazine, MSN, Sympatico.ca, Matador Travel Network, and my long-running blog, Modern Gonzo.

APPENDIX: IN THE MEDIA

When media spawns media: I was interviewed and profiled in various publications, TV, radio stations and blogs, usually about my "dream job". These included CNN, MSNBC, Forbes Travels, METRO, the CBC, Travel Channel, CTV, Global News, Breakfast TV, pretty much all the newspapers I wrote for, and some weird ones like Finland's TV guide, and a Kazakhstan in-flight magazine

AFTERWORD

It's taken me years to put this book together, and as you'll tell from the (hopefully few) typos and formatting errors, it was completely built by hand. The show continues to broadcast around the world, and while our team has moved on to other projects and different lives, *Word Travels* continues to inspire millions of viewers with its stories, images and words. We were never a true "hit" show, and I never became a celebrity. Occasionally I get recognized at airports, where seeing the travel guy on TV might make more sense. I did, however, get recognized when it counted - on one of my first dates with my future wife. Some kid was star-struck in a mall, and wherever he is, well done! *Word Travels* was nominated for a Canadian Gemini Award in the Best Documentary Series category, no mean feat, since we never really saw ourselves as a documentary series, and were up against some pretty meaty competition.

Viewers often assume Julia and I are romantically involved. We joked that we were like a married couple: we fought all the time and never had sex. Our two different personalities appealed to some and put off others, but there's no denying it took our show to some very interesting places. Did I get rich making it? Even though the show is broadcast worldwide, there are no residuals in lifestyle programming. It was contract work with perks. We are perhaps the most successful Canadian travel series ever produced, but once we wrapped, I continued to be a travel writer, fighting for penny assignments, living like a king on the road, earning less than a KFC dishwasher at home. We stopped shooting more episodes because the money ran out, the broadcaster shifted its programming focus, and after 36 countries, the series had simply run its course.

I often wonder how the show would look if it had been picked up today, after I've been to so many countries. Would we be the jaded, cliché travel writers so despised in the failed *Travel Channel* "Confessions of a Travel Writer" series? Certainly, by the end of our third season, the pure joy of travel was replaced by schedules, exhaustion and personal challenges. Filming the show had become something of a job - a wild, thrilling, crazy job, but a job nonetheless. I continued to travel without the crew, writing, filming and photographing on my own, visiting two-dozen more countries, hitting that 100-country mark. Before I had a chance to finish this book, I accepted my next great challenge: defining the things to do in Canada before you die, for my first major book release entitled *The Great Canadian Bucket List*. After seeing the world, it's time to see my adopted home, and of course, bring along everyone while I do so.

I guess travel writers don't die. They just travel at home.

ACKNOWLEDGMENTS

Word Travels was the collective work of many people. I've thanked them before, and will continue to do so for many years to come. On the advice of my friend Andréa Fehsenfeld, I sent a cold email pitch to Brian Hamilton at Vancouver's Omni Film Productions. He forwarded it to their Lifestyle head, Heather Hawthorn-Doyle, who then oversaw every aspect of the project, including getting it sold, getting it made, and making sure everyone got home in one piece. Heather mentored us, played referee at times, and, like all of us, put in hours and dedication way beyond the call of production duty. *Word Travels* will always be "our baby." Omni Film was supportive and a great company to work with, so to everyone involved - Brian, Michael, Gabi, Lori, Gary, Corinne, Christine, Sue and everyone else - a tip of the hat in your direction. *Word Travels* wouldn't exist were it not for my co-host Julia. Together we were a package no broadcaster could refuse... OK, maybe three or four. Sean Cable was director of photography in every single episode, throwing his six-figure camera about like a trusty backpack. He sweated to get his shots, literally, much to the pain of our able and hard-working production assistants Chris Mennell, Neil Maclean and Ian Mackenzie. They carried the tripod, gathered releases, checked us into hotels and picked up Sean's sweat rags. You can hear us courtesy of our sound guys, Whistler's own Paul Vance, and, in season one, Zach Williams. Both did terrific camera duty as well.

Special thanks to everyone for the fantastic production photos.

Our directors - Mary Frymire, Michael Bodnarchuk, Jordan Kawchuk, Peter Steel and Cathy Parke steered the ship away from the rocks that threatened to topple it. Back in the office, Leah Kimura and Caroline Manuel literally put the show together, tirelessly organizing everything from flights and meals to story segments and music clearances. Without them, *Word Travels* would be a no-show. Deb Wainwright, our senior producer, created the scripts and a watchable show from hours and hours of footage, including great shots of me barfing in the bushes. Our editor Peter Steel doodled more cars than any sane person should in his editing cave, slicing and dicing the footage to make it relevant decades after it was filmed. Thanks are also due to Ben, Erin, Janet, Jessica, Randy, Tasha, Barton, Gordon, Neil, Nicholas, and everyone at

Omni Post for helping create the final product. Gratitude is extended to my sponsors throughout the series: Keen Footwear, Sugoi, Panasonic, Chlorophyll, MEC, Timex, Ray-Ban, Ryders, Alternative Apparel, Crumpler, Tatonka, Sony, Olympus, Columbia, Arson, Tilly and all the national and regional tourism boards. Patrice Baillargeon, the OLN broadcasting executive, should really get the credit for creating *Word Travels*. It was he who saw the potential in Julia and I just being ourselves, as opposed to chasing someone else's dreams. Special thanks to Marlene MacIsaac for proof-editing the book and making it that much more readable. My friends and family have always been supportive of my crazy ventures, even when they didn't quite believe all of this was real. They helped when I was sleeping on couches, sometimes their couches, and saw me through the incredible rebirth of my career. Keeping them in touch motivated me to record my travels in the first place. My wife Ana and I began dating during the third season, and somehow she put up with a boyfriend with one foot at home and the rest of him around the world. I love you guys.

Finally, thanks to the hundreds of people around the world who helped us, guided us, transported us, organized us, protected us, fed us, housed us, insured us, sponsored us, published, promoted and broadcast us. And the millions who watched the show, and read the wonderful stories they helped create.

Word Travels
www.wordtravels.tv

Developed for Television Heather Hawthorne-Doyle, Robin Esrock and Julia Dimon. **Senior Producer** Deborah Wainwright **Produced by** Leah Kimura **Director of Photography** Sean Cable **Series Editor** Peter Steel **Music Supervisor** Caroline Manuel **Associate Producers** Robin Esrock, Julia Dimon and Caroline Manual **Executive Producers** Brian Hamilton, Michael Chechik and Heather Hawthorne-Doyle

Produced in Association with OLN and the Participation of the Rogers Cable Network Fund, Rogers Telefund, Government of Canada: Canadian Film or Video Production Tax Credit, and Province of British Columbia Film Incentive

ABOUT THE AUTHOR

Born and raised in South Africa, Robin Esrock is a travel writer, author, TV host, public speaker and producer. He has been a regular travel columnist for The Globe & Mail, Outpost Magazine, MSN, Bell, The Vancouver Sun, Chill Magazine, SHE, The Gulf News and others, and his stories have appeared in over a dozen major publications including National Geographic Traveler, The Chicago Tribune, The Guardian, The Sydney Morning Herald, South China Morning Post, Cape Town Argus, Dallas Morning News and Toronto Star. Robin has been profiled as a travel expert on the CBC, CNN, CTV, Forbes Travel, Travel+Leisure, Explore, and in many other outlets. In 2012, Robin was honoured as Master of Ceremonies at the Explorer's Club Annual Dinner in New York. Robin is the author of The Great Canadian Bucket List, which took him to all 10 provinces and 3 territories in search of the nation's best experiences.

He currently lives in Burnaby, British Columbia with his wife and daughter.

Made in the USA
Charleston, SC
21 September 2013